1971

Literature and Society

General Editor: Herbert Tint

Tradition and Revolution

German Literature and Society
1830–1890

Eda Sagarra

BASIC BOOKS, INC., PUBLISHERS

NEW YORK

To the memory of my father
Kevin O'Shiel

© 1971 by Eda Sagarra
Library of Congress Catalog Card Number: 75-150810
SBN 465-08682-9
Printed in the United States of America

830.809
$129

Contents

58301

Part I

The Social Background 1830-90

Germany after Napoleon

'So peculiarly and insignificantly good-natured' said Carus, physician and well-known German man of letters, of his countrymen in 1844.[1] It was the kind of remark often made about Germans in the years between the Congress of Vienna (1815) and the Revolution of 1848. It was also one which was generally acceptable to them. Revolutions and wars tended to encourage bouts of self-analysis among intellectuals: this happened after the Napoleonic wars and after Germany's two unsuccessful revolutions in 1830 and 1848. On the whole, however, Germans seemed content with their well-regulated sedentary lives in the early years of the period 1830–90, and content too with the impression of amiability and predictability which they gave abroad. Germany as a country was not well-known to outsiders in 1830, nor even to the Germans themselves, nor was her courtesy title of 'great power' taken very seriously. One of the best informed British visitors in the thirties, Dr Hawkins of Edinburgh, suggested in 1837 that things were changing. With his contemporaries' fondness for painting optimistic pictures of the future, he declared: 'this obscurity is, happily, daily yielding to a bright dawn.'[2] The Germans were industrious; he thought they should be able to make something of themselves in this age of change.

Germany's political system seemed however to elude change; it was antiquated and complex, and most observers agreed that it provided a serious obstacle to her development in the nineteenth century. Germany in 1830 was a federal state, dominated by Austria. The thousand year old Holy Roman Empire had been brought to an end by Napoleon in 1806. In 1815, after Napoleon's defeat and the Congress of Vienna (1814–5) which had assembled to restore peace and order to Europe, a German Confederation had been set up, comprising thirty-eight states including the German territories of Austria. (This number was increased to thirty-nine in 1817 with the restoration of Hesse-Homburg.) Switzerland's destiny in this period was of course separate from that of Germany and German Austria, although her intellectuals in the German speaking cantons continued to identify themselves with the German cultural heritage. The population of the Confederation numbered about 35,000,000 in 1830, and comprised Germans, Slavs and Jews, living almost entirely on the land; there were only thirty-four towns with a population above 20,000 and the largest cities, Vienna and Berlin, had not yet more than a quarter of a million. Life in the German states was generally lived in small units. Germany had no capital, and so the horizons of the inhabitants were bounded by the *Residenz*, the seat of the administration and of the territorial ruler. There were few essential differences in the way of life of the different states, but there were considerable variations and some significant differences of attitude towards prevailing circumstances in the regions of Germany, which will be dealt with in greater detail later. Thus the South and West, which lay closer to France, were more in touch with the times than the North and East. The Napoleonic wars had affected Germany profoundly, yet peace brought not recovery, but a severe and widespread depression in agriculture and manufacture. This, as well as the agrarian way of life common to almost all regions, prevented social change. An undeveloped transport system, neglected roads, as well as hard work all round, kept Germans at home. The passport system and police vigilance dampened initiative to see the world. And so, despite the prolonged experience of war and unrest, the small political units and the censorship succeeded in confining people's attention and interest to local affairs. Only the regular soldiers, the students and journeymen provided an intermittent link with other parts of the country. After 1815, Prussian officials who came to work in the newly acquired Rhenish provinces were stared at as strangers.

Although such things as the censorship and the necessity to apply for separate passports on taking a trip to two places five or ten miles apart were irritating, in general people in Germany were much less restless than the inhabitants of France, Italy or Switzerland. Considering the revolutionary character of nineteenth-century Europe, there was withal relatively little dissatisfaction with the status quo. Germany's few firebrands were dreamers, not practical men. The consensus of opinion among foreign visitors was that the Germans were pedantically self-sufficient, contented and well-mannered, and this view was shared by Germans returning home from other countries. Depending on one's point of view, these characteristics were seen as positive qualities or merely as a lack of a national personality. It is fair to conclude from the numerous accounts by contemporary English and American travellers, such as J. Russell in his *A Tour of Germany, and some of the southern provinces of the Austrian Empire*, which appeared some six years before the opening of our period, or Dr Hawkins in his book already mentioned, that this was the generally accepted 'German type', not very different from his father and grandfather before him, but fundamentally distinct from the popular image of the German fifty years later.

Social structure

Germany's social structure in 1830 amounted to something halfway between western bourgeois society and the autocratic regimes of Eastern Europe. That is to say there was a large middle class which was gradually beginning to launch into commercial enterprise. It was educated but not wealthy. As in other Central European countries, the main body of the German middle class were state officials, on low salaries and exercising less influence on public life than their education and talents warranted. In subsequent decades there was plenty of evidence of a specifically bourgeois culture in Germany, but the middle classes did not seem animated by the self-confidence one associates with their counterparts in Victorian England. In political and social life their influence never outweighed that of the aristocracy. The authoritarian tradition of German life in all its aspects kept the middle classes on the whole willingly subservient to their hereditary superiors even in the nineteenth century. Although the desire to equip their minds and improve their financial status was generally characteristic of the bourgeoisie at the beginning of the period 1830–90, this did not carry with it the urge to challenge the existing order. Individual initiative was not at a premium in Germany before 1848, neither, with some exceptions in the service of the state and in commerce, were its rewards attractive before the 1850s. Even later, in the sixties and seventies, middle class intellectuals argued that since a self-confident middle class did not yet exist in Germany, it was best to leave the management of affairs to the hereditary rulers: in the words of Baumgarten, regarded by his contemporaries as a liberal historian: 'the citizen is born to work, not to be a statesman.'[3] Social discrimination between the nobility and the middle classes existed and was made apparent in all sorts of ways. The latter were excluded from their rulers' courts or admitted only to gape from afar: in some states a rope separated the classes at court functions, at balls and in the theatre. In the inns separate tables were reserved for the nobility, the military and for the merchants. As late as 1848 a middle class girl had to be termed *Demoisell,* not *Fräulein,* and even a teacher could be denied the title *Herr.* In Prussia a junior officer of aristocratic birth might remain seated while his superior officer stood.

The hereditary rulers were the thirty-nine sovereigns of the confederate states and their nobility. The latter was not homogeneous. It ranged from the great magnates of the Rhineland, like the Metternichs, those of South Germany and Silesia, like the Hohenlohes, who were equally at home in Germany, England or Russia, to the Prussian Junkers in the North and Northeast, provincial, uneducated, close to the soil; the latter aided their mortgaged estates by service in the Prussian army, and sent their younger sons into the civil service. There were also the country gentry in Central Germany and the South, whose patents of nobility derived from service to the local ruler; their sons, with a university education but without a fortune, entered the service of the state and provided the material from which many excellent appointments were made in the first half of the nineteenth century. These men, like Maaßen or Vincke in Prussia, the majority of them non-Prussian, became the pioneers of the industrial revolution in its characteristic German form of initiative by the state. The Prussian nobility on the other hand was less flexible and much less cosmopolitan than the Austrian or South German aristocracy; they were looked on as stiff and unimaginative by their fellows in other parts of the Confederation; certainly they had little conception of the reality of change in their time. Their attitude offended the more liberal inhabitants of Prussia's new western provinces, the Rhineland and Westphalia, and of Prussian Saxony which she had also acquired at the Congress of Vienna.

German visitors to England were invariably impressed by the social role of the aristocracy in that country. In Germany, particularly in Prussia, the nobility were much more concerned with preserving their privileges than with justifying their position. The fate suffered by the French nobles after 1792 had made a deep impression on Germany's rulers and her upper classes. They tried successfully to close their ranks. A glance at the effect of the concessions made to the French middle classes in 1830 and 1848 seemed to prove them right. Their exclusiveness was as much political as social; the landed aristocracy acted as magistrates and police on their estates, they retained a monopoly of seats in the local assembly in Prussia even after 1871, and they always enjoyed preference in the army and the civil service.

Instances are rare of that remarkable social conscience of the English upper classes. The reasons for this, however, are predominantly economic. 'The German nobility,' wrote Hawkins in 1837,

does not possess all the moral influence, which it is essential to the well-being of society that this order should exercise. This is partly to be attributed to their excessive number, and to the careless and sometimes sordid manner in which the rank has been multiplied; partly to the circumstance of the title being participated by all the sons; partly to their former reluctance to engage in any pursuit except the army and the court.[4]

After 1811 the nobility had become subject to some taxation and their land could be acquired by commoners. Their economic position declined steadily throughout the nineteenth century, but as the ethos of their kind forbade them, at least in the early decades of the century, to farm their estates for profit, the Prussian landowners became increasingly dependent on the court to maintain their privileges. They were able to retain their social position and their domination of the army because of the conservative sympathies of the Prussian rulers throughout the period 1830–90. Successive critics of the German, and more particularly of the Prussian nobility, from Hawkins to the sociologist Max Weber (in his inaugural lecture at Freiburg in 1895), pointed to their restrictive influence on progress owing to their relative poverty. Despite this, as Max Weber was to point out, the nobility maintained their privileged position in the nineteenth century because they had what the German bourgeoisie so signally lacked: an instinct for power.

Like the nobility the German sovereigns behaved before 1848 as if the French Revolution had never taken place. The concern of the Prussian and Bavarian monarchs, Frederick William III and Ludwig I, with the former glories of Germany showed the influence of Romanticism grown old. Their young contemporaries in the thirties, particularly the group of writers known as the Young Germans, mocked at their habit of living in the past, but did not reckon that such notions would exercise a much more lasting influence on German public opinion than their own versions of progress, plagiarised from the Saint Simonists in France. Most German sovereigns were on familiar terms with their nobility, distrusted the middle classes and had at least a sentimental view of their paternal bond with the common people; this bond did in fact exist in many states, such as in Austria under Francis and Saxony under King John. The German courts could indeed even be cosy. In 1858, when Castelli, the Viennese conversationalist and dialect poet, came to pay his respects to the Queen of Saxony, the sister of the Dowager Empress of Austria, he found the royal palace guards knitting. The Queen assured him that this kept them out of mischief.[5] Life at a German court was rarely flamboyant: on her marriage to the heir to the Prussian throne in 1858, Queen Victoria's eldest daughter, Vicky, was taken aback by the poor appointments of the royal palace and the frugality of the fare. Despite the royal suspicion of the bourgeoisie there was not much in their way of life to distinguish between them.

The German middle classes lived frugally before 1871. This was dictated as much by necessity as by principle. The German officials, who constituted the greater part of the middle classes, worked long hours on low salaries. In Bavaria salaries were so low that village teachers were known to take work as navvies on the roads to supplement their meagre incomes. To compensate for these privations, the German middle classes set great store by the possession of a title or order. Orders were first granted to the middle classes in 1804. They also helped to differentiate the various sectors and to buttress the general respect for the social hierarchy. They were easier to come by in the South than in the North, and were perhaps even more greatly coveted there. The respect for orders and titles was prevalent throughout the Confederation, and remained a useful comic device after the manner of the successful dramatist August von Kotzebue in his comedy *Die deutschen Kleinstädter* (1803), a favourite play for many decades. It was by no means only the civil servants who coveted titles: the commercial classes also proved susceptible to their lure. To be accepted in society, the rich man found he needed an order or title, and he gradually came to share the ethos of the official. During the Empire, the award of the title of *Kommerzienrat* (Commercial Councillor) or even *Geheimrat* (Privy Councillor) assured the loyal allegiance to the Crown and confirmed the conservative sympathies of many a businessman.

It was the wholesale merchants who were the first to acquire wealth in Germany, and by the 1850s they were attempting to associate with the aristocracy and looked down on the middle class officials. However, the wholesale merchants and factory owners were initially regarded with some suspicion both by the nobility and the bureaucracy, with the effect of inhibiting their self-confidence as an independent and progressive class. Large-scale industrialisation and transport development was too closely linked to state planning and banking for a merchant class to emerge that could compare with that of England in the nineteenth century. The attitudes of society towards the capitalists did undergo a change during the so-called Promoter's Boom (1850–73), which was the first stage of the industrial revolution in Germany. By the time of the founding of the Empire, in 1871, names like Krupp and Siemens in industry became the object of veneration. By the end of our period a tremendous sense of power and self-importance was characteristic of the captains of industry, many of them now ennobled. In 1870 the King of Prussia travelled by ordinary train; at the end of the century the big industrialist had his private coach linked to the express.

The relationship between the new rich bourgeoisie and their employees in the last decades of the century was similar to that of the aristocracy and the middle classes in 1830. The capitalists shared the official view that the workers were a potentially dangerous element in the hands of disgruntled middle class agitators, and that social policy was the means of rendering them harmless. In the large workers' colonies set up by the big industrialists – such as that of Stumm in the Saar – informers were placed to report on the workers' sentiments toward their employers. With some exceptions, the middle classes as a whole retained a conservative and often provincial outlook throughout the nineteenth century; their reluctance to commit themselves to liberalism, despite the wide interest shown in liberal ideas from about 1840 to 1870, derived largely from what they regarded as its cosmopolitan taint. The factory workers gave their support to socialism after 1875 (the Gotha Conference of workers' parties), but the urban clerical workers, who increased rapidly in numbers after 1871, were no less authoritarian than their employers and looked on themselves, as did the minor officials, as the backbone of society. They were antagonistic towards the factory workers and were probably the most reactionary group in Germany at that time.

In one regard at least the German middle class at this time was more united than that of France or England. A common bond was their concern for education. The frugality of the middle class home was maintained for a purpose: Germans saved for their children's education. In voluntary co-operation with state planning, they ensured that the general educational standard of their country was the highest in the world and the number of illiterates minimal. The rapid rise of Germany to being a leading industrial nation in the late nineteenth century owes a very great deal to the ambition of middle class parents. A far-sighted policy on the part of the rulers of the German states allowed technical education to develop early in the century, and an ever-expanding number of courses anticipated the needs of industry. One section of the middle class in particular set very great store by education, but, unlike the rest, was abreast of contemporary European developments and aware of the implications for Germany. This was the Jews. It was the Jews who helped to bring about change in political and social life at the beginning of the period through their contacts in other parts of the country and beyond the German frontiers. It was easier for the Jews, at least for the established families, to think of themselves as Germans rather than Prussians, Bavarians or Hessians. The Jews had relations in other cities and countries, and their business interests and their desire to educate themselves gave them greater impetus than other Germans to move about.

One of the most distinguished of such families in 1830 was the Mendelssohns. Moses Mendelssohn (1729–86), grandfather of Felix, the composer, had come to Berlin in 1743 from Dessau in Saxony and had become one of the most revered thinkers of the

Enlightenment, a friend of Lessing, who had modelled his *Nathan* on him. Felix's father had owned a bank in Hamburg, but had fled from Napoleon and was now living in Berlin. In 1830 Felix, a young man of twenty-one, was already a well-known composer, whom the great Goethe had invited to visit him, and in May 1830 had asked to instruct him about the development of modern music. Felix's aunt, Dorothea, was the wife of the Romantic writer Friedrich Schlegel; his sister Fanny, herself a distinguished musician, married Wilhelm Hensel the painter. The Mendelssohns were wealthy, highly cultivated and most hospitable: on occasions they welcomed over one hundred guests to their house in the Leipziger Strasse in Berlin to a concert or a theatre performance. Famous men visited them constantly, astronomers, philosophers and men of letters; Alexander von Humboldt, the explorer and brother of Wilhelm, stayed with them for weeks at a time and had an observatory in their garden. The Mendelssohns, like many Jewish families in similar circumstances, were baptised, the children, Felix and Fanny, while they were still quite small, their father, Abraham, some years later. Heine called his own baptism 'the ticket of admission into European culture' and many Jews grudgingly acknowledged that he was right. Such well-connected Jews were not actively persecuted, but they experienced several disabilities in their careers if they were not baptised. Thus Fanny Lewald's father decided to have his numerous family made Christians because of the restrictions on the number of marriages permitted to the Jewish community in Königsberg.

The Jews, whether baptised or not, played an important role in shaping public opinion in the course of the nineteenth century, and in focussing public interest on topical matters. Before 1830 communications in Germany were very poor; there was no capital to attract the Julien Sorels of Germany to conquer society and make a fortune: most people lived and died within a few miles of where they had been born. Even after the advent of the railways (1835) and the improvement of the highways, there was a certain stigma attached to those who were mobile, and the Jews, especially the Jewish journalists of the 1830s and 1840s, were widely criticised on this account.

One of the features of the opening years of the period 1830–90 is the decline of the artisan class all over Germany. They were affected, as the peasants were, by poor harvests, and the high price of food in towns. The general depression of the post-war years, when cheap English goods undercut the German products after the continental blockade had been lifted, hit them hard. The artisans resisted the idea of taking employment in the factories, which began to open in steadily increasing numbers in the 1830s. 'A factory isn't like a master's house,' wrote a travelling journeyman in 1837, 'there's no bond between the workers. Everyone goes his own way and doesn't care about the rest.'[6] Despite the difficulty of getting employment, the guild system lingered on longer in Germany and the Austrian Empire than in the rest of Europe, and even in the late 1830s young artisans were to be seen on almost every German highway, each with his pack on his back. Each journeyman had to have the sum of ten *gulden* travelling money lest he became a burden to the community; if he spent or lost this money, he could be put to work for the municipality in which he found himself until he had earned it. He also had to carry a *Wanderbuch* which contained details of his trade and also his movements; this gave him the right to apply to a master of his trade for a small sum, or for lodging, and work if it was available. It also allowed him to pass through state boundaries with relative ease at a time when frontier guards, particularly on the Austrian border, were all too ready to see in every healthy young man a revolutionary. A vivid account of life on the roads survives in the diaries and letters of a tanner's apprentice, Johann Eberhard Dewald (1836–8), who travelled through Germany to Hungary and from there to Italy and France in the pursuit of knowledge of his craft. Many times on his wanderings zealous officials demanded that he and his companions strip naked to prove they were carrying no seditious material: in liberal Baden they were actually arrested and clapped into irons for a night 'because we sang a song in praise of German unity; they (the authorities) don't make it easy for a man to be proud of his Fatherland!'[7]

The decline of the artisans was precipitated by the growth of Germany's population, which rose by 25 per cent between 1816 and 1831. The population growth was, with the notable exception of France, a European phenomenon; it was in part the result of a fall in the death figures and, in Prussia, of the liberal agrarian and trade reforms of Stein and Hardenberg in the first decade of the century. The middle classes in Germany were not prosperous enough to provide for those unable to support themselves. The philosopher Hegel voiced a general concern when he warned of the 'sinking of a large mass below subsistence level and the loss of a sense of honour and law.' Unemployment became a serious problem in the late twenties. Schinkel, the architect of the new Berlin, was approached in 1831 for his opinion on the possibility of starting public works for the unemployed. The situation was temporarily alleviated in the mid-thirties, but real hardship and discontent among the artisans helped to cause revolution in 1848. Yet despite the hopes which Marx placed in them, they were far more concerned in 1848 with government protection in times of stress and free education as a means of self-government than with the dictatorship of the proletariat.

There was no real industrial proletariat in Germany before 1848. Although the numbers of factory workers grew steadily, they still formed only a relatively small proportion of the working classes at that time and in the Hungry Forties were better off than the artisans or the peasants. The authorities and the middle classes were however much concerned with the question; proletariatisation of the domestic workers in Central and Eastern Germany – the best known example being the Silesian weavers – was common in the 1840s. The proletariat as such emerged after 1850 and the bogey of revolution soon undermined relations between employers and labour. The rest of the community became hostile to the workers after 1848. One notes that the urban working classes are neither successfully nor sympathetically portrayed in nineteenth-century German literature, with the exception of Gutzkow (*Die Ritter vom Geiste* 1850–2), in his portrait of the construction workers, the tender-hearted giant Danebrand and his level-headed young companion Karl Eisold. Yet by all accounts the factory workers were more sober and self-respecting in German cities than in London, Manchester or Glasgow. They were also better educated; workers' educational associations were fairly common in mid-century Germany and yet most sections of German society mistrusted and actively feared the workers from about 1870 onwards. This was part of the complex reaction to change which characterised Germans in the late nineteenth century. They tried to rationalise their own dread of change, seeing revolution as a foreign import and the urban proletariat as its arm. The emergence of the Social Democrat party as a mass political party in the eighties and of organised trade unionism in the nineties was interpreted by public opinion as a symptom of foreign influence in Germany. People ignored the fact that the workers showed more concern for their economic condition than for revolution. Indeed the German urban working classes played virtually no part in the political history of their country, a remarkable fact in a revolutionary age. Although its members joined the socialist party and acquired through it a sense of identity as a class, the suspicion with which they were regarded by the rest of German society and by the state did not drive them to extreme measures. They did not react to their enforced isolation as a class because they acquired this sense of identity at a time of prosperity in Germany. In the long run their concern with financial rewards and with the traditional desire of the German lower classes for self-improvement enabled them to accept bourgeois ideals, including, eventually, nationalism.

The German peasantry suffered badly from the depression of 1830. This was partly because of the wars, bad harvests and epidemics of the last twenty years, partly also the long term effect of the liberation of the serfs and other reforming movements at the beginning of the century. The liberation was not merely an agrarian question: it postulated a complete re-organisation of the structure of society and the relationship of the different classes to each other. There was a very great variety of systems of tenure within the German Confederation. The efforts of statesmen and others to reform and simplify met with a varying degree of success in different areas. In the kingdom of Prussia, which comprised about three-fifths of the Confederation, the personal bondage of the peasants and their feudal obligations were, with some exceptions, abolished in the years 1799–1816; however, they still remained subject to patrimonial justice until 1849. The Prussian reform was therefore rapid but incomplete. Despite the intentions of Baron Stein and other reformers, a strong peasantry did not emerge: quite the reverse happened. The new smallholders were often unable to meet the payments due, since the period after liberalisation coincided with some of the worst years for farmers in the century. A number were then forced to sell part of their land, and ultimately surrendered it all to become landless peasants, who, however, now no longer enjoyed the protection of a local landlord in times of stress. Agricultural labourers were to be drawn from this growing pool; the Junker estates were gradually transformed into capitalist enterprises. This was only done with reluctance: the Junkers needed the profits but feared to be thought engaging in trade. In Bavaria, Württemberg and the Grand Duchy of Hesse, personal servitude was abolished, but not manorial dues and patrimonial justice. Accordingly agriculture in South and parts of Central Germany revived more slowly after the middle of the century than elsewhere. In Saxony, Hanover and Electoral Hesse the liberation of the peasants was delayed until the 1830s, but was more successful owing to the work of enlightened legislators. The commuting for money payments of manorial dues, that is, of one or more days' labour per week owed to the local lord of the manor, was more common in Central Germany than Prussia. From the middle of the century, the creation of credit banks for small farmers helped to prevent the widespread debts and bankruptcies which had depressed the peasants earlier in the century. In Austria the *Raiffeisen* credit banks (named after their founder) saved the small farmer from virtual extinction.

In general the emancipation of the peasantry benefitted the landowner and the well-to-do farmer rather than the peasant, who generally bore the brunt of natural catastrophes such as cholera, cattle disease and the bad harvests of the twenties and the forties. There was a surplus population on the land all over Germany until the industrial revolution gathered sufficient momentum in the second half of the century to absorb it into the towns. A high birth rate and advances in medical knowledge and hygiene proved a further burden on the small farmer who struggled to support a large family. Even if personally free, the German peasants also failed to prosper because of the uneconomic nature of their holdings and their old-fashioned methods. Cultivation of unenclosed land in common was still practised in the early decades of the nineteenth century. In South Germany in particular holdings were scattered and the practice existed of continually subdividing land among all the sons. In the 1840s speculation in land on a large scale created a feeling of insecurity among the peasants, while the distress occasioned by repeated bad harvests was a most important social cause of revolution in 1848. The authorities failed to do much about this before 1848 for political reasons: they feared to lose an important source of manpower for the army. The kings of Prussia and even as late as the 1860s Bismarck himself were in no doubt as to the value of the peasantry for this purpose. In the non-commissioned officer and farmer's son, Sandrart, Gutzkow (*Die Ritter vom Geiste*) left a portrait of the loyal if somewhat simple soldier as the authority liked to see him.

However, apart from the *Jacquerie* in Austrian Galicia in 1846 (recorded by Marie von Ebner-Eschenbach in *Jakob Szela*, 1883) and the serious incidents in South Baden in 1848, the peasants rarely associated themselves with efforts to improve their lot. Indeed they usually acted as the arm of the state in repressing revolts. It was this which persuaded Bismarck in the sixties that the lower orders were naturally conservative and which led him to introduce universal suffrage in the Empire. Bismarck was thinking of the agricultural classes and in particular of the East Elbian landowners, of which he was one, when he took another more far-reaching decision: to make Germany capable of feeding herself despite the industrial revolution. His decision was aimed to serve those sections of the population which were in favour of the status quo. As so often with Bismarck, an economic decision was dictated by political considerations. To meet this need and because of the continued rural exodus in Germany, the Prussian landowners brought in hordes of seasonal workers from Poland and Russia in the 1880s. By 1890 these numbered almost a million, and as illiterate migrants they fed the perennial dislike of the Slav among the native Germans.

Daily life

The distribution of Germany's population altered more rapidly between 1830 and 1890 than at any other time in her history. The population rose steadily in these years, reaching 40,000,000 in 1871 and over 55,000,000 by 1890. At the beginning of the period some four-fifths lived on the land, at the end only two-fifths did so. Yet, except at the extremes of the social scale, daily habits showed surprisingly little variation between 1830 and 1890. In the country, and even in the towns until the middle of the century, people grew their own garden produce and made their own clothes and even household utensils. Wandering carpenters, masons and glaziers helped out where necessary. The traditional frugality of the German home was not lost in the age of the industrial revolution. The German housewife was justifiably proud of her thrift, and visitors to Germany in the nineteenth century commented on the general satisfaction derived by all classes and both sexes from small and sensible economies.[8]

In Victorian England it was not thought good form in polite society to praise the food offered by one's hostess as the servants must be assumed to have cooked it; in Germany even the well-to-do lady of the house took care to supervise its preparation. The family diet was based on rye bread, dairy produce and vegetables in large quantities, with veal on Sundays. Outside Vienna white bread was regarded as injurious to health and meat, except in the Baltic provinces, as much the same. Sausages and potato salad were popular, and coffee and cake was regarded as the mark of a festivity. Then, as now, the cost of the coffee and cake was almost that of a full meal.

Mealtimes were much the same as they are today; the main meal at 12 or 1 o'clock seemed excessively early to English visitors who dined at four, and a certain snobbery for things English made some Germans change their dinner hour to the afternoon, especially after the marriage of Princess Victoria to Frederick of Prussia. In Hamburg and elsewhere in Northern Germany after mid-century, people liked to talk of 'lunch'. A cold supper was eaten at about 8 o'clock. People rose early and retired early, the King of Prussia, Frederick William III, setting the example. Shows usually began at 6 pm and ended before 10. Everyone was used to working long hours, including the children. School began at 8 am in winter, 7 in summer, and continued with a two-hour break for dinner until 5 pm. School and university holidays were a little shorter than they are now.

The frugality of daily life at all levels, except in the courts of some of the princes, was reflected in the homes. Even the nobility and the professional classes were accustomed to let rooms and even storeys of their houses to strangers. These were not well-appointed; polished floors were a substitute for carpets, and the stairway and entrance hall of the homes of even high officials had nothing of the luxury of a London or Paris townhouse. But in the first decades of the period they were certainly elegant: every detail was attended to, and the style of the *Biedermeier* period (c. 1820–50) was expressed in porcelain, in pictures, in the draping of the white voile curtains, in the furniture and even in the cooking utensils. On the walls hung portraits and miniatures from the family circle and rustic landscapes: nature was drawn into the room to offset the rather stark simplicity. A vogue for window boxes and for indoor plants at this time spread right down the social scale and outlasted the Biedermeier era. In the poorer homes furniture was made of pearwood, in the bourgeois homes of mahogany. People began to acquire more household possessions in the thirties; linen and kitchen utensils, and, much later, furniture and hangings. Wilhelm von Humboldt, for a time a Prussian Minister, owed his large household to a private fortune and not to his official position: when he moved back from Rome to Prussia his luggage included one ton of linen, three-quarters of a ton of books and half a ton of bedding.

Home life between 1830 and 1890 was invested with a certain ritual solemnity which survived longer in Germany than elsewhere. Certain pieces of furniture acquired a special significance, notably the sofa. The publisher Cotta was admired in Tübingen for his possession of one early in the century, and Gabriele von Humboldt received one as part of her dowry. The sofa became more general from the mid-century onwards and its possession helped to illustrate the increasing stratification of bourgeois society: it was the place of honour in the home. Thus, should a university professor and a mere lecturer be present in the room with their wives, the lecturer's wife would not dream of taking her seat on the sofa. Such niceties of protocol in bourgeois circles were the product of increasing self-consciousness; they became most marked among academics after 1871: in the very circles which before 1848 had been noted for their simplicity. In the same way, under the Empire, the modest elegance of the German home gave way to the current European fashion for crowded rooms, draped walls and dark and cumbersome furniture.

Social habits were modified in other ways in the first half of the century. People began to wash more. Karoline von Humboldt was one of the first to install a bathroom in her house, influenced by English fashion. Bathing was thought frivolous and immodest, but the habit caught on. The association of water and health gave impetus to the vogue for sea bathing and taking the waters, both of which first became fashionable at the beginning of the century. In Germany people became health-conscious and this provided a delicious subject of conversation for the better-off right through the period. Already in the late twenties women began to discover fashionable doctors who 'understood' their complaints. Fontane tells of his mother's insistence on taking a wearisome journey to Berlin to consult the currently fashionable *Geheimrat* Horn.[9] But it was not really until the Empire that people, especially women, started to take an almost morbid interest in medical details, so much so that a popular journal like the *Gartenlaube* could increase its high circulation with diagrams and figure drawings to indicate the effect of tightlacing on the internal organs. Friends now fell out over such questions as the medical effects of open windows in home or school.

The popular image of women in Germany had changed some years before the opening of this period, from one of independence of character, even among women and girls of the people, to a domesticated docility, accepting without question the superiority of the male and the woman's dependence on him. In German Romantic circles, where they played a prominent and sometimes dynamic part, women were portrayed as both capable of intense feeling and as the intellectual equals of men. But under the impact of the defeat of Prussia at Jena in 1806 and the emergence of the national movement, the feminine ideal changed. Writers such as Kleist (in *Das Käthchen von Heilbronn,* 1808), Chamisso or Eichendorff may have projected their own desires into the portraits of women that appear in their work, but they were also recording the change that perceptive contemporaries had observed. The feminine ideal of the post-Napoleonic age owes a good deal to Queen Luise of Prussia, consort of Frederick William III. She and her household shared the hardships of life in Prussia after the French occupied the greater part of the country after 1806. The frugality of her way of life in Memel, Königsberg and Berlin in these years brought her close to her people, and her early death in 1810 made her into something of a legend.

The new image was specifically German – even in 1808 Wilhelm von Humboldt spoke of 'German womanliness' – a motherly figure yet full of girlish innocence. Fanny Lewald, later a highly successful novelist, who was born in 1811 in Königsberg, complained bitterly in her diaries of the difficulties encountered by women who tried to break free of the family circle. In German literature women are presented as mothers and sisters to their menfolk, rarely wives and lovers; there are very few successful examples of passionate women in nineteenth century German literature. This interpretation was common in portraiture also between 1820 and 1840; in literature it lasted much longer – it was still to be found in the *Heimatkunst* at the end of the century and was revived in a highly sentimentalised form in the Third Reich. The German girl and woman was 'unspoilt'; any trace of sophistication was foreign to her. (It was nòt until the second half of the century that sophistication became suspect and German women complacent about their provincial manners.) The German woman, both in literature and life in the mid-nineteenth century, found her whole *raison d'être* in her husband and family; she had no substance out this role. As in Eichendorff's lines

How often have I realised that a girl's soul
is her lover's, not her own.[10]

The bourgeois practice in nineteenth-century Germany of giving a married woman her husband's title suggested the satisfaction to be derived from reflected glory (Frau *Kommerzienrat* Treibel in Fontane's novel, *Frau Jenny Treibel*, 1892). The familiar image of the German *Hausfrau* is a creation of this period, a source of complacency to society generally; she was rarely the object of satire in German writing. The *Hausfrau* was not confined to one social class, but seems to have been the accepted feminine idea of virtu- ally all classes, including even the aristocracy. Frau *Justizrat* Zeisel, born, as she liked to emphasise, a von Dünkerle, in Gutz- kow's above-mentioned novel, was an example of the model German wife for society, as was the eccentric Princess von Ippe- Büchsenstein (Fontane, *Der Stechlin*, 1898), who expressed her satisfaction repeatedly and at some length that she bore her middle-class husband a child every year because that was what was expected of a good *Hausfrau*.

Attempts made in the nineteenth century to widen the horizons of German women beyond their domestic circle generally found their sternest critics among women themselves. Feminism was rare in Germany, although the Young German movement under the stimulus of French Saint-Simonian thinking provided an interest- ing if short-lived exception to the rule. The unusual ideas of Saint Simonism about women had been part of the progressive and often practical reform of the French movement. It is characteristic that its German followers largely disregarded the social reform and advocated the emancipation of the flesh and, as a corollary, of women. Many of them attacked contemporary attitudes by rejecting the institution of marriage as degrading to women, although they did not go as far as the Saint-Simonists in attributing the supreme role in society to women. The feminism of the Young Germans found few converts among women. It was provocative in Gutzkow (*Wally, die Zweiflerin,* 1835), idealistic and ironic by turns in Mundt (*Madonna, eine Heilige,* 1835), and moderate in Wienbarg; all of these owed a special debt to three women of the time: Rahel von Varnhagen, who died in 1833, Bettina von Arnim, sister of Clemens Brentano, and Charlotte Stieglitz, who committed suicide to inspire her poet husband in 1835. In the words of another Young German, Mundt, 'Bettina's love, Charlotte's death and the dark prophecies of Rahel pierced our hearts'.[11] Perhaps the frustrations of these young men, their bitter feeling that being German put them at a disadvantage in the world, were assuaged by the knowledge of what women such as Rahel and Bettina had achieved in their spheres, and they were thus drawn to proclaim support for feminism.

Rahel Levin (born in 1771) was regarded by her contemporaries as one of the most interesting women of the age. Like Schleiermacher's wife Henriette and Friedrich Schlegel's Dorothea, she was the daughter of a wealthy Berlin Jew, and after a late marriage to the diplomat Varnhagen von Ense, she presided in the years after the Napoleonic wars over one of the most brilliant salons in Berlin. She staunchly upheld Goethe's reputation in the twenties and early thirties, when he was under attack from Wolfgang Menzel and others, and she died one year after Goethe, in 1833. It was the cult of Rahel in her husband's three-volume *Rahel* (1834) which impressed the Young Germans, for they had not known her personally. Bettina von Arnim (1785–1859), sister of the poet Clemens Brentano and wife of the writer Achim von Arnim, shared Rahel's concern for social and political questions, but she played a more active role on behalf of the poor and underprivileged. In 1843 she appealed personally but unsuccessfully on their behalf to Frederick William IV of Prussia in *Dies Buch gehört dem König*. The popularity of women writers in Germany from about 1840 onwards, of Fanny Lewald, Countess Hahn-Hahn, Betty Paoli and the prolific dramatist Charlotte

Birch-Pfeiffer owed a good deal to the attention focussed on their talents and social disabilities by the Young Germans.

Interest in women's rights dates back to the late eighteenth century. Writers and thinkers of German classicism had valued the role of women in polite society and stressed the importance of education for women. Throughout the nineteenth century women's education was the primary goal of those distinguished women who concerned themselves with the condition of their fellows. These included (besides Rahel and Bettina) Malwida von Meysenbug, Luise Büchner, Lou Andreas-Salomé and particularly Luise Otto-Peters (1819–95), who helped to pioneer the Froebel Kindergarten. Frau Otto-Peters also led the agitation to permit women to go to university. It was not until 1891 that they were admitted to university; the first doctorate was awarded to a woman in 1896. A topical reference is to be found in the figure of Anna in Hauptmann's *Einsame Menschen* (1891) who is depicted as a fiery supporter of revolutionary causes. 1848 and the issues it raised helped to formulate specific goals within the women's rights movement, but it was not until the founding of the *Allgemeiner Deutscher Frauenverein* in Leipzig in 1865 by Frau Otto-Peters, that the efforts of individual women were channelled to a common end. Women of intellectual stature and compelling personality like Luise Büchner, Lou Andreas-Salomé, Auguste Schmit and Helene Lange, and the aristocratic socialist Lily Braun, achieved notable success in the improvement of the legal and social position of women. The achievement of these women was all the greater because the vast majority were apathetic towards the efforts made on their behalf and largely uninterested in life outside their homes. Caroline Pichler in the early nineteenth century, who could bring up her family, entertain and still find time to write numerous patriotic dramas – sixty volumes of collected works – became a rare type after mid-century, and already in 1842 William Howitt could observe with some justice that 'literary ladies are looked upon as a sort of pretty monster'.[12] The greatest woman writer of the nineteenth century in Germany, Annette von Droste-Hülshoff (1797–1848), won little recognition outside her immediate circle of friends.

Regional and class differences used to be apparent in Germany in the way people dressed. This changed between 1820 and 1850.

Cheap English cottons revolutionised women's dress, in particular after the end of the continental blockade; all classes wore them in their daily life. Middle-class manners and fashions began to set the tone in mid-century. Even the nobility followed the fashion for trousers and boots, discarding the traditional breeches, stockings and shoes. Although the academics clung to their well-loved slippers and quilted dressing-gowns even after the 1848 Revolution, the tail coat became the standard dress for social occasions for all classes by the thirties. One's class was no longer expressed in what one wore. Even individual taste could only be expressed in one's choice of waistcoat. Men's clothes became hard-wearing, made of leather and heavy cloth, and the wealthy proclaimed the solidity of their fortunes in massive blue overcoats with up to five collars. Young people in the twenties and thirties rejected overcoats, and even in Germany tentatively took up dandyism. Brummel had made black a popular colour and when Börne, the journalist, returned to Germany in the twenties, he found every tenth woman mourning some distant relative, as an excuse for donning the fashionable colour. In the next decade white became all the rage and German girls began to diet. The cantankerous Wolfgang Menzel, critic and journalist, voiced a complaint at the beginning of the period that would become drearily familiar later on: that German women, who should know better, were aping French fashion. Although German women remained as thrifty in their dress as in their housekeeping, French fashions were always copied in Germany, with a time lag, from the crinoline to the bustle and the muttonchop sleeve. After 1848 the moustache became popular among men. Germans, always excessive smokers, began in the 1850s to show their growing prosperity in cigars rather than pipes; and the cigar has remained a cherished symbol of prosperity to this day.

As standards of dress and behaviour gradually became more stereotyped around mid-century, certain articles retained symbolic value. One such was the *queue*. The pigtail had been abolished in the Prussian army as far back as 1808, but it was still worn quite commonly in the provinces and around the time of the 1830 Revolution. The *queue* was worn as a mark of political dependability. The Landgrave of Hesse had handed out rewards on his return to his capital in 1815 to those officers whom he saw wearing this symbol of reaction. Immermann's satirical comments in *Münch-*

hausen (1839) showed that it was still a topical issue.[13] Another such symbol was the hat. In 1848 slouch hats became the mark of a revolutionary, so officials were careful to wear top hats, and the anxious citizens in revolutionary Vienna attested their loyalty by wearing them as well.

Germany was a cheap country to live in, at least until late in the century. An educated Scotswoman spent a summer house-keeping in Hanover in 1865 and kept an exact record of the price of individual items of food and household necessities over the period.[14] The cost of living compared very favourably with that of Scotland or England at the time, and she commented, as did other visitors, on the relatively high standard of living Germans could enjoy despite their low incomes. Although salaries and wages were low in Germany until after 1871, prices were low as well and the staple products which made up the simple German diet were cheap. After 1871 wages began to rise, with brief fluctuations in 1873 and 1880. At the same time prices rose less, and the income per head of the population actually doubled between 1871 and 1913. The cost of living varied according to region both at the beginning and end of the period. On the whole life was more costly in the towns of the North than in the South.

As for salaries, the disparity between earnings at the top and bottom of the professional ladder was considerable in mid-century, and was made to seem greater, since men at the top of their professions were not expected to keep up appearances to the extent usual in England or France. If they entertained at all, it was on a modest scale. A minister of state in Prussia, or a general, might earn 12,000 *thaler* (one *thaler* was the equivalent of about three shillings in 1830), while a sergeant earned 102 and a private 60.[15] There were considerable differences between the earnings of skilled and manual workers in the North and West and in the East of Germany, notably Silesia and the Baltic ports, between 1850 and 1870. Wages in the Rhineland were as much as twenty-five per cent higher in the 1860s and 1870s than in the East, where the population increase was greatest, unemployment high and the roads and railways less developed. By the end of the period regional wage differentials, as well as those between the various classes of workers had almost disappeared.

There were two periods of general social distress in Germany in consequence of sudden inflation: one was at the end of the the Napoleonic wars, the other in the so-called Hungry Forties. On both occasions city dwellers and agricultural workers were hard hit and there were bread riots in East Germany and in Berlin. There was considerable poverty all over Germany around 1830 and the authorities began to fear the consequences of a population explosion and legislated accordingly. It seemed that the writings of Malthus had penetrated Germany. In Württemberg, Bavaria, Baden, Hanover and Hesse, laws were passed requiring a prospective couple to give evidence of their adequate means of support before marriage. The result of the law was a general increase in illegitimacy.

The cost of accommodation was modest in Germany, and an estimated three-quarters of the population of the city of Berlin in mid-century paid less than 50 *Reichsthaler* annually in rent (that is, about £8). Clothes, apart from articles of fashion like the cashmere shawls for 1500 *thaler,* were also inexpensive. In 1822 an overcoat cost between 16 and 22 *thaler,* a pair of trousers 5 to 8, though these might seem a considerable item for a clerk in a government office who earned 200 *thaler* yearly (in 1835). The cost of education need not be large: a Silesian merchant, Simon, paid one *thaler* a month for his son, Henry, to attend the *gymnasium* in the 1820s; there were opportunities for poor boys to attend both school and university on scholarships. Henry Simon spent 565 *thaler* in one calendar year while a student of law at the university of Berlin from 1825–6. This included the cost of his journeys home to Breslau, plus presents for his family, but as the son of a well-to-do merchant he was likely to spend more than most. Students often lodged at the houses of their teachers. Half a year's lodging at Tübingen or Heidelberg in 1845 cost a student some twenty five florins, but in Bonn or Berlin, then the fashionable universities, it would cost the same in *thaler,* that is, twice as much.

The payment of artists' work varied greatly; the fee was generally determined by demand. Painters and musicians, especially the newly popular *virtuosi,* could often command a high price; so did some authors. Clauren, the most popular author of the mid-nineteenth century, could command twenty-four *louis d'or* a sheet, but Grillparzer got only six ducats from Weimar for his play *Sappho*. Austrians were generally content with less. Of course Clauren was exceptional: he happened to produce the sentimental pieces that the reading public wanted. E. Th. A. Hoffman earned a salary of 1600 *thaler* as a senior civil servant, but he got 330 for a short story in the twenties. Karoline von Humboldt learned 'as a secret' from her husband that Goethe had managed to get 1000 *thaler* for his *Hermann und Dorothea*. That worked out at twelve *groschen* or a shilling a line, she mused, but then Goethe was a good business man. Zelter earned 1550 *thaler* for his Good Friday music, but this too was unusually high. Piracy and the lending libraries kept low the number of copies of books and of musical scores sold at the official price. Goethe's *Conversations with Eckermann,* his most popular book in mid-century, sold only 3,000 copies in thirty-two years. On the whole writers were not paid well before 1880, but then few of the major figures were professional writers: they did not depend on their literary works for a living. The great majority, like Hoffmann, Grillparzer, Eichendorff, Stifter, Keller, Storm, were civil servants; Mörike and Gotthelf were clergymen; Heine, Börne, Gutzkow and Fontane were journalists for much of their lives. To many, writing was initially a form of escape or compensation, but few wished to risk making it their sole means of support. They even felt that it would not necessarily be good for their writing: Keller and Storm in their correspondence blamed the aridity of Paul Heyse's later works on the fact that he had no other means of employment and lacked the stimulus of limited opportunity to write.

Visitors to the German states in the 1830s–40s rarely refrained from criticising the repressive policies of their rulers; but most admitted the existence of a positive side to the regime. The German sovereigns showed unusual interest in the arts and made generous provision for the recreation of their subjects. King John of Saxony could publish a translation of Dante under the pseudonym of *Philalethes* and correspond on Virgil with the intelligent Frederick William iv of Prussia. This belonged to the private sphere: what mattered was the monarchs' public patronage of the arts. Almost every ruler was interested in the theatre; King Frederick William iii of Prussia attended it every night of his life in these years; the Landgrave of Hesse acted as his own producer and even conducted the orchestra. In Germany in the

1830s there were fifty-two resident theatres, the best of which were thought to be those of Vienna, Berlin, Weimar, Munich, Düsseldorf (under Immermann), Dresden (under Tieck), Hamburg, Frankfurt and Brunswick. There were thirty travelling companies and an estimated 3,500 persons employed in the theatre at this time.

The wide interest in music was common in all sections of society except the very poor. The rulers fostered it for the sake of what Ilse Barea calls 'officially attested harmlessness'[16] which was the ideal of the more reactionary rulers for their subjects. The Berlin *Singakademie* for the daughters of the well-born, under the direction of Goethe's friend Karl Zelter, his pupil Mendelssohn's encouragement of public subscription concerts, and the numerous choirs which were formed in local circles at this time, are instances of growing interest. And everybody joined the craze for opera in the twenties and thirties. Humboldt as Minister of Education had done much for the teaching of music. In consultation with Zelter he had found ways to make music accessible to all classes. Even the poor schools were now supplied with instruments.

Another amenity enjoyed by the populace was access to the possessions of their rulers. The Austrian Emperor took the lead in opening his park and gallery in Belvedere to the public, the Margrave of Baden and even the unpleasant Landgrave of Hesse followed suit, and soon it became general practice to let the public promenade in royal and ducal grounds. The people took full and careful advantage of the opportunities. Germans had the name for enjoying themselves on little, but what city dwellers in England had the parks and tea- and beer-gardens specially built for them by the city fathers as had the Germans of all classes?

The general habit of the family constitutional, so aptly illustrated decades later by Wilhelm Busch, was formed in these years. The streets in the main towns were paved in the twenties and thirties, so one could walk without getting splashed with mud. Contemporaries frequently expressed their pleasure at this innovation. It became a habit in mid-century for middle-class women to drink coffee and eat ices, and for the men to drink white wine on holiday afternoons. Bavarian beer penetrated North Germany and began to oust the watery white or Prussian beer with which the monarchy had assured the sobriety of its citizens. The coffee house began to spread outside the bigger cities, and men to go there to

27

read their newspapers. There were no clubs in Germany in the English sense. The cakeshop also became popular and was one of the first bridges between the aristocracy and the middle classes. There were ninety-six cakeshops in Berlin in 1840, but there were also sixty bookshops and thirty-six lending libraries to cater for the tremendous public demand for light reading.

Alongside the institutions created or patronised by the paternalistic rulers, the professional middle classes began to form associations of their own. Henry Simon, a lawyer from Breslau, who later participated in the 1848 Revolution and then fled to England, joined such a social club during his time in Magdeburg in 1835. It was limited to 400 members and the written regulations declared that 'members of the officer corps and the professions are suitable associates'.[17] The entry fee was a *thaler,* about three shillings, and the monthly subscription the same. The object was mainly social, and wives and members of the family were invited to the regular balls and festivities in the winter months. The balls began at 6 pm and ended about 9.30 to 10. The clubs, like the one Simon later joined in Greifswald, sometimes indulged in charitable activity, and sometimes in aesthetic pursuits; art societies, or *Kunstvereine,* sprang up all over Germany in these years. The Society for the Protection of Animals, which Castelli, with not a little self-advertisement, founded in Vienna in the thirties, and which had a large following, is another example of the need for contacts and interests outside the immediate family circle. These activities are also instances of the first tentative steps in bourgeois self-assertion, which in western countries by now took the form of commercial enterprise. After 1848 associations in bourgeois circles tended to be more within the professions, and later many were nationalistic.

In time, even non-political associations in Germany did serve the creation of national self-consciousness. Associations came together at festivals and congresses from all parts of the country, from the Dürer and the Naturalists' festivals in 1828 to the economists' conference in 1858 and the famous Schiller centenary of 1859. The National Liberal Association, formed in the same year, 1859, represented a new stage in Germany's development, both as a social phenomenon and evidence of political achievement. The national character of the association was taken for granted and it was largely created by middle class opinion, though its active president was Duke Ernst of Coburg, elder brother of Prince Albert. Despite the rigid separation of the classes in Germany, Germans soon proved themselves susceptible to nationalist appeal. When in the seventies and eighties sporting clubs became a popular form of association, particularly for hiking, climbing and fencing, these had peculiarly nationalist overtones. In the Jahn tradition the Alpine Club was the first to exclude Jews, and other athletic groups gradually followed suit.

In the smaller towns and among the petty bourgeoisie, the *Stammtisch* or regular table at the local inn was the centre of masculine social life. Germans sat down to drink. They discussed too, but more usually it was 'Life' they discussed, not public affairs. At the beginning of the period people were conditioned into leaving politics to the authorities. They were not particularly interested in politics. The heavy polls of the seventies and eighties indicated the change that had come over the Germans in the last fifty years. In the circumstances, as in Nazi Germany or the German Democratic Republic today, people in the 1830s and 1840s cultivated hobbies and pastimes: skittles, cards or stamp collecting, or literary or musical interests. Such pursuits, if engaged in by a group, could of course be suspect; Grillparzer and Castelli witnessed the seizure of the archives of the *Ludlamshöhle,* their literary club in Vienna, by thirty-two policemen and a commissioner. Germans also liked to entertain at home, but standards of hospitality varied according to region. The aristocratic and the Jewish salons in Berlin declined after about 1830, and it was some time before the middle classes could offer a substitute. By the late 1850s the 'evenings' of academic circles, again mainly in Berlin, began to be talked about. Here authors read their works, and painters and musicians were welcome. The cultural tone was high, humour absent, and weak tea replaced alcohol at these *'Spree soirées'* as their critics called them, referring to the river on which Berlin lies. The guests were expected to go home at ten. The warmth of welcome was nicely graded according to status and title. Spielhagen's *Problematische Naturen* contains a splendidly funny account of such a gathering, featuring a reading of Schiller's *Wallenstein* by guests and hosts: the important roles are reserved for those whom the hosts consider socially superior;

29

Primula, the vicar's wife, has ambitions as a poetess and an actress and has rehearsed her performance of the heroine Thekla; finding another preferred to her for this chosen role and herself cast as one of the murderers, she bursts sobbing from the room and refuses to take further part in the entertainment.[18]

The South of Germany was much less formal in its manners and generally less pretentious than the North. The rulers there had the common touch, none more so that King Ludwig 1 of Bavaria (1825–48) in his role as the German Maecenas. He summoned leading scholars and artists to his court and treated them as his intimates. In Vienna the high nobility, although very caste-conscious, patronised young men and women of humble origins who showed artistic talent: this was the only part of the Confederation where the aristocratic salon still survived into the middle of the century. Despite the decline in the Jewish salon, Jewish intellectuals and businessmen liked to entertain at home and it was they who offered the most socially mixed hospitality in all regions of Germany. In the thirties and early forties, when Germans were beginning to feel the need for contact with a more cosmopolitan world than their own, the Jews were in a position to satisfy this need through their family and business connections. The Jews entertained their friends with concerts and lectures as well as good food, and contemporary novels and memoirs, for example Imermann's *Epigonen* (1836), Felix von Mendelssohn's life and the letters of Meyerbeer contain many examples from life of the importance of the Jewish or part-Jewish home as a bridge between class and region.

The German public's appetite for reading material at serious as well as popular level excited considerable comment at home and abroad from the late eighteenth century onwards. There were some 296 bookshops in Prussia in the 1830s, and 114 in Bavaria. Books seemed to play a less important role in the life of Austrians; at any rate in the same decade there were only 89 bookshops in the whole Austrian monarchy. Illiteracy was rare in the Confederation and it was popular demand, rather than the booksellers and publishers, which encouraged the setting up of lending libraries in all towns and even in some larger villages. Books were expensive, not least because the activity of the pirateers made it necessary for publishers to cover their costs with the first hundred or so copies. No national law of copyright existed, although in the states a system of privileges still operated which protected a particular publication in that state. But if a privilege was obtained for a book in one state the pirateers merely published it in the neighbouring states at a much lower price and on cheap paper. The official situation was such that when Perthes and his associates planned to publish Goethe's collected works, they had to apply separately to each of the thirty-nine states of the Confederation and received the copyright as a privilege, not a right. Only in the 1830s did several German states attempt to combine to protect publishers and therefore authors from the pirateers. Until then the case of Goethe's brother-in-law Vulpius was typical. His *Rinaldo Rinaldini* was the most widely read novel of the early nineteenth century, but only five editions were printed by his publisher: the pirateers had provided the rest. Vulpius' only revenge was to introduce a pirateer into the fifth edition of his novel and have Rinaldo hang him without further ceremony from a tree. When a national law of copyright was introduced in the 1860s, the publishers were able to lower the price of Gutzkow's nine-volume novel, *Die Ritter vom Geiste,* by half.

Geography, travellers' tales and devotional literature had been favourite reading matter in the eighteenth century. In the nineteenth it was the novel. Novels were generally serialised in almanacs and 'pocket books' until about 1850; thereafter cheap editions of novels, often up to 1,000 pages long, appeared and enjoyed considerable success. Political and social questions, the position of the nobility and of the Jews, German unity, and Darwinism were all treated in novels, the most successful of which, such as those by Freytag and Spielhagen, went into scores of editions. Novels about local life and sentimental tales of family life remained popular throughout the period. The chief literary achievement of the time was the novella, a form of short story requiring great technical mastery. However it was never popular with a wide reading public nor with the majority of critics. Lyric poetry became less popular in Germany in the second half of the nineteenth century, as Keller noted in 1880. Ballads on the other hand retained their appeal and the national movement of the sixties increased their popularity.

The weeklies, such as *Die Gartenlaube,* which first appeared on a national scale in the fifties, fostered discussion of national issues in the home. It is interesting to trace the change of public attitudes from liberal to exclusively nationalist in successive issues of *Die Gartenlaube* from the date of its first issue, 1853, to 1866, the year of the battle of Königgrätz.[19] After 1848 the number of national and local newspapers increased and circulation rose steadily. At the end of the period German newspapers reflect the character of educated German public opinion: a high cultural level in the serious press, but much less straight political reporting than was customary in the British or French press of the time. On a more popular level, the regional press more than held its own against the centralised national press throughout this period and well into the twentieth century.

The greatest change in social habits was brought about by the revolution in transport which is of course the most far-reaching single cause of change in the century. The roads were extremely bad in 1830 owing to troop movements in the wars and neglect ever since, but this began to be rectified in the following decade. Outside Vienna, where stone posts stood on street corners to protect the houses from temperamental drivers, the pace of travel was slow before 1835. Travellers noted that Germans were notoriously careful drivers, five to six miles an hour being considered by them an excellent average on a coach trip. The *Eilwagen* or fast coaches on the road between Frankfurt and Leipzig reached nine miles an hour. The authorities reinforced native caution by imposing fines of six florins or ten shillings on coachmen who did not attach a drag to their loaded vehicles when descending an incline.

Yet the Germans showed immediate enthusiasm for the railways and steamships, and people who had formerly never considered leaving their province now began to become acquainted with other parts of the Confederation. Steamships had run regularly on the Rhine since the twenties and English engineers introduced them to the Danube and the Elbe ten years later. The famous Danube steamship company, the *Donaudampfschiffahrts-gesellschaft,* was opened in 1835, and six years later the traffic on the company's steamships had increased from 17,000 to 170,000 passengers a year. The first German railway was opened between Nuremberg and Furth, also in 1835, and ten years later a network of some 1,500 miles existed in Germany. Varnhagen wrote in the early forties that some 2,000 people used the line from Berlin to Potsdam daily. Better transport and a slowly improving economy started a vogue for travel which by the 1850s spread rapidly right down the social scale. No longer were young gentlemen on the Grand Tour, their tutors, soldiers, students and journeymen the only travellers in the Confederation. Even middle-class families of modest means began to take annual holidays in different parts of Germany. This coincided with the vogue for the 'waters'.

The spas, of which there were about one hundred in Germany in mid-century, were nicely graded accordinging to the rank of those who patronised them. Aachen and Baden were the most expensive, Karlsbad, with its association with crowned heads and of course Goethe, the most elegant. Even conferences of statesmen, at Karlsbad, Teplitz and Troppau, and later Gastein, combined business with the waters. The most fashionable spas attracted some 5,000 visitors annually in the thirties, the less well known, where one could get furnished accommodation and the baths for as little as a couple of shillings a day, about 500 to 1,500. The Prussian government, however, soon began to show concern for the amount of money spent on this new fashion. In 1834 the doctors of Berlin were instructed in a special circular to prescribe a visit to the spas for their patients only in exceptional circumstances. It tended, the Prussian authorities alleged, to lead families into debt, and furthermore aroused bitterness among those who were unable to afford the journeys from which they hoped so much. There was also the loss which the state incurred if the destination of the trip lay outside its frontiers.

Contemporaries were not slow to grasp the implications of the new mobility and the revolution in transport. Even before this happened, Goethe had written in 1828: 'I do not fear that Germany will never be one. Our fine roads and the railways of the future will play their part here.'[20] The importance of the Customs Union of 1834 in stimulating mobility of people as well as goods became a significant factor in the growth of national consciousness.

Education

The nationwide interest in communications was new in Germany: interest and pride in their educational system had long been characteristic of Germans of almost all classes. These attitudes had been formed under the Enlightenment, for benevolent despots in the eighteenth century in Prussia, Austria, Württemberg and elsewhere had shown personal interest in primary and secondary schooling and in university education. Humboldt's reforms in Prussia in the early nineteenth century had aimed to make good educational facilities available to almost everyone in that state. However staffing and housing especially in the primary schools left much to be desired. As late as 1864, Raabe's literary depiction of a poor primary school in *Der Hungerpastor* was felt to be disturbingly accurate. In the early chapters of Raabe's novel, the idealistic young teacher, Hans Unwirasch, sees the hopelessness of trying to teach children who are undernourished and who often contract tuberculosis in the squalid schoolhouse. Grossly underpaid himself, he strives in vain to alleviate their misery. Humboldt's policy was particularly effective in secondary school education. His brief but fertile period as Minister of Public Instruction was informed with secular humanism, and his efforts were imitated to some extent in other states, notably Bavaria. Education was broadly based as regards curriculum, and aimed at creating, at least in Prussia, self-reliant, well-informed citizens in the wider context of Prussian liberal reform which was initiated and carried through by the ministers of the Prussian crown in the years 1806–19, by Stein, Hardenberg, Gneisenau, Humboldt and others.

Several other features of German education in the nineteenth century deserve to be mentioned. In his secondary school reform Humboldt had distinguished between the *humanistisches Gymnasium,* which taught mainly the humanities, and the *Realgymnasium* which gave prominence to scientific subjects. The latter prepared a substantial number of men for the industrialisation of the country in mid-century. Technical colleges also received attention. The first had been founded many decades earlier in Brunswick in 1745, Vienna (1815), Karlsruhe (1829), Hanover (1831) and several others followed. These were so-called *Polytechniken* and were succeeded after the middle of the century by technical universities, such as for example that of Munich, founded in 1868. Experimental schools were a further notable feature of the educational scene. Many of these, such as the Francke Foundation at Halle, with its stress on crafts and the sciences, or the pietist *Herrenhuter* schools go back to the eighteenth century. Basedow's *Philanthropinum* at Dessau had not survived into the nineteenth century but it had created the precedent for teachers' training colleges, which were adopted by Prussia and other states. In the field of *Kindergarten* and primary school teaching, Germany was well in advance of the time; the greatest pedagogues of the century applied and developed Pestalozzi's ideas: Froebel, who founded the first *Kindergarten* in Thuringia, Herbart, Stifter, and Gotthelf.

The traditional relationship between the state and the universities was deeply affected in Germany by the revolutionary upheaval and the war years. Many German universities owed their origin to an enlightened Protestant prince, who had looked on his foundation as a support to his cause: for instance Marburg and Jena. Others were the fruit of the new interest in scientific inquiry in the eighteenth century, such as Halle and Göttingen. By 1815 a number of universities had disappeared, or survived merely as theological colleges, such as Salzburg. The Prussian authorities showed an interest in the founding of new universities and the re-invigoration of older ones. Berlin, Bonn and Breslau were the creation of the Prussian liberal reform era. The particular interest of Berlin University, which Humboldt founded as the crowning achievement of his period as minister of education in 1810, was his concept of it as a 'privileged corporation', as against the traditional view of a university as a state institution. This permitted a considerable degree of freedom within the university, of academic self-government, whereby members of the faculties elected their own rector. The faculties themselves were largely independent of the senate. The centralised administration and extreme specialisation of French universities had no place in the German system. Furthermore academic freedom had a beneficial influence on teaching and scholarship. Freedom to teach and study what one wished and the flexible and wide syllabus encouraged the pursuit of knowledge for its own sake, if it did perpetuate the type of scholar who is cut off from the rest of the world. As the century progressed, facilities for research were greatly extended in every field.

There were naturally some distinctions between the twenty-two universities of the Confederation. A small number retained their exclusive character of academies for the sons of noblemen – this was true of Bonn, the 'princes' ' university, which Frederick William, later King of Prussia (1840–61), and Prince Albert of Saxe-

Coburg attended; in general however the German university was socially much more broadly based than comparable institutions in other countries. No religious or other test was imposed on students entering the university. They were also protected from the law of the land in that they were subject to the jurisdiction of the university. Tradesmen could not sue them for debt above a small sum, nor landladies for unpaid rent of more than a term. The relatively low cost of a university education and the students' independence of any rigid course or examination system fostered an enthusiastic spirit of scientific enquiry.

However students laboured under one distinct disadvantage between 1819 and 1848, namely the constant vigilance of the authorities in the spirit of the Carlsbad Decrees (1819). These had been the work of the leading statesmen of the Confederation under Metternich, who had imposed strict measures on universities in order to guard against radicalism. Duelling was suspect in these years and, according to the regulations of several universities (Berlin, Breslau etc.) duellists risked punishment of between three and six years' imprisonment in a fortress. In her memoirs the novelist, Fanny Lewald, described the effect of such rigorous punishment on her cousin Heinrich Simon. The real reason for this harsh policy was the political association between duelling and the fraternities or student associations. These had been founded after 1815 with the object of achieving the liberal reform and national unity which the Congress of Vienna had failed to give. But duelling continued right through the century, often arousing intense public interest, as for example in the case of the social reformer, Ferdinand Lassalle, whose career was cut short by his death in a duel. After 1866 when the national movement became respectable, duelling was actually condoned as the action of a brave and manly German. Apart from individual cases like the 'demagogues' or radical student groups in Prussia after Carlsbad, the social reformers like Georg Büchner and his friends, the body of the students did not draw the attention of the authorities to themselves. Many took part in the Revolution of 1848, but only in Vienna could the student body be compared to the political groups of the universities in Latin countries. In general the German student was sober and hardworking, his limited means forcing him to pay attention to his studies, and like his seniors he tended not to be interested in politics. Student numbers remained steady between 1830 and 1870 at about 15,000. After 1871 there was a rapid increase, until by 1900 the number had doubled. The technical universities had some 3,000 students in 1869 and by 1900 over 10,000.

In the first half of the century the universities often provided the most significant criticism of the authoritarian system, in particular of the 'alliance of throne and altar' which had been restored after 1815; Schleiermacher at Berlin, Görres in the Rhineland and at Munich, and the Tübingen school of theology in the 1830s were prominent here. In the second half of the century such criticism became rare, although the causes for this lie in the earlier period. It was one of the consequences of the post-war years that universities in the greater part of Germany lost control over their own finances; as they were rarely endowed they thus became subordinate to the Ministry of Religion and Instruction. Though it consulted the faculty in question, the Ministry made its own appointments to chairs. Some appointments, like those of Hegel and Ranke, had far-reaching effects on current attitudes to the state and authority in the next generation. By the middle of the century it was apparent that the authorities tended to appoint to chairs men whose political views were acceptable to them. Until 1867 a man whose convictions were unacceptable could usually find preference elsewhere in Germany; after the establishment of the Empire, this possibility, apart from Austria, was closed. For these reasons the tradition of German universities as critics of authoritarian assumptions was largely lost. In the last decades of the nineteenth century the German academics, like other members of the intelligentsia, became increasingly anti-liberal.

Apart from the Prussian landowners Germans of all classes retained a deep respect for the educated man and set great store by the education of their children. But although the average German was well taught and acquainted with a wide variety of subjects, he was not encouraged to think for himself nor to relate his knowledge to his political and social circumstances. The system in Germany was as authoritarian as any and the nineteenth century, instead of modifying authoritarian assumptions, confirmed them. The approach to teaching became noticeably anti-aesthetic from about the 1830s onwards. The love of learning characteristic of the early decades of the century degenerated into a desire to accumulate mere book-learning: even Hegel, who died in 1831, admitted that the German pupil acquired merely a knowledge of facts, a preparation adequate to a career in the civil service. He himself was partly to blame for this. As a teacher he had paid little regard to the importance of criticism and discussion by the student. Two leading Prussian state officials, Altenstein, the minister, and Schulze, the secretary of state for secondary education, helped to put Hegel's ideas into practice during their period in office in the 1820s and 1830s. Although 1848 brought a revival of interest in liberal educational policies as an important instrument of political reform, paternalist rulers successfully eradicated this tendency in the fifties. The educational reforms at the time of the *Kulturkampf* attempted to free secondary education from the strong influence of the churches, but they did not try to check the tendency to believe that there was a right and wrong answer to every question, or to connect book-learning with political and social reality.

The influence of school and more particularly university was probably greater in Germany than elsewhere: it affected a more considerable proportion of the population, since the middle class attended grammar school and university in increasing numbers. For many it was the one time in their lives that they moved freely outside their family circle. The seminar system gave individual professors considerable influence over their students and helped to create schools within a particular discipline. Whatever their shortcomings, beyond the boundaries of Germany her institutions of learning acquired a growing reputation throughout the nineteenth century.

German scholarship achieved fame in Western Europe and in the United States partly through the mediation of Carlyle and Emerson; however it was above all in Eastern Europe that German scholarship and culture enjoyed the greatest esteem and influence. 'Whoever wears a decent coat here, speaks Italian', reported the Tuscan ambassador to the Viennese court under Leopold I: the same could have been said of German in East and South East Europe two centuries later. For the Czechs, Hungarians and Southern Slavs, German culture appeared to be a bridge to the restoration of their own national culture. The lustre of Herder's name drew increasing numbers of students to Germany, and in the first decades of the nineteenth century there was room in German minds and hearts for the national aspirations of her neighbours; there was, for example, Hoffmann von Fallersleben's enthusiasm for the Flemish cause, that of Lenau and Laube for Poland, especially in 1830–31, and that of the historian Luden for the Czechs. German cultural nationalism still made converts in Eastern Europe at a time when in Germany it had been superseded by an exclusively political programme. Panslavism itself was the by-product of German thought, of men like Herder, Hegel and the German Romantics.

It was in the historical sciences that German scholarship made its most significant contribution to Europe in the nineteenth century. To this was added, at the end of the period, the achievements of German doctors and chemists. Slav students attended German universities in large numbers, and between 1848 and 1914 more than half of all doctors, lawyers and teachers in the Balkan countries and almost every leading writer had been educated in Vienna.[21]

The churches

If religious questions aroused less passion and controversy in nineteenth century Germany than in England and, to judge from literature, the clergyman seemed a less necessary part of the social scene, the history of the churches is of fundamental importance to an understanding of German political and social attitudes in the latter half of the century.

The decisive event in the history of the Catholic Church in Germany during this period was the secularisation of ecclesiastical estates and church lands which had taken place in 1803 in the wake of the revolutionary wars. Hitherto the German Catholic Church had been a significant political force in its own right. Its bishops and abbots, generally scions of noble houses, were often immensely wealthy men. In addition the church owed a very great deal of its influence and prestige to its ancient association with the Holy Roman Empire. In 1803 the French were planning to use ecclesiastical territory to compensate the German secular princes who had been forced to surrender their estates on the left bank of the Rhine. Accordingly a deputation of the *Reichstag* or Diet of the Holy Roman Empire decreed that church property should be redistributed and the ecclesiastical rulers compensated for their loss. This upheaval was followed in 1806 by the collapse of the Holy Roman Empire, 1,006 years after its creation, then by the Napoleonic occupation of Germany and finally by the peace conference at Vienna in 1815. Contrary to expectations the Congress made no provision for the regulation of Catholic affairs in the new Confederation.

All these events had a profound effect on German Catholicism, although the pessimistic prophecies of contemporary writers as to the disintegration of the Catholic Church itself were not fulfilled. In the short run injustice was done to individuals, and the secular princes often proved harder taskmasters to their subjects than their ecclesiastical predecessors, and were less mindful of their obligations to the educational and charitable institutions which they now took over. In the long run, however, the secularisation and its consequences proved the source of renewed spiritual strength to the Church as a whole. It also healed some of its most painful antagonisms, and it solved one problem which had bedevilled the Church in the previous century: the gulf between the aristocratic and often worldly hierarchy and the parish clergy was bridged. Henceforth appointments were made on merit and the German episcopacy in the following decades included men of singular moral and intellectual stature such as Archbishop Ketteler of Mainz, or Archbishop Geissel of Cologne.

The rulers and representatives of the various states at the Congress of Vienna in 1815 strenuously avoided committing themselves to a general agreement on the future organisation of the Catholic Church and its relations to the civil power. They did this in the hope of being able to revise diocesan boundaries in their own favour, appoint their own territorial bishop and retain a decisive influence in ecclesiastical affairs. The papal legate Cardinal Consalvi, having failed to achieve the desired settlement at Vienna, now worked to obtain a series of concordats between the Vatican and the German states. Only Bavaria actually signed a concordat in 1817, which gave assurance to the Church that her rights would be protected and that the secular ruler would contribute to the support of the Church. In return for this, the King received extensive rights in nominating bishops and members of cathedral chapters, and even parish priests. Papal bulls settled diocesan arrangements for Baden, Württemberg and Nassau in 1821, and subsequently for Prussia, Hesse-Kassel and Hesse-Darmstadt. In practice the secular power benefitted at the expense of the church, for it took its rights more literally than its obligations. After 1830 ecclesiastical stipends were paid by the state governments and though areas of conflict remained, both Protestant and Catholic representatives sat on management committees of state schools, and Catholic schools and faculties of theology at the universities were promoted.

The only major decision affecting the future of the churches which was taken at Vienna was contained in Article 16 of the *Bundesakte* or Federal laws (June 1815). The Confederation was to be based on religious equality in place of the old confessional states, whereby each state was identified with a particular denomination. Equal civil and political rights were now granted to the Christian subjects of states. The secular princes jealously guarded their sovereign rights at the expense of those of the churches, and the Catholic hierarchy and faithful clashed with the secular power on many occasions in the nineteenth century. This was something which had been quite rare before the French Revolution of 1789. The wording of the Bavarian Concordat of 1817 and the Papal bulls of 1821 was made purposely vague in order to avoid conflict, but this instead proved the source of endless controversy. The most celebrated clash between church and state occurred in Prussia in the 1870s. This was the so-called *Kulturkampf*, when Bismarck, supported by the liberal parties, introduced legislation to curtail the influence of the churches, particularly the Catholic Church, in public life, education and marriage. The opposition to Bismarck from the clergy and laity, and more especially from the Catholic Centre party, acerbated the conflict and led to the imprisonment of a large number of the clergy. At one time some 30 bishops and 1,800 priests were imprisoned or under house arrest. The quarrel was complicated by the fact that the Centre party had become the focal point of the extensive opposition to German rule in Poland, Alsace and the areas along the Danish border acquired by Prussia in 1866. It eventually ended in a compromise largely in favour of the Catholics after more than a decade of conflict. Nearly forty years previously the *Kulturkampf* had been anticipated in the celebrated Cologne Incident of 1837, involving the redoubtable Archbishop Droste-Vischering of Cologne, and its sequel, the quarrel between Archbishop Dunin of Posen, and the Governor of the Grand Duchy of Posen, Flottwell. In Cologne and Posen the archbishops were arrested; Dunin actually spent ten months in a fortress. The quarrel concerned principally the Church's claims that the children of mixed marriages should be Catholic. This was an issue of relevance at that time since Prussian civil servants coming to work in the Rhineland frequently married Catholic women from the region. The quarrels in 1837 dragged on for many months, for the authorities had underestimated their opponents as well as the degree of loyalty of the faithful. The incidents aroused a widespread reaction among the intellectual laity as well as the masses, and although bitter criticism of the clergy flowed from the pens of public figures – such as the Young German Gutzkow – the issue was eventually settled for the time being in a manner generally favourable to the Church. When Frederick William IV came to the throne in 1840 he made a point of conciliating public opinion in the Catholic Rhineland in order to win support against growing revolutionary unrest. One of the means he chose was to start a fund to finish Cologne Cathedral, a project which aroused a good deal of public controversy. However, up to the time of the *Kulturkampf* the Catholic Church was better situated in Prussia than in the other German states.

The secularisation of church lands in 1803 had given the German Protestant princes an ascendancy over the Catholic rulers which was to be significant in subsequent decades. Before that date Germany had been fairly evenly divided between Protestant and Catholic rulers. Now the former ecclesiastical princes were reduced to being subjects of secular rulers, most of them Protestant. Even where the ruler was Catholic, as in Bavaria, he usually tried to imitate his Protestant peers and treat the Church and its institutions as part of the state. Only in Austria, where Metternich was well aware of the value of the Catholic Church as an ally of conservatism, was the civil authority anxious to conciliate the Papacy and the Church.

An interesting consequence of the German rulers' encroachments on the Church was the changed relation of German Catholics to the Papacy. Whereas formerly the hierarchy had resisted what they regarded as papal interference, now they looked to Rome for guidance and authority. A few individuals did challenge papal authority in the nineteenth century – there was the case of the Bonn theologian Hermes in the thirties or Bishop Döllinger's famous rejection of papal infallibility after the First Vatican Council in 1870 and his subsequent founding of the Old

Catholic church – but these incidents had little long-term effect in Germany.

The shock administered to the Church as a whole by the secularisation of church property in 1803 and its consequences gave members of the Church at all levels a new self-awareness. A number of Catholic intellectual circles were formed, notably in Vienna and Munich. At the beginning of the century Clemens Maria Hofbauer introduced to Vienna the missionary order of the Redemptorists, who were famous for their preaching and their zeal. Hofbauer won an enthusiastic following both among the aristocracy and the artisan classes. He attracted controversial figures to his cause: the Romantic writers Friedrich Schlegel, Zacharias Werner, Adam Müller, all of them converts to Catholicism. In Munich the Rhenish publicist Görres, who had fled there in 1827 to evade the Prussian authorities, attracted others, men like the scientist and social reformer, Franz von Baader, and Bishop Ignaz Döllinger. Throughout the nineteenth century German Catholics associated the decline in the secular authority of their church with the influence of liberalism and the ideas of the French Revolution. During the Prussian reform era and in the years of bureaucratic domination which followed (1819–40), Catholic publicists sided with the old feudal society and were the spokesmen of a Romantic conservative philosophy which remained attractive for many decades to come. The contribution made by Adam Müller, Görres and von Baader to philosophy, theology, history, political and social thought had an important influence on conservative thinking between 1815–48. These Catholic thinkers and those who shared their views resented the power of the state to intervene in church affairs and hoped to curtail it. They felt closer to Rome than had German Catholics for many generations and they made skilful use of the press to spread their ideas, e.g. the journals *Eos* in Munich and *Der Katholik* in Mainz. After 1848 the emergence of a Catholic political party gave a new cohesion and sense of unity to Catholics; it anticipated the Catholic Centre Party (1871–1933) in its high degree of organisation and its ability to unite all classes and all interests.

In the early years of the century Clemens Maria Hofbauer had attracted large numbers of artisans back to the Church in Vienna by his preaching and his personal piety; in South and West Germany the reintroduction of processions, pilgrimages and other popular devotions which had disappeared during the Enlightenment had a widespread appeal to the masses. The custom of holding missions, consisting of sermons and devotional exercises all over the country proved an effective way of winning back many who had left the Church. The fact that these were often prohibited by the police did not deter worshippers: when the police intervened in Baden enormous crowds streamed across the Rhine to attend the services in Alsace. In the second half of the century the Catholic masses, unlike the Protestants, remained in general faithful to their religion. Catholicism even managed to gain a foothold in the Trade Union movement: by 1913 approximately one sixth of all trade union members belonged to the Christian Trade Union.

An important aspect of the religious revival was the movement known as social Catholicism; here, too, Adam Müller and Franz von Baader were influential figures in its early days. Like other Catholic social thinkers in the nineteenth century, they looked at the question of labour relations from a patriarchal point of view, in terms of the duties of employers, not of workers' rights. Social Catholicism found two great apostles in the priests von Ketteler (1811–77), later Archbishop of Mainz, and Adolf Kolping (1813–65), founder of a nationwide network of hostels for artisans which still exist in Germany today and are known as *Kolpinghäuser*. The two men came from very dissimilar backgrounds: Kolping was an artisan and had become a priest only in middle life, while Ketteler was a nobleman. Both had been educated in Jesuit colleges in Switzerland (the Jesuits were banned in Germany and Austria between 1773 and 1848). Kolping decided to devote his life to helping the apprentices who were so hard hit by the Hungry Forties and he founded the first Catholic Clubs for working men. Ketteler's book, *Die Arbeiterfrage und das Christentum* (1864), showed the influence both of Catholic social thinking and of the author's contacts with Lassalle, the socialist leader. Somewhat unexpectedly for a distinguished prelate, he advocated universal suffrage as a means of encouraging working class self-help. Ketteler and Kolping embodied in their different ways the new type of priest who was socially active and involved in topical affairs; during their lifetime the Church showed increasing awareness of its social role. The Society of St Vincent de Paul, founded in France in the thirties, opened its first brotherhood in Munich in 1845, with the support of the nobility, members of Görres' circle, and working men. The care of the poor, sick and destitute was undertaken by various bodies within the Church, both religious and lay.

Yet despite the real revival of Catholic life and worship in Germany, and of its relative success as compared with Protestantism in retaining the support of the masses of the faithful in a secularist age, the position of the Catholic Church in nineteenth-century Germany was something of an anomaly. Individual Catholics made relatively little contribution to the national life: it was men from Protestant or humanist backgrounds who determined the future of life and thought. Catholics had a very small share in the original work in philosophy, history, science and statecraft. Northern Germany set its stamp on Central and Southern Germany, and after 1848–9 the genuine popular and democratic elements of Rhenish and South German Catholicism failed to provide a balance to the more rigid political and class system of Prussia. Catholic thinkers had virtually no part in the liberal bourgeois movement of the industrial era; they did not share the prevalent belief in progress, nor the cultural pessimism of the minority. Politically, Catholics preferred the federal form of state for Germany, because it safeguarded their position and approximated more closely to the Holy Roman Empire, whose passing many now regretted. When in 1866 Austria was defeated by Prussia and was excluded from Germany, the German Catholics were deeply affected. Austria was their natural ally and a counterweight to Prussia and Protestantism in Germany. After this date Catholics tended to be on the defensive, and they became sensitive to the repetition of a charge levelled against them decades earlier by the nationalists, Arndt and Jahn, that they were un-German. The earlier association of the Catholic Church and the Holy Roman Empire became a liability for German Catholics in the age of nationalism. Yet for all the variety of opinion and personality within the fold, German Catholics strove successfully towards greater unity in religious life in the face of what they regarded as the disintegration of traditional culture and society. As subjects of the state, the Catholic population accommodated itself with surprisingly little protest to the social and political conformity of the Empire; apart from the *Kulturkampf* there was little in their outward demeanour to distinguish them from their fellow Christians.

The history of the Protestant Church in Germany in the nineteenth century differed significantly from that of the Catholic Church. Even the growing awareness of secularism as the common foe did little to draw them nearer, except perhaps socially. While the Catholic Church undoubtedly experienced a revival of religious life after the upheavals at the beginning of the century, the Protestant revival was more limited and often occurred outside the main body of the Church. Where the Catholic stand against state intervention inspired both the educated and the masses of the faithful, the peculiar relation of the Protestant Church to the state, particularly in Prussia, ultimately had an injurious effect on its spiritual authority. The Lutheran Church in Germany had also been more affected by the Enlightenment than had the Catholic, and rationalist theological views among the clergy played no small part in the gradual alienation of the lower classes from religion. Humanism had virtually supplanted Christian belief among educated Protestants during the German Enlightenment and in subsequent decades. The absolutist rulers generally associated themselves with this trend with far-reaching consequences for religious life. The influence of the classical humanists, of Kant, Goethe, Schiller, Humboldt and others, was decisive in the early decades of the nineteenth century when belief in orthodox Protestant doctrines was already tenuous.

The relationship between Protestantism and political authority in Prussia in the nineteenth century was determined by the developments under the absolutist rulers and by the Stein–Hardenberg reforms (1806–19). Although the nineteenth century Hohenzollerns were personally pious – unlike Frederick II (1740–86) or Frederick William II (1786–97) – their views on the balance between state and church authority did not differ fundamentally from those of their predecessors. During the Prussian reform movement Stein set up departments of religion and education in the Ministry of the Interior. These became one autonomous ministry under Hegel's disciple Altenstein in 1817 under the title of Ministry of Cults and Public Instruction. The old consistories were abolished and civic deputations for church and school questions were appointed to the provincial diets in their stead. Stein had tried to encourage lay participation in church affairs by granting some autonomy in local appointments. Here he was largely unsuccessful; the central bureaucracy in Berlin perceptibly took over control of church administration and was encouraged to do so by Frederick William III (1797–1840) and his ministers. While eighteenth-century rulers had been basically indifferent to religious questions, they had been glad to make use of the capabilities of the clergy and tended to treat them virtually as civil servants, employed in school and charitable work. State intervention under Altenstein continued this practice. Furthermore the appointment of clergymen of accommodating views served to widen a gulf between the clergy and people in the nineteenth century, which was only bridged by exceptional individuals.

For the officials in the Ministry, the re-organisation of church affairs after 1815 was merely one aspect of the regenerated monarchic state. Frederick William III took his role as head of both the Lutheran and Reformed Churches in his dominions very seriously, but his somewhat amateur enthusiasm combined with intolerance of criticism were damaging to true religious fervour. On the three-hundredth anniversary of the Reformation, 31 October 1817, Frederick proclaimed the Union of the two Protestant Churches under the title of the Evangelical Church, and after initial local reluctance, the churches of Baden, Nassau and the Bavarian Palatinate followed suit. Without sufficient consultation the Prussian King imposed a new uniform liturgy and a centralised constitution which aroused the keenest resentment. The old territorial system was replaced by an episcopal one, and the synods were set aside. Acting as he thought right in his person as head of the Church in his dominions, Frederick took over authority in matters such as the appointment of the general superintendents who were to be the highest ecclesiastical authority. On the basis of a cabinet order, he assumed powers such as his absolutist ancestors had never claimed. The King even forbade the use of the term Protestant. He thought it redolent of rebellion. It was, as the great reformer, Schleiermacher, remarked, a court church. The use of threats and expressions of displeasure or the judicious award of the highly coveted Prussian Order of the Red Eagle persuaded the majority of clergy and faithful to accept the King's will. In the provinces dissent lasted longer, and in Silesia, always a law unto itself in religious matters, thousands of Lutherans emigrated to the United States. In spiritual terms the cost of the hierarchical church was considerable. Religious life seemed to take second place to the endless discussion of constitutional questions. Moreover, the new church had little contact with the masses and meant little to them. This fact, and of course the immigration of the agricultural workers to the cities after 1850, helps to account for the astonishingly rapid decline of religious belief among the working classes in North Germany.

It was particularly among the opponents of the new bureaucratic monarchy of Prussia, the upholders of the old feudal order, that a Protestant religious revival occurred. In the Junker families of East Elbia, such as the Thaddens or the Gerlachs, and also among the peasants and artisans of the Lower Rhine and Württemberg, Pietist devotion flourished and preachers gained a large following. Pietism had begun as a reform movement within the Lutheran Church in Germany. In the early eighteenth century many Protestants had rejected the excessive concern with dogma characteristic of orthodox Lutherans at the time, and had set out to foster personal piety, especially in the home. Associated with this Pietist revival in the nineteenth century, was a renewed concern for charitable work, akin to social Catholicism, though with less contact with the working classes. Friedrich Schleiermacher (1768–1834), who had been a pastor, philosopher and university lecturer, gained great renown among the upper classes of Prussia in the early 1830s as a preacher. He stressed personal piety and experience of God as being more important than questions of dogma. Further aspects of this revival were the founding of theological faculties at the universities and the encouragement of religious instruction in the schools and in the home. The Pietists had always been interested in education; their teachers brought warmth and understanding to the task of educating children. There were several Pietist boarding schools in northern Germany and Silesia, including some for girls, although these were of a rather low academic standard. (Literary references to these are to be found in Spielhagen's *Problematische Naturen* (1861) and Fontane's *Unwiederbringlich* (1891).) Pious Protestants preferred the traditional feudal order, feeling that democracy and the revival of absolutist government after 1835 were equally destructive of genuine religious values. Bismarck himself was deeply affected by his contacts with a Pietist circle in Pomerania at the age of thirty, and his own personal dislike of an all-powerful church was one of the motives in his *Kulturkampf* policy many years later.

One of the most significant aspects of nineteenth century German Protestantism was the attempt, following on the rationalist theology of the Enlightenment, to harmonise Christian beliefs with contemporary liberal thought and scholarship. The failure of this attempt if not always acknowledged, was real, and had a profound effect on the attitudes as well as the actual religious practice of the middle classes. In Tübingen F. C. Baur (1792–1860) first applied the historical critical methods of Hegel in a systematic manner to Bible criticism, with disruptive effects he had not foreseen. He cast doubt on the authenticity of St John's Gospel, and to some contemporaries his research seemed to reduce the Evangelists to the stature of rival scholars, capable of resorting to deliberate forgeries. Following his methods, the so-called Tübingen school, which included Strauß, author of *Das Leben Jesu* (1835) and F. Th. Vischer, supplied the Hegelian Left (or Young Hegelians as Strauß named them) with radical arguments against Christianity. A feeling became prevalent among the educated middle classes that research must necessarily erode the foundations of Christian belief still further, while religious dogma became equated, at least for many liberals, with an unsound, unscholarly approach. Orthodox Christians allowed themselves to become absorbed in discussions of the finer points of Biblical criticism, thereby stressing the gulf that separated them from the mass of the people. The variety of opinion within the Church seemed to many contemporaries to give substance to the current phrase about 'the slow suicide of Protestantism'. The universities played a supremely important role in mid-century as centres of religious controversy. Thus Tübingen represented the historical critical position while Dorpat, Rostock and Erlangen were staunchly orthodox. Halle was still a centre for rationalist theologians, but was replaced in mid-century by Jena and Heidelberg. Berlin for its part contained representatives of nearly every position. The clergymen educated at these institutions taught their different ideas to their congregations and pupils.

When Frederick William IV of Prussia came to the throne in 1840 his ambition was a revival of Protestantism which would overcome social and political barriers. He thought in terms of the old feudal classes, held together by a personal bond with the monarch, Christ's representative. In Friedrich Julius Stahl, a baptised Jew from Munich, he found his philosopher. Stahl was an anti-Hegelian, author of *Die Philosophie des Rechtes* (1830–7). His monograph *Der christliche Staat* was written on the occasion of the debate on political equality for Jews and dissidents in the United Diet, and published first in the *Evangelische Kirchenzeitung* (founded in 1827 by Hengstenberg in defence of the new orthodox Lutheranism and edited by him until his death in 1869). Here Stahl provided the governing classes in Prussia with the defence of the status quo which they needed. In his eclectic portrait of the Christian state, elements of German history, Prussian tradition and Luther's teaching on sovereignty were blended with a regard for the constitutional and national movements of the age. Stahl won acclaim because he exactly answered a contemporary need, but his work made little provision for any religious crisis of conscience in the face of modern scientific and social thought. After 1850 he became associated with the *Kreuzzeitung* party, which included the most active element of Prussian conservatism, the Gerlachs, Wagener and the Prime Minister Manteuffel.

In the forties, and particularly during the Revolution of 1848, the Protestant Church became too closely identified with the reactionary state not to alienate those who desired political and social reform. Philosophic radicals of the Hegelian Left, many of whom were atheists at this time, were closer to the 'people' and their needs than their own pastors; nor did this situation change during the reaction after 1848. There was no-one to look after the religious needs of the urban masses in Germany. There was no tradition of non-conformity in Central Europe, nor did the urban working classes have a share in the Pietist tradition of the artisans of Württemberg, Silesia and the Lower Rhine. Only in the 1880s was a belated and unsuccessful attempt made to convert the factory workers by Pastor Stöcker. Stöcker, formerly a court preacher, won a following among the petty bourgeoisie by means of his attack on 'Jewish capitalists': he made little headway however with the urban working classes. They refused to betray their belief in socialism, which had colourful and forceful leaders, and which also contained a messianic element to satisfy a natural human need. By the time Stöcker appeared, the alienation of the working class from religion was virtually complete.

In middle class families women remained and were expected to be faithful to their religion; for men, devotion to duty, whether Lutheran or Hegelian in origin, was considered a satisfactory substitute for Christianity. Besides, the state in Germany was well able to play the role of social stabiliser which in other countries was played by the Church.

The state and the individual

Attitudes to state and church in Germany were profoundly influenced, at least among civil servants and the liberal middle classes before 1848, by Hegel's philosophy. From 1818 to his death from cholera in 1831 Hegel held the chair of history in Berlin, an appointment which carried great moral authority as well as intellectual influence, and one which Ranke and Treitschke were also to occupy. His ideas found favour with the state, which encouraged the appointment of his disciples to university chairs throughout Prussia in the thirties. Reading Hegel's vision of the historic role of the Prussian state as set forth in his *Grundlinien des Rechtes* (1821) and his lectures on the philosophy of history (published in his collected works in 1832), the ordinary German might feel that he had a vicarious share in shaping the national destiny. In Hegel the state replaced the earlier Romantic concept of the *Volk* as the repository of authority. The rapid growth of the state bureaucracy in numbers and influence, the increasing responsibility of the state in the public and private spheres gave substance to the idea of state patriotism, at least in Prussia. In Austria or in Saxony this was not so; for here dynastic loyalty still prevailed and state patriotism meant little.

Hegel obtained his chair at a time when views on the purpose of university education were undergoing a change particularly in Prussia. The new universities of Berlin, Bonn and Breslau bore the name of Frederick William and celebrated their founder's day on the King's birthday. Humboldt's humane vision was lost sight of. Instead these universities became the training ground of future civil servants fostering in good and dutiful subjects acceptable attitudes towards the state. Hegel encouraged such views in his teaching, as the state did in its appointments. In his writing he rationalised such contemporary developments as the increasing invasion by the state of the private sphere and the open subordination of the rights of the individual to those of the state. The body of Hegel's philosophy was difficult to digest, but it was easy to find quotations to substantiate the claims of the state such as: 'the state has the supreme right over individuals ... whose highest duty is to be members of that state;' or the one most often cited: 'what is real is rational and what is rational is real.' The following generation, which came to maturity in the fifties and sixties, was attracted by Hegel's emphasis on power and its acquisition by the state. The average citizen of the thirties – though not of course the intellectual radicals, the Young Germans or Young Hegelians – saw in Hegel above all the philosopher who was satisfied that the rule of law obtained in Prussia and who propounded the state's responsibility to provide an ordered existence for its subjects.

The state interfered in the lives of Germans in a way that must have been incomprehensible to an Englishman or an American, as visitors invariably noticed. How far were Germans themselves aware of actual oppression? Apart from a small number of dissidents the nation as a whole was not really troubled by the oppressive conditions of life. In Prussia, at least, discipline was virtually the same for everyone, and since contact with the outside world in the early years of the period 1830–90 was so limited, it was the visitors and only rarely the natives who commented at all on these aspects of life. Schooling here was compulsory from the age of five unless parents could demonstrate their fitness to educate their child at home. Even where a child of poor parents had to go to work at an early age, state inspectors saw to it that he had some form of schooling up to the age of fourteen. Certain subjects were compulsory and the civil service was only open to those with a university training. At some stage of his life, every Prussian had to enlist in the army. Conscription was for two years, although those who had passed their school leaving certificate (*Abitur*) could do the *Einjährige* or one year voluntary service without pay. From twenty-five to thirty-one a Prussian belonged to the first class, from thirty-two to forty to the second class of the militia (*Landwehr*) and from the age of forty-one to fifty he could be conscripted in an emergency. In the other states, as for example in Bavaria, every man was liable for conscription once he reached the age of twenty-one, but might not necessarily have to serve.

The watchfulness of the authorities impeded movement in the

Confederation, though it did not actually prevent it. In 1819 when Grillparzer wished to visit Italy, he had to get personal permission from the Emperor or his representative. A new passport was required in Prussia for every journey made and this demanded particulars of physical appearance in addition to the usual information: colour of eyes, hair, eyebrows, beard, shape of face and chin, forehead, height, and colour of skin. If the traveller stayed more than twenty-four hours in any place, he was required to report to the local police. The abstract authority of the state must have seemed personal to its subjects, even in the larger states: when Henry Simon (1805–60), then a young lawyer, sought official sanction in the 1830s for his annual holiday or leave of absence from his post in the Ministry of Justice in Prussia, his request was perused and signed by the minister himself.

The same was true of a teacher applying for a post at a grammar school; then as now teachers were civil servants. An applicant for a post in the civil service was subjected to the most manifold inquiries: it is hardly surprising that, since he had to be prepared to answer them, the Prussian civil servant surrendered not only his skill but his very soul to the state he served. Apart from the usual particulars as to birth and parentage, place of origin, education and qualifications, the candidate had to report on his property, his health, record of military service and general suitability for the post. Certificates had to be produced in evidence of every statement. As to his character he had to say whether he was 'honest, honourable, persevering, economical, discreet, courageous, disinterested, veracious, regular, polite, temperate, diligent, sociable, friendly, obedient'; he was required to state if he was 'prone to debauchery, chicanery or frivolous intrigue? passionate, or timid or retiring? . . . inclined to gambling, dissipation, and turmoil? . . . inconsiderate, vindictive or servile?' In addition he was asked if he understood chemistry, what other sciences he was conversant with, and whether he could draw, ride and use firearms. The final question was whether he had any 'reasonable and proper wishes'.[22]

The restrictions imposed by the authorities on the press limited personal freedom: the worst of these was the censorship. There was a censor in every Prussian town with a printing works, and in the large towns he was almost always identical with the chief of police. In Austria the censorship was more rigid, but the state officials were literal and usually managed to censor the letter rather than the spirit. Castelli tells of the satisfaction to be derived from seeing what subversive material one could slip in under the noses of the censors. Up to 1832 all censored words were replaced by blanks, and it had become something of a national sport to guess the original when the Federal Diet intervened to forbid the practice. The most effective way of getting subversive material past the censor was the fictitious memoirs or traveller's tales in which the German political system was described in detail as what the writer had witnessed in France, Belgium or some other country. For the authorities were in general concerned only with their own state and were prepared to countenance satiric references particularly to western states. The heroes of several contemporary popular novels in the 1830s and 1840s were depicted as taking part in foreign revolutions, which gave the authors an opportunity for general observations in politics. Had all these numerous heroes been assembled in one place, Wolfgang Menzel observed in 1831, 'indeed with such fine fellows I could conquer the whole world'.[23]

The censorship could in fact be very onerous, as the case of the Young Germans shows. Their works were proscribed by federal decree in 1835, and as they largely depended on their pens for a living, this exposed them to considerable dangers. It was particularly frustrating for men like Grillparzer, who was by no means a subversive writer but who felt that the poetic intention of his works was misunderstood and debased. It had economic disadvantages as well. Publishers of books and periodicals had to pay the censor for his pains, yet when they had their proofs returned with a certificate from the censor, they were still liable to have publication seized without compensation. Furthermore a writer might not have material published abroad without first having obtained the approval of the censor at home. Such petty tyranny was quite without its positive side, since the publishers and authors were offered no protection by the state against pirateers.

The German governments, above all in Austria, were morbidly sensitive to the dangers of the written word, particularly the dangers of a free press. There were many newspapers in the Confederation, and their number grew every year: in the mid thirties there was one newspaper for every 43,000 inhabitants in Prussia, for every 347,000 in Austria. Most newspapers were government sponsored although there were famous papers of moderate liberal tendency: the *Augsburger Allgemeine Zeitung*, the leading organ in the Confederation, the *Frankfurter Zeitung*, the oldest in the country and the *Voßische Zeitung*, known affectionately as Tante *Voß*. The circulation of these was between 8,000 and 10,000 in the thirties; the *Voßische* doubled its circulation in the years 1840–8 showing the Germans' increased interest in current affairs. But the press was dominated by the governments. Editors of all newspapers in Prussia were instructed to mention military affairs first. The *Preußische Staatszeitung*, the official paper, printed foreign news, usually in the form of extracts from foreign journals, but without leading article or commentary. Home news was hardly referred to apart from occasional mention at the end of the paper. In the different government districts, including the new western provinces with their more liberal traditions, twenty-five political journals existed in the thirties. These were under the supervision of the local censor and might only print what had already appeared in the *Staatszeitung*. They enjoyed a monopoly of advertising in their districts and therefore virtually enjoyed a government subsidy, unlike the independently owned papers.

Yet the situation of the press aroused little opposition among the public before 1848, apart from a few isolated groups. Spielhagen wrote in 1861 of his countrymen in the forties: 'These harmless fellows, *au fond*, politics do not interest them'. (*Problematische Naturen*). The authorities encouraged the lengthy discussion of art in newspapers and periodicals. Bourgeois interest in the arts had been fostered through the lack of outlet for their talents and imagination in the public sphere, and in the thirties aesthetic problems were discussed with passion. It would be mistaken to think that people generally objected to the lack of political comment and news, even after the Revolution of 1830. Except for brief interludes, such as the highly emotional response to the Polish rising of 1831 and to its colourful refugees, or the Hambach Festival of 1832, where several thousands met to fête leading radicals and to demonstrate in favour of a free press, or the Cologne Incident, the picturesque and the anecdotal had more interest for the German reader at this time than politics.

The situation changed rapidly in the forties. Interest in politics became widespread, though the reasons for this were often economic. Not unnaturally the German commercial classes took the lead. The German state system brought with it a bewildering variety of freight and customs regulations, quite apart from the different weights, measures and currencies in use. Any attempt to simplify the process of transporting goods and selling them across state boundaries was bound to attract businessmen. For these reasons entrepreneurs began to look to Prussia for leadership after the initiative she had taken in the united Prussian (Maaßen) tariff of 1818, and more particularly after the *Zollverein* of 1834. But the commercial classes, despite the gradual increase of business enterprise in the thirties and early forties, could not yet be regarded as representative of public feeling.

In general it is therefore true to say that the authoritarian and in places thoroughly repressive political system in Germany had the effect of smothering individual initiative in both the practical and imaginative fields, though it was only in individual cases that this was experienced as a hardship before the Revolution of 1848. Throughout the period 1815–40 only a comparatively small number of Germans argued from the particular case of repression to a general criticism of the system. After 1840 criticism became more common, but among those who began to advocate a different state and society, there were very few indeed who could agree as to the practical form this might take.

It is not possible in a short survey of social life in Germany in this period to distinguish in detail between the different states and regions. But in 1830 Germans themselves considered the different parts of the Federation to be very distinctive. They only gradually became aware of this: Wilhelm Hauff was probably the first to make the sense of difference between North and South the subject of a short story, *Das Bild des Kaisers*, in 1828. In many ways provincial, even rural, the cities of Germany in 1830 give the most helpful guide to regional variety. The populations of cities like Vienna, Berlin or Hamburg in 1830 were less than one tenth of the figure they reached at the end of the century, and a town like Düsseldorf, which in Heine's youth was the rather sleepy capital of the small duchy of Jülich-Cleve-Berg, became less than a century later one of Germany's wealthiest industrial cities. There was no capital of Germany in 1830, a fact Mme de Staël had stressed some decades earlier in *De l'Allemagne* (1801); the Diet of the Confederation met at Frankfurt and the President of the Confederation, the Emperor of Austria, resided at Vienna. The historic German cities represented different aspects of German life and character: Vienna and Dresden were considered the most cultured and elegant, yet with a pronounced local air; Düsseldorf was already striving to be included in this category; Hamburg and Frankfurt were wealthy commercial centres with a patriarchal merchant class. Munich was being rebuilt under Ludwig I as a Renaissance city, the Mecca of artists, but the countrified manners of its inhabitants made his efforts seem merely eccentric. Berlin, the capital of Prussia, seemed early in the nineteenth century a cross between a garrison town and a scattered village. Lagarde commented on the croaking of the frogs there at night, as late as 1852. After Frederick William IV came to the Prussian throne in 1840 his taste for the pseudo-historic was matched by that of the city fathers and public buildings, and later even factories were erected, created in the 'Gothic', 'Byzantine' or 'Renaissance' manner.

Vienna was the capital of the Habsburg multiracial Empire and was also the seat of the President of the German Confederation, Francis I of Austria (1804–1835). The city exploited its renown for charm and gaiety in the mid-nineteenth century as it does in the twentieth. There was no city better paved or lit, with better – or faster – transport than Vienna. The city fathers made a successful effort to foster that civic pride which is still characteristic of Viennese of all classes. The huge numbers of Czechs and Croats and Hungarians who flocked into the city after mid-century did not alter its character, but demonstrated the celebrated Viennese powers of assimilation. Vienna offered plenty of amusement to her inhabitants: the Austrians enjoyed themselves more than other German subjects. Vienna was the first city in Germany to open her museums and galleries to the public, and the great popular park, the *Prater,* lay along the road to one of the Imperial hunting lodges and racing parks. The authorities opened the enormous Apollo dance hall after the Napoleonic wars, in order that their subjects should forget their troubles in dancing, and they made the fullest use of the opportunity. The theatres were actively encouraged for the same reasons. Even in hard times an air of gaiety and, in parts of the city, of luxury prevailed: seven hundred fiacres rolled through the streets and there were some seventy-five coffee houses. Although the different classes did not in general mix socially, social distinctions were less formal in Vienna than in other German cities and all classes spoke a form of Viennese dialect, even the Emperor himself. There were six-hundred Jewish families who enjoyed historic privileges not granted to Jews in other German states. The Jews who did not belong to these families – and there were many – suffered the usual disabilities of the German Jew.

The paternalist attitude of the city fathers extended to all sorts of matters and Vienna, like Munich, was one of the first cities in Europe to show an active interest in social medicine. Its renowned medical and hospital facilities were extended to the poor and the disgraced without the moralising tone of most contemporary charitable bodies. Unmarried mothers were admitted to labour wards under a pseudonym. There was strict control over the sale of poisons, and food was examined by public inspectors; a corpse could not be buried without first being seen by the state physician of the district. During the cholera epidemic (1830–1) Prussia sent soldiers to guard her frontiers: the Viennese city fathers tried to find the cause of the scourge.

Visitors to Vienna liked to see it as a city of carefree gaiety, while philanthropists praised the real achievements of the authorities. But the realism, even cynicism, of the majority of its inhabitants under their veneer of sentimentality was amply justified by living conditions. The aftermath of state bankruptcy (1811) and of the wars, recession and famine, had hit the civil servants and small craftsmen who made up the greater part of the population of some 200,000 in 1830. Typhus was one of the worst scourges in nineteenth century Vienna (Schubert was one of its victims) and the city, as indeed the whole of the Austro-Hungarian Empire, was badly hit by the cholera epidemic of 1830–1. In the subsequent years there was actually a population deficit in Vienna, and it was only the influx of foreign workers after 1848 that redressed the balance. Nowhere was the revolution more violent and bloody than here. The Biedermeier era (1815–48), the age of 'roast chicken' in popular legend, was in fact a time of rising prices, unemployment and depression for craftsmen and agricultural labourers alike in Austria. Economic difficulties go far to account for Austria's failure to retain supremacy in nineteenth-century Germany. The patriarchal system was politically repressive, stunting both artistic and commercial initiative: Hawkins called the authorities 'indulgent parents to the docile and submissive, but stern and unyielding to the restless and discontented.'[24]

Unlike Vienna, Berlin in 1830 was a town of merchants and poor labourers. Few of the Prussian nobility lived there, apart from the officials, nor was there at that time a 'season' to attract the magnates of Silesia or the better-off Rhenish bourgeoisie. The Berlin character, hardheaded and caustic, is the product of these years. The Berlin tradesman had a name for discourtesy, but his life was hard. The first slums were created in the forties. In the slum areas the roads were not paved and great barrack-like tenements shot up to accommodate the innumerable immigrants from the eastern provinces of Prussia who flocked into the city from the fifties onwards. Such conditions worsened in the 1860s; they help to explain the appeal of socialism in the following decades.

In 1830 Berlin had a population of about 180,000; by the end of the century it had reached almost 2,000,000. Gas lighting had been introduced in 1826, the streets in the main part of the city were paved in the same decade and given names and the houses numbered. The drainage problem was not satisfactorily solved until later in the century; even the King's palace as well as the houses of the citizens had in front of it, in the words of a contemporary English traveller, 'a stinking festering gutter, rank with bubbles of a putrid effervescence'.[25] But the citizens of Berlin found nothing incongruous in the royal priorities: Berlin under Schinkel, one of the few distinguished architects of the age, was made into a modern city with fine streets and representational buildings before the sewage question was considered. The rebuilding of the city after the devastation of the French occupation was carried out under royal patronage and impressed the population. People took pride in the new landmarks and monuments of the city, particularly Schinkel's Old Museum and the statues executed by Rauch of Queen Luise and of the heroes of Prussian resistance to Napoleon, Blücher, Gneisenau and Scharnhorst.

The King's daily appearance at the theatre at the stroke of six, and his departure at eight for supper and early bed, helped to stress the bourgeois character of life in Berlin. As in Vienna, august patronage of the arts was meant to compensate for the authorities' intolerance of political aspirations in the subjects. The court also patronised opera, music and the ballet, and the official papers reported on performances. But *'Berlinisch'* was synonymous with 'philistine' when Arnim, Chamisso and Hoffmann were writing in the first three decades of the century, and it remained so even under the rule of the aesthetically minded Frederick William IV (1840–61). In Berlin, in contrast with Vienna, there were early signs of middle class self-help. Marriage societies began to be formed in the thirties and forties among the salaried to provide for daughters' dowries. Schools for the poor, the blind, the deaf and dumb existed in 1831, as well as facilities for feeding the unemployed. As in Vienna the population of Berlin grew rapidly from the late thirties; there was little immigration from the south and west, but a great deal from Silesia, Posen, Pomerania and East Prussia. In the second half of the nineteenth century the typical Berliner was reputed to have at least one Silesian grandparent and also a Jewish one.

Frankfurt in 1830 was a far wealthier city than Berlin, more exclusive in conferring the privilege of citizenship than Vienna. In 1815 it was made a sovereign state once more and the seat of the Diet of the German Confederation. The city was the natural capital of Germany, both for geographical reasons and because of its long mercantile tradition. It traded in manufactured goods, spices and wine and became the financial centre of the Confederation. The administrative and military bodies of the constituent states also had their headquarters there, and it was the clearing house for the major currencies of Germany up to the creation of a uniform currency in 1867.

There was a long established Jewish community in Frankfurt; Börne, the journalist, was one of its sons as was the founder of the Rothschild dynasty. The authorities in the city were thought to be rather tolerant towards their Jewish community. How limited this tolerance was is seen from the rules governing the movements of Jews. They lived in one particular part of the city and were confined to this ghetto at night and after four o'clock on Sundays. On holidays, even on the occasion of the first balloon ascent from the city in 1831, they were not allowed to leave the ghetto. The number of marriages per annum which the Jewish community might celebrate was restricted to fifteen in an effort to limit the number of Jews. In Frankfurt as also in South Germany the cruel cry *'Hep, hep'* (*Hierusalem est perdita*) was still occasionally heard on the streets, or even *'Jud' mach mores'* whereby a Jew was obliged to step down from the pavement on to the roadway. Such taunts were usually made in an occasional outburst of rowdyism, more commonly in South Germany than elsewhere, and should not lead one to suppose that antisemitism was generally prevalent in Germany. The Jews who lived in ghettos (not all did) retained their traditional dress and many wore the long Jewish side curls. In Germany, as in other countries, to be different was to invite comment from bystanders. Despite their disabilities however even the wealthy Jews of Frankfurt lived in the ghetto. In the course of the nineteenth century their sons tended to travel abroad and to enter the professions, to be less strictly orthodox than their fathers. The well-to-do and successful began to be more widely accepted socially and by mid century contributed much to the prosperity of the city. In this Frankfurt was fairly representative of other cities with sizeable populations, such as Hamburg, Breslau or Königsberg. In 1866 Frankfurt was annexed to Prussia. Bismarck decided to punish the city for having sided with Austria in the Austro-Prussian war of 1866 and he imposed a heavy levy: the Jews made by far the largest contribution towards meeting this obligation.

Hamburg, like Frankfurt, was a former Free Imperial City of the Holy Roman Empire and was the largest of the four city states included in the Confederation – Hamburg, Frankfurt, Bremen, Lübeck. Both cities retained their reputation for being freer and more sophisticated than other German cities, but whereas Frankfurt suffered the ignominy of annexation in 1866, Hamburg was guided by self-interest when she agreed to form part of the Empire in 1871. This was the commercial capital of Germany, connected by trade agreements with all the major foreign powers, notably England and the Americas. The businessmen of Hamburg had enterprise and in their way of life a certain elegance, both qualities uncommon in Germany of the time. They usually sent their sons abroad to gain experience, usually to England, and they liked to feel as English as their ships, often affecting English phrases in their speech. The people of Hamburg were outward looking and tended to patronise other Germans. They resisted joining the *Zollverein,* and felt resentment towards Prussia for her success in politics. After 1871 there was considerable rivalry between the new Imperial capital of Berlin and Hamburg with its more homogeneous patrician society. *Frau Jenny Treibel*

(1892) satirised the anxious efforts of the new rich Frau Treibel to appear at ease in her recently acquired mansion and not to allow the cool self-satisfaction of her Hamburg daughter-in-law to fluster her.

Hamburg remained a patrician society even after 1871 and bankers and merchants set the tone in society: in Munich it was the King. It would be hard to find a greater contrast in Germany in 1830 than that between these two cities; there was in Munich hardly a trace of that cosmopolitan character which was the pride of the citizens of Hamburg. It was the ambition of King Ludwig I (1825–48) to make Bavaria second in importance only to Austria in the Confederation. Even as a young prince he planned to rebuild Munich as a great city; when Bavaria acquired Salzburg in the Napoleonic era, Ludwig had had some of Salzburg's historic buildings dismantled and the marble and stone carted to Munich. In the 1820s and 1830s the neo-classical Munich was erected, and both Ludwig and his son and successor Maximilian II (1848–64) took pride in the name given their capital by a contemporary: Athens on the Isar. They encouraged poets, painters, architects and academics to come and settle in Munich by offering them sinecures. For some years, until about 1860, it seemed as though Munich might indeed offer a more cultured court and congenial environment to German men of letters than Prussia could provide. Although many contemporaries depicted Ludwig as a somewhat parochial Maecenas who attracted worthy artists to Munich and wrote bad poetry, the population of Bavaria was largely indifferent to their King's cultural efforts. He understood his people well enough and satisfied them by erecting vast beer halls alongside the neo-Renaissance buildings with which he had adorned the city. The Bavarians took pride in the fact that Bavaria, according to themselves, was the only pure German state. The population of all the rest, they alleged, was either part Slav or French, part Danish or Dutch. They even shrugged off the highest crime rate in the Confederation as evidence of their manly German spirit, though the nature of the crime, pilfering and an illegitimacy rate of 1:1 in the early decades of the century, seemed hardly to corroborate this assertion. Certainly people in Bavaria allowed themselves to be little influenced by what was going on in other parts of the country. However it was in Bavarian territory that two interesting economic developments took place in

Ludwig I's reign: the Rhine and the Danube were linked by canal
in the 1830s and the first German railway line was opened between Furth and Nuremberg in 1835. Ludwig was personally
interested in matters of transport, but politically, like his subjects, he became more and more conservative as the years passed.
The Revolution of 1830 had frightened him and he attributed it
to the effects of industrial development: he therefore undertook
a deliberate policy of retarding such development. There was
virtually no urban working class in Munich, a fact which helps to
explain why there was no revolutionary unrest there in 1848. The
state of Bavaria was peopled almost entirely by peasants and artisans and the economy based on small farming and handicraft.
The Bavarians began to voice their growing dissatisfaction with
the King's unpopular liaison with the dancer, Lola Montez, in
1848; Ludwig promptly abdicated in favour of his son, and the
revolution, which was throwing the rest of Central Europe into
a ferment, passed Bavaria by.

The cities and towns of Germany, from the larger ones just
mentioned to the smaller state capitals of Stuttgart, Karlsruhe,
Göttingen or Brunswick, struck visitors as quiet homely places before the 1848 Revolution. They noted again and again that the
presence of the bureaucratic administration, not commercial
enterprise, constituted a town in Germany. The lack of shops, the
country air and slow pace of life was generally characteristic. Outside the free cities of Frankfurt, Hamburg, Bremen and the now
declining Lübeck, efforts to improve facilities were usually made
by the rulers, not the citizens. The reason for this was partly the
absence of a moneyed class, but also partly the tendency of the
Germans to let the authorities do things for them. The criticism
levelled at German domestic servants, 'they are so willing, but you
have to tell them everything', could be applied to their masters
also. Baron von Stein's reforms had strengthened the power of the
municipal administrators, but it had not had the effect of creating
the initiative that Stein knew his countrymen needed. When the
accelerating pace of industrialisation began to have its effect on
Germany, the countrified air of its cities largely disappeared. But
century-old habits were less susceptible of change, and the direction of local administration as well as of political affairs remained
closely associated with the established hierarchy.

Conclusion

When Carus, physician to the King of Saxony, returned to Germany after accompanying his royal master on an extensive visit to England, he recorded a little breathlessly in his diary (1844): 'I felt with pleasure that I was again on German ground, where, though the material part of life, and all that relates to its attainments, is less cultivated, a higher and more enthusiastic feeling for the ideal of life, as represented in philosophy, art and poetry, has taken root among the people, and continually gives evidence of its presence'.[26] The writer Börne was scornful about the Germans' passive character – a nation of flunkeys, he called his people. The French journalist Girardin laughed at their idealism when he remarked to his German colleague Gutzkow in 1835 'you want to liberate Germany with Sanskrit'. Few Germans felt the need to make such criticisms before 1848. One of the most interesting features of the years 1830–90 is the change observable in the Germans' own opinion of themselves. At the time of the Polish uprising in 1831 the Germans undoubtedly merited Wolfgang Menzel's censure that they were more interested in the fate of other nations than their own. They fully accepted the current view of their docility and their impractical idealism. Whether they condoned or approved of the rather rowdy attempts at reform by young men in the 1830s, they did not usually see the relevance of such action to their own situation and were not much attracted by the idea even if they did. Despite the example of the Romantics, the German people had not yet learned to think historically or even nationally. Yet well before the end of the period 1830–90, the average German proudly believed that his country was more efficient and successful, better organised and more cultured than her neighbours. He took pride in what he regarded as the superiority of his country's achievements, but it seemed as though he needed to compare Germany with other nations in order to reassure himself. Despite this or perhaps because he had not had time to digest its rapid transformation, the German of 1890 was unable to take himself for granted.

The French Revolution of 1789 and the Napoleonic wars began a process which at last brought change to Germany. However, the effects of this process became visible only gradually. In the years 1815–48 Germans were only beginning to become aware of the ideas and issues which were in 1848–90 to change the character of their country. In 1830 German society was still virtually static and was to remain so for almost twenty years to come. After 1848 it underwent a sudden and rapid change. The so-called Promoters' Boom came upon Germany in 1850, easing the unresolved tensions of the recent revolution; it lasted for almost a quarter of a century. The advent of the first industrial revolution in Prussia and in the rest of Germany coincided with the political unification of the country. Germany changed, and both the Germans themselves and foreign observers believed that the character of the nation had altered too. From being static, Germany became dynamic in military affairs, commerce and industry, though to a much lesser extent in her society; from being a nation long regarded as philosophic, a-political and unpractical, she became highly organised and excessively self-conscious.

The industrial revolution was largely responsible for making Germany one of the great powers of Europe and her people prosperous. Men from narrow provincial backgrounds rose to become prominent in commerce, industry and banking. The expansion of the administration after 1871 and the accessibility of higher education created opportunities for civil servants of lower middle-class origin. One of the most significant features of the revolutionary period in Germany was that it did not greatly alter the basic structure of society. The nobility retained their privileged position and their control over government, the higher administration and the army. The middle classes who acquired wealth and influence retained the attitudes of mind of their former station. A disinclination for politics, as well as lack of opportunity to win position and influence through a political career, prevented them from questioning the validity of their political views. Even the new industrial proletariat, which by the end of the century was the largest homogeneous section of the community, tended to become increasingly conformist in outlook.

Regional differences in manners and outlook, which were still quite apparent in 1830, had modified considerably by 1890. The sentiments of a Württemberg businessman or official sound as Prussian as those of their counterparts in the North. Distinctions of occupation and class, real as they were, disappeared when confronted with the emotional appeal of national unity. Even the Socialists, often branded as traitors to their country because of their allegiance to an international movement, and the people of Bavaria, the most independent of the regions, did not find it in them to resist the appeal of a threatened Fatherland in 1914. The tremendous changes of recent decades had caused many tensions in German society and in political life, but the extent and significance of these did not become apparent until the end of the Great War. In 1890, at the close of the period under discussion, the conformity of German society, and the single-mindedness of German endeavour created an image of unity and harmony of which the majority of Germans felt proud.

Part II

Literature and Society 1830-90

The Literary Scene 1830-90

Like England and France, the United States and Russia, Germany had an extensive literature in the nineteenth century. Yet Germany's literature is not well known to the educated non-German reader today, nor is it highly regarded by him. At the beginning of our period English men and women of letters, such as Carlyle, George Eliot and Ralph Emerson, showed great interest in Germany, but ever since the view has been widely held that the nineteenth century was a period of decline, even decadence, in the history of German literature.

How did this come about? The English reading public (in particular) regarded, and possibly still regards German literature – apart from lyric poetry – as excessively philosophical and in general inferior to English and French creative writing. The difficulties of appreciating Germany's achievement in this period lie in the fact that German literature is so different. German writers were aware of change in their society and in the world beyond their provincial homes; this was the age of the industrial revolution, when Germany changed from being an agrarian economy to a great industrial nation; in 1871 the much longed for unification of Germany took place. In what he wrote and in what he felt he ought to write the German was concerned to comprehend the age in all its diversity; he was less concerned to reform society or to entertain, as for example English novelists such as Dickens and Mrs Gaskell did. In order to present the changes around him, the political and industrial revolutions, the decline of the authority of the churches, the new spirit of scientific enquiry, the German writer in this age of realism preferred to depict the world symbolically. Both the thematic and the formal characteristics of German literature in the nineteenth century suggest that it had more in common with American literature than with that of England or France; an American reading German novels and short stories is often reminded of Poe and Hawthorne. Another common feature of the German and the American literary scene is self-consciousness. Each is concerned with creating a new tradition or reviving an earlier one.

In the case of Germany with her long cultural history this may seem surprising. But modern German literature was still a relatively new phenomenon in 1830. The very brevity of the period of classical literature in the age of Goethe made many of the generation of writers born about 1800 – such as Grillparzer, Mörike or Immermann – regard the ideas it embodied as a sacred heritage. They tried to demonstrate in their work that these ideas were still relevant to the German-speaking world in the nineteenth century. As late as 1857, the Austrian Stifter wrote his major work, the novel, *Der Nachsommer,* with this intention. Such pious regard for past achievement helps to explain the great emphasis placed by most writers of this period on form, as well as their fondness for lengthy discussion of aesthetic questions. The desire to comprehend the diversity of the age also explains writers' preoccupation with the ethical foundations of their world. The reflective tenor of much of German literature has tended to put off the would-be reader.

Our present concern with social conflict and our tendency nowadays to judge literature according to the awareness it shows of the social context in which it was written, provide a further obstacle to a general appreciation of nineteenth-century German literature. One looks in vain in Germany for the social novels we admire in Victorian England and which were usually the work of middle class authors. For historical reasons a strong self-reliant middle class was slow to emerge in Germany. Even in the nineteenth century this class was made to feel socially inferior by the aristocracy and it had only a restricted influence on public life. Most writers in the period came from a middle-class background and their influence on society was less marked than in other West European countries. The writer was not highly regarded by German society until the late eighteenth century, and even then only exceptional individuals, such as Goethe, won the esteem of the wellborn.

The German writer did not look upon himself as 'the spokesman of his age'. However, for a brief period during the Napoleonic wars, the attitude of society towards his function changed:

writers and scholars actually seemed to be expressing the sentiments of the whole German nation. The Romantic philosopher
Fichte, later Rector of Berlin University, delivered a rousing dia-
tribe against the French occupation in *Reden an die deutsche
Nation* (1807–8), within a stone's throw of the French garrison at
Berlin; Heinrich von Kleist wrote patriotic dramas and edited a
local newspaper in the same city; the poet and university professor, E. M. Arndt, wrote patriotic poems and marching songs
which were sung all over Germany; the Lutheran theologian
Schleiermacher, who was also well known as a philosopher of the
Romantic movement, preached uplifting sermons to the German
nation. After the defeat of Napoleon these voices were suppressed
by the authorities who feared that nationalist sentiments were
dangerous to law and order. To be a writer was to make oneself an
object of suspicion to the rather timorous bureaucrats who ruled
the German states from 1815–48, particularly if one touched
upon political or social questions. Despite this, the Revolution of
1830 caused great excitement, especially among young writers,
and aroused a dormant interest in public affairs in the reading
public. The example of France acted as a powerful stimulus to the
imagination of creative writers, such as the journalists Heine and
Börne, and the so-called Young Germans, Gutzkow and his associates, as well as the political philosophers known as the Young
Hegelians. Women writers also began to make a name for themselves as novelists. Very many new journals were founded and
avidly read. Novels, essays and reviews were filled with allusions
to current affairs.

A significant if gradual change became apparent in the relationship between the writer and society. The public's appetite for information and comment increased rapidly with technical progress
in communications (the railways, the electric telegraph, the steam
press). The public's demand for literature was much greater than
it is today: in Germany as elsewhere, people living in the provinces felt that it kept them in touch with modern developments
and improved their minds; it also provided them with useful
dinner-table conversation. To cater for the wide interest of readers,
writers created new genres or revived forgotten ones. In particular
the historical drama and the historical novel enjoyed great vogue
in the 1830s. The former generally drew their themes from Germany's great past – for example there was a plethora of 'Hohen-

staufen dramas'; the latter were generally set in a patriarchal world, which reflected the conservative society in which most Germans still lived. Peasant literature became popular; some of Germany's great writers excelled in this genre. All sections of society enjoyed travel books, especially those depicting far-off lands. People showed a keen interest in the United States; many had relatives who had emigrated there. Charles Sealsfield won a deserved reputation for his novels on American life. This extraordinary man, born in Austria in 1793, became a monk, but fled from Austria to America in 1823 after deserting his order. He returned to settle in Switzerland in 1832 and wrote novels in English and German; he had attained such fluency in both languages that few were able to tell his origin. Willibald Alexis, a writer of historical novels, founded a journal for criminal literature in the 1830s and fostered a wide interest in criminal literature among the public; at the same time the vogue for phrenology led even the editors of magazines for women to include illustrations of the human cranium in order to warn susceptible ladies against 'criminal types'.

Germany's lack of a capital influenced her literature profoundly. There existed in Germany no educated and sophisticated society with its focus in a capital society. In the Austrian Empire Vienna provided its musicians and artists with the advantages of an enthusiastic and critical public and with noble patrons; but for various reasons, of which the most notorious was the censorship, Vienna did not benefit her writers in the same way. The regional capitals sometimes provided individual writers with a centre, such as Weimar until the death of Goethe, but this was exceptional. The Bavarian monarchs Ludwig I (1825–48) and Maximilian II (1848–64) tried to provide such a centre in Munich by attracting diverse talents to the city and by paying writers like Emanuel Geibel and Paul Heyse handsome sums to talk on cultural subjects and read their works to the court and polite society. These efforts failed because the artistic community thus assembled so obviously had no link with the local population. The case of Karl Immermann (1790–1840) shows how a flourishing city could influence a writer's development favourably: his major novels were written after he had transferred his home from the culturally rather remote Magdeburg to the lively Rhenish town of Düsseldorf. In general however most regional capitals were from a literary point of view rather philistine. Raabe's caricature of the literary life of the *Residenz* in *Abu Telfan* (1867) corresponded to the view of many. German writers who travelled to Paris or London always commented on the stimulating atmosphere there and their own sense of being made to feel provincial by contrast.

A by-product of Germany's lack of a capital city was the regional inspiration of her literature. It so happened that almost all her major writers in the period 1830–90 were born and worked in the provinces. The immediacy of their work owes much to its local inspiration. If the background of the German writer was provincial, his works were not, despite the impression conveyed in numerous histories of European literature which deal patronisingly with Germany.

The overall impression given by the body of German nineteenth century writing is of a literature less uniform, more highly differentiated than that of England, France, Italy or Russia. Germany certainly failed to achieve distinction in what must be regarded as the foremost literary achievement of the century in Europe and America: the novel. Drama declined after mid century despite the continued cultivation of the stage and the great attention paid to production in the many German theatres. But German literature in this period is distinguished for its exploration of new themes and for its experimentation in literary techniques whose originality has only recently been recognised. Intellectual life as well as literature lacked a clear profile in Germany 1830–90, and one cannot trace the development of a specific literary tradition without leaving many major figures unaccounted for, but yet it is full of originality, of discoveries and observations which were to be exploited only very much later.[1]

2

What was Biedermeier?

In the first decades of the nineteenth century educated Germans were well aware that their country's political and social development had not kept pace with her advances in philosophy and literature. Moreover they saw the hopes of the patriots and liberal reformers, during and after the French occupation of Prussia, stifled by the authorities at the Congress of Vienna and even more ruthlessly at Carlsbad in 1819. There was however remarkably little protest at this situation. Numerically the patriots – whatever later popular legend might assert to the contrary – has always been few. The penalties inflicted on those who protested were severe, as was shown in the case of Georg Büchner's associates in the 1830s, many of whom died in prison as a result of torture or neglect, or the harsh prison conditions to which the dialect writer Fritz Reuter was subjected for seven years over a trifling political offence. The main reason for the political quietism characteristic of Germans in the years of the Restoration (1815–48), was that the authorities and the public at large welcomed the stability and security offered by a return to the old pre-war political system. Life had been so tranquil for more than a generation in Prussia, in Saxony, in Bavaria and in Baden before Napoleon's wars. The length of these wars, which lasted intermittently from 1792–1815, the constant upheavals they forced on a people unused to change, the destruction of the Holy Roman Empire, brought no obvious benefits, except perhaps to the citizens of the left bank of the Rhine who enjoyed the advantages of a liberal administration for twenty years during the French occupation. The turbulence and the privations suffered by Germans in other parts of the country made people begin to talk of the 'good old days before 1789'.

The Germans associated their sufferings and losses less with the war or the person of Napoleon, whom many admired, than with the phenomenon of revolution. The French Revolution had

been responsible for killing a king and for sending countless noblemen to their death or into exile. It had stirred people's minds, it
was said, in a way that made them strive for things beyond their
station. Not only Napoleon but the whole French nation had been
filled with ambitions which had disturbed the peace of Europe
for a generation, and had almost succeeded in destroying the
order of society. Germans knew that their own country was especially vulnerable to European unrest because of its position in the
centre of Europe and its lack of unity. Accordingly, people in
general were not dissatisfied with the outcome of the Congress of
Vienna and did not think to criticise the omission in the Final
Act of the Congress of Vienna of clauses guaranteeing individual
rights and liberties. If stern measures seemed to the authorities
necessary in order to protect the restored order, these very
measures also served to reassure the citizen that the settlement
was going to be a permanent one. Prussia and Bavaria, both of
which were later to strive for supremacy in Germany, welcomed
the restoration of Austria (in 1815) to her former position of
authority in Germany. This was a pledge of peace in the present
and of security for the future.

Most German writers between about 1820 and 1848 shared the
political attitudes described above. They were usually more suspi-
cious of liberalism than critical of the paternalism of their rulers.
Writers in England, France or Belgium might advocate liberty,
free enterprise and individual initiative as the virtues of the nineteenth century. In Germany most writers – there were of course
notable exceptions – felt that these ideas had little immediate relevance to the German situation. The term *Biedermeier* has been
applied to those major and minor writers of the period of the
Restoration who believed it was possible to counteract the subversive influence of the French Revolution on political and social
life by recreating a harmonious society based on humanist principles. There were in fact two distinct trends in German literature
in this period, the Biedermeier, which was traditionalist in its
literary ideas and conservative in its political views, and that of
the Young Germans, who in the 1830s and 1840s were interested
in liberal reform. The latter included many talented journalists;
there was a polemical side to their writing at all times; they thrust
themselves forcibly on the attention of the public and enjoyed
an occasional *succès de scandale,* the most notable being the

court case again Gutzkow for his audacious novel *Wally, die Zweiflerin,* which led to his being imprisoned. These writers will be discussed in Chapter 6.

Unlike the label Young Germans, the term Biedermeier was not used by any of the writers to whom it is now applied. It was coined by a certain Eichrodt and his colleague Kußmaul who published in the satiric journal *Fliegende Blätter* their *Gedichte des schwäbischen Schullehrers Weiland Gottlieb Biedermeier und seines Freundes Horazius Treuherz* in the year 1855. The word conjured up a picture of contented and frugal domesticity, of law-abiding citizens, like those depicted in the paintings of Richter, Schwind and Spitzweg, talented and popular painters of mid century, who also painted interiors and landscapes. Biedermeier was not used in any serious sense until the early twentieth century when art historians used it to describe a specific style of architecture, painting and domestic art in South Germany and Austria which roughly corresponded to what we understand by early Victorian. Its meaning is much more precise as a term of art than of literary criticism. Biedermeier is used to characterise the simple two storey dwelling houses, their façades adorned with elegant stuccowork, which one still sees today in Salzburg, Graz or Linz. Great attention to detail and workmanship was a feature of this style; indoors there were cupboards and wardrobes with gently curving doors or drawers, fashioned by the skilled cabinetmakers of the age; there were tea and coffee sets, the products of the Imperial porcelain factory at the Augarten in Vienna or similar factories in Bohemia. Every object used for work or leisure in the household reflected the sense of style characteristic of the Restoration period in Germany and Austria, including even those beautifully engraved and hand-coloured playing cards still found today.

As a term of literary criticism however the Biedermeier evokes less the grace of life than the narrow environment of the bourgeoisie during these years. Efforts have been made in recent times to make it more respectable, but it remains largely a convenient label, not a precise description, for a period in German literature about which it is extremely difficult to make accurate general statements. It embraces a large number of minor if interesting writers, such as the novelists Willibald Alexis or Alexander von Ungern-Sternberg, but it also includes some of Germany's greatest writers, the dramatist Grillparzer, the lyric poets and novella writers Mörike and Annette von Droste-Hülshoff, and the early work of Adalbert Stifter and Gottfried Keller. The attitudes of these writers towards politics and society were representative of the German people as a whole at this time. That is, they regretted the political excitability of their younger contemporaries and regarded innovation in this sphere as suspect and even subversive. They themselves were not however enthusiastic about the political order. The paternal relationship between ruler and subjects which existed in most German states was not seen by the subjects as an ideal one, but rather the best to be obtained in the circumstances. The prevailing note of literature and thought, especially up to about 1840, is accommodation to reality, a somewhat passive acceptance of an imperfect world. Many of those who were middle-aged in the 1830s were politically passive because they had been disillusioned in their youth: firstly by Napoleon, who had disappointed the hopes placed in him that he would create a liberal and prosperous Germany, later by the statesmen at Vienna in 1815, who had disregarded the patriotic ambitions of writers and thinkers formed in the Wars of Liberation (1813–15). These disappointments bred a distrust of the 'great world'. After the war writers in Germany tended to withdraw into a domestic or local world. They were certainly aware that great changes were taking place outside Germany, despite the apparent stability of their own environment, but they instinctively withdrew from representing these in a realistic manner in their work. This was in fact only an intensification of tendencies inherent in German literature from the eighteenth century onwards, the result of the restricted environment of the bourgeois intelligentsia in that country.

The narrowness of their world encouraged writers to stress the ethical nature of art. Every-day life was informed with a higher purpose and in novels and short stories the objects used in the household or at work were given a symbolic significance as agents of that purpose; duty was made to seem a noble concept: 'Diligence,' wrote Immermann, 'is our Apollo and effort our Muse.'[1] The German rulers and their governments exemplified such views and indeed, despite the social inferiority of the middle classes, it can be said that the ideals of this age were bourgeois. The King of Prussia rose at six and retired at nine as did his diligent subjects. He, like they, lived frugally. The Emperor Francis 1 of

Austria (1804–35) liked to be seen out walking in the streets of Vienna, his consort on his arm. They visited Vienna's new canals together to show that they shared the enthusiasms and preoccupations of their subjects. In contrast with France or England at this time, bourgeois values did not initially include material advancement or enthusiasm for progress through scientific discovery. These became features of German life from 1850 onwards, after the industrial revolution began. Until this date the characteristics of the world in which most writers lived, and which they portrayed in their work, were conservatism, self-sufficiency and devotion to work well done for its own sake and not for any material reward. For all the stress on contentment with one's station in life, neither society nor the writers (except Gotthelf) were noticeably Christian.

Literature and the arts were closer to the life of ordinary people than at any time since the 1770s. The most talented writers owed much to their contacts with popular forms and taste – for example Grillparzer's theatrical plots, Mörike's folksong metres. Artists strove to be popular, to write, paint and compose for as wide a public as possible. In contrast with the preceding generation of Romantic writers, the difference between 'art' and 'popular culture' was in practice very slight. People enjoyed the arts in their own homes and in public on a much wider scale than hitherto. Theatre audiences included artisans as well as the middle classes and the nobility. A study of the cutlery workers in Solingen about 1848 has shown that they regarded music-making and reading in their own homes as an important leisure activity and it was not uncommon for some of them to own pianos.[2] The subscription concert was introduced in the large towns in the 1820s and 1830s and immediately became popular. The many weekly journals in which major writers published their work reached an audience the range of which was wide both as to class and age. The bond thus created between classes in the enjoyment of the arts is a feature of the period, which its political problems make us all too easily overlook. Contemporaries were aware of this achievement, and wrote about it enthusiastically.

The theatre in particular epitomised the communal enjoyment of the arts. This was the time when popular enthusiasm for the theatre was at its keenest. It was not an age of great dramatists – with the obvious exception of Grillparzer, Büchner and Hebbel – but of great performances. The appointment of theatre directors was one in which the public took the keenest interest – as when Tieck was appointed to Dresden in 1819 and to Berlin in 1840, and the former Young German Heinrich Laube to Vienna in 1849. Official appointments showed the taste of the authorities to be more enlightened in the world of theatre and of music than it was where books were concerned; thus Weber was made director of the court orchestra in Dresden in the 1820s and Wagner held the post two decades later; Mendelssohn conducted the *Gewandhaus* orchestra in Leipzig from 1835 onwards and was able to found the Conservatory there in 1842 where Clara Schumann's father taught.

Local rulers contributed generously to the support of theatres and orchestras. A number of them even took part personally in their court theatres, to which the general public were admitted. German rulers and their courts sat regularly in the theatre with their subjects ; in Austria members of the court even attended the suburban popular theatres. In fact the theatre was the centre of public life at this time, a substitute, it was aptly said, for parliament. Performances gave people plenty to talk about – in Vienna Adolf Bäuerle's *Theaterzeitung*, a daily paper, devoted wholly to the theatre was able to survive for fifty-four years. The authorities regarded the theatre as a valuable distraction from politics and cultivated the taste for it accordingly: when Franz Liszt started to give regular public concerts in Vienna he was required to play at night, after the theatre performances were over; even still the great concert hall of the *Musikverein* was filled to capacity at each of his appearances.

The function and meaning of art during the Biedermeier period was a social one. People believed that the creation and enjoyment of art drew men together and strengthened their sense of community. Eduard Mörike (1804–75) made this point in his most famous novella, *Mozart auf der Reise nach Prag* (1855) when he depicted the assembled company performing a scene from *Don Giovanni* under Mozart's own direction. The writer came to be regarded as a kind of bourgeois poet laureate, celebrating domestic events in a poem which might then be set to music by a composer friend. The most widely appreciated forms of writing in these years were the idyll or epic poem for domestic enjoyment, and the drama for public performance. The sociable character of Biedermeier writing is further illustrated by the popularity of certain genres: satire, epigram, travellers' tales and, in particular, diaries, letters and memoirs which were read aloud to a circle of family or friends. An ubiquitous society figure, the diplomat and *causeur* Varnhagen von Ense (1785–1858) created a fashion when he published the letters and writings of his wife Rahel after her death in 1833. On the other hand the long novel of ideas which was to become so popular in the fifties was scarcely known in this period. People fought shy of political discussion or were simply not interested, while radical social ideas were frowned upon as offending good taste.

Another aspect of the Biedermeier, which is both confusing and interesting to the critic, is the variety of literary styles often found in a single work. Most writers of the time were staunch admirers of their own classical literature and condemned what they considered the formlessness or lack of discipline of the German Romantic movement but they could not help being influenced by many of its ideas. Both major and minor writers paid the greatest attention to formal questions in their works, and many proved themselves quite as ready to experiment in form as their Romantic predecessors had been. They also owed many of their themes to the same source: interest in history, in nature, in customs and legends. In their interpretation of these themes, the Biedermeier writers showed a new sense of realism. Thus in the novel, short story or epic poem details of everyday life were appreciated: Tieck has the cabinet-maker Leonhard in his story *Der junge Tischlermeister* (1836) give an exact account of his craft to his aristocratic friend, Baron Elsheim, while Gotthelf's novels are full of details about farm work. A number of writers catered for the public's interest in local and national history: Wilhelm Hauff (1802–27) wrote historical tales about his native Württemberg, W. Alexis historic novels about Prussia, while Droste-Hülshoff evoked the atmosphere of her native Westphalia in poems and short stories. Writers were concerned primarily with discovering meaningful historic tradition, as embodied in still extant social customs and in living legend. The interest in history on the part of the public was also a response to a need for security in an age which threatened to bring change. In the same way Grillparzer stressed in his historical dramas the continuity and the authority of the Habsburg dynasty; it is noteworthy that Grillparzer's last two plays on patriotic subjects, in which destructive forces threaten the kingdom of

Bohemia (*Libussa*) and the Holy Roman Empire (*Ein Bruderzwist im Hause Habsburg*) (both 1848), were never offered by him to a publisher.

Many writers, and especially those whom we regard today as the major figures of the time, Grillparzer, Mörike, Droste-Hülshoff and Tieck, were intimately concerned with the position of the artist in the society of their age. While the 'pose' of the artist is something quite alien to the Biedermeier which is why the poet Platen, who seemed to affect such a pose, was so often satirised by his contemporaries – many viewed the changing position of the artist with some distress. Although the influence of a writer in Germany had never been comparable to that enjoyed by a writer in France or England, Grillparzer, Mörike and many others detected a lack of understanding by the public of the true role of the artist, and they condemned the current tendencies among young writers to get too involved, as they saw it, in ephemeral issues at the cost of their art.

Both Grillparzer and Mörike made the artist the subject of a novella. Grillparzer's *Der arme Spielmann* (published 1848) and Mörike's *Mozart auf der Reise nach Prag* (1855) are among their creators' most perfect works of art. They were written towards the end of the creative life of each writer and appeared after the outbreak of revolution in 1848; this seemed to give greater point to the views expressed. The novellas are nostalgic in that they look back to an age when art was readily understood in its social function. They are in an ostensibly Romantic form, the *Künstlernovelle* or artist novella, but neither Jakob, the poor musician, nor Mozart have much in common with the obsessed figures of Hoffmann's tales, Rat Krespel or Anselmus.

Mörike tells the story of Mozart at the time he was engaged on writing *Don Giovanni* and was invited to Prague for the first performance of the work. He leaves Vienna with his wife Constanze at a time when he is beset by malicious criticism and money troubles; they stop at an inn on the journey. Mozart takes a walk, finds a beautiful country mansion with an orangery in the grounds, and is accosted by an angry gardener when in a moment of abstraction he picks one of the oranges. He is brought before the owner of the estate, but to his surprise he finds he is known and his work admired by the family. He and his wife spend an evening at the castle; Mozart plays the piano and his hosts sing excerpts from the opera. In Mörike's portrait of Mozart the universality of the great musician's genius is seen to owe almost as much to his human qualities as to his natural gifts. The artist is not a creature apart from society, although he is blessed with keener insight than most; he is part of the society in which he works and lives and his work brings its members closer together. The degree of sensibility of each person is different; some penetrate more deeply into the mysteries of creative art than others. However each in his way is able to share the bond which art creates and to experience through it a deeper understanding of life. Thus the young niece of Mozart's host, Eugenie, understands the sublimity of *Don Giovanni*; her uncle admires the jollity of the peasant scenes, while the old aunt is reminded of the days when she too was young and beautiful. In this story, surely one of the great works of art written in the Biedermeier period, with its language subtly imitating the music of Mozart's opera, Mörike created out of his imagination the ideal audience which he lacked in his own day.

In an age more self-confident than the Biedermeier, this lack of a perceptive audience might have transformed the artist into a sort of Cassandra figure. In Grillparzer's story of the poor musician he becomes a lovable but eccentric figure. In *Der arme Spielmann* Jakob exemplifies his creator's sense of inadequacy with regard to the earlier, classical age of German literature. This sentiment oppressed many of Grillparzer's contemporaries such as Immermann, Platen or the young Stifter.

The figure of the artist in *Der arme Spielmann* is in fact divided between the two main characters, the narrator, who is not named, and Jakob, the poor musician. The narrator, we are told, is a dramatist who claims to have a deep interest in his fellow human beings. As he unfolds his tale, the limits of his sympathy and sensibility are made clear to the reader: he lacks the human feeling which would allow him to understand Jakob. At the same time, his professed affection for the populace of Vienna enjoying the festivities outside the city is that of a somewhat clinical observer: he has none of the naiveté of a truly popular writer. Jakob is in every way the reverse of the narrator. Grillparzer could easily have enlisted our sympathies by contrasting his human qualities with the arid intelligence of the narrator, or by showing, as Stifter was to do in *Kalkstein,* the power of simple goodness to change the world. Instead he presents in Jakob a grotesque figure, whose biography is a distorted version of Grillparzer's own. In Jakob's attitude to his 'art', Grillparzer reveals the problem of his generation: with a devotion that is the equivalent of antique piety, Jakob practises the works of the old masters and finds fulfilment in the discipline he imposes upon himself, but alas, he completely lacks the ability to communicate the beauty of these works in his performance. His playing is a travesty of the original music, it is a ghastly shrieking noise which arouses mingled horror and amusement among his listeners. What need have the great masters of the past of the unfortunate tribute paid them by the poor musician? Grillparzer's diaries, for all the sense of superiority he showed in them towards his younger contemporaries and their preoccupation with non-literary matters, have a good deal of masochism in their estimation of his own achievement. In his *Künstlernovelle* we see the same quality: his cruel picture of his own inadequacy in relation to his great predecessors, memories of the feeling of inferiority which overcame him when he visited Goethe at Weimar in 1825. Apart from the personal portrait he gave of himself here, Grillparzer suggested that the work of his generation was neither part of a local culture such as that which had formerly existed in Vienna, nor part of a living literary tradition. This profound and beautiful story can of course be read on more than one level and the moral implications are in a strange way uplifting to the reader. As a portrait of the artist in his own day, Grillparzer is pessimistic; inevitably he was drawn to the conclusion that the efforts of the artist to preserve the past for future generations are arid and fruitless.

Many other writers shared Grillparzer's pessimism about their future. Such concern is not of course a phenomenon exclusive to Germany, but a symptom of nineteenth-century doubts as to the purpose and function of art in a bourgeois society. It was aggravated in Grillparzer and Stifter and many other great writers of the century by their failure to win recognition for their achievement. Some writers, such as the novelist Wilhelm Raabe, won acclaim for their early works but failed to make an impression on the public with their mature works. There is indeed a striking discrepancy between the esteem in which Grillparzer, Mörike, Droste-Hülshoff and Stifter are held in the twentieth century and the somewhat patronising reception accorded to them in their own lifetime. It was characteristic of Germany that literary critics should fail to appreciate major poetic achievement in what was, in Heine's apt phrase, an age of prose. Even Goethe's fame declined in Germany before his death in 1832. Indeed of the writers of the period who are still read today, only Tieck and perhaps Hebbel were recognised as great names in the years 1830–50.

Related to this general pessimism and sense of failure is the theme of loneliness and isolation which occurs often in the works of the writers to be treated in the next chapter, though contemporary critics often attributed it to the fashionable melancholia of the thirties. The sense of being misunderstood or superficially interpreted is constantly mentioned in their diaries and letters, forcefully by some, such as Grillparzer, resignedly by others. A feeling of being out of tune with the times accounts for the withdrawal of many talented writers in these years from social concerns; it accounts also for the unrealistic and negative solutions offered to the crises of the times in novels, notably at the end of Immermann's *Die Epigonen* (1836).

In the novels of Immermann, in Tieck's short stories, in Grillparzer's dramas and Mörike's love poems, the characters or the speaker often commune with themselves rather than each other, the lack of social intercourse reflecting the situation of their creators. Thus despite the tranquillity of the German Confederation under Metternich's guidance, which was enjoyed by the average citizen, a sense of unease haunted many Germans, contrasting with the rather cosy provincialism of their lives. Their fear had no concrete object, unlike that of English people in the years of recession at the end of the 1830s and at the beginning of the 1840s when Chartist agitation seemed to presage a wild uprising of starved workers. The major writers of the Biedermeier expressed in their works the dread of an impending crisis in society and in art, although they did this indirectly or by implication. If they gave more immediate expression to their fear, as Grillparzer did in *Libussa,* they did not publish such works; Grillparzer left instructions that his play be destroyed after his death.

Thirty or forty years ago, the writers of this group were cited as evidence of the serenity of German life in the years before the Revolution of 1848. Their work seemed to give substance to the argument that Germany was then a placid haven in a turbulent world and that her writers, apart from Heine and his imitators, were profundly uninterested in the world outside the frontiers of their imagination. Mörike's fluid lines: *Laß, o Welt, o laß mich sein* (*Verborgenheit*, 1832), provided a handy and mellifluous heading for the whole group. Obviously the physical circumstances of the writer in Germany influenced his choice of material; these men rarely sought the contact with other cultures which is so notable in the case of the even more isolated Russian writers. On the other hand, the basic themes in their work, the formal problems of the drama and novel which preoccupied them and which few succeeded in solving, show a deep involvement with their age. The fact that they did not openly challenge the status quo did not mean that they ignored it. The passages expressing contentment, such as Raimund's *Hobellied* in his comedy *Der Verschwender* (1834), Grillparzer's lines on the joys of self-abnegation in Act IV of *Der Traum ein Leben* (1834), Mörike's verses, Immermann's and Nestroy's happy endings, are at variance with the general tenor of the works in question. Although the general impression of the Biedermeier age is one of contented enjoyment of the modest pleasures of life, of which art is one, there is in the work of the great writers and of many minor figures also, a current of unease that such a world cannot last. The discordant imagery of so many works communicates the underlying pessimism of their creators more persuasively than does the harmonious life they depict.[3]

3

The Biedermeier Writers
1820-50

I Narrative prose

After the death of Goethe in March 1832, Ludwig Tieck, who
lived in Saxony, was looked on by Germans as their greatest living
writer. Tieck had settled in Dresden when he was appointed
director of the court theatre in 1819 and he now enjoyed a nationwide reputation. Born in 1773, he was one of the last surviving
members of the early Romantic movement; Eichendorff, the author of *Aus dem Leben eines Taugenichts* was almost a generation
younger. Contemporaries rated Tieck higher than we do today,
though the edge of this admiration was directed against Goethe,
who had not chosen to be as accessible. Tieck had the quality of
recognising greatness in others, and he had a fluid style as well
as considerable receptivity to new ideas. It was he who had stimulated and encouraged the Romantic poets Novalis, Wackenroder
and Friedrich Schlegel; later he had published Kleist and the
Sturm und Drang playwright Lenz when few recognised their
genius. In the 1830s he gave sympathy to Immermann and
Grabbe at crucial points in their artistic development. His long life
– he was still active up to the year of his death in 1853 – and
involvement in literary affairs made him a public figure, which
his younger colleagues were not, and enabled him to help promising talents.

Tieck had always been a voracious and adventurous reader.
His tastes were catholic: he explored foreign and medieval litera-
tures and by his translations from English, Spanish and Italian,
as well as medieval German, he made little known works familiar
to his countrymen. Up to 1819 he was known primarily as a lyric
poet, dramatist and critic. After that date he wrote no more poetry
or plays, and instead concentrated on narrative prose. Influenced
by his reading of Cervantes' prose tales, he started to make contemporary issues the subject of his stories. In his preference for the

novella with its exacting formal demands, and the social criticism contained in these late works, he exercised an important influence on his younger contemporaries.

Like many of the surviving Romantics, Friedrich Schlegel, Adam Müller and Zacharias Werner, he determined to use his talents for the benefit of mankind, as he understood it. His late work was an attempt to understand and interpret his period for contemporaries, and he tried to stress the positive and sustaining elements in social life. The characters of his stories have an absorbing interest in their own times; they discuss, often at length, those forces which help to mould men's characters and the society in which they live: religion, historical tradition, art and music. Although he frequently used the form of the historical tale or novel, Tieck was really only concerned with the present. He made little attempt, as did W. Alexis in the wake of Sir Walter Scott, to create a sense of period in the past. (Tieck in fact disliked Scott which was rather an original thing to do in the 1830s.) He used historical costume to lend distance and show how the past was responsible for the present. The historical settings of many of his works between 1820 and 1840 are always analogous to the time of writing; times of decline or decay in human history when new social forces are released. Thus in *Der Hexensabbath* (1823) and *Der Aufruhr in den Cevennen* (1826), Tieck treated emotional religious movements of earlier ages, but he made the parallel with the situation in Germany in the 1820s apparent, when many Romantic writers and late Romantic painters, known as the Nazarenes, were becoming converted to the Catholic Church. Tieck's intention was to see these movements as social phenomena; his readers misunderstood him and accused him of not making his own sympathies sufficiently clear.

Their constant concern with their past makes Tieck's characters tireless storytellers.[1] This slows the pace of the tale and permits the inclusion of long discursive passages. Critics have seen in this evidence of the decline of Tieck's creative powers, but quite apart from their considerable literary merit, these novellas show a more comprehensive survey of the issues confronting society between 1820 and 1840 than any other writer of fiction was providing at the time in Germany. They are set in a bourgeois world and the values which inform them are middle class ones, although they are significantly different from those current in Western

Europe generally. The German middle classes, composed of officials and craftsmen, are pictured trying to enlarge their horizons through education. One of the most interesting examples is Leonhard, the hero of the short novel, *Der junge Tischlermeister* (1836), which describes the way of life of a master craftsman in South Germany in the 1830s. Leonhard is well-educated, he even reads Homer in the original, but he is also a successful and tenacious businessman; his paternalistic attitude to his employees is described in loving detail. The work is particularly worth looking at for the light it throws on the current attitudes of conservative German society towards the age and on the ideals which animate the middle class. Usefulness is stressed as much as beauty, both in people and in possessions. The heroine is not a well born lady, but a practical housewife, her bunch of keys occupying her attention, as did the comb and mirror her literary predecessors. In art the social function is regarded as of prime importance. Speaking of his work, cabinet-making, Leonhard tells his aristocrat friend, Baron Elsheim, why he chose to be a craftsman rather than an academic. His words are suitably sententious in such a serious young man, but what he says could be quoted as an instance of the Biedermeier aesthetic : 'I have always felt elevated by the instinct in man to want everything in daily use to be both functional and beautiful; thus a rich man and an educated man will want no object in his house which is not transformed by the addition of ornament into something higher.'[2] Satisfaction with a task well done and a high standard of workmanship are seen as the ideals of the age and also as a substitute for the lack of creative genius which is felt to be characteristic of it. The contentment with one's station which these ideals imply has a pronounced ethical undertone.

Tieck has been criticised for the uncomplicated picture he drew of this bourgeois world, a criticism which might seem to have all the more force since the thirties were a time when 'problems' were the prerequisite of serious social or political commentary. In fact his world only *seems* uncomplicated. He was keenly aware of living at the beginning of an age of great social change, and in his stories he tried to record a way of life which he believed would shortly disappear. He portrayed the German middle classes on the eve of the industrial revolution, in particular the artisan class. His account has much in common with the impressions of artisan life recorded in the diary of the journeyman Dewald in 1836–8.[3] Already the artisans had largely lost their privileged positon as members of guilds and were facing competition from overseas which they were not able to meet. The decline of the guilds caused concern to writers of conservative sympathies up to the middle of the century. The demands of the artisans for protection in times of stress took up a disproportionate amount of the energy of the 1848 revolutionaries, whatever Marx might allege to the contrary. Although Tieck's vision of society in *Der junge Tischlermeister* and his other prose works of the thirties is admittedly somewhat utopian, it showed his most distinguished quality as a writer and critic, namely his intuitive grasp of the fact that the unease felt by his contemporaries had its roots in social change; he understood that the real significance of the factory system lay in its social consequences. The factory system would wipe out the type of man whom Tieck and others like him considered the backbone of the nation; it would rob them of their dignity by robbing them of pride in their work; it would erect still higher barriers between classes, which even in an ideal society are hard to bridge. The decline of the guilds, like the decline of aristocratic patronage of the arts (a theme treated in this story and in many other novellas written in the same period) was but a symptom of the disappearance of a society which provided material security and made life meaningful to the individual.

Karl Immermann

The influence of Tieck on other writers was widespread and diverse. One of the most interesting of such writers was Karl Immermann (1795–1840) whose prose works offer such an excellent guide to the climate of the 1830s. Immermann is stronger on detail than most, though less sure on general issues. He called his *Die Epigonen* 'a novel of the times' and produced a splendid compendium of the attitudes, habits and obsessions of a large section of German society in the thirties. Twenty years later most of the novel was dated. In it the objectionable smell of the first mackintoshes seems as important as the neo-Gothic revival, the convert Jew in German society as significant as the vogue for Hegel. An inordinate amount of space in this novel, as in *Münchhausen* (1839), was devoted to satiric portraits of contemporaries, some clever, some inept and even vicious. *Münchhausen* purports to be a satirical novel of the times, but its author was too over-whelmed with the seriousness of his criticisms for it to succeed in amusing the modern reader, as does the Romantic novelist Hoff-mann's earlier satirical novel, *Die Lebensansichten des Kater Murrs* (1821). *Die Epigonen* was the first German novel to deal with the rise of the new commercial class at the expense of the hereditary nobility. Like many German writers since, Immermann regarded social change of this kind in the nature of cultural and spiritual loss.

As is the case with his contemporary the dramatist Grabbe, the disparity between intention and achievement makes Immermann a particularly interesting figure. Grabbe defied inherited literary conventions and achieved in many scenes of his plays a new idiom: even in his failures we are aware of his quality. In Immer-mann's case we see Germany's literary achievements in the past as a burden which prevented him from developing a style ade-quate to what he was saying. 'The poet,' he wrote in 1818, 'must be responsible for everything in his work, everything, that is, ex-cept the influences on him; these are a burden laid on him by fate.'[4] Thus he was a self-confessed epigone, one who is born of a later, less distinguished generation, and this feeling he shared in some measure with every other writer discussed in this chapter, with the exception of the popular Viennese dramatists. The bit-terest satire in Immermann's work, the episode of the *Wiederkäuer* in *Münchhausen,* the goats who chew over and regurgitate what they have eaten, is directed against himself. In his earlier novel, *Die Epigonen,* he made no attempt to match his 'contemporary' novel with a contemporary style. He simply took over the external form of Goethe's great novel, *Wilhelm Meisters Lehrjahre* (1795–6). Wilhelm and Natalie are renamed Hermann and Cor-delia; even Mignon appears as Flämmchen.

The unifying theme of *Die Epigonen* is a social one, and it is not surprising that people were excited about it when it was pub-lished in 1836. Besides portraying the topical quarrels and pre-occupations of the time, in which most of its readers took sides, it dealt with the clash between the position and claims of the feudal aristocracy, which was suffering economic decline, and the grow-ing power of bourgeois capitalism. Immermann was critical of the aristocracy, with whom he had become acquainted through his mistress, Countess Ahlefeldt, while the prototype of the industrialist in the story, the hero Hermann's uncle, was modelled on a certain Nathusius, who bought up mortgaged estates around Hanover during the depression of the 1820s to build factories. Immermann admits a certain reluctant admiration for the efficiency of the business machine and the network of commerce throughout the world, but the industrialist is condemned because he disparages the arts and has no true feeling for nature; he thinks only in terms of profit or loss. His aristocratic opposite number, the Duke, is a man of wide culture, but selfish and degenerate, while his wife is a prey to hysterical religious crises. The faults of both render them incapable, in Immermann's eyes, of assuming leadership in society. The solution is found, as so often in nineteenth-century German novels, in the next generation, in the marriage between Hermann and Cordelia. Hermann, the symbolic hero, is, like the hero of Sue's *The Wandering Jew* (1844) and Dankmar Wildungen in Gutzkow's *Die Ritter vom Geiste* (1850–2), related to both social spheres. His wife Cordelia is also discovered to be part noble, part bourgeois in origin. At the end of the novel Hermann inherits his uncle's vast commercial empire, and, deeply disturbed by the depression of the factory workers and the unhealthy appearance of their families, decides to close the factories and resettle the workers as craftsmen and agricultural labourers.

The end of the novel does not ring true; but Immermann's solution is none the less illuminating. Unlike many other writers of the Biedermeier he was not an obscure provincial, but a judge in the Court of Appeals at Düsseldorf. He had opportunity to observe at first hand industrial developments in the Rhineland. But in Germany acquaintance with the problems of industrialisation generated none of that moral energy for the improvement of the human lot which animated the middle classes in England in the nineteenth century; at any rate not until the advent of socialism in the 1860s. Industrialisation is inevitable, but we must do our best to ignore it, seems to be Immermann's answer. Unlike many of his contemporaries who so admired Hegel, Immerman believed that the state was a necessary evil, but like his generation he automatically discounted the power of the individual to shape the world in which he lived.

The inherited social structure is the theme of *Münchhausen*, the novel a parody of romantic feeling. The central character of the story, Baron von Münchhausen, who lives with his daughter in the crazy castle Schnick-Schnack-Schnurr, is an example of the degenerate and antiquated feudal aristocracy of Germany, but also a symbol of the absurdity of the world. Immermann contrasted the absurd fantasies of Münchhausen with the vigour and practicality of the farming community which he depicted in the celebrated section of the novel entitled *Der Oberhof*. This portrait of an agrarian community is connected with the body of the novel through the hero, Oswald, and it won Immermann great acclaim, even from those such as the Young Germans who had been satirised in other sections. Tieck said it was the best modern novel; Hebbel, the dramatist, praised it highly. It was published on the eve of the forties, in the last year of Immermann's life, when the literary and political climate was already changing. 'We must leave the romantic behind us and go on to the realistic, the pragmatic,' wrote Immermann in his posthumously published memoirs, the engaging *Memorabilien* (1840–3).[5] The *Oberhof* might well have represented a stylistic breakthrough for Immermann, an indication of his future development, had he lived. It brings him near the great prose writers of the middle of the century, Gotthelf, Droste-Hülshoff (in *Die Judenbuche*) and Stifter, in whose works the peasant community, the primordial forces, were central themes. The *Hofschulze,* the patriarchal head of this farming community, is not presented as an ideal figure: he is sly, hard and even brutal, and his character is presented as realistically as that of any farmer in Gotthelf's novels. Like Gotthelf and their younger contemporary Stifter, Immermann was more interested in the community than the individual. The *Hofschulze* embodies a way of life and it is on this that his character rests. The community is not without human shortcomings, even absurdities, shown for example in the comic picture of the village bride. The way of life is 'natural' and every event meaningful, giving evidence, as in the christenings depicted in Gotthelf's stories and novels, of a stable world. Immermann contrasted the 'real' agrarian community with the falseness of the feudal aristocracy and with the unfeeling world of business, which also appears in the novel; in this he gave nineteenth-century German fiction one of its most fertile themes. It belongs to both serious and popular literature. The nostalgia of the uprooted peasant for the countryside became a widespread phenomenon in German society, especially among the lower paid office workers and officials. Towards the end of the nineteenth century the representation of country life found a new popularity as *Heimatdichtung,* a sentimental version of the real thing. Another feature of Immermann's novel had a more delayed influence: this was the idea of 'regenerating' the blood of the effete nobility through the marriage of the hero Oswald with Lisbeth, from the *Oberhof.* Ironically this tribute to the moral strength of the *Volk* earned for Immermann the doubtful honour of a place in the Nazi gallery of their spiritual ancestors.

The realistic section of *Münchhausen* tells the story of the courtship of Oswald and Lisbeth and ends with their marriage. Immermann made it clear that this was not the conventional happy ending: marriage is a serious task, as well as the source of great happiness. He made the point in a letter appended to *Münchhausen*: 'It was my aim to record the story of love, to follow love to a point where it makes men wise, and ready to serve their home and country, their age and their fellow men.'[6] We are aware of the relevance of his own late marriage here, for the letter records the change it brought about in the actual writing of the novel. Tieck had anticipated Immermann's treatment of married love in his novellas (such as the delightful story *Des Lebens Überfluß,* 1839); the younger writer looked forward to the novellas of the later realist writers, Storm, Raabe, Paul Heyse and Otto Ludwig, with their fine portrayal of marriage and family life.

Immermann therefore is one of a group of writers who were keenly and regretfully aware of change and attempted to record it in their work. Apart from a small number of innovations, they did this within the framework of inherited literary forms, and this often diminished their impact and set bounds to their imagination. The confusion as to the purpose and function of literature in their generation, the turning – in their eyes the degradation – of literature into a preaching platform, increased their reverence for the past. The ethical consequences of social change preoccupied them, and a most penetrating aspect of their work is their portrayal of men on the threshold of a new age.

Willibald Alexis

The current preoccupation with the changing world found a

very different expression in the work of the novelist and critic, Alexis, whose real name was Wilhelm Häring. He was born in 1798, two years after Immermann, and he died in 1871, a year before Grillparzer. His first novel was published in 1823 and he followed this with a series of historical novels set in Brandenburg, which proved very popular. The reception of Alexis' novels is as relevant to a discussion of literature and society as the novels themselves. The reading public now showed that they were beginning to share a sense of the conflict between tradition and change which was to preoccupy Germans throughout the period 1830–90. Awareness of the past shows itself at specific points in a nation's history either as tradition, which is taken more or less for granted, or rediscovery, which occurs at a time when the form of the state or the bonds of society seem jeopardised. The French Revolution of 1789 and the European Romantic movement had awakened in the nations of Europe a consciousness of their own past. This changed the character of historical writing in the nineteenth century, whether it was in the form of serious history or of fiction. The novels of Sir Walter Scott, coming at a time of revolutionary upheaval, made this new sense of the past vivid to a large reading public. Writers of fiction, of drama and ballads tried to satisfy the demand for historical works; they tried to present the past in the great German historian Leopold von Ranke's phrase, 'as it really happened', by making an effort to include genuine touches and to avoid anachronisms.

In Germany the desire to recreate the past remained strong throughout our period. In the world of scholarship German historians, the pioneers Niebuhr (1776–1831) and his pupil Ranke (1795–1886), and later the students at their seminars, devoted their creative abilities to the first extensive historical research based on the systematic use of contemporary sources. The years when Ranke was a young scholar saw the compilation and publication of an immense amount of material from the past on which future historians would draw for many decades, notably Baron von Stein's foundation, the famous *Monumenta Germaniae Historica,* under the able direction of the Hanoverian historian George Pertz; the first volume of the series appeared in 1826. During these years a very large number of historical studies were made at both local and national level, national and civic museums were opened, antiquarian societies sprang up all over the country, all these things testifying to the very wide interest in Germany's past.

Willibald Alexis was the first German historical novelist in the modern sense. He owed his overnight popularity to the fiction that his *Walladmor* (1823), published when he was twenty-five, and *Castle Avalon* (1827) were, in his own words, 'free translations from two unknown works of Sir Walter Scott'. Scott's popularity was already something of a publisher's phenomenon in Germany at this time. As Fontane remarked many years later, his name replaced that of Napoleon in the conversation of the nation.[7] Germans were attracted to Scott because here was a novelist who aroused a sense of national consciousness among his readers by his treatment of patriotic themes. It was this quality which inspired Wilhelm Hauff, a gifted writer who died in 1827 at the early age of twenty-five, to write *Liechtenstein* (1826), a historical tale about his native Württemberg in the hope that his story would awaken in his fellow countrymen a sense of their past and thus inspire them with self-confidence.[8] Willibald Alexis set his novels in the provincial world of the Electorate of Brandenburg which was eventually to become the kingdom of Prussia. He satisfied his readers' curiosity about the past by his vivid record of everyday life in the seventeenth century. He was an observant writer with an eye for humorous detail and he made the past live by his inclusion of realistic touches, such the problem of draughts in the castle at Bredow in his best known novel, *Die Hosen des Herrn von Bredow* (1846); the satisfactory outcome of the plot in this novel is made to depend on whether the harassed Frau von Bredow can get her warrior husband's trousers dry in time for enemy action after she has washed them against his express wishes.

Alexis was popular also because he drew analogies between the historical world he depicted and the society of his day. In common with many of his generation he expressed in his novels nostalgia for the moral values and close-knit society of an earlier age. As in the case of the writers of peasant literature, he was admired for his portrayal of a local world which had managed to resist change. Thus the German historical novel in the first decades of our period, like the village tale and in poetry the idyll, which was much cultivated in these years, was to some extent a form of escape from the present, a symptom of the general reluctance of Germans to accept change. Before 1866, when Prussia defeated Austria and the unification of Germany seemed at last in sight, writers of historical tales and novels wrote about patriotic subjects in Germany's past and interpreted them in a way that strove to make the past seem warm and familiar to the reader. After 1866 historical novels, plays and poetry became even more popular than in the Biedermeier period, but they were charged with a pathos which was quite foreign to Alexis and Hauff, or the less well known historical novelists Wilhelm Meinhold and Robert Prutz. The patriotic pose of Geibel's much read lyrics, of Felix Dahn's highly successful novel, *Der Kampf um Rom* (1876) or Ernst von Wildenbruch's dramas distinguishes the later period clearly from the earlier one.

II   The theatre

'Now that people no longer go to church, the theatre is the only public place of worship left,' Grillparzer remarked in his diary in 1839–40.[9] The ritual character of the visit to the theatre, the solemn if enthusiastic devotion of German theatre-goers, gave substance to his contention. The creative years of Franz Grillparzer's life, 1817–48, which coincide almost exactly with the Restoration era in Germany and Austria, were at first sight favourable to the dramatist. Stimulated by the interest of the public and encouraged by the authorities who, in the view of the then Austrian chief of police, Count Sedlnitzky, saw the theatre as an antidote to politics in the 'dangerous evening hours', dramatists of note and almost every aspiring writer attempted to cater for the demand. And yet if we look at the records of the repertories for these years, few names are known to us today. Contrary to common belief Lessing, Goethe and Schiller did not dominate the theatre in Germany during their lifetime nor in the period we are speaking about. August von Kotzebue (1761–1819) and Wilhelm Iffland (1759–1814) and, in nineteenth century Vienna, Eduard Bauernfeld (1802–90) were much more popular and more prolific. In Vienna Kotzebue's plays were performed some 3,650 times up to the year 1867 and Bauernfeld's works were put on 1,100 times in the *Hofburg* or Vienna Court Theatre alone in 1828–92. Their works reflected the aspirations and foibles of their largely middle-class audiences, who increasingly determined the choice of play and type of production. Though Grillparzer, Austria's greatest playwright, was distinguished in being, apart from Hebbel, the only living dramatist of note whose plays were actually performed, outside Vienna only his early plays were known.

Grillparzer was born in Vienna in 1791 and lived all his life there apart from a number of journeys abroad. He owes his unique position in German drama to a combination of literary influences on the one hand and theatrical influences on the other. He 'discovered' Goethe for the first time when he was almost eighteen years old; he never lost his admiration for Goethe and his delight in his achievement as a writer of poetic drama. Although the date of Grillparzer's birth would seem to place him among the younger German Romantic writers, he belonged by virtue of the language and ideas of his plays to German classicism. He felt keenly the distance separating him as an Austrian and as one of a later generation from Goethe's Weimar; he cherished the works of classical humanism with an almost religious reverence. He was convinced of the inferiority of the work of contemporary dramatists and in his own dramas sought to raise the standards of the theatre and the taste of the public by producing 'something in between Goethe and Kotzebue, what the theatre needs' – great poetic drama but good theatre as well.[10]

Though perhaps to a lesser extent than his contemporaries in the popular theatre in Vienna, Grillparzer is also a dramatist who must be seen rather than read. In his essays on the theatre and in his diaries he constantly referred to the immediacy of appeal which a successful drama must have. He frequently used words like 'picture' (*Bild*), 'painting' (*Gemälde*), 'mirror' (*Spiegel*) to indicate the visual impact of a scene. 'A true dramatic poet *sees* his work being performed as he writes it,' he said of Raimund in an essay on this popular writer for the theatre whom he so admired.[11] Grillparzer owed his keen sense of the stage to his native city. His earliest memories were of sitting on his nursemaid's knee reading with her scenes from Schikaneder's text of *The Magic Flute*.[12] He always wrote with the public in mind. On a number of occasions he referred to the audience as a jury who represents common humanity. If he did not have a high opinion of the artistic sensibility of his Viennese audiences, he did rate their intuitive reaction highly, and when they ceased to respond enthusiastically to his works and in 1838 rejected his comedy, *Weh' dem, der lügt,* he offered no more of his plays for performance. From the popular theatre in Vienna he learned to employ visual effects on the stage:

the great tableaux in his historical dramas such as the entry of the flamboyant Bohemian king Ottokar before the assembled court at the end of Act I of *König Ottokars Glück und Ende* 1825, or the entry of the aging Emperor Rudolph II in the first act of *Ein Bruderzwist im Hause Habsburg* (1848). In all his plays, most memorably perhaps in *Des Meeres und der Liebe Wellen* (1831), his poignant love tragedy, and in *Ein treuer Diener seines Herrn* (1828), he represents emotional developments by a concrete equivalent on the stage. The 'spectacle' which Viennese theatre-goers demanded is evident in all his plays, from his first work, *Die Ahnfrau* (1817), a brooding drama of fate, onwards. He made the point that 'a tragedy, however sad it may be, is still a play'[13] and even in *Sappho* (1818), his most classical work, a superb portrait of the great poetess who yearns to be loved as a woman rather than revered as an artist and tries to force this love from a young man of her retinue, he satisfied his public's desire for entertainment by Sappho's dramatic suicide at the end. He paid close attention to stage effects to enhance the aesthetic appeal of his plays – for the first performance of his most popular play in Vienna, *Der Traum ein Leben* (1834) the handsome sum of 1,100 gulden was spent on stage effects, costumes and scenery.

Grillparzer is not only a master of the theatre but a writer of historical dramas of the first order. As the subject of a multinational Empire and as a citizen of Vienna which had enjoyed a much longer unbroken cultural tradition than any other city in the Confederation, he had a keen sense of his country's past. To his dramatic work he brought an informed interest in ancient and modern history and an intimate knowledge of Shakespeare and the Spanish dramatists. Grillparzer is one of the few writers in German who was passionately interested in politics, not as a speculative study of systems, but for the light it throws on human behaviour. The lack of outlet for political comment in Austria therefore never stunted his powers of observation as it did those of many of his contemporaries. His diaries are full of notes on human types and their eccentricities, on the characteristics of a nation or a city expressed in the form of epigram or aphorism. The patriotic figures and themes from Austrian history in the dramas of his middle years – *König Ottokar, Ein Bruderzwist,* already mentioned, and *Libussa* (1848) – eventually won him the high regard of his countrymen and he was hailed as their national dramatist.

This is still the main source of his popularity in his own country today. In these dramas Grillparzer was primarily concerned with the nature of man as a political animal, the effect of ambition for power on a man's character, the nature of authority. It should be stressed that this concern is if not unique in the German dramatic tradition certainly a formidable achievement.

Grillparzer owed the maturity of his vision to a variety of causes: his first plays were written immediately after the defeat of Napoleon and the collapse of his Empire. The poet was both attracted to and repelled by the figure of Napoleon who had had a decisive effect on Grillparzer's own life and the fortunes of his family; like all his generation, he never forgot the impact of Napoleon's fall. He was sceptical of greatness; he never portrayed a truly dynamic figure on the stage. Jason in *Das goldene Vlieβ* (1821) or Ottokar may at first seem to be such, but the course of the drama reveals their strength to be a sham. Critics have interpreted this as the heritage of the baroque in Austria; it is more likely to have been the impact of Napoleon's fate. Grillparzer is tremendously convincing in his portrayal of decline and defeat, and it is in this sense, and not as a literary epigone, that he is the child of his time. His touch is surest when he shows observers of life, men grown old or wise, or those who have not yet known life, the adolescent.

German drama has always tended to draw its inspiration from ideas rather than from the passions and conflicts of human beings. Similarly German political thought is speculative rather than pragmatic: knowledge of human nature has not been considered of great importance in the equipment of a ruler. Grillparzer as an Austrian based his political philosophy on an analysis of human behaviour. *Libussa,* the product of political wisdom rather than dramatic talent, and *Ein Bruderzwist* are among his last plays; in the long political speeches of the mythical Bohemian princess Libussa and those of the Emperor Rudolph II his language achieves a rare sonority and he gives evidence of a pragmatic political philosophy which is almost unique among German literary figures. However his heroes – and Ottokar and the King in *Ein treuer Diener seines Herrn* must be included here as well – achieve a knowledge of human nature, become wise rulers in Grillparzer's view only through failure. Insight into the ways of men is bought at the cost of exclusion from their affairs. His last plays were finished under the impact of the Revolution of 1848, which was a severe shock to Grillparzer as to his fellow-countryman Stifter. The fear of the destructive power of the masses is starkly present in *Libussa*, the fear of change and distrust of the contemporary adulation of progress in *Ein Bruderzwist*. Like his younger contemporary Büchner Grillparzer feared that human beings were going to be debased in the name of scientific and political advance; in his cultural pessimism he anticipated Jakob Burckhardt, the art historian, like himself a man of wide culture. He was naturally conservative, a typical early nineteenth-century Austrian in his dynastic rather than national loyalties; he justified his traditional allegiance both in his plays and in his diaries on the grounds that the Habsburg dynasty provided a living tradition, which, though not ideal, was meaningful to the individual. He was typical of the Biedermeier in his sceptical accommodation to reality, he constantly pointed out that those politicians, critics and journalists who advocated change in the thirties and forties for the sake of an abstract ideal had little knowledge of society and its needs. The patriotic themes from the history of the house of Habsburg, the famous lines spoken in *Ein Bruderzwist* by the Emperor to those who are agitating for concessions which begin : 'Do not test the supports, do not seek to improve', are the essence of his political moderation but also of his political realism.[14]

Both as a poet and a political commentator, Grillparzer was invariably critical of theorists. In this he reveals the difference between the Austrian and the German mentality. Wherever he travelled his first visits were not to libraries, but to the theatre and the national assembly or parliament, as for example on his visit to France and England in 1836. These institutions taught him, he believed, something of the nature of the people and their traditions, and led him to understand what another might condemn, merely because it was different. It was essential to take temperament and tradition into account when judging a nation and the behaviour of legislators and theatre-goers told him much about national character. While never an opponent of change as such, he grew fearful of the effects of too rapid change, especially as regards his own country. In his plays his recognition of the influence of environment on psychological development and character point towards the future course of European drama. He saw in the Habsburg monarchy the sustaining tradition, the symbol of the living community, in which the individual flourishes and his life is made meaningful. His plays are not primarily patriotic plays in the narrow sense Germans used it in the nineteenth century. Grillparzer rather reminds us of Shakespeare: he is Austria's national dramatist in the same sense as we think of Shakespeare and England. The political settlement of the 'German question' in 1866, when Austria was defeated by Prussia and excluded from Germany, had a decisive effect on Grillparzer's reputation. Austria after 1866 became increasingly preoccupied with internal problems, particularly with the jealousies of the subject nations. German-speaking Austrians grew inward-looking and her popular culture provincial. In Austria Grillparzer continued to be played as a reminder of former times, but in the Germany of the second half of the nineteenth century his broad political vision had little appeal.

Grillparzer suffered more than most from the pettiness of the Austrian censorship and by the end of the 1840s the fertility and spontaneity of his genius was impaired. At the same time his insight was sharpened. He became aware of the social as well as of the political consequences of the upheavals he was witnessing around him. His insistence on the importance of authority and loyalty in his historical plays suggests that he foresaw the course of development in Central Europe over the next decades. The fragmentation of society so powerfully portrayed by another Austrian and a great admirer of Grillparzer, namely Hugo von Hofmannsthal (*Der Turm* 1925), is anticipated in the figure of the libertine, who appears in all his major plays – Zawisch (*Ottokar*), Otto von Meran (*Ein treuer Diener*) and Don Cäsar (*Ein Bruderzwist*) etc. The conflict between traditional conservatism with its stress on the community and the increasing claims of the individual, the narrow boundary between liberty and licence, between permissiveness and anarchy, are pinpointed by Grillparzer as acute modern problems, to which he, great writer that he was, would offer no escapist solution.

The Viennese Popular Theatre

When Grillparzer's first plays, *Die Ahnfrau* and *Sappho,* were being produced in Vienna, the popular theatre in the city was dominated by the so-called 'Big Three', the playwrights and actors

Bäuerle, Meisl and Gleich. Adolf Bäuerle (1786–1859) was a well-known figure in the city, editor for many decades of the *Theater-zeitung,* which the Viennese read then, as today they read the local *Bild-Kurier,* to confirm their own views of the previous night's theatre performances. He also wrote some 200 plays for the local popular stage, as well as directing and acting in many of them. It is hardly surprising, in view of his many activities, that most of these are hastily contrived pieces, the plots filched from wherever he could get them, or the whole play a crude parody of some successful piece. This was common practice in the popular theatre and elicited no comment, since the public was there to be entertained, and the same piece was rarely repeated more than a couple of times. There were three main popular theatres catering for the local inhabitants in the suburbs – hence the title *Vorstadt-bühne* or suburban stage – most of whom were middle class officials, shop owners, artisans. The largest was the *Theater an der Wien,* where *Die Ahnfrau* was first performed, then there was the *Leopoldstadt* theatre in the north of the city, near the river Danube, and the *Josephstadt* theatre in the west. The mainstay of these were the *Zauberposse,* a sort of burlesque with magic elements which indulged the audience's taste for spectacular productions and lavish scenery, and the parody. The public clamoured for novelty; its enthusiasm has been compared to that of late nineteenth-century audiences for the music hall. Parody had the advantage of being easy to arrive at – and topical. Thus Meisl, Bäuerle's son-in-law, produced *Die Frau Ahndles* only a short time after Grillparzer's play was staged. Most of these had a very short run indeed, although *Die verhängnisvolle Limonade* (The Fateful Lemonade), a parody of Schiller's *Kabale und Liebe,* was revived successfully over a century after it was written.

Bäuerle was undoubtedly the most able of the *Großen Drei* and he made an important contribution to the repertory of the popular stage when in 1811 he created *Parapluiemacher Staberl,* the timorous umbrella maker, the 'average Viennese'. Staberl made his appearances in several successive plays, either by Bäuerle or his imitators, and encouraged the vogue for the *'Lokalstück'* or comedy based on local manners which Nestroy was to exploit in the 1830s and 1840s. Bäuerle's most successful play was *Die falsche Primadonna in Krähwinkel* (1818), a satire on the public's indiscriminate appetite for celebrities. Krähwinkel was of course Vienna, and Bäuerle's success inspired a host of imitators, including Meisl and Gleich. The *Krähwinkliaden,* as these plays came to be called, offered great possibilities for social and political satire, but apart from the creation of the dogged informer *Ratsdiener* Klaus, a familiar figure in Metternich's Austria, it was not until the censorship lapsed for a while during the 1848 Revolution that Nestroy seized the opportunity to write his splendid satire on the Austrian political system, *Freiheit in Krähwinkel* (1849); even then he did not waste time thinking out a plot but borrowed Bäuerle's *Primadonna*.

Bäuerle, Meisl and Gleich catered for the Viennese public's desire to be entertained; box office success was really all that mattered to them. Ferdinand Raimund (1790–1836), who began his career in the theatre at the age of fourteen selling sweets in the interval, deplored what he regarded as the debasement of taste in the popular theatres of his time. He aspired to be a tragic actor; there is a touching if slightly grotesque anecdote told of how he used to stand for hours practising grimaces in front of the mirror to make his mouth as large as that of the tragedian Ochsenheimer, whom he had chosen as his model. In vain; a speech defect thrust him willy-nilly into comic roles. He had already made a name for himself as an actor in the *Leopoldstädter* theatre when in 1823 he ventured to improve public taste by writing *Der Barometermacher auf der Zauberinsel,* the first of some eight plays which both regaled and instructed his audiences. Raimund provided the Viennese with an illusion in the lean years after the war and the state bankruptcy in Austria. He presented in his plays native types who are watched over by benevolent spirits, and to the accompaniment of music and dancing the virtuous are rewarded and the wicked made to see the error of their ways. Material security is added to moral improvement (as in *Der Alpenkönig und der Menschenfeind,* 1828 and *Der Verschwender,* 1834) to convince the audience of the happy end. Raimund achieved his greatest triumphs in the presentation of what the Viennese enjoyed so much: complicated stage machinery by which the supernatural forces could be transported through the air, spirits, ghosts and fairies in whom they no longer believed, but whose imaginative presentation delighted them the more. Other playwrights might mock Raimund for his naive belief in allegories, but Fortune, Youth, Age and Hope conquered the audiences by

103

the ingenuity of their costumes and the catchiness of their songs. Raimund had a splendid sense of the theatre – for example the scene in *Der Bauer als Millionär* (1826) in which Youth bids farewell to the grasping farmer, prematurely aged through greed, in a lovely song set to music by Schubert, and before our eyes the farmer becomes old and grey. In his equally accomplished play, *Der Alpenkönig und der Menschenfeind*, a kindly spirit brings about the reformation of a misanthrope, Rappelkopf, who is plaguing his family, by confronting him with his own intolerable character in a psychologically and theatrically brilliant scene.

The immediate social and political environment had little relevance for Raimund. The characterisation of the poor charcoal burners in *Der Bauer* or the quietism expressed in the faithful servant Valentin's *Hobellied* (*Der Verschwender*): *Da streiten sich die Leut' herum, Oft um den Wert des Glücks.*[15] (People will go on quarrelling about what good fortune is) are not intended as criticism of the time; they simply express the conditions and the philosophy of life of most of Raimund's audience in these years. In the middle of the 1830s however even Viennese audiences in the suburban theatres began to prefer political and social allusion and to transfer their allegiance from Raimund to Nestroy. Raimund felt this deeply, for like Grillparzer he believed passionately in poetic 'truth', the revelation of unchanging human nature in an aesthetically pleasing way as the purpose of drama, and he ranked Nestroy with contemporary polemical writers who debased the noble nature of dramatic art. Grillparzer held Raimund in high esteem; he did not mention Nestroy. Although Nestroy was the product of the Viennese popular theatre, both the subject matter of his plays and his parody of popular theatre conventions brought him closer to the political writers of the forties and to that novel product of the mid-nineteenth century theatre, the political cabaret.

Even today Viennese audiences continue to take sides over the relative merits of their two great popular dramatists, and whereas most of them agree that Raimund is 'a greater artist', Nestroy's verbal brilliance continues to be immensely successful on the stage. Although the son of a well-to-do lawyer and educated in Vienna's famous school, the *Schottenkloster,* Nestroy (1802–62) became an actor and like Raimund began later to write his own plays. He had no lofty poetic purpose in mind, but wrote some eighty plays to provide roles for himself and the company with whom he acted. With his long bony frame and his talent for long speeches full of word-artistry, he rapidly became one of the biggest box-office attractions on the local stage. In his earliest success, *Der böse Geist Lumpazivagabundus oder das Liederliche Kleeblatt* (1833), where the fairy Fortuna determines to show how three vagabonds can be reformed, Nestroy seems to deride his audience for succumbing to illusions. One of the characters wins the lottery, *das große Los,* a recurring symbol in Nestory's plays of human happiness, with which he mocks the material values of those who believe they are motivated by higher things. Fortuna wins her wager, for of course, Nestroy seems to say, the spectators have to have their happy ending, but in fact two of the wastrels remain just as they are, while the third, who is 'reformed' by being married and becoming a houseowner, turns into a prig, which is much less attractive.

Although the popular theatres were of course subject to the censorship, improvisation was not prohibited as it was in the court theatres; so actors naturally made plenty of use of the opportunities provided by the text. Nestroy had done this as an actor, and most of his own plays are built round a central character who could respond to the mood of the audience or his own inspiration to expand a speech into a witty disquisition on topical events. Like comedians in more recent authoritarian states, Nestroy frequently used mime and gesture to emphasise a provocative remark. He was naturally an acute observer of his surroundings; his plays abound in local types and references to the way of life in his native city, but it was not until the censorship was lifted for a brief time that his great gifts as a satirist became evident. *Freiheit in Krähwinkel* (1849) is one of the most hilarious satires in German on the political system and society as well as a witty portrayal of the recent revolution. In the following years he wrote several successful parodies, a literary form which has never been popular in Germany as opposed to Austria. He employed a technique long familiar in the popular theatre of de-bunking portentousness or destroying pathos by translating the characters into Viennese types, and blank verse into Viennese dialect. He parodied Meyerbeer's *Robert the Devil* (*Robert der Teuxel*) in this way, and Wagner's *Tannhäuser* (1857) and *Lohengrin* (1859). Hebbel's *Judith* appeared in 1849 as Nestroy's *Judith und Holofernes,* with the character of Judith transformed into Judith and her identical twin brother Joab, who braves Holofernes' tent and leaves Judith modestly outside. However, the fact that Nestroy was successful with his parodies of such works showed that the Viennese popular theatre was changing. The audience was a more educated one: to enjoy parodies of this type you have to know the original. After the 1840s the local population of shopkeepers and artisans could in general no longer afford to pay the higher prices demanded by theatres. Many such theatres were closed or rebuilt to cater for a more sophisticated audience. Nestroy's expansion of the musical aspect of his comedies and his introduction of the fashionable French composer Offenbach to Vienna in the fifties pointed to the future when the operetta was to become virtually synonymous with popular entertainment. After 1848 the population of the city of Vienna increased rapidly from 300,000 to 2,000,000 in 1900. Although Vienna showed its usual powers of assimilation as regards the mass of Czech, Slovene, Croat and Hungarian immigrants, it is possible that the language difficulties of such a large immigrant population encouraged the trend away from the spoken word in the city's theatres towards music.

III *Lyric poetry*

We now turn to lyric poetry. At first sight the period 1820–50 seemed favourable to the writing of lyric poetry. In middle-class circles the poet was called upon to act, as has been said, as a kind of bourgeois poet laureate, celebrating the various birthdays, namedays and anniversaries which broke the monotony of provincial life. Some of the finest as well as the most trite poetry in German has been written about the domestic scene, and the great poets as well as the minor ones produced occasional verse of this kind. The German lyric in this period has frequently been called sentimental, and if this is often so, the English or American reader should remember that the German language is particularly rich in expressions of feeling and sentiment, and that the institution of friendship between members of the same sex was widely cultivated in Germany at this time. Friends marked an occasion by reciting verses or inscribing them in an album. Many of Germany's leading poets catered for the demand for such 'album verses', Uhland, Heine (in his *Buch der Lieder*, 1827), Rückert the orientalist,

Lenau, and Geibel (from 1840), who was later known as the German Tennyson.

Those poets who today seem to tower above their generation, Eduard Mörike and Annette von Droste-Hülshoff, suffered from the prevailing taste in so far as their poetry required greater effort from the reader than he was prepared to make. What did not fit in with the current ideas on simplicity and accessibility was generally rejected as not poetry. The story of the changing reputation of these two poets is a fascinating one. In Mörike's case it has been told from his own lifetime until the present day in an absorbing study by S. S. Prawer;[16] it was not until our own day that critics agreed in acclaiming their achievement, thus fulfilling a wish expressed by Droste-Hülshoff that she might be read in one hundred years time.

Mörike (1804–75) lived all his life in or near the confines of his native Swabia. His vocabulary is not unlike that of the Swabian poets Uhland and Kerner who were so widely read in the early decades of the century; he derived inspiration from lyric verse forms popular in his time, notably the idyll. Close examination shows Mörike to be a sophisticated and difficult poet. His blend of exacting metres of classical origin and naive folksong rhythms elicited the comment from Gottfried Keller that he was 'the son of Horace and a fair Swabian girl'.[17] His poems are usually set in nature or the domestic scene but they evoke a world that is unfamiliar. A contented uneventful life is suddenly threatened with destruction as the poet becomes aware of the darker forces of existence: *Peregrina, Denk' es, o Seele, Mein Flusz*. Art becomes a private affair, communication with others difficult. In his love poetry Mörike rarely speaks to the beloved, but reflects in the 'lonely' hours of dusk and dawn. His surroundings bring him consolation: objects in nature and domestic things reveal their essence to the poet in moments of heightened awareness; they do so with such immediacy and such lyrical felicity that it seems as though no poet had spoken of these things before: *Auf eine Lampe, Die schöne Buche* and many more. Although the titles and ostensible themes of his poetry make Mörike a typical Bierdermeier figure, an impression that seems confirmed by the outward story of his life as a country parson and schoolteacher, his poetry has little direct relevance to his age.

Unlike most other poets of his time, he wrote of things that had no reference to the time of writing nor to society, either directly or by inference. His prose showed a perceptive understanding of the position of the artist in the contemporary world (his novel *Maler Nolten*, 1832 and *Mozart auf der Reise nach Prag*, already mentioned). In fact his real concern was with the nature of artistic creation and the mind of the artist.

Mörike had many affectionate friends among contemporary writers and critics. The second great poet or rather poetess of this time, Annette von Drost-Hülshoff (1797–1848) pursued her career for the most part strangely isolated from her contemporaries and their preoccupations. She lived the sheltered existence of the unmarried daughter of an old Westphalian noble family and was in poor health for almost all her life. It was accepted by her family that she should share their cultivated interest in the arts, but they reacted with shock and horror to the outspokenness of her first poetry. She was inevitably influenced by the Romantic movement, by Lord Byron and Sir Walter Scott in her early work, but her major poetry, written between 1837 and 1845, highly individual and passionately felt, has no real place in the German literary scene of the 1830s or 1840s. In the late 1830s Droste-Hülshoff made the acquaintance of a young journalist named Levin Schücking, who introduced her to the political poet Freiligrath, and to Friedrich Engels, who showed a surprising regard for her work. She reacted immediately to this new stimulus: she shared their interest in contemporary social problems and planned a work on the customs of her native Westphalia. She wrote some patriotic verses in imitation of Freiligrath and of Geibel, while her ballads, which still have a merited place in anthologies, often had a social theme – *Das Fegefeuer des westfälischen Adels,* or *Die Schwestern* with its marvellous opening and refrain : *Sanft pochte der Käfer im morschen Schrein* (Gently knocked the beetle in the crumbling chest). How different these ballads were from the current favourites about popular figures of national or local legend written by Uhland, Strachwitz or Scherenberg! She imbued hers with a sense of apprehension, of horror at the powers threatening man, which is only partially explained by his environment.

Droste-Hülshoff was not in fact influenced by her belated contacts with contemporary literary circles. She needed reassurance about her poetic gift, but once released, her singular genius created a number of marvellous lyric poems and one novella, which owe little to contemporary society. The novella *Die Juden-buche* (1842) was originally conceived as a psychological study of a murderer. It is the story of the young Friedrich Mergel, who murders a Jew, escapes human justice, is captured by Turkish pirates, and after nearly thirty years in captivity returns home and is found hanging from the tree which was the scene of the crime. After the first draft its author departed from her original concept and in vivid scenes alternating between brightly illuminated encounters and dark unexplained happenings traces the uncanny fate of Mergel. It is a tremendously compelling tale. Mergel's heredity and environment is realistically portrayed but the sinister forces of existence are evident throughout. From the beginning a strange duality is apparent in the characters and in nature; it becomes more pronounced as the tale progresses: concrete individuals merge into supernatural beings, the devil himself, the spectre of original sin. Nature herself is ambiguous in her relation to man; the trees in the forest are now tangible objects, now they are the groaning of creation as a mysterious and evil fate approaches. In the end the reader is not sure whether Mergel was hanged by the Jewish community in revenge for his deed or whether, compelled by a sinister impulse, he hangs himself from a tree in the forest he had desecrated. It is in this work that the point of comparison between Annette von Droste-Hülshoff and Emily Brontë becomes clear. A strange affinity links these two almost exact contemporaries. Each felt an instinctive bond with the grim landscape of her homeland, and each created from her imagination a haunting passionate world which contrasts strangely with their secluded lives.

Droste-Hülshoff's lyric poetry is imbued with the sense of fear and foreboding engendered by human guilt. The precise and unusual imagery of her poetry seems often an attempt to cling to her immediate surroundings in the chaotic world which menaced her. The fact that she was myopic made her prefer small objects about her, such as insects, shells, flowers and stones. Like the English novelist Hardy, she was both extremely exact in her observation of nature and poetic in the expression of what she saw. She never tried to create atmosphere with embellishment, as the Romantics had done; although foreign and dialect words are common in her poetry they came naturally from the speech of her educated family circle. Similarly her use of military terms in *Die Schlacht am Loener Bruch* (1837) or the technical expressions of many epics and ballads came simply from her familiarity with them. She was a regional poet and drew much of her vocabulary as well as her inspiration from her homeland. *Die Schlacht am Loener Bruch,* the second part of *Das geistliche Jahr* (1839) and the *Heidebilder* (1841–2) contain some of the best examples of her local inspiration. Images like *aschgrau, dürr, modermorsch, moderschlamm,* recall the bogs and heaths of Westphalia. She used them however as religious images to express the turmoil of her soul, her sense of sin and guilt, and the loss of grace.

For Droste-Hülshoff is essentially a religious poet, the only major religious poet of the nineteenth century in Germany. She belies the traditional picture of the busy German woman of simple faith; her entire work expresses her struggle against unbelief, a struggle which failed time and time again. Her religion rarely brought her comfort, nor did she find solace among her fellow Catholics. Her love poetry is primarily religious; many of the poems addressed to Schücking, nearly twenty years younger than herself, speak of the soul's longing for compassion. Her extraordinarily vivid experience of nature heightened her sense of man's existential guilt. In her last great religious poem, *Die ächzende Kreatur* (1846) she showed how man in all his contacts with nature inflicts pain and incurs guilt. She found nature in need of redemption, since every living being shares the curse of man's original sin. Her work contains many features associated with the twentieth century, notably man's alienation from nature and the overwhelming sense of fear (*Angst*) he feels in consequence. At the heart of her work lay the conflict between faith and knowledge which she knew to be a contemporary one. Later commentators have linked her name with that of Kierkegaard.

With the tremendous courage which was typical of her, she sought to link her life, 'my little, my rich kingdom', 'my little green space', of which she speaks in the second part of *Das geistliche Jahr,* to humanity. Occasionally she breaks out of her isolation in some of her finest lyric poems: in the passion and exaltation of *Im Turme,* the expectation, the terror and release of *Mondesaufgang,* in the intense experience of nature in *Im Grase* or *Durchwachte Nacht.* But these are but felicitous moments in a solitary existence. Annette von Droste-Hülshoff is perhaps unique among the Biedermeier writers or indeed her generation in that she gave expression to fears, conflicts and experiences to which they refer only by implication.

She is a difficult poet, the rhythms of her lyrics are harsh and jerky, her meaning occasionally obscure. She made few concessions to popular taste, and her sudden fame after the publication of her collected poems in 1844 was more probably the result of the vogue for women writers at that time, and to her somewhat romantic noble origins and solitary life.

If anyone had enquired in 1830 or 1840 who was Germany's most popular poet, the answer almost certainly would have been that Ludwig Uhland was both the most popular and the greatest living poet in Germany. Uhland did not in in fact belong to the Biedermeier generation. He was a late Romantic poet, born in 1787 and writing nothing significant after about 1820. He was a Swabian like Mörike or the better known minor poets Justus Kerner (1786–1862) and Gustav Schwab (1792–1850). He became a well known figure throughout Germany for his stand in defence of liberty, both in his native Württemberg and later, in 1849, at the Frankfurt Parliament (see p. 168). His poems, mainly idylls, ballads and occasional verses were read and recited in countless German households, and many, such as *'Ich hatt' einen Kameraden'* passed into familiar speech and were set to music. His simplicity, sincerity and humour found the approval of critics as well as the public, even as exigent a critic as Hebbel who declared : 'Uhland is without doubt the leading lyric poet' (of our time).[18] Uhland was nationally popular. To the middle-aged in the 1830s his ballads, written mostly in the Napoleonic wars, recalled the ideals and hopes of their youth. Uhland expressed exactly the nostalgic patriotism felt by so many, a sentiment which recalled a noble past but in no way demanded positive action. The younger generation who were inspired to national feeling by the brief Revolution of 1830, found much to admire in him as well. By 1840 a different nationalism made itself felt in Germany, prompted by fears of aggressive French action on the Rhine; people now started to read the political poets Herwegh and Freiligrath, and they gradually forgot Uhland except when they chanced on an anthology.

In the late 1820s and in the 1830s two other poets, of a very different complexion, Count August Platen-Hallermünde (1796–

1835) and Nikolaus Lenau (1802–50), whose real name was Niembsch Edler von Strehlenau, were widely talked about. Public interest in them derived as much from their unusual personalities and lives as from their poetry. Platen, a South German aristocrat and officer, was a man of broad education and somewhat eclectic culture, who also had a command of some twelve languages. He was one of a generation of cultured Germans who, coming to maturity at the end of the Romantic movement, felt at odds with the intellectual climate of their native country. In 1824 he wrote in his diary 'poetry is in a state of rapid decay and is becoming more and more an article of luxury, instead of being of the people.'[19] In his own poetry he tried to reimpose the exacting discipline of complex verse forms, such as the sonnet, the Persian ghasel and the Pindaric ode. Platen's sense of conflict with his age was given poignancy by a personal tragedy, his homosexuality, which was paired with a deeply emotional nature. He found refuge from loneliness in art, which he believed was the only reality of ultimate significance. In 1824 he went on his first visit to Venice, which proved to be the most important experience of his life. Venice, symbol for him of beauty in decay, inspired his splendid *Venetianische Sonette* (1824). Platen was by the nature of his work not a popular poet, but the educated reading public responded to the classical beauty of his verses. They did not always appreciate the mental discipline which went into their making; even Goethe, who admired him, thought he was unfeeling, that 'he lacked love'. He made his permanent home in Italy, like many German painters of the time, who, like him, felt ill at ease in Germany. It was not until the end of the century that Platen's art found appreciation among his peers: C. F. Meyer, Friedrich Nietzsche and later still Thomas Mann, who made Platen's life the basis of his finest novella, *Der Tod in Venedig* (1911).

Nikolaus Lenau (1802–50) was a Byronic wanderer, and in his restless pursuit of his art, his inability to lead even outwardly the life of a 'normal' German, somewhat akin to Platen. But Lenau was much more accessible to his readers. He was a virtuoso performer on the guitar and the violin which he had learnt in his native Hungary; in his lyric poetry he combined great musicality with realistically observed natural phenomena and found favour with a wide public. He wrote exquisite nature poetry, but virtually all his poems, whether the theme is love or nature, liberty or faith, breathe an air of pessimism at the transience of things. Lenau's fascination lies in his being so apt a representative of certain tendencies in the 1830s, and in contemporaries' awareness of the fact. He seemed to incorporate, in the then fashionable phrase, the *Zerrissene,* the one who is torn asunder by conflicting claims and beliefs. He lost his early religious faith when his mother, to whom he was very closely attached, died of cancer in 1829; his unhappy love affairs made him lose his faith in human virtue also, and his hope of human happiness. He had liberal aspirations, pleading for political liberty for the Poles in his *Polenlieder* (1831-3), and for religious freedom in *Die Albigenser* (1842), and in his posthumous verse epic, *Don Juan,* for emancipation from social and sexual convention. His contemporaries sympathised with Lenau's feelings of frustration at the inertia of ordinary people; they laughed at his satire on Metternich in the scenes, *Die Lektion* and *Das Lied,* in his *Faust* (1836): they, as he, lacked clear political objectives. He went to America in 1832 in search of a new and happier world, but returned, bitterly disappointed, three years later. His fruitless wanderings expressed his spiritual rootlessness, and his friends and his many admirers watched in horror as his *Weltschmerz* affected his mental balance; he died insane in 1850. He is best remembered for his wonderful evocation of his Hungarian homeland in such poems as '*Rings ein Verstummen, ein Entfärben*' (All around sounds, colours die away), '*Auf dem Teich, dem regungslosen ...*' (On the still pool ...), both from the *Schilflieder.*

One further lyric poet deserves mention, not least as an example of the unexpected talents and emotions which a study of apparently quiet domesticated Biedermeier figures reveals. Friedrich Rückert was born one year after Uhland, in 1788, but unlike him was active as a writer as well as a scholar until the middle of the nineteenth century. His was a minor poetic talent if one measures his enormous lyric output against the achievements of Mörike. But continuous assessment has no relevance to art, and we remember Rückert best on the one hand for his poignant *Kindertotenlieder* and his deeply-felt occasional verse such as the poem beginning: *Du bist die Ruh* (Thou art stillness), and on the other for his fascinating and beautiful translations from Sanscrit, Arabic, Ethiopian, Persian and Hebrew. It was not merely that he translated oriental poetry – he was a professor of Eastern

Studies at Erlangen – but he identified himself so completely with the world of the original that it seems as if an oriental is using German as his poetic medium.

The 1840s brought about a marked change in the public's taste in poetry. Though the ballad retained its appeal, and continued to do so almost to the end of the century, the nationwide enthusiasm for political poetry of the type written by Freiligrath, Herwegh and Nikolaus Becker indicated a new development in Germans' attitude to their literature, a desire that poetry as well as prose should more closely reflect the preoccupations of the nation as a whole.

4

Peasant Literature in Nineteenth Century Germany

The work of Johann Peter Hebel (1760–1826) inspired many German writers to explore peasant literature as a serious literary form. His *Schätzkästlein des rheinischen Hausfreundes* (1811) was his best known work. When he addressed himself to an educated audience he used his native Alemannic dialect; for his country readers he wrote in the kind of standard German prose which they were familiar with in their Bibles. Hebel died four years before the opening of our period, but he continued to be read, as he would have wished, by the simple country folk who are the protagonists of his stories and poems, as well as by educated people who delighted in his fine mind and human wisdom. Hebel was a man of wide culture, a professor of Hebrew and dogmatic theology in Karlsruhe, and an ex-officio member of the Baden Diet. His work never lost its appeal; children who learned his poems, like the whimsical one on porridge (*Das Habermus*), recalled them again and again when they were grown up. Goethe admired him; he was loved by Kafka and by Hofmannsthal, whose *Das Bergwerk von Falun* was inspired by Hebel's *Unverhofftes Wiedersehen*. Hebel's wonderful narrative gifts, his humour and naturalness disguise the sophistication of his art, yet, despite his wide culture, he wrote about rural life as one who was part of it.

Two men of great narrative talent in nineteenth century Germany, the Swiss Jeremias Gotthelf (1797–1854) and the Mecklenburger Fritz Reuter (1810–74), wrote novels of peasant life. Gotthelf was a parson who regarded his literary activity as an extension of his pastoral work: he interspersed his numerous novels and stories with encouragement and fatherly admonition to his parishioners. He had little time for literary theories or movements; unlike his contemporaries he was almost wholly unaffected by literary tradition. Popular devotional works and his own epic gift determined the form of his novels. For a long time Gotthelf, whose real name was Albert Bitzius, was a source of embarrassment to literary historians. This was caused by his characteristic mixture of dialect and standard German, which although a major source of his expressiveness, made it difficult to fit him into the literary movements of the century. His lifespan coincides with the Biedermeier period and for many years he was classified as belonging to the periphery of that type of writing. However neither the style nor the content of his writing resemble the work of Grillparzer, Tieck, Mörike or Immermann, although there are inevitable points of contact (thus the novella *Das Erd-beer-Mareili*, 1850, has several features in common with the short stories of the time). His ideas on education and portraits of young people in his work bring him close at times to Adalbert Stifter. In his avowed didactic purpose and the clear confrontation he permits between good and evil, the spirit and the flesh, Gotthelf shows his affinities with the devotional writing of the time. In other ways he has much in common with realist novelists in countries other than Germany; his novels are distinguished by a concrete imagination, realistic observation of the everyday world, and, un-like German novelists of his century, he took for granted that the social and political context of his time was relevant to his writing.

Gotthelf's parents came from the educated and well-to-do bourgeoisie of Berne. When he was nine years old his father ac-cepted a country living; the writer's most characteristic trait, his concrete imagination was apparently awakened by his child-hood contact with the countryside and farm life. He was educated at home, and later at Berne and in Germany. He attended the university of Göttingen which had a traditional association with Berne ever since the great anatomist, naturalist and much revered Swiss poet Albrecht von Haller (1708–77) had gone there. Gott-helf's father died shortly after his return to Switzerland. He had acted as his father's curate and in 1832 he became vicar of the parish of Lützelflüh in the Emmenthal, a post he held till his death.

Gotthelf's intellectual background was the Enlightenment; he was deeply influenced by the great Swiss educationalist, Pestalozzi (1746–1827), who had at one time been a neighbour of his family. Gotthelf later grouped Pestalozzi together with Christ and the

Old Testament prophets because of the influence he exercised on those who came after him. His own enthusiasm for educational reform amounted to a passion: as a minister of his church he proved to be headstrong but enlightened. He gave a broad interpretation to the task of preaching the word of God : the material conditions of life, the challenge of the times to traditional beliefs and modes of existence, above all the education of children and the unlettered masses, claimed his attention. He was intimately involved in the ferment of ideas about him – it must be remembered that Switzerland in the 1830s was far more radical in temper than either Germany or Austria. It was not until he was nearly forty that he turned to creative writing, but his reasons were none of them aesthetic. He brought to his writing the same drive, the same moral purpose, the picturesqueness and earthiness which had already marked his activities as a preacher, political reformer and publicist. As a pastor he had rich experience of human behaviour, and his assertive yet warm personality made him respond to human happiness and suffering. Within a couple of years of his first literary efforts and the appearance of a most original theoretical work on poverty – *Die Armennot* (1840)[1] – he wrote his four great novels and his major novellas. All of these are memorable for his powerful and intensely moving portrayal of human weakness and resourcefulness.

Gotthelf's approach to his writing is fundamentally unlike that of his contemporaries in Germany. For him literature always served a polemical purpose. His prime intention was to arouse controversy and to bring about a change of heart in an apathetic public. He wrote more than one of his novels on commission, to denounce modern abuses, such as the novel *Anni Bäbi Jowäger* (1843–4), which showed up the evils of medical quackery. He made strenuous efforts to get his books published and was fortunate in finding in 1845 a Berlin publisher, Julius Springer, who enabled him to reach a wider audience. Gotthelf soon showed that his lofty purpose did not exclude a sound business sense; Springer complained that he paid Gotthelf more than any other writer on his list. Grillparzer, Mörike and Stifter looked on their poetical integrity as an ethical duty, but for Gotthelf didactic elements, the demands of a popular audience and political necessity could take precedence over aesthetic matters. Gotthelf has in fact some link with the tendentious Young German writers whom he so despised. As H. Waidson observed in his study of the Swiss writer: 'even if they fought each other tooth and nail, they fought each other with the same weapons.'[2] Virtually all modern Swiss writers with the exception of C. F. Meyer and perhaps Carl Spitteler have been politically committed. In his early manhood Gotthelf had taken an active part in local politics but was debarred from holding political office because he was a clergyman. This and other, more personal reasons, made him turn to writing. 'This life must consume itself or else burst forth in some way or other,' he wrote to his cousin Karl Bitzius. And further on : 'if I had been able to ride out every day or two, I would never have written.'[3]

The immediate intention of his novels was to direct his readers' attention to their duties to family and community. *Uli der Knecht* (1841) is to be read by farmhands and maidservants, he wrote. They must improve their minds through contact with men and women wiser than themselves and by reading. Gotthelf, like Keller, wished people to become involved in the life of the community and thus become politically responsible, and he saw the means to achieve this in education. The rationalist ideas of the Enlightenment, particularly with regard to education, survived longer in Switzerland than in Germany; while Germans took pride in their educational system as producing men of culture and learning, Gotthelf, like another educational reformer of enlightened views, Humboldt, believed that education was primarily important for making men into good citizens. He felt it necessary to bring home to people the duties which political emancipation had imposed. He was very much aware of the discrepancy between the rights of citizens in Switzerland and their ignorance of their responsibility. Keller's early recognition of Gotthelf's stature as a writer, despite their different political views, shows the influence of their common background. They reached different conclusions in their work, but each realised the demands their country made on the individual, and the opportunities it offered. To be sure, political responsibility was a more tangible thing in the small Swiss state than it could be for civil servants of a bureaucratic Empire under which the Austrians, Grillparzer and Stifter, lived.

In the views expressed in the novels on education of young people Gotthelf shows a sensitive awareness of how children learn and also plenty of sound common sense. His emphasis on fostering natural ability rather than repressing inclination looks forward to

Stifter, as does his belief in the importance of love and patience,
and the usefulness of stories (*Uli der Pächter*, 1847). The many
moving portraits of grandmothers and parents, as in *Käthe, die
Grossmutter* (1847), in the *Uli* novels, and the magnificent *Geld
und Geist* (1843–4), remind us of similar, if perhaps less earthy,
figures in Stifter's tales. 'So many children,' he wrote in *Uli der
Pächter*, 'owe their grandmother far more than ever they do the
learned professors, who are most of them dried-up wigs.'[4]

Gotthelf attributes an important role to environment and the
use of meaningful objects in the educational process. This is
typical of his age. Stifter, Keller, and even Storm stress these
things. The symbolic significance of concrete objects in the novellas
of all these writers derives from the fact that a way of life is embodied in simple household things and their users feel that this is
so. A conscious importance attached to household possessions and
ritual is characteristic both of bourgeois and peasant life (at least
in the prosperous regions of Central Europe) in the years 1830–50.
For both classes a certain material level of comfort is also the
pledge of solid virtue. Such attitudes suggest a gradual improvement in the general standard of living. In the generation which
came to maturity in the 1860s and later such reverence for the
spiritual significance of possessions was lost; they merely indicated
social status.

Gotthelf's pedagogic ideas owed their impact to his powers of
presenting relationships within the family. In German-speaking
lands the family unit was strong, and remained so even in the
industrial age. Cases of cruelty to children were comparatively rare
and rarer still, despite the familiar image of the stern German
father figure, was cruelty in the name of discipline. Parents of all
classes felt more immediately responsible for their children's upbringing than parents in Victorian England; they were not inclined to entrust them to servants or institutions. Gotthelf raised a
monument to family life in all his major works. It was his fear of
the threat to the family and hence to the community as a whole
which caused him to abandon his earlier liberal views in the
1840s and, like Tieck, Grillparzer and Stifter, to advocate a return
to an earlier paternalism. The community, not the individual, is
the hero of his great novels; it is represented by the unforgettable
figure of the mother in *Geld und Geist,* by Johannes, the father,
and by Vreneli, the young orphan, in the *Uli* novels.

To discover new literary types and to portray them with compelling psychological realism was probably the finest achievement of German writers of mid-century, to whatever literary group they were considered to belong. This quality is perhaps nowhere more persuasive than in the many portraits in German literature of this period of children and adolescents. In the two *Uli* novels, the character of the remarkable heroine, Vreneli, is motivated by her earlier experience of being an unloved child. Vreneli's language at those points in the story where her character is revealed is quite without sentimentality or pathos; it is so adequate to the situation and so much the language that reticent peasants would use that the reader is deeply moved. Gotthelf's portrait of young people reminds us of Keller in the early chapters of *Der grüne Heinrich* or *Romeo und Julia auf dem Dorfe;* Storm too in *Viola tricolor* shows similar psychological penetration of the mind of a child.

Gotthelf shared certain themes and interests with writers such as the above-mentioned. He set himself apart from them by his avowed moral intention and his tremendous conviction in an age of doubt. He was the last great Christian writer in nineteenth-century Germany. Personal loss and setbacks in his career caused him to modify his political views in middle life: his natural ardour was transformed into an almost apocalyptic pessimism as regards human nature. This allowed him to create in his literary works portraits of unredeemable human wickedness which were quite unique in his time. Harter Hans, the Dorngrütbauer in *Geld und Geist,* the selfish children in *Uli der Knecht* are cases in point. Gotthelf makes no effort to soften the impact of their evil natures by including mitigating psychological or environmental factors, as his contemporaries Grillparzer or Droste-Hülshoff, Hebbel or Stifter do. Whereas for example Holofernes' depravity in Hebbel's *Judith* is in some way accounted for by his isolation from his fellowmen, or the evil life of Friedrich Mergel in Droste-Hülshoff's *Die Judenbuche* is the product of his heredity and educational environment, Gotthelf's villains are wholly responsible for what they are. At times he seems almost to be obsessed with man's base nature; even his heroes and heroines have an alloy of meanness and pettiness.

However Gotthelf's pessimism was contained and balanced by his faith. The conflict of these two forces gives dynamism to plot and characterisation in every one of his works. The immediacy of feeling in his prose springs from his character and experience, while his imagination and dramatic powers combine to create powerful symbols. These were drawn from his immediate environment with a decided preference for the archetypal. The elements fascinated him as the voice of God in nature; in his works they are transformed into myths. Thus the popular image of the river as a snake appears in one of his earliest works, *Die Wassernot im Emmenthal* (1838), a mighty creature tearing down the valleys, devouring men and homesteads. Then there are the many fire images, given substance by his own experience in helping to combat village fires: there is a marvellous account of such a fire in *Geld und Geist,* the turning point of the novel. The best known of Gotthelf's works, the novella *Die Schwarze Spinne* (1845), takes its title from his most powerful image, the black spider, with its mythological and erotic associations. Here, as elsewhere Gotthelf's imagery, like his faith, orders and gives perspective to his narrative.

The world of his novels, with the exception of the unpublished *Der Herr Esau* dealing with urban society, is that of prosperous farming communities of the Emmenthal. It is a static world, aware of contemporary upheaval beyond its horizons, but scarcely affected by the reality of historical change. Against this background, which varies only according to the seasons, the ancient struggle between spirit and flesh is fought again and again. The strength of human passion, the violence of personal conflicts, the variety of human types, are in no way limited by the local setting. Yet although the human situation may be primary, Gotthelf's novels are social documents in a sense that the so-called novels of the age (*Zeitromane*) of Immermann, Spielhagen or Freytag are not. He takes for granted the social dimension of literature which his fellow writers regarded with unease. As described by him, the precise habits of life, the execution of tasks on the farm could be incorporated almost as they are into a social history of the time. They also serve to describe the material world of the protagonists of the story, which conditions their actions and their affections. The imagery which they employ in speaking of their faith is frequently drawn from the commercial language of the time. Thus Johannes in *Uli der Knecht* says 'God has given us capital goods which we must make bear interest, namely strength and time.' Further on he speaks of the desirability of 'a good income in this

121

life, then heaven and its treasures.'[5] The two are in tacit and permanent association, and Gotthelf demonstrated in all his work that he shared the nineteenth-century belief in the moral virtue and conservative force of property and success gained through hard work. He was perhaps the only great novelist in the German language in the nineteenth century who was not ashamed to say so.

The Mecklenburg writer Fritz Reuter had a far more adventurous life than Gotthelf, which he made the subject of two of his great novels written in Low German or *Platt*. He was arrested on the charge of conspiring to rebel against the Prussian government in whose territories he happened to find himself in 1833, and after ill-treatment including even torture, was sentenced to thirty years imprisonment. He spent seven years in a number of fortresses, although his only offence seems to have been a connection with radical student fraternities in his youth, and was not set free until 1840. His was unable to find employment, became an alcoholic, but was rescued from his plight by a resolute woman, Luise Kuntz, whom he married in 1853. The same year saw his first collection of stories and verses in the dialect of his native Mecklenburg; he was most surprised by their success. This encouraged him to write the three major novels for which he is remembered, *Ut de Franzosentid* (1859), on the French occupation under Napoleon, and the autobiographical *Ut min Festungstid* (1862) a resilient account of his experiences in prison, wisely humorous, and *Ut min Stromtid* (1862–4), which tells of his life as a farmer. All three abound in earthy humour, local colour and memorable characters, avuncular and eccentric, such as Onkel Bräsig in the last-named novel. Like Klaus Groth (1819–99), author of the lovely lyric verse collection in *Platt* entitled *Quickborn* (1853), Reuter enjoyed the admiration of almost everyone who could read North German dialect 'from Holland to the Baltic East'.[6] Reuter's is one of the rare cases where opinion of the time and the judgement of modern literary historians coincide: he is very highly thought of to-day, while in his own day his novels earned him a fortune and several public honours.

Hebel, Gotthelf and the North German writers, Fritz Reuter and Klaus Groth, wrote, as it were, from within the rural society they depicted. The aesthetic appeal of their work owed a great deal to the idiom in which it was written. Many other literary figures in the same period wrote about peasant life in standard

German, as for example Heinrich Zschokke (1777–1848), Immermann (see above) or Berthold Auerbach (1812–82), but they wrote for the urban reader. Zschokke was a zealous philanthropist, moved by the plight of the peasants in the years after 1815. In his novel *Das Goldmacherdorf* (1817, a year of crop failure and plague), a democratic schoolteacher restores to life a spiritually and economically decayed village. In a later work *Die Branntweinpest* (1834) he depicted the evil influence of alcoholism in a peasant community. Immermann's *Der Oberhof* is something of a landmark in peasant literature. He introduced here a theme which inspired a host of imitators for almost a century, when he contrasted the nobility and dignity of rural life – which is not however without its villains – with the artificiality of urban life. Immermann wrote persuasively about the countryside in this section of his novel *Münchhausen*. The colours and forms of the countryside are effectively woven into the everyday life described. His account of the village wedding is splendid (Marie von Ebner-Eschenbach, the Austrian novelist, took over almost every detail in her story, *Die Unverstandene auf dem Dorfe*);[7] the scene where the stout perspiring young bride is forced in her stiff wedding dress by her bridesmaids until her face becomes scarlet with effort is very funny. The last named of those writers, Berthold Auerbach, something of a literary lion in Berlin in the 1850s, was the son of a Württemberg Jewish pedlar and had intimate knowledge of the rural life which he described in his immensely popular *Schwarzwälder Dorfgeschichten* (1843–54). Auerbach, like Immermann, stressed the healthy moral and physical life in the countryside and as editor of the *Deutsche Volkskalender* he promoted interest in peasant literature throughout Germany.

Austria produced many works of peasant literature in the nineteenth century both in dialect and in standard German. Adalbert Stifter obviously had close affinities with the tale of country life, but Peter Rosegger (1843–1918), a self-taught writer from Styria, who began life as a tailor's apprentice, is much more representative of the cheerful, didactic portrayal of a local world which is typical of Austrian popular writing. Rosegger's stories and novels started to appear in the decade following Austria's defeat in 1866 at the hands of Prussia and her exclusion from Germany. This severance of Austria from her cultural hinterland had the effect of exaggerating those features that were characteristic of Austrian writing: a close bond between writer and his regional background, and the didactic quality of Austrian humanism. This last was clearly marked in the plays and novels of Ludwig Anzengruber (1839–89), certainly the greatest dramatist of peasant life of the century. Like Grillparzer Anzengruber lived at Vienna but had connections with the countryside, the *Innviertel* in Upper Austria, through his grandparents. He started life as an actor in the provinces, but came back to the capital and joined the police force. He had little experience of the people of whom he wrote, and sometimes the blend of dialect and standard German in his plays appears unnatural. He had great dramatic talent and an urgent social message, which conquered the Viennese suburban theatres from the first performance of his *Pfarrer von Kirchfeld* in 1870. Anzengruber attacked the power of the clergy in the Austrian countryside: the priest in this first play is a holy man who in trying to fulfil his vocation is accused of being a freethinker by the older clergy and parishioners. In *Die Kreuzelschreiber* (1872) he made the abuse of privilege the subject of a hilarious comedy: the farmers' wives of a local community are persuaded by their priest to attempt a marital strike in order to overcome their husbands' dislike of modern church doctrine. The social and political message of Anzengruber's plays (and of his prose works, as for example *Der Sternsteinhof* 1883) belongs to the era of the liberal parties in Austria and German politics and the anticlerical atmosphere of the *Kulturkampf*, but his theatrical talents are the products of a more indigenous tradition: the Viennese popular theatre which enjoyed in his work a late flowering. Most of his plays were performed for the first time at the *Theater an der Wien* which once had seen the premières of Mozart's *Die Zauberflöte* and Grillparzer's *Die Ahnfrau*. His most powerful work, *Der Meineidbauer* (1871), a peasant tragedy, gained the singular honour (for a dramatist of the popular theatre) of being performed at the *Hofburg* in 1893. On this occasion Katharina Schratt, friend and confidante of the Emperor Francis Joseph in his old age, played the female lead.

There is perhaps something artificial about separating literature about peasant life from a general discussion of nineteenth-century German literature, as has been done in this chapter. Some of the writers mentioned here could be said to belong to the Biedermeier or the later realist groups; others, and minor writers not included, have their roots in an older tradition of popular almanacs read by a wide public but having few pretensions to literature. It is, I believe, justifiable to make this separation to draw attention to the special achievement of German writers in making the peasant and his environment the subject of serious literature. Up to this time the peasant had been almost always a figure of comedy in literature or was used to give 'local colour'. In consequence of the new literature about the countryside, the reading public was made aware of the conditions of life and the needs of that section of the population which in mid-century still constituted more than half of the population of Germany, Austria and Switzerland.

5

The German Writer between Revolutions, 1830-48

Students of German today are invariably introduced to the Biedermeier and to the works of Gotthelf, and yet, from a social and political point of view, quite a different set of writers are important. In the years between 1830 and 1848 the journalists Börne, Menzel and Heine and the young writers associated under the name of Young Germany commanded the attention of the public. These years are remarkable in Germany for the new importance of the press and of journalists, and also because in this period something like a consistent public opinion emerged in the Confederation. To all those who had felt oppressed by the political stagnation after the Carlsbad Decrees in 1819, the revolution which broke out in France in July 1830, overthrowing the Bourbon monarchy, marked both an end and a new beginning; in particular it inspired students and young intellectuals in Central Europe to call for changes in their countries. In Germany a young lecturer called Ludwig Wienbarg provided the programme, as it were, in his *Aesthetische Feldzüge* (1834) with its crusading title; in these essays he unwittingly gave the young writers of his day a name when he addressed himself to 'Young Germany' and called on them to involve themselves in the questions of the day. 'The poets and writers of fine prose no longer serve the Muses alone, but the Fatherland; let them be allies in the great causes of our time!'[1] Not only youth was excited; many German academics with an established reputation saw the justification of their work in its relevance to the present time. Jakob Grimm wrote that German scholarship was 'worthwhile', insofar as it 'benefits the present generation'.[2] In a more systematic way Gervinus, one of the seven university professors who protested against unconstitutional action by King Ernst of Hanover in 1837 and lost his chair, presented a similar view in his national history of German literature.

Gervinus published his *Neuere Geschichte der poetischen National-Literatur der Deutschen,* the first of its kind in Germany, between 1835 and 1842. This immensely heavy work, with its close print and exhaustive information, became a political document in its time and as such was widely read. This 'writer without style, scholar without method, thinker without depth, politician without prophetic powers, this man without charm', as his critic Karl Hillebrand put it nastily half a century later,[3] made up for his defects by an overpowering and contagious moral earnestness. Contemporaries were impressed by the novelty of his arguments: 'let us not believe that this nation, which has such magnificent achievements in art, religion and literature, is impotent when it comes to affairs of state.'[4] Gervinus' argument met with a positive response because it expressed what many people were instinctively beginning to feel. Whether expressed in such emotionally charged language or with the Viennese urbanity of Count Auersperg under his bourgeois pseudonym of Anastasius Grün (in the delightfully misleading poem entitled *Spaziergänge eines Wiener Poeten* 1831) the arts, especially literature, were now to be pressed into the service of political causes.

This sudden quickening of interest in public affairs was perceptible in the thirties and became widespread in the next decade. Even school textbooks were affected. Thus in his preface to a two-volume anthology for German teachers which appeared in 1843, the poet Gustav Schwab declared that he had purposely avoided including too much purely literary material: 'religion, science, plastic and graphic art, nature, public, domestic and social life, history, patriotic writings and popular works enjoyed equal representation.'[5] The new didactic note in the writing of these years reflected the growth of self-awareness arising from the July Revolution; it did not indicate a greater degree of political liberty. 1830 had relatively little effect on German political institutions, though excitement and apprehension were widespread. A couple of rulers were sent, in Charles II's famous phrase, on their travels, but they were not molested by the people; they were expelled because they were personally unpopular. Thus the Duke of Brunswick was replaced by his brother; the Landgrave of Hesse and his mistress gave way to his son and the latter's mistress.

There was, however, a definite revival of interest in affairs of state which had not been there in the twenties, and a gradual breach in Germany's isolation from the events of the rest of Europe. Events in France, Poland and the Netherlands were referred to in novels written in the thirties, and Germans read the newspapers with avidity.

The press stimulated these changes and also made capital out of them, particularly the many periodicals owned by the influential publisher Baron Cotta, whose *Augsburger Allgemeine Zeitung* was at that time Germany's leading newspaper. The habit of subscribing annually or bi-annually to a newspaper became current in the 1830s, enabling proprietors to budget; a further innovation, letters to the editor, increasing circulation considerably. As has been said, political news was suspect to the censorship, but the arts were encouraged. The marshal of the Prussian court commented a trifle grimly in 1832 on the occasion of a visit of a famous dancer, Taglioni, to Berlin: 'Taglioni will dance ... the mimic graces of this great artist have obliterated the fearsome portents of our time.'[6] The feuilleton was imported from France in the thirties, and for many decades (and in Austria even still) was known as *'unter'm Strichl'* or 'below the line', as reviews of performances, new books and exhibitions were printed below a line drawn across the printed page, separating these from the reports of state affairs. Very soon clever journalists such as Heine and Börne learned to exploit the popularity of the feuilleton and write about political matters under the guise of literary criticism.

The current notion of the political and social purpose of literature was certainly well-timed. The exploits of the Young Germans would scarcely have been possible without the new role of the press. Heine spoke of the journals as the 'fortresses of the Young Germans' – a remark which, coming from Heine, could of course be interpreted in two ways. Financially, few of these young writers could have survived without the regular payment they received for their articles. The lack of a centralised national press in Germany encouraged the mobility of the journalists; e.g. Gutzkow worked successively in Berlin, Stuttgart, Frankfurt and Hamburg. This had the effect of disseminating ideas more widely and overcoming the lack of interest hitherto felt in one part of Germany for the preoccupations of the rest. The process was naturally accelerated by the revolution in transport. The press was not without its enemies in the thirties, and these were not confined to the conservative writers. The argument that it prostituted culture was used against it, and in Germany this seemed the more reprehensible because cultural values had largely supplanted religion among the educated classes. Individuals were singled out for special abuse, notably the diplomat and writer Varnhagen von Ense, 'the renegade aristocrat', and the Viennese critic Saphir, 'the matador of the gutter press'. In another way, and one less commented on, the press exercised an important influence on public opinion: in economic affairs. In 1834 the Customs Union (*Zollverein*) was formed on Prussian initiative. Few, apart from some liberally-minded officials, grasped its significance at the time; they were too used to thinking in terms of political authority and did not in general link political and economic progress. In 1835 Friedrich List, the great political economist of Germany in the middle of the nineteenth century, instituted the *Eisen-Journal* to overcome people's prejudice against the railways; from 1843 to his death in 1846 he edited the *Zollvereinsblatt* to propagate the idea of economic unification for Germany. In the forties other technical and trade journals became common and had great educative value.

Through the medium of the press a number of Germans now began to exercise considerable influence on their countrymen. Foremost among such writers in the early thirties was Wolfgang Menzel (1798–1873) who brought himself forcibly to public notice by his scurrilous attacks on Goethe, even before the latter's death in 1832; indeed the hatred expressed by politically-minded writers for Goethe was almost as great as the veneration in which he was held by the more conservative. Rather ironically the literary hotheads and the Protestant Prussian orthodoxy were at one in their attitude to Goethe, though they differed in their expression of it. The Prussian minister Hengstenberg, a leading theologian, condemned the great poet in the *Evangelische Kirchenzeitung* as 'a pagan influence', while Menzel poured scorn on Goethe's alleged lack of patriotic feeling. After fighting at Waterloo, Menzel had become a member of the nationalist athletic association formed by the eccentric patriot Jahn during the French occupation of Prussia. (Jahn had instructed his followers to knot their kerchiefs and smite with these any German they heard using

Tradition and Revolution

a foreign expression in their own language.) Menzel's patriotism was less eccentric but equally intolerant. He spent five years in exile in Switzerland after Jahn was imprisoned for his activities. Menzel was able to return to Germany in 1825 through the good offices of Baron Cotta, and he became editor of the *Morgenblatt für gebildete Stände*. It is hard to understand the reasons for his immense if brief moral authority in Germany in the late twenties and early thirties, analogous to that of the Russian journalist, Katkov, in the *Moscow Gazette* at the end of the century. Menzel preached hatred of the French at a time when public opinion in Germany was generally rather sympathetic to France; he was virulently anti-Jewish, while he lauded the manly virtues of the Germans and the national aims of their literature and their art. The negative bias of his ideas became more pronounced as he grew older; his earlier radicalism gave way to reactionary conservatism and he lost no occasion to fulminate against the influence of Jews, foreigners and women in German life. Something of the flavour of his personality and his prose is contained in the following criticism of Gutzkow's controversial novel, *Wally, die Zweiflerin*: 'Gutzkow has again taken it on himself to bring to Germany that infamous French ape, who, in the arms of a harlot, mocks at God. Yet vice was foiled by the national virtues of our people.'⁷ Like many a nationalist after him, Menzel had the narrow moral code of his humble origins and it was on moral grounds that he based his attacks on Goethe. Goethe's private morality, according to Menzel, made him unfit for the position of respect in which he was held; Menzel's former colleague Börne and a successful journalist himself called Goethe 'a groveller before princes'; both agreed that Goethe's cosmopolitanism was un-German and to be deplored. Wolfgang Menzel was one of the first to popularise in Germany the notion that the quality of an artist's work depends on his character and political opinions. Börne, unlike Menzel, was sufficiently imaginative to distinguish between the moral grounds he used to judge Goethe's personality and the aesthetic canons he applied to his work.

Very many young Germans shared a feeling of bitterness towards Germany's greatest poet. Although many felt bitter because he had not chosen to use his nationwide authority for national and liberal ends, the quarrel was essentially one of generations, with an admixture of jealousy for his unique achievements and re-

130

nown. Tieck and Varnhagen von Ense, both members of an older generation, helped to cast aspersions on his name. In fact the whole question of German attitudes to Goethe in the early 1830s is symptomatic of the change that was taking place among German intellectuals. As Goethe's stature seemed to diminish, Schiller was acclaimed. Schiller's humanism was disregarded, his democratic ideals stressed; he was exalted as the great national poet of Germany, his blameless life and self-discipline singled out as typical German qualities. This image was augmented throughout the nineteenth century and even abroad Schiller clubs were much more numerous than Goethe societies; these clubs were popular and social as well as serious in purpose; the Goethe societies were, in so far as they existed at all, academic in nature. The first Schiller Club was founded in 1840 by the Saxon radical Robert Blum, then secretary to the Dresden theatre. During his speech at the opening of the club he declared that Schiller's love of liberty destined him to the poet of the German bourgeoisie. Two decades later the centenary of Schiller's birth was widely celebrated in Germany and in Europe; Goethe's centenary ten years earlier had passed almost unnoticed.

The second journalist who made a name for himself at this time as a thoroughly partial commentator on affairs was Ludwig Börne (1786–1837). Like Heine, Börne was a Jew. Both were born in cities which were about to become important commercial centres, Börne in Frankfurt, Heine in Düsseldorf, and both became exiles in Paris. Heine went to Paris in 1831 as a republican and ended his days as a supporter of tried political systems; Börne started as a monarchist and became a violent republican. Both were concerned to awaken the German people from their political apathy, but Börne's judgement was affected by a terrible moral earnestness which he shared with his former mentor Menzel. 'The German has too little political enlightenment,' wrote Börne in 1819, coining a phrase that has since come to be seen as the panacea for democratic ailments in the German Federal Republic.[8] In that year Börne had gone to Paris for a time, returning again for two years in 1822 and eventually settling there permanently in 1830. He looked on himself as a voluntary exile, and, like Heine, suffered many allegations against his good name for remaining there. He came back to Germany in 1832 to take part in the Hambach festival (see p. 170) and was fêted by crowds;

yet despite his advanced opinions he was not molested by the authorities. Börne, like other educated Germans, was attracted to Paris for the way in which the French state put the talents of its citizens to good use. What appealed to them in particular was that men of letters actually held state appointments: 'Thiers ... is going to be Undersecretary of State for Finance, Mignet a minister or its equivalent! The way people get on here! ... It's as though friend Heine had been made a minister or Menzel or myself. And what are we?'[9] wrote Börne to a friend in 1830. He and Heine made it the aim of their careers as journalists to create a genuine public opinion in Germany.

The chief means employed by Börne was his publication of reviews of contemporary events in the arts. That is to say, they were ostensibly aesthetic comments, collected under the title of *Briefe aus Paris* (1834) and *Dramaturgische Blätter* one year later. Frequently Börne ignored the actual book or performance named in the heading and rode off on his favourite political hobby horse. He managed to get an astonishing amount of political comment past the censor; for this alone he was appreciated by his readers. Drama, according to Börne, was the mirror of contemporary society, and as such must be tendentious; the human situation was not enough. The conflict of ideologies, the clash of different social codes, turning points in the history of a nation, such themes began to attract both critic and reader or theatregoer. Even at a popular level the same is true: novel titles reflected this current interest such as *Degen und Palette* (The dagger and the palette), *Hie Zoller, hie Welf* (Hohenzollern contra Guelph) and so on. When the distinguished Dr Hawkins made the observation in 1838 that 'in our days politics usurp all attention and have almost driven literature from the field', he was witnessing a real transformation in the German scene.[10] Börne would have put it rather differently. Literature, he believed, was part of politics, albeit its handmaid. He pronounced Shakespeare and Calderón to be democratic and therefore good writers, Racine a monarchist and therefore bad. In a similar vein Friedrich Engels, who was influenced by these ideas as a young man (he was born in 1820), asserted that Genoveva and Griselda in the dramas of Tieck, Halm and others were obsequious figures; they were not calculated to awaken in the people a love of liberty and they were therefore quite unsuitable to the contemporary theatre.

Engels went so far as to recommend the imposition of a censorship in order to protect the theatre from such plays.[11]

Heine's verbal brilliance has tended to obscure Börne's achievements as a stylist and to let us forget the great influence he enjoyed in his lifetime. He was very readable and had a keen knowledge of the German character. He was the author of a number of pithy remarks which continued to be quoted, even by those who had never heard of him: Austria is the China of Europe, Germany its ghetto; the Germans, a nation of flunkeys; of the ridiculous literalness of the censorship he said: 'if chance should reveal a mathematician among the Spanish Jacobins, the Federal Diet would proscribe logarithms.'[12] Menzel was made unforgettable in an essay Börne wrote shortly before he died: *Menzel, der Franzosenfresser*. In this essay he warned against the folly of assuming the superiority of things German; more emphatically he ridiculed the idea of a specifically German scale of values, the assumption that justice and virtue were peculiarly German qualities, not simply human ones. Börne brought wit and energy and a degree of common sense in his campaign to awaken German public opinion. But Menzel and not Börne continued to be read. Although Menzel's popularity declined in relation to what it had been in the thirties, he was still being read many decades later; in the years before his death in 1873 he began to anticipate the grotesque fantasies of twentieth century nationalists by a confession of faith in the German pagan god Odin.

Although Börne offers pleasures even to the modern reader, few are attracted to him by anything except historical interest. The opposite is true of Heine (1797–1856). Heine is one of the few nineteenth-century German figures who needs no apology or explanation. English and American readers have always been attracted by his lyrical gifts, his wit, and not least by his penetrating vision and constant awareness of the relevance to literature of the social and political context of the time. They have regarded it as a virtue that Heine does not preach; for though he shared the contemporary view that politics and poetry were compatible, his views on the nature of poetry were fundamentally at variance with those of the political writers. Thus when Menzel or the Young Germans, Engels or Marx talked of literature, they often meant what Heine called unkindly 'rhymed newspaper articles'. In *Atta Troll*, an epic poem in several cantos ostensibly about a dancing bear, Heine satirised the politically committed poetry of his younger contemporaries to great effect; he began to be regarded by them as a renegade from a cause to which he had never wholly belonged.

Heine has never been popular in Germany except for a short time during his life. He was one of the first victims of antisemitic discrimination at the end of the nineteenth century, but long before that he had made himself suspect by the very facility with which he wrote on serious matters. The influence of the philosophers Fichte and Schelling, still more of Hegel, had established the view fairly generally in the educated German mind that profundity of thought was dependent on a certain obscurity of expression. Heine made this observation many times in his *Geschichte der Religion und Philosophie in Deutschland*. Heine, like Goethe, was attacked for his moral character, but he did not make it easy for his admirers. He continually and often unnecessarily insulted contemporaries by his scurrilous attacks, such as the scarcely veiled accusation of homosexuality against Platen in *Die Bäder von Lucca* (1830–1) or by his attacks on Börne's character in *Ludwig Börne* (1840), a work his temperament made him singularly unfitted to write. Of the popular poet von Fallersleben he wrote in 1840: 'after, or rather with, Hoffmann von Fallersleben, all poetry is at an end.'[13] Heine's fault, in his countrymen's eyes, was his lack of a moral standpoint. Turncoat he might be – he would not have been the first among German men of letters – but to attack all parties at once was proof indeed of a lack of moral earnestness. The disillusionment of those who had believed Heine was on their side made them all the more enraged in their condemnation of him. Furthermore he seemed excessively concerned with personalities. It escaped his critics' notice that these were for him symbolic of contemporary issues and universal attitudes, which is why we can still read his satirical writings with such pleasure.

His manner of writing, the deceptive simplicity of his satirical verse, his eye for the weak spot in his opponent and his economy in expressing it have more affinity with the best French and German political cartoonists of the nineteenth century than with the so-called political poetry of the time. He made every human and every topical issue the subject of poetry, from the most exalted to the most banal. It was not a lyrical age, although Uhland was

still so popular, Uhland, whom Heine gently mocked while con-
fessing his own early indebtedness to him. Heine's verse form was
based on the German folksong and contemporary popular idiom;
he always remained drawn to German popular culture. Every
modern reader of Heine at some time echoes Nietzsche's remark
on reading him: 'How he manipulates the German language!'
though without always realising that his art is a highly conscious
one. Heine's interest in the context of this book lies less in the
simple beauty of his love poetry or the great lyric poetry of his last
years, *Romanzero* (1851) and *Gedichte* 1853 and 1854, than in
his almost uncanny perception of the political changes taking place
in Germany and Europe. He expressed his opinion in both prose
and poetry. In the decade 1831–40 he made German prose a
vehicle with which to instruct and amuse and irritate his countrymen which has earned him the title of 'grandfather of modern
journalism'.

Heine came to Paris in consequence of the July Revolution to
act as a kind of foreign correspondent for Cotta's *Augsburger
Allgemeine*. Cotta's tactful editing of Heine's articles before he
submitted them to the censorship and the cuts made by the censor
drew incessant complaints from their author, but they still remained lively enough to draw comment from readers all over the
country. Heine wished to make his fellow Germans more familiar
with French civilisation and to use the press as a means of liberating Germans from what he regarded as their intellectual and
political isolation in modern Europe. Paris exhilarated him in
these first years. The sense of being cut off from the present, which
had previously haunted him, gave way to a sense of history in the
making. It was not just the overthrow of regimes but his perception of a new social order emerging: the rule of the financial and
industrial bourgeoisie taking over in France from the feudal aristocracy. He was attracted to the teachings of the philosopher Saint-
Simon (1760–1825) and his followers: to their acceptance of the
modern world of technological advance, their belief in progress,
above all to their optimistic view of man's nature and preoccupation with his material wellbeing. As with Börne, Heine's articles
from Paris were simply an excuse for discussing whatever happened to excite him at that moment. Coming as he did from Germany everything seemed fascinating. At the same time Heine was
determined to educate the French public about Germany. His

famous history of German religion and philosophy, published in 1834, was certainly the most readable account of the subject ever written; it was intended to acquaint Frenchmen with the modern history and, not least, the complex character of their German neighbour. It served an additional purpose in providing an antidote to Mme de Staël's idealised *De l'Allemagne* (1801), which was still widely read. *Die Romantische Schule* (1836) provided the French with Heine's colourful and highly partial account of recent German literature.

Unlike other Germans Heine looked upon France and Germany as complementary, although he became increasingly convinced, as the years went by, of the complexity of the German character. No-one has ever written more perceptively in prose or poetry on the German mentality. The irony or ambiguity of his observations does not affect the sincerity nor the accuracy of his analysis. In *Atta Troll,* perhaps the most perfect satire he wrote, and in *Deutschland, ein Wintermärchen,* the irony was often a subterfuge to get audacious comment past the censor. A fictitious journey through Germany provides the opportunity for sly and witty comments on contemporary situations, on habits and attitudes which make up the national character.

In the forties Heine became fascinated with Communism. He never was a Communist nor was he tempted to be one, but the vision of the egalitarian society haunted him in the last decade of his life, and he was quite as convinced as Marx, whom he met and became friendly with for a time in Paris, that a revolution of the proletariat would occur. Through Marx and his associates Heine was able to publish some of his more outspoken political poems. He did not, however, feel happy in the association, because they so obviously regarded him as 'won' for the cause. He brought wit to a serious subject, as in his exposé of the premisses of Marxism beginning: *'Es gibt zwei Sorten Ratten/Die Hungrigen und die Satten.'*[14] (There are two types of rat, the hungry and the fat), but the quality of his mind made it impossible for him to contemplate allegiance to any political cause or party. If he shared for a time the nineteenth-century belief in social progress leading to a utopia, his detachment reminded him that it was only a vision.

In 1848 Heine was struck down by spinal paralysis which made him bedridden and in continuous pain for the last eight years of his life. Even before then his interest in political affairs had re-

ceded. His comments on the Revolution in 1848 were full of disillusionment; his admirers felt that he was out of touch with the
times. The German character as manifest in contemporary personalities still inspired an occasional satire, such as the splendid
poem on the proposed German navy *Unsere Marine* (published
1855), but the substance of the poetry he wrote after 1848 is
religious.[15]

To the end of his life Heine was a controversial figure and he
has remained so since. Even today critical accounts of his work
both in and outside Germany present contradictory evaluations.
In a social and political context the assessment can only be positive. Nearly everyone who has written on nineteenth-century
Germany since 1945 interprets the period through twentieth-
century eyes and as a result Heine has been often made to seem a
man born before his time. But Heine was in fact completely of his
time, and in spite of his occasional sense of being alone and misunderstood by contemporaries, he made his poetry and his prose
out of the stuff and language of contemporary experience.

6

Young Germany 1830-48

One could say that the group of writers associated under the name of Young Germans were unfortunate in being Heine's contemporaries. Had they belonged to another generation, the contrast between his lightness and their pedantry might not have been as striking. Coming from Heine to the Young Germans, one is at first reluctant to attribute anything more than limited historical importance to their work. Heine influenced them greatly and for a time he felt kindly towards them, since they so obviously admired him. They seized on his idea of creating an informed public opinion through journalism. Their name derived from Wienbarg's dedication of his *Aesthetische Feldzüge* to 'the Young Germany, not the old',[1] but members of the German movement were much less radical than their counterparts in other European countries. They lacked a leader such as Young Italy had in Mazzini; they were enthusiastic in a general way about the idea of a united Germany but were not active politically; nor did they leave any of the stirring melodies or patriotic poems such as those written by Thomas Davis and members of Young Ireland which inspired later generations of Irish nationalists. Although the works of a number of the Young Germans were banned by the Federal Diet on the instigation of Wolfgang Menzel in 1835, the authorities did not appear to take them very seriously.

The general public took a different view especially from about 1835 onwards. Almost all these writers were born in the second decade of the nineteenth century; seizing on the word 'modern' they made it as popular as the term 'Romantic' had been a generation earlier. People who read the early novels and dramas of Gutzkow and Laube, and the poems of Freiligrath and Herwegh felt stimulated by the controversial issues they treated. Furthermore the public enjoyed their affirmation of the modern age, the way they wrote about the practical achievements of the time such as the railways, which the conservative writers ignored or attacked. Under the influence of Saint-Simonian ideas these young writers discussed notions of a general emancipation from social and sex taboos, as for example in Gutzkow's novel *Wally, die Zweiflerin* and Mundt's *Madonna, eine Heilige* (both 1835). In the forties they began to be concerned with the urgent social problems around them. They were impressed by Heine's poem on the starving Silesian weavers' revolt in *Das Lied der schlesischen Weber*; the historical novelist and critic Robert Prutz wrote a novel about them called *Das Engelchen* (1851) and Ernst Willkomm exposed the abuses of the millowners in *Die Sklaven* (1845). Freiligrath translated Ebenezer Elliott, the poet of the Corn Law disturbances. Young Germany can be seen as part of a wider movement, the origins of socialism in Germany, and despite the differences which soon arose between the Young Germans, with their rather theoretical revolutionary fervour, and the radical political writers including Marx, there were many points of contact between them in the thirties and early forties.

Censorship in the Confederation was in general limited to journals, pamphlets and books of less than twenty printed sheets. Political writers in the thirties therefore chose to express their ideas through the medium of the novel. When Gutzkow's *Wally* appeared in the summer of 1835, Wolfgang Menzel appealed to the Diet to have it banned; his motives were very largely injured pride because Gutzkow, a former associate of his in Stuttgart, had turned against him. The Federal Diet duly banned not only *Wally*, but the works of Gutzkow, Wienbarg, Laube and Mundt, and also of Heine, declaring that they were 'unchristian, blasphemous, they trample underfoot all morality, modesty and decency.' The prohibition gave these writers a cohesion they had not formerly possessed, but, unlike the Romantics, they really got on better apart from one another. Gutzkow alternated between Stuttgart, Frankfurt and Hamburg, Laube, who for a while edited the popular literary journal *Zeitung für die elegante Welt,* was based in Leipzig, Wienbarg in Kiel and Mundt in Berlin.

Karl Gutzkow (1811–78) was the real leader of the Young Germans and influenced many of his contemporaries, who were not actually associated with the short-lived group, to write on political and social matters. He fascinated people not least because he had rejected a theological career for journalism, although religious questions continued to engage him throughout his life. He was one of the first Germans to earn his living entirely by his pen, for Börne and Heine had both been able to supplement their earnings by allowances from reluctant relatives. Before 1830 politics had had no interest for Gutzkow; the fall of the Bourbons in Paris had changed all that. In his memoirs he described how as a student at Berlin university, he was about to receive a gold medal for distinction as a student from the hands of the rector of the university, Hegel, when he was electrified at the news from Paris. His only thought was to get the ceremony over as quickly as possible so as to learn more about what was happening in France. History, he declared, lay before him, learning behind. He hoped, rather ambitiously for a young man of nineteen, to model himself on the French politician and writer Thiers. Thiers' newspaper articles had helped to precipitate the outbreak of revolution by their affect on French public opinion; like many aspiring young Germans in this decade, Gutzkow looked constantly to France for inspiration. When the Polish revolt against Russian oppression broke out in 1831 he addressed *Polnische Lieder* to the Crown Prince, later King Frederick William IV of Prussia, who was thought to be accessible to liberal views. Throughout the next ten years, despite the ban on his works in 1835, Gutzkow continued to excite his German readers by his treatment of topical issues in the various journals with which he was associated as editor or sub-editor.

In 1842 the ban on his works was lifted and he accepted a post in 1846 as resident dramatist to the court theatre in Dresden. Always a prolific writer, his personal and intellectual frustrations found an outlet in the forties in intense hard work. He wrote nearly fifty plays, almost all of them on topical issues, although to defeat the censorship he usually set them in other countries or centuries. This simple device was most successful. Thus an audacious satire on German society, *Richard Savage* (1839), was on the programme of some eighteen German theatres after its publication, for Gutzkow had set the action in England. The Prussian censor was also quite willing to pass for performance *Patkul* (1844), a dramatisation of a peccadillo of King August the Strong of Saxony, despite the protests of the Saxon ambassador to the Prussian court. Gutzkow's best plays were *Uriel Acosta* (1847), a tragedy which bears comparison with *Nathan der Weise,* and a comedy *Zopf und Schwert* (1844) about the proposed marriage between Frederick II's sister, Wilhelmine of Prussia, and King George III of England. This play was immensely successful in Germany. Had Gutzkow been a playright in France, where authors were paid royalties on the performance of their works, *Zopf und Schwert* would have made Gutzkow a rich man. In the years after the Revolution of 1848, Gutzkow turned to the novel again and in his attempt to depict the whole canvas of modern life made an important contribution to the technique of the novel in Germany. This aspect of his career will be treated in Chapter 10.

One of Gutzkow's early associates was Heinrich Laube (1806–84), who was some seven years his senior and who encouraged him as a writer. Laube's association with Young Germany was a brief one. He showed a degree of political opportunism in his break with the group after the Federal condemnation, and he went on to enjoy a successful career. During the early thirties he was much influenced by Saint-Simonian ideas and wrote a novel called *Junges Europa* (1833–7). The novel is in three parts and is interesting, on the one hand for its picture of the current enthusiasm for Polish liberty, on the other for the manner in which Laube's youthful idealism evaporated as the book progressed. Even in the early part, *Die Dichter,* a discordant note is struck when the young hero Valerius announces his intention to depart for Poland: 'Tomorrow I go to Warsaw to fight for the sacred right of a nation to overthrow tyranny. I am not very fond of the Polish people, I must confess, but I will bleed and die in their cause.'[2] Those who are inspired by abstract ideals without relation to their human implications are often disillusioned. This was true of a number of Young Germans besides Laube. The second part *Die Krieger* is a drab account of participation in the Polish revolt, while in the third, *Die Bürger,* the hero settles back to the daily round in Germany and vaguely hopes things will get better in Europe.

Condemned to seven years imprisonment by the Diet in 1835, Laube in fact merely spent eighteen months at the home of Prince Pückler-Muskau in a pleasant form of house arrest. In 1836 he went so far as to proclaim publicly his total lack of interest in politics. He was not the only opportunist among the political writers: Dingelstedt accepted a title from the Prussian government and Freiligrath a pension, though he later renounced it; Anastasius Grün solicited a court appointment. Academics published statements daily after the 1835 ban denying their connections with a journal Gutzkow had been proposing to edit, the *Deutsche Revue*. Laube later entered the Frankfurt Parliament during the 1848 Revolution alongside many writers and scholars of liberal opinion. In 1850 he took up an appointment as director of the *Hofburg* theatre at Vienna, and his activity here for almost two decades brought him more lasting fame than his brief notoriety as a Young German in the thirties.

If Gutzkow, Laube, Mundt and other prose writers associated with them shocked or titillated contemporary opinion by their treatment of topical issues and for the sensuality of their love scenes, the lyric poets, Freiligrath, Herwegh and Hoffmann von Fallersleben delighted their public. Freiligrath (1810–76) was a merchant's son who became suddenly famous for some poems he published in Gustav Schwab's *Morgenblatt* and Chamisso's *Musenalmanach* in 1833. On this occasion Chamisso declared somewhat fulsomely: 'since this nightingale began to sing, the rest of us are as sparrows.'[3] He was excited by the younger poet's choice of social themes and his realistic portrait of the times. Chamisso himself had been one of the first Germans to write poetry about the lower classes – *Der Bettler und sein Hund* (1829) and *Die alte Waschfrau* (1833), but in common with the Romantic generation to which he belonged (he was born in 1786) he treated these idyllically. Freiligrath developed into a revolutionary poet in the forties; in 1844 *Ein Glaubensbekenntnis* attacked Prussian institutions and government policy, although its author had earlier received his state pension from King Frederick William IV for his poems about the sufferings of the poor. *Ein Glaubensbekenntnis* was instantly proscribed by the censor but this only encouraged clandestine sales. Freiligrath began to be talked about all over Germany. Two years later his most famous poems appeared under the title of *Ça ira,* where the author portrayed the proletariat as the real force in the nation and a potential threat to the state in its present form. One of the poems in this collection entitled *Unten auf* (from below) contains the lines: *Wir sind die Kraft! Wir hammern jung das alte morsche Ding, den Staat,/Die wir von Gottes Zorne sind bis jetzt das Proletariat!* ('We are the power!' We'll crush and renew with hammer blows that rotten thing, the state!/We whom, till now, God's anger has condemned to be the proletariat!')[4] The speaker is the stoker of the Steamship bringing the King and Queen of Prussia across the Rhine. It says a good deal about the literary tastes of the time that this and the rest of the poems in *Ça ira* were so successful that Freiligrath was able to support his wife and family entirely by his earnings as a poet. He was not in Germany at this time. In 1844 he had left Germany and become friendly with Marx, whom he met in Brussels and who had a strong influence on the ideas contained in *Ça ira*. He returned to Germany to take part in the Revolution of 1848, serving a brief term of imprisonment in Düsseldorf. On his release he was surrounded by crowds of workmen who acclaimed him as their champion. He then joined the Communist League and proved an excellent organiser and fundraiser, even after he settled in England where he lived until 1865.

In 1865 his friends raised money in Germany, England and the United States to enable 'Germany's greatest revolutionary poet' to return to his native country; the fund realised 60,000 *thaler,* a very considerable sum, but he was thoroughly disillusioned with the new materialistically minded Germany he found on his return. Freiligrath's most notable achievement in the mind of his contemporaries and of later writers was to have made a man of letters a force in the public mind. Although he lacked sophistication and could write verse which it was a joy to parody, his obvious enthusiasm for a cause and his instinctive grasp of the temper of his age appealed to Germans in their brief revolutionary period. It is thus we are to understand his fame and the tributes paid to him by writers far greater than he, such as Fontane, who wrote in 1853: 'we are indebted to him as to perhaps no poet since Schiller, and hardly pay him too much honour when we call him the Bürger of his age.'[5]

Georg Herwegh (1817–75) was the most radical of the political poets of his time and an early associate of Marx. His poems were published by Marx during the latter's brief spell as editor of the *Rheinische Zeitung* and also in Arnold Ruge's progressive *Hallische Jahrbücher. Die Partei,* a strident call for partisanship in poetry, appeared in the latter in 1842. Herwegh advanced ambitious claims for the poet in this age of unrest: 'Princes dream, let poets act!' he trumpeted. Varnhagen commented rather nastily in a letter to the English writer Monckton Milnes: 'Instead of playing their lyres, our poets are beginning to use them to whack their opponents over the head.'[6] In his poetry he called upon the King of Prussia to defend Germany against her enemy France; he evoked visions of future German greatness which inflamed the imagination of German youth, and when he travelled through Germany to Berlin to appeal in person to the King, he was acclaimed vociferously and fêted by the populace. Heine's incomparable satire, *Die Audienz* (1853), has made this meeting memorable; he depicts the naive incomprehension of the King who hoped to gladden the hearts of his subjects by receiving a poet of the people; Herwegh plans an impassioned plea for freedom. Instead they talk about this year's dumplings in Herwegh's native Swabia and when the poet tries to change the subject he is marched off by two armed guards. But although we remember Heine and tend to forget the 'iron lark' as Heine called him, in his own time Herwegh was numbered among the great. He lived up to his revolutionary principles in 1848 by leading six hundred German volunteers and a few French radicals into battle against the Prussians in Baden. The skirmish ended in slaughter and Herweigh went into exile. On his return in 1866 he was even more critical of his country than Freiligrath and desired to be buried not in Germany but in free Switzerland where he had spent part of his exile.

Hoffmann von Fallersleben (1798–1874), traditionally associated with Freiligrath and Herwegh, came from Silesia. His chief claim to fame is seen to lie in his having written *Deutschland, Deutschland über alles,* the national anthem of such different subsequent regimes in Germany: the Second Empire, the Weimar Republic and the present Federal Republic of Germany. He wrote it in a moment of patriotic exaltation, when rumours of French aggression on the Rhine were current. Schneckenburger's *Die Wacht am Rhein* and Nikolaus Becker's *Sie sollen ihn nicht haben, den freien deutschen Rhein* inspired this quiet professor of German at Breslau university. He lost his chair when he published his collected *Politische Lieder* in 1842. In fact Hoffmann von Fallersleben was a political poet only by accident; most of his lyrics are occasional verses of sensibility and include many charming children's poems. His chief interest in this context is as a type of cultured provincial of liberal sympathies who was drawn to the national movement in the forties because he saw it as the most likely agent of reform.[7]

The Young Germans and those political poets associated with them believed not only that literature has a messianic world-changing function, but also that it is directed at the whole nation. The name given to these writers was an apt one, they were German, not regional figures. They came from all parts, they travelled incessantly, they were known all over the country. This quality excited their countrymen, as was proved by the ovation given to Herwegh on his journey through Germany in 1842. A cynic might add that, since the banqueting habit had been formed among south German liberals, any occasion was an excuse, but it was clear that the reception given to Herwegh was a tribute to the political role of the poet. These men believed that revolution must come to Germany and that literature in such an age must be radically different from what it had been. The effects of better education meant that the people, not the courts, were now, in Herwegh's words, the Maecenas of the poet's talents; they judged him and they rewarded him.

In another country these men might indeed have realised their ambitions in politics; they might never have become writers, or they might, like Disraeli, have gone on to greater things. In Germany political repression and the limited social mobility of the time allowed few opportunities for young men of ambition; writing seemed to offer them the only chance of making a name for themselves. It was a remarkable achievement for writers without position or connections to be taken seriously by public opinion. They were not merely youthful iconoclasts, though most of them were successful in attracting public interest when they were still in their twenties. Their enthusiasms were as seriously meant as Menzel's inquisitorial zeal and Börne's didactic tone. In his preface to the second edition of *Wally, die Zweiflerin* in 1851, Karl Gutzkow looked back with a certain nostalgia to the unpractical idealism of sixteen years earlier and contrasted it with what he considered to be Germany's growing materialism. He excused the occasional fantasies of himself and his associates by asking what the alternative would have been: 'to write opera texts perhaps, or edit a history of Germany, in which all the other nations figured wretchedly, the sons of Thiuskon alone throned on their dizzy heights?"[8] The possibilities indeed were limited. In assessing the achievements of the Young Germans we are forced to admit that they are less than contemporaries believed. It should however be emphasised that their work represents a potential which was not realised in Germany afterwards: namely a positive appreciation of contemporary innovations and a concern for the condition of man in society. Though they wrote no major work, German literature is in their debt: they gave great impetus to the novel and to literary criticism, by direct influence and by way of reaction; the drama benefited from the innovations in Gutzkow's plays, as later from the policies of Laube and Dingelstedt as directors of the *Hofburg* theatre. Though circumstances made them doctrinaire, they strove to forge links between Germany and the rest of Europe at a time when she was for political reasons isolated.

The Young Hegelians

Another aspect of the contemporary rejection of tradition is represented by a group of thinkers who were first interested in religious studies but soon turned their attention to man's social condition. Members of this loosely associated group included the philosopher Ludwig Feuerbach (1804–72), the political publicist Arnold Ruge (1802–80), as well as Karl Marx (1818–83) and Friedrich Engels (1820–95), who were almost a generation younger than these. It also included David Friedrich Strauß. Strauß was the author of the controversial *Das Leben Jesu* (1835) in which he convincingly cast doubt on the historic figure of Christ by applying historical critical methods to Bible studies. This was one of those books which excited tremendous public reaction both in and beyond Germany. Because many educated people were unsure of their beliefs at this time, *Das Leben Jesu* seemed to mark a turning point in history: the errors of historical Christianity were here, they felt, conclusively demonstrated. This feeling of an occasion was not confined to Germany: George Eliot was profoundly moved by it and provided English readers with a translation in 1846.

All the above-mentioned German writers were intoxicated with Hegel's thought and became known in Strauß' phrase as the Young Hegelians or Hegelian left. Hegel's vision of the continual dialectical progress of history fascinated all of them and in the publications, journals and newspapers with which they were associated at various times Hegel's thought was given a topical interpretation. They rejected Hegel's idealism and declared his conservatism to be utterly at variance with his revolutionary method. The principal organ of the Young Hegelians was Ruge's *Hallissche Jahrbücher* (1838–43) which appeared for a time six days in the week. In this periodical Strauß' historical critical method was applied to philosophy and politics. At first they attacked Christianity for its alleged part in undermining the state, but after the renewal of the 'alliance of throne and altar' on Frederick William IV's accession to the Prussian throne in 1840, the state too came under their fire. Philosophy seemed to hold the key to political upheaval in their minds; as Marx wrote in 1844 in the *Deutsch-Französische Jahrbücher,* the successor of the *Hallische*: 'Revolution is dawning in the mind of the philosopher as once it dawned in the mind of the monk' (Martin Luther).[9] Feuerbach, Ruge, Bauer and Moses Hess, who was one of the leaders of the democratic movement in the Rhineland during 1848, used Hegelian methods to reveal the falsity of the premises on which Christianity and contemporary society rested. Bruno Bauer actually rejected the state altogether, asserting that it exploited the same human weaknesses and fears upon which religion depended. Though they lacked political experience and their radicalism was often of an abstract character, the Young Hegelians did not shrink from the implications of their thought. These were explosive indeed, and helped to condition Germans to the idea of an imminent revolution, although when revolution actually came in 1848 their influence was minimal.

It was only natural that the Young Hegelians, with the zeal of the converted, should condemn the Young Germans for their political timidity. Gutzkow shrugged this off: 'The young are all the same. We teach them to read and write and the first thing they do is to commit intellectual parricide.'[10] Engels recorded that the poems of Freiligrath entered his narrow Pietist home like a liberating vision. Both he and Marx came from solid middle class families; Engels' father was a well-to-do merchant, Marx's a civil servant. They met in Paris in 1845 after the suppression by the Prussian government of the *Rheinische Zeitung* which Marx had edited for a time, and settled in Brussels after Engels had published his *Condition of the Working Class in England.* They now began one of the most famous intellectual partnerships of the century. Marx had been much influenced by one of the Young Hegelian group, Ludwig Feuerbach, 'the pious atheist'. Feuerbach inverted Hegel's idealism and asserted that nature (matter), not spirit, was the true reality. Nowadays, he said, love of God should give place to love of man, religion to social ethics. Atheistic humanism, the struggle to free man from suffering and exploitation, was Marx's chief debt to Feuerbach. The Marxist critic Bulgakov and the Czech statesman Masaryk both alleged that one learned more of Marx from reading a little Feuerbach than from three volumes of *Das Kapital*.

Marx and Engels soon distanced themselves from the Young Hegelians and began work on the *Communist Manifesto* which was published anonymously a few weeks before the outbreak of revolution in Germany in February 1848. Engels' human qualities were complementary to Marx's formidable intellect and his literary ability helped Marx to communicate his ideas. The concepts of class war and political revolution as the instrument for liberating the masses were contained in this historic document, which, although it was soon translated into four languages, became effective only much later. The powerful language of the *Manifesto,* its rousing propaganda slogans – 'workers of the world, unite!' – have long become household words, but in its time it had little practical influence. Marx's intellectual arrogance was the subject of much adverse comment and irritation among his contemporaries. This and his obsessive dedication to his cause made him a solitary figure, and yet the ideas which he regarded as his own unique contribution to the age were very much in the air on the eve of 1848. The fear of class war and of the proletariat in particular was a vivid one to contemporary philosophers, poets and governments; the idea of the continual and immutable progress of history was, more than anything else, the epoch's debt to Hegel. Marx, a Rhenish Jew as was Heine, had a strong messianic streak in his nature and was singleminded in his conviction that history would develop as he anticipated. He was firmly convinced of the philosopher's ability and duty to change the world. In March 1848 Marx, accompanied by Engels, hastened back to Germany to put his ideas into practice. Marx was thirty years of age, Engels twenty-eight. However, despite their assertions to the contrary, despite their arrest and trial in 1849, neither they nor the League of Communists for which the *Manifesto* had been written played a significant role in the revolution. However, on his acquittal by a jury after his trial, Marx, who had conducted his own defence, was thanked 'for an unusually instructive lecture'.[11]

The events and perhaps even more the expectations of the inter-revolutionary years 1830–48 had far-reaching effects on German writers and their readers. And yet, although writers in general felt more involved in public affairs in the forties than they had in previous decades, and people demanded now of literature that it be topical and 'problematic', there were few men of real ability in prominent literary circles. Moreover the actual political influence of men of letters was much less than they assumed, and though many took part in the events of 1848–9, their deliberations were not very effective. After the revolution itself had been suppressed they accepted, as did the German middle class in general, their lack of political influence with surprising equanimity.

7

Revolution in Drama:
Grabbe, Büchner, Hebbel

Although German theatres continued to entertain large audiences with an extensive repertory between 1830 and 1848, the Young Germans produced no major dramatic work. Nor, with the exception of Gutzkow, did current interest in social and political matters in the forties find expression in stage plays.

Germany had at least four great dramatists who were writing in these years: Grillparzer, Grabbe, Büchner and Hebbel. Of these Grabbe and Büchner won virtually no recognition during their lifetime and their work, apart from one or two of Grabbe's plays, remained unperformed for nearly three quarters of a century after their deaths. Christian Dietrich Grabbe was born in 1801 and died in 1836; Büchner and Hebbel were born in the same year, in 1813, but Büchner died in 1837; exactly a century after his birth his finest play, *Woyzeck,* had its first performance and exercised an immediate influence on the dramatic style of that time. Hebbel lived until 1863; he wrote his first play in 1839–40 and enjoyed success almost from the first. His career as a dramatist was crowned by the reception given to his trilogy, *Die Nibelungen* (1861), for which he was awarded the Schiller Prize.

I Grabbe

Had Grabbe lived longer, he would surely have been bitterly jealous at Hebbel's success, for like Hebbel he came from a humble background in North Germany. Grabbe's father was a prison warder and Grabbe's early memories included one of taking a murderer for a walk in the prison yard, as Immermann recorded in his *Memorabilien*. In appearance, he was almost grotesque, with fine and sensitive hands, a noble forehead, weak mouth and uncouth movements, which in later life became exaggerated as a result of dypsomania and mental illness. Although Grabbe attracted the attention of prominent literary figures such as Tieck, Immermann and Heine, only one of his plays, *Don Juan und Faust* (1829), was successfully performed in his lifetime (it captured the German stage again in 1870–90). Grabbe was a typical provincial writer frustrated by poverty and lack of contact with congenial minds. The sense of the futility of life haunts his work, expressed in the frequent image of the merry-go-round; his excesses and what we see as a lack of taste in his work derive also from his frustrated intellect. The more publishers refused his work, the more violently he responded. To those who knew him he seemed the incarnation of *der Zerrissene,* a disillusioned observer of humanity, torn by conflicting loyalties. But whereas in the case of most other writers of whom this term was used, it was a pose, with Grabbe the mask and the man were one: his schizophrenia is often visible in his work. The bitterness of ill-health, a wretchedly unhappy marriage combined with his disgust at the state of affairs in Germany in the 1820s and 1830s gave substance to Grabbe's nihilistic view of life. In vain Tieck counselled him in a fatherly letter: 'I must warn you not to give in to this destructive force, this cynicism, which is importuning you under the guise of its deadly enemy, poetry.'[1] Essentially a late Romantic writer, Grabbe showed evidence of his generation's disillusionment with idealism: 'war and peace, love and happiness, God and faith are but empty phrases for what they once meant.'[2] He tended to use Romantic irony to excess, but whenever he came to speak of Germany, his pathos was genuine and deeply felt: 'Germany, Europe's heart, alas, torn apart and disillusioned.'[3]

Grabbe wrote one comedy *Scherz, Satire, Ironie und tiefere Bedeutung* (1827), humorous and grotesque by turns, which anticipated the theatre of the absurd. It is of particular interest for its parody of contemporary intellectual attitudes as embodied in the various figures of the play: the romantic poet, the pedantic schoolmaster and the nihilistic devil etc. Apart from this play, which has seen many successful performances in recent years in Germany and abroad, all the rest of his plays are tragedies, the most relevant in this context being his historical plays, particularly *Napo-*

leon (1831) and *Hannibal* (1835). The first of these was written under the impact of the July Revolution and its failure in Germany. It is an uneven play and lacks a convincing conclusion, but it has enthralling scenes and typifies the originality of Grabbe's dramatic view of his age. One of the few advocates of Grabbe in the nineteenth century, the literary historian Hans Herrig, wrote in 1874: 'In Grabbe history comes alive for the first time.'[4] In Grabbe's *Napoleon* the French Emperor is not in fact the central figure: the dominating personality is the *Zeitgeist* as represented by the masses. Grabbe's presentation of the crowds is undoubtedly the most interesting feature of a play that is full of psychological and technical innovations. The play is broken up into short scenes reflecting the multiple interpretations of the great man, until the audience eventually gets the impression that he is no longer a person but a kind of a myth, an impression that is in fact reinforced by the scenes in which Napoleon himself appears. History is made to seem a thrilling but pointless spectacle through the eyes of the masses, compounded of every social class – street mobs, soldiers, courtiers, jacobins, pedlars and passers-by. The characters and speech of the members of the crowd are crude and sensual, sentimental or cynical by turns. The dramatist skilfully suggests the potential violence of the crowd, which can so easily turn to a mob; he also allows the sense of isolation and impotence of the individual to emerge, a feature he shares with Büchner. The sum of their views does not give us a consistent interpretation of Napoleon or of the times, for to Grabbe history is not meaningful. The great historical personages, Marius, Henry IV, Emperor of medieval Germany, Napoleon and Hannibal, heroes of his tragedies, who might seem to prove the contrary, are invariably destroyed by the meanness of their environment. Although Grabbe always sets his plays in the past or in foreign countries, it seems clear that his despairing view of history and humanity was prompted by his contemplation of his native country. His last play, published posthumously, was on the patriotic subject of Arminius' defeat of the Romans in the battle of the Teutoburger forest, a subject Kleist had treated in *Die Hermannsschlacht* in 1810. He had hoped to write the great national drama of the century, but despite himself his theme remained that of the sacrifice of a great individual to the pettiness of his times and the passions of the masses. Grabbe tried valiantly to prove that the heroic was not dead, but was continually forced to display the contrary. He incorporates much of the disillusionment of the post-Napoleonic age and the failure of the Revolution of 1830 to change things in Germany. He did not live long enough or have sufficient contacts among his fellow writers to foresee the possibility of another revolution, but his last drama, and implicitly some of his earlier works, express a feature of German political writings in the 1830s and 1840s: to seek in the idea of a resurgent Germany the answer to a despairing view of mankind.

II Georg Büchner

At the beginning of Büchner's comedy, *Leonce und Lena* (1836), there is a prologue which serves as a kind of programme for his whole work. It consists of six words spoken by the Italian writers Alfieri and Gozzi: *'E la fama? E la fame?'* (What of fame? What of hunger?); not lofty ideals but everyday life and the sufferings of man are the stuff of art, in Büchner's view. The political philosophers Marx, Engels and Ruge strove at one time to harness the literary talents of such men as Gutzkow and Freiligrath (whom Engels repeatedly plagiarised) to the cause of political radicalism. They were scarcely aware of the existence of the agitator and dramatist Georg Büchner who had died at the age of twenty-three when Marx and Engels were still very young men. Yet Büchner combined extreme radical views with literary and theatrical talents of a very high order. Such qualities were in themselves no recommendation, since aesthetic merit has never been high in the priorities of effective political literature, but Büchner had other things to recommend him. He had made a name for himself as a political agitator on a local scale when he wrote and distributed with the pastor Weidig (see p. 167) the pamphlet *Der Hessische Landbote* (1834), urging the oppressed peasantry of his native Hesse to revolt against their landlords. Büchner combined a social radical programme with that intense sympathy for the sufferings of humanity which has always drawn people to the theory of Communism. Like Communists then as now he wished to ameliorate the lot of the oppressed regardless of the feelings of those concerned. He believed that he must first make people aware of their misery and he therefore thrust copies of his pamphlet on the passive and bemused peasantry. As with

Marx, the components of Büchner's thought were very much part of his age; he did not however become a Communist, even at a time when social radicalism and Communism were still much the same thing.

This brief political activity nearly cost Büchner his liberty: he was forced to flee to France and later went to Switzerland. It proved however to be only a stage in his development. He chose a scientific career and already had made a name for himself at the time of his death. Literature was in fact something of a sideline for him and it is quite possible that he would have concentrated on scientific rather than imaginative writing, had he lived to realise his early promise. He wrote five literary works, two trage-dies, *Dantons Tod* and *Woyzeck,* a story *Lenz* and a comedy *Leonce und Lena,* an amusing parody of the Romantic comedy, eminently performable if dramatically weak. The fifth, a drama *Pietro Aretino,* has not survived.

Dantons Tod was Büchner's first literary work, written in five weeks to finance his flight from his home; his brother kept watch of the stairs as he wrote, for he went in fear of arrest for his political activity. Gutzkow was the first to recognise his talent and published the play in truncated form (because of the censorship) as soon as Büchner finished it in the spring of 1835. Büchner had an instinctive sense for what is effective on the stage. Like Grabbe he made use of mime, song and dance to enhance the vitality of his crowd scenes; these provide a kaleidoscope of contemporary society and the characters express themselves in an earthy idiom which is quite unlike the conventional language of the drama in his time. For Büchner art was no longer concerned with the beautiful and noble, but the vital, even if it be ugly or obscene; unlike the Young Germans who had sympathy with such views, he possessed the talent to create a new dramatic idiom and technique to express his ideas. Whereas Grabbe accepted the current theatrical con-vention that serious drama was written in blank verse (that is, up to the time he wrote *Napoleon*), Büchner wrote all his plays in prose.

Dantons Tod is set in the French Revolution of 1789 and ex-presses its author's own disillusionment with revolution: when-ever man strives to change society for the better, he finds that he is a mere instrument of history and that his efforts are so ineffective as to be grotesque. Büchner does not exploit the obvious dramatic moments of his play, which is in general historically accurate: thus he allows two opposing principles of life to confront one another in the scene between the epicurean Danton and the fanatic Robespierre without following this up. The action of the play is really the intellectual and emotional response of the participants to the revolutionary situation. The nihilistic musings of Danton and his friends, who are imprisoned in the course of the play, are interrupted by a sudden upsurge of human anguish: the cynics who would sneer at life cling for a moment to those whom they love. These moments of tenderness, such as that between Danton and his wife Julie or Danton's young friend Camille and his Lucille, are evoked with delicacy and with economy of words and gestures; they are the only relief in an oppressive and fatalist atmosphere. In all Büchner's works the capacity and need of human beings for tenderness is expressed with great feeling and conviction. His deepest concern was not with 'the frightful fatalism of history',[5] of which he wrote to his fiancée Minna Jaeglé in 1835, nor yet the destruction of bourgeois society. Certainly he poured scorn on the latter, both in his letters and his plays, but it is wrong to emphasise this aspect of his work exclusively, as Marxist critics tend to do. In all his works it is the human condition which is primary.

This is made clear in his last two works, the wonderful prose fragment *Lenz* and his tragedy *Woyzeck*: Lenz's madness and Woyzeck's suicide are not the immediate result of the sufferings they endure from society, but because this is the way of things. The social and political context is less evident in *Lenz* than in any of Büchner's other works. It is the story of the *Sturm und Drang* writer Lenz, who was a friend of Goethe in their youth but failed to realise his early promise. It is one of the most original works of the century, both in form and in language: in nervous fragmentary prose, Büchner showed a human being who is unable to integrate himself into society and is driven mad by his gradual awareness of his own isolation. Like the tragedy of the poor Woyzeck, it is intensely felt; the feelings of the protagonists are communicated through rhythms rather than through the actual meaning of the sentences. As J. P. Stern observed: 'The depths of soul uncovered in *Lenz* give one a feeling that it belongs to a period much more recent that the ' 'thirties of the last century.'[6] Lenz is an extraordinary individual and his condition might be ascribed to his genius: however Büchner is clear that this was not his meaning, when he chose as the hero of his last play a human being at the lowest possible level of existence: Woyzeck earns his daily bread by acting as a human guinea pig for the pseudo-scientific experiments of a pedant. As we follow his tragic fate through the loss of his mistress Marie to a dashing soldier, to her murder and his own arrest, we know that Büchner's concern is not the eccentricity of genius but the grim fact of human existence.

For all his contact with contemporary ideas, Büchner is a solitary figure. He was determined to debunk the idealistic belief in man's capacity for enlightenment because observation of life around him had convinced of its falsity. He also rejected the liberal optimism of Gutzkow and the Young Germans: when still unknown as a writer he rejected Gutzkow's offer to make common cause with them. He did not share the political radicals' conviction that the future would produce a better world, although his sympathy with human misery was at least as great as theirs. Unlike the political writers of his times he created in the language of his plays a perfect vehicle for his thought; his style is racy yet poetical. How well he conveys the politician's bombast, the self-hypnotism of academic verbiage, the scarcely coherent but intensely emotional utterances of Woyzeck and Marie! The form of his dramas, with their numerous short fast-moving scenes and constantly changing locations, emphasise in an extraordinarily vivid manner the individual's oppression by his circumstances.

III Hebbel

Grabbe and Büchner provide striking examples of the variety of response by nineteenth-century German writers to their tradition and environment. To twentieth-century readers both are astonishingly modern, but they had virtually no influence on the dramatic writing of their time. Thus when critics and the theatre-going public spoke of the decline of drama in the Restoration period, 1815–48, no-one thought to mention either of these as evidence to the contrary. While drama continued to be held in high regard – 'the highest form of poetry and indeed art' in Hegel's phrase[7] – the great tradition of German drama which began with Lessing was widely acknowledged to have come to an end. It was frequently alleged that the age was unfavourable to the writing of great plays. Against this climate of opinion it is difficult to account for the phenomenon of Friedrich Hebbel and for his considerable success. Hebbel is the one dramatist of genius between 1837 and 1889, when Gerhart Hauptmann's first play appeared. He was not unaffected by contemporary moods and events; he was influenced by a small number of older contemporaries, by Hegel and the Romantic philosopher and scientist Schubart, but in his unremitting absorption with metaphysical, existential and aesthetic problems, he largely disregarded the preoccupations of those around him with a changing world. He had all the dedication as an artist which we find in Grillparzer, Mörike or Stifter, but he also had a passion they appeared to lack. He applied these qualities to his self-appointed task of restoring German classical drama in his own age, for he was keenly aware of the decline of the dramatist's art in Europe. His own art was at all times highly self-conscious and he brought awe-inspiring mental powers to the analysis of tragedy and the creation of his own plays. He made as great demands on his art as on those around him. He argued with F. Th. Vischer, Hettner, Gervinus and other leading critics. He discussed his own aesthetic position in essays, letters and in his diaries, which provide an absorbing account of his creative life. Some of his own dynamism rubbed off on the characters of his plays. Though the extremist positions they take up bring his heroes and heroines rather close to bathos at times, the urgency of their creator communicates itself to the audience and convinces them in spite of themselves. His dramatic work was distinguished by his technical mastery of the theatre and his insight in psychology, history and philosophy. Contemporary writers found him rigid, excessively philosophic; they could not ignore him. The theatre-going public rewarded him with an enthusiastic reception of his first plays and he was fortunate in attracting some of the best actors and actresses of the day to take the leads.

Hebbel accepted the recognition accorded to him as an artist as something that was due to him from society. He had suffered years of hunger and privation as he prepared to be a writer. His earliest works, short stories and lyric poems, expressed something of the spiritual desolation which he had experienced in the poverty of his childhood home in Wesselburen. 'I will never get over that, never, and so I have no right to forgive what I have suffered', he wrote in his memoirs.[8] *Judith,* his first play, was written during a crisis in his life in 1839–40. He was fortunate enough to attract the interest of Tieck, who arranged for its first performance in Berlin in 1840. Encouraged by this confirmation of his own belief in himself, Hebbel went on to express his dramatic vision in seven major plays. He received a scholarship from the King of Denmark – Wesselburen in Holstein was ruled by the Danish king although it was part of the Confederation – and spent three years travelling in Europe. He settled in Vienna in 1845 and in the following year, at a critical stage in his career, married the *Hofburgtheater* actress Christine Enghaus, who frequently played the lead in his plays. She brought him security, important connections with the theatre and in his private life he experienced a serenity he had not known before. From then until his death in 1863 he was an accepted if somewhat awkward figure in the cultured society of the Austrian capital.

In *Judith* Hebbel interpreted a biblical subject in a highly unusual way. Judith believes herself appointed by God to save her town Bethulia by murdering its oppressor Holofernes. Holofernes bears some resemblance to the historic Napoleon and the play contains reflections on the relationship of the individual and history which preoccupied Hebbel in many of his plays. The central theme of this play however is the motivation of Judith's act of murder and its consequences for her. She enters the camp, confronts Holofernes, but instead of carrying out her mission, she surrenders herself to him. She kills him later in anger and humiliation because he has treated her merely as a convenient instrument to satisfy his lust. It says something for the persuasiveness of Hebbel's psychological portrait of Judith that we accept this as convincing, despite the woodenness of Hoofernes. (Nestroy's parody, *Judith und Holofernes* (1849), made a good deal out of Hebbel's rather ineffective portrait of the tyrant.) Judith's realisation that she has killed Holofernes, not to avenge her people, but from motives of personal outrage, destroys her belief in a divine order. In his drama, if not in its theoretical basis, Hebbel owed much to the Young German view of the emancipated woman (which he sharply rejected). In almost all his plays he showed perception in deomonstrating the blend of rational and emotional factors which motivate a woman's action and in portraying her need to love and be loved. Such love is capable of any sacrifice without moral conflict (*Genoveva* or *Agnes Bernauer*); its rejection is identical with the destruction of the woman's personality. An interesting feature of Hebbel's work is the disparity between the conscious and unconscious motivation of dramatic action. He was aware of this and said that he occasionally changed motivation in the course of writing a play; absorbed with his ambition to revive the classical drama of ideas he tended in his theoretical writings to ascribe ideas to his works which are not necessarily their real subject. Thus the alienation between the sexes as an indication of man's guilt and isolation is often far more convincingly represented – in *Judith* or *Herodes und Mariamne* for example – than (as Hebbel would have us believe) the relationship between the individual and history or mankind at a turning point of its destiny.

Judith was followed by *Genoveva* (1841), a play prompted by his criticism of the tragedies on the same subject by Maler Müller and Tieck. In the course of writing the original theme was modified. Golo, who covets and destroys Genoveva, dominates the play. He embodies, like Judith and other memorable characters in Hebbel's works, the dualist principle of life, but Hebbel adds, almost incidentally, astonishing psychological detail. His next major play was *Maria Magdalene* in 1843, a formal achievement unequalled as yet by Hebbel. This play is a powerful indictment of the petty bourgeois world which Meister Anton, his daughter Klara ('Maria Magdalene'), his son and Klara's fiancé Leonhard inhabit, but it is not a social drama. Bourgeois society is an image of his central theme of isolation; there is no 'message' for the social reformer. The manner in which the individual is conditioned by the narrowness of the physical and moral horizons of his life looks forward to Ibsen. Hebbel managed to communicate all the intensity of his own experience without distortion; indeed he himself confessed to being shattered by his own characters. There is no light relief; the possibility of humour is excluded. The 'dramatic necessity' so dear to the theorist Hebbel's heart is wonderfully blended with the degrading social necessity which drives Klara to her death.

After eighteen months in Rome and Naples, where he met the art historian and literary critic Hermann Hettner with whom he later corresponded, Hebbel wrote *Eine Trauerspiel in Sizilien* and *Julia*. He now overcame his 'titantic subjectivism' and began to take into consideration religion and the state. Somewhat like Grillparzer and Stifter, Hebbel underwent a transformation from moderate liberal to conservative views under the impact of the Revolution. He had taken an active part in the first weeks, offering himself as candidate for election, and had commented on the events of 1848 in Vienna in a long series of articles for the *Augsburger Allgemeine*; by the end of 1848 however, his attitude had changed from one of enthusiastic support of constitutional government to a critical resignation. Against this background he wrote *Herodes und Mariamne* which was first performed at the *Hofburg* in April 1849. He considered this work as his masterpiece and believed it to exemplify his view of tragedy. In this typical of his age, he sought to lend significance to the action by placing it at the watershed between the pagan and the Christian worlds. The power of the tragedy for the audience lies rather in the complex relationship of the two main characters and in the forceful representation of the Judith theme of the debasement of human love and personality. Mariamne is a scion of the Maccabees, Herod her husband, the upstart Tetrarch of Jerusalem. Herod loves his wife with possessive jealousy. He tried to force her to promise to kill herself as proof of her love if he should not return from the war. This she refuses to do, not out of a lack of love, for she herself loves him passionately but because her self-respect demands freedom of choice. In the end husband and wife destroy each other by the unreasonable and excessive demands they make.

If the revolution brought no radical break in Hebbel's outlook it did bring a certain change of emphasis in favour of conservative forces in the world. Some years afterwards, when he was already engaged on his last play, he looked back on the works he had written since 1848 in a letter to Baron Cotta: '*Herodes*,' he wrote, 'celebrates Christianity as the most noble cultural force, *Michelangelo* preaches humility, *Agnes Bernauer* sees the state as the foundation of all human welfare, entitled to demand any sacrifice; *Gyges* draws attention to the eternal rights of tradition and custom.'[9] It indicates some change in Hebbel's relations to the outside world that he now felt the obligation to address himself directly to the public. He wrote on topical affairs in the fifties, on political and aesthetic matters, and published a large number of reviews of plays and books. Unlike Grillparzer, Stifter or Raabe he cultivated an extensive correspondence with leading intellectuals. His civil conscience was, as it were, awakened by recent events and by his discovery of the works of the philosopher

Schopenhauer; and there was, besides, a strong element of satisfaction at what he, once an impoverished student, had achieved by his own efforts. Hebbel's conception of the writer's role in society and his need to speak directly to a public was similar to that of the Young Germans or the liberal positivisits of the fifties, for all his peremptory rejection of their views.

In the years 1849 and 1850 he wrote a comedy, *Der Rubin,* and a two-act drama *Michelangelo*; one year later he wrote *Agnes Bernauer* in the space of twelve weeks. His first concern here was to write a tragedy without guilt, as embodied in the figure of Agnes, the daughter of an Augsburg barber in the fifteenth century. Albrecht, heir to the Bavarian duchy, marries Agnes secretly, but his father, Duke Ernst, decides that for reasons of state she must be killed. Hebbel's diaries contain some contradictory comments on the play which critics quote in defence of their interpretation. It strikes one as a little glib when he asserts that 'the individual however great and splendid, however noble and beautiful, must submit in all circumstances to society, because society and its formal expression, the state, embodies the whole of humanity, whereas the individual represents but a single aspect.'[10] The persuasiveness of the play owes much to the author's interpretation of the figure of Duke Ernst, representing the state, whose stature grows as the action proceeds. His decision that the peerless Agnes must be killed so that the succession be assured and peace preserved in Bavaria is only taken after much thought and in full knowledge of what he is doing. The one person in the drama who challenges Ernst's right to put the good of the state before the claims of the individual to happiness is Albrecht, but he allies himself with the hereditary enemies of his duchy and unleashes civil war in what is essentially a quest for vengeance, not the vindication of a principle. The analogy between the latter part of *Agnes Bernauer* and the recent Revolution of 1848 is obvious: it was the violence of the autumn clashes between radicals and the armed forces and the fear of the disintegration of the Austrian Empire which had made so many Austrians and Germans alter their attitudes towards liberal reform in the course of 1848. In the last act of *Agnes Bernauer* Albrecht acknowledges the authority of the legate of the Holy Roman Empire, who has come to put him under the ban of the Empire if he should continue to challenge his father; in the final scene of the play Ernst hands over his staff of office as Duke of Bavaria to his son and successor, telling him to rule for a year and see what effect the exercise of power will have on his judgement of his father's conduct. Ernst's last long speech gives evidence of a pragmatic conservatism,[11] and the audience is made aware of the complexity of the issues at stake: this play is not simply about the conflicting claims of the state and the individual, but the whole question of authority in society. It is symptomatic of Hebbel's own political views that the character of Ernst is by far the most impressive in the play.

Although not in the strict sense of the word a popular writer, Hebbel enjoyed greater success in his lifetime than any other contemporary German writer of similar stature. Everyone of his major plays was performed within a year or two of its completion, except *Gyges und sein Ring* (1854), in Vienna, Berlin, Munich or Weimar. His later plays however had no more than a *succès d'estime*, and it was with the deliberate intention of achieving popular acclaim that he started to write the *Nibelungen* in 1850, and started a sort of one-man propaganda drive to prepare critics and the theatre for the reception of the finished work. He experienced great difficulty in writing it, but when it was performed in Weimar in 1861, the success was all that Hebbel could have hoped for. The moment was particularly favourable. The theatre-going public was still experiencing the newfound sense of national purpose, stimulated by the founding of the liberal association, the *Nationalverein* in 1859, by Schiller centenary in the same year and by the policies of new liberal Prussian government formed by the Prussian regent, later King William of Prussia, in 1858.

The idea of resuscitating the *Nibelungen* as a national myth goes back to the Romantics. Fouqué had written a version in 1810, Uhland had planned a drama, and in 1848 Wagner wrote *Siegfrieds Tod*; the popular writers Raupach in the *Nibelungenhort* (1834) and later Geibel in *Brunhilde* (1857) had won public acclaim. Hebbel criticised both these last works with his customary frankness. His idea was more ambitious: he saw his tragedy in terms of a restoration of the classical role of the theatre as a national act. 'The modern theatre . . . has always been mere entertainment,' he wrote disparagingly.[12] His satisfaction at the way he had solved his task was generally shared by his contemporaries, though for different reasons. Hebbel did not live to see others outbid him for popularity in this field, like the nationalist historian Jordan who wrote a successful play on the subject in 1868. Later critics have been more guarded in their tributes. Hebbel's effort to digest the vast material and fit it into his philosophy of history is often apparent. He did not always heed the warning of his friend F.Th. Vischer against the dangers of distorting the naive epic by modern psychological motivation. Kriemhild, as Jost Hermand points out, has more of Strindberg in her make-up than of the figure of the saga, Siegfried at times speaks like a follower of Jahn.[13] The mixture of passion and analysis which often mars Hebbel's heroes is evident here too. The last play of the trilogy, *Kriemhild's Rache,* is the finest, with an impressive confrontation of personalities and principles. The villain Hagen, the noble Dietrich and Kriemhild grow in stature and his verse achieves a pathos which had eluded him in *Herodes und Mariamne.*

Perhaps the chief interest of the *Nibelungen* in this context is the reception it had. Among its foremost admirers were Julian Schmidt, who edited the very influential journal *Die Grenzboten* and who had hitherto been a virulent critic of Hebbel. Treitschke, at the time undergoing a change from liberal to extreme national historian, praised it; the Emperor Francis Joseph of Austria ordered a gala performance for the opening of the Austrian parliament, Wagner, Grillparzer and Gutzkow were in the minority who rejected Hebbel's achievement. This trilogy represents a stage in the evolution of the German public's relation to its literature : 'the national motif, the subordination of the individual, the idea of state, the monumental character, all these (are) traits which indicate its intermediary position between the rejection of the 1848 Revolution and the spirit of the new Empire.'[14] It is tempting to conjecture whether Hebbel, his success crowned with the award of the coveted Schiller Prize for literature, might not well have become the national poet of the Empire, a much better Wildenbruch, had he lived, in the same way as Wagner came to embody the new Germany in his music. Thus he spans almost the whole of our period, looking back to the classical German drama of the Goethean age, though always keenly aware of the gulf separating him from it, while in other ways, and particularly in his portrayal of the relations of the sexes as a symbol of human guilt and isolation, he looks forward to Ibsen. Although he has so many qualities of character and talent which identify him with the age in which he lived, Hebbel, more than any other writer discussed here, defies the efforts to 'fit him in' to a chronological account of German literature.

8

The 1848 Revolution

Students of Germany in the nineteenth century tend to find the 1848 Revolution a dull affair. There was in Germany little of the bravado nor indeed the bloodshed associated with revolutionary disturbances in Poland, Italy or France in the same year. The very divisions of Germany add to the confused picture and general lack of profile of the revolution in that country. It produced no great popular leaders or stirring events to catch the public imagination, although for a few weeks the parliament which met in Frankfurt in May 1848 seemed to constitute such an event. Karl Marx cast himself in the role of revolutionary leader but had only a minimal influence on events; Robert Blum, the Saxon publisher and leftwing liberal, had a better claim, but his career was abruptly terminated in October 1848 when he was shot by the Austrian authorities; Gustav Hecker and F. Struve were democratic leaders of some potential who led the revolution in Baden; there it was fed by German exiles from Switzerland and had a more radical and violent character than in any other part of Germany, but their influence was local only and their fame did not outlive the events of 1848–9. The somewhat pedestrian character of the German revolution derives from the fact that it was almost entirely the creation of middle class liberals who wanted to secure constitutional rights and to overcome the fragmentation of Germany and who hoped to realise their ambitions by strictly legal means.

If the final causes of revolution were economic ones, the long-term cause was the political disaffection of the educated. In Germany as elsewhere the growth of political awareness during the recent decades had created a natural demand for participation in public affairs. As Agatha Ramm observes in her recent history of Germany: 'From Sicily and Naples to Scandinavia, from Poland and Croatia to France, the common denominator was one of ideas;

for there was an underlying intellectual cohesion among these classes in their essentially bookish world.'[1] The liberal movement in Germany grew not from an indigenous tradition of protest, but rather from the German pastime of political theorising. Harassed by petty restrictions and occasionally – as in the case of Büchner's political associates in Hesse – brutally persecuted if they engaged in political activity, educated Germans in the thirties liked to quote Kant's observation that people were free when they were subject to laws, not to individuals. From 1830–49 they discussed aspects of liberal reform, and hoped to persuade their rulers to adopt their proposals by means of parliamentary resolutions if their state had a parliament, by public meetings if they had none. 'They call it liberty when they get together to drink beer and found a journal,' thus Domina Adelheid, Dubslav Stechlin's formidable sister, summarised the amateur character of German liberalism half a century later in Fontane's novel *Der Stechlin*.[2] Her observation was accurate in characterising the social appeal of liberal ideas in the years before the Revolution. Educated people all over the country were drawn together to exchange their views and to try and convert others to their beliefs by the most effective method they knew: the popular journals. They were moderate, influenced by Kant and Humboldt in their respect for the authority of the state as the guardian of the laws. Hence the preoccupation of the makers of the German Revolution was with constitutions and assemblies in 1848.

Although the more articulate and extreme exponents of reform, the Young Germans, Young Hegelians and those associated with their ideas, generally lived in North Germany, political attitudes and institutions were generally more liberal in the south and west. Certain historical and geographical factors favoured this development: the proximity to France, the survival of a number of former free imperial cities, the commerce of the Rhine and Main, and the greater material prosperity of the region. The period of the French occupation of the Rhineland had a significant effect on political thinking over the next decades: Napoleon had introduced a system of local government which was both liberal and efficient; its success prejudiced the population in its favour. After 1815 many Rhenish businessmen contrasted their new Prussian masters unfavourably with the enlightened French. The growth of liberalism in this region had much more in common with developments in England and France some years earlier: liberalism was the natural creed of businessmen who were expanding their enterprises under the difficult conditions prevailing in Germany, men like the Hanoverian banker Hansemann, who settled in Cologne, Camphausen, who collaborated with him on the Cologne-Aachen railway line and himself pioneered the Leipzig-Dresden stretch and founded the first German insurance company, or Mevissen, one of the proprietors of the progressive newspaper, the *Rheinische Zeitung* which Marx edited 1842–3. In their liberal sympathies they had practical aims, and unlike the South Germans who concentrated on the theoretical justification of their beliefs, they looked around for the most effective agency to support them. They decided, like the Prussian liberals of the fifties and sixties, that Prussia was in the best position to satisfy their needs. Camphausen entered the Prussian government and was active for a brief period as Prime Minister with Hansemann as his Minister of Finance in 1848.

Alongside the liberal movement in the Rhineland there grew up democratic agitation under its leader Moses Hess, who was for a time one of the Young Hegelians and later became a Communist. In Hesse-Darmstadt a pastor, Weidig, friend and mentor of Georg Büchner, attempted to rally support for democracy among the peasants. Subsequently he was arrested and hounded to death by a sadistic magistrate, Georgi, who according to current practice examined the defendant in private and presented his report to the court who tried the prisoner on this basis only. Büchner had called the German judiciary 'the whore of the German princes'.[3] Georgi was decorated for his efforts, but the case aroused sufficient public disquiet to make judicial reform a prominent feature of liberal and democratic policy.

Although Hesse-Darmstadt under its unpopular Grand Duke William was not a congenial place to live in, the other larger states in South Germany, Baden, Württemberg and Bavaria were relatively liberal. The oldest liberal institution in the South was the Württemberg Diet which had managed to limit the power of the princes for many years. Its unique feature was its bourgeois composition, consisting of Protestant prelates and the sons of middle class families with a university education. The Swabians had resolutely resisted attempts by the notorious despot of Schiller's youth, Duke Karl Eugen, or the grotesque Frederick I whom

Napoleon raised to be King of Württemberg, to create an absolutist state. The poet Uhland expressed the individualistic attitude of his countrymen in his *Vaterländische Gedichte* and in his actions: he resigned from the civil service of his state in protest over an injustice and on another occasion refused decorations from Prussia and Bavaria on liberal grounds. Later, in 1848, Uhland was to take part in the National Assembly at St Paul's Church in Frankfurt where he coined the famous phrase: no sovereign could rule over Germany whose head had not been anointed with a drop of democratic oil.[4] The saying can be seen as a kind of symbolic dividing line between the period of moderate South German liberalism up to the middle of the century and the Prussian type of state liberalism which predominated thereafter.

The sturdy Swabian middle class had no counterpart in Bavaria, if we exclude the territories of Franconia and the Palatinate which Bavaria had received from Napoleon. However Bavaria could boast of being the first constitutional state in Germany; in 1818 her king had granted his people a constitution, which, although scarcely more than a formality, satisfied their political aspirations. Society in Bavaria was more homogeneous than in other German states and in the historical territories, that is, excluding Franconia and the Palatinate, almost uniformly Catholic. It was composed of tenant farmers and artisans, as well as a large bureaucracy, whose outlook became progressively more reactionary in the thirties and forties. To contemporaries, Bavarians were simply being true to type in demonstrating their fundamental lack of interest in politics, when rioting broke out in 1843 and 1844 solely because the government tried to raise the price of beer. Bavaria's ruler Ludwig 1 (1825–48) shared his Habsburg brother-in-law's view: everything for the people, nothing by the people; he had considerable confidence in his own ability to rule wisely and was indeed an enlightened administrator. He introduced into Bavaria the system of local government which Napoleon had imposed on the Palatinate, and he interested himself in a practical way in economic welfare; he furthered the project of a Rhine-Danube canal, while his commercial treaty with Prussia facilitated the creation of the Customs Union in 1834. In 1848, as her envoy to the Austrian court Count Luxburg had prophesied with a certain smugness in February of the same year, Bavaria remained unaffected by the turbulence around her.

The most liberal state in Germany was Baden, which lay in the South-west. Before the railway network was extended throughout Germany, Paris lay nearer than Munich or Berlin, and the people of Baden were sensitive to developments in France. In parts of the state Napoleon's civil code was still in force. Baden's peculiar claim to fame in this time was the fact that it possessed two chambers of deputies elected on a property qualification. English travellers found this rather pedestrian but visitors from other parts of Germany streamed to Karlsruhe to marvel at the active participation of the people in the process of government. In practice it was less ideal. Two notable liberals, Rotteck and Welcker, who were professors at Freiburg university and members of the Baden Diet, supported a liberal press policy and lost their chairs through the intervention of Metternich in 1832. The event won them considerable fame, and Welcker, who had introduced a motion into the lower house to abolish censorship, found himself a hero. Banquets were held in his honour and toasts made to his name. North Germans liked to deride this sort of thing, but the fact remained that moderate liberal opinions became generally representative of the South Germans between 1830 and 1848, not only because they corresponded in a certain sense to local tradition, but because people could identify them with a popular and congenial figure; the liberal movement gave the more sociable southerners a chance to meet and broaden their small horizons. No doubt Domina Adelheid was right up to a point.

The challenge of Rotteck and Welcker to authority marks the beginning of the rise of the academics to leadership of public opinion in Germany, some years before the incident of the seven Göttingen professors in 1837. As teachers and writers these two exercised a great influence on liberal thought at least up to 1848. Rotteck's *General History* in six volumes became in every sense a popular work in South Germany, where it was to be found in most educated homes. Thus when Gutzkow in *Die Ritter vom Geiste*, written in 1849–51, wanted to indicate the liberal sympathies of his pub-owner Justus Heidecker, he described his library in which Rotteck's *History* and his *Staatslexikon* had pride of place.[5] This latter work appeared between 1834 and 1844, fifteen volumes written in collaboration with Welcker and for many years a standard reference work on liberalism and parliamentary democracy. From his rational and liberal standpoint Rotteck condemned in his *History* the annexation of Polish territory by Frederick II of Prussia; he called it an outrage against national and human rights. On these grounds alone nationalist German historians in the second half of the century had little time for Rotteck; Treitschke barely mentioned him in his influential *History of Germany in the Nineteenth Century* (1870 ff). The dilemma of the post-1848 liberals in Prussia, namely the priority to be given to liberal principles or nationalist emotions, never confronted Rotteck. For Rotteck as for Welcker, if national unity curtailed individual liberty it was not worth having. 'Rather freedom without unity than unity without freedom', Rotteck declared in a speech at Baden-weiler shortly after the Hambach Popular Festival of 1832, where tens of thousands had met to commemorate the Bavarian constitution of 1818 and to fête the Polish refugees. Treitschke's patronising tone in his work towards Rotteck is indicative also of the change in German public opinion between the 1830s and the 1870s: in the former period it was possible to criticise Frederick the Great and to feel solidarity with the Poles; in the latter it was morally reprehensible to do so.

The South Germans and the people of the Rhineland felt an instinctive hostility towards North Germans, which Prussia's reputation for conservative and occasionally repressive policies only served to increase. In 1837 there took place in Hanover an event which almost overnight drew north and south close together. This was the so-called affair of the Göttingen Seven. On the accession of Queen Victoria to the English throne, Hanover, where the Salic law obtained, passed to her uncle, Ernst August. The new king, allegedly the 'wickedest of Victoria's wicked uncles', has been maligned by historians; by German standards at least he was not excessively reactionary when he abrogated the 1833 Basic Law of the state. The vast majority of the bureaucracy in Hanover, including university professors and school teachers, were quite ready to disregard their oath to the former law and to make their declaration of obedience to the new king. Unexpectedly seven professors at the university of Göttingen, which had enjoyed a reputation for greater freedom than other institutions in the Confederation, lodged a protest. These included Dahlmann, the architect of the 1833 law, the Grimm brothers and Gervinus, the literary historian. All seven were instantly dismissed by the king and given three days to leave Hanoverian territory. The reaction was without precedent. The familiar adjuncts of political activity in mid-nineteenth century Germany: collections, founding of clubs, banquets, speeches, took place all over the country. Enough money was collected to pay the professors their salaries until they could find employment elsewhere. Old hostilities, such as a long-standing quarrel between Welcker and Dahlmann, were forgotten. What was quite novel was a sense of a unified middle class opinion throughout Germany. Moreover the incident confirmed the university professors as leaders of German liberalism; for the next decade university and grammar school teachers were to exercise a formative influence on political opinions if not to the same extent on political events.

Three years after the affair at Göttingen a long-awaited event took place: Frederick William IV succeeded his father as King of Prussia at the age of forty-nine. The new king was generally if erroneously looked upon as a man of the times. In the quality of his mind he was unlike the traditional Hohenzollern, who were usually disciplined and single-minded; he resembled rather his great-nephew, Kaiser William II, who had the same artistic temperament, the same power to charm and quick grasp of things as well as the same weakness for the Romantic trappings of power. Both monarchs felt they had the common touch and both reacted almost hysterically when they were made to see that this implied a two-way relationship. In mental powers Frederick William's only equal among his fellow rulers was King John of Saxony (who was known as Philalethes and had translated Dante's *Divina Commedia*); the two kings corresponded on scholarly projects. Frederick was warm-hearted and could be excellent company, but he became increasingly subject to fits of rage and melancholia. He belonged by birth and experience to that generation of rulers who resolutely refused to accept the hard fact that the Revolution of 1789 had actually taken place. He had a sentimental feeling about liberal aspirations, which soon evaporated once he had come to power; gifted with little knowledge of human nature, still less of contemporary reality, he remained prone to sudden bursts of enthusiasm. 'The King is so fond of beauty', remarked one of his courtiers to a colleague; 'yes,' replied another 'but he finds everything beautiful.' This remark summarises the limitations of a man who in 1848–9 unexpectedly found himself in a position to determine the future of Germany.

171

However in the best Hohenzollern tradition, the reign started off well. Contemporaries did not overlook the fact that his accession coincided with the centenary of the great Frederick II's accession. The new king – in this also similar to his grand-nephew William II – showed initial enthusiasm for social welfare; he also ordered the release of Jahn who had been confined during the persecution of the radicals after 1819, he recalled the patriotic poet of the Napoleonic wars, Arndt, to his chair at Bonn university, which he had lost in 1819, and summoned Tieck and Schelling to Berlin. These were elderly men now; to the young he was less gracious. There was the affair of Herwegh's interview (see p. 144); the progressive *Rheinische Zeitung* was proscribed, as were Ruge's *Hallische Jahrbücher*. Ruge moved across the border into Saxony and published the journal under another name. The self-deception of those who had placed their hopes in the King was made evident within three years of his accession. Frederick made his own position clear when he remarked to the Governor of East Prussia, Theodor von Schön, a man of considerable influence in Prussia and one who was known for his liberal views: 'Believe me on my royal word that as long as I reign no prince, no peasant or peasant body, no Diet or Jewish school shall appropriate anything which has hitherto *rightly or wrongly* appertained to the Crown, unless I have first given it away.'[6]

One of Frederick's few concessions, but one which enriched the life of the individual and added considerable zest to politics, was his abolition of the censorship on illustrations. The fashionable caricaturist Gavarini was working at this time for the Paris *Charivari*; the taste for political caricature spread quickly to Germany. The Munich *Fliegende Blätter,* founded in 1845, and *Kladderadatsch* in Berlin (from 1849) became immensely popular in middle class circles, while Adolf Glasbrenner's cheap illustrated pamphlets, which were full of topical allusions, were widely read among the working classes. Frederick William himself was nothing short of a gift for cartoonists. Although he was that rare thing, a Hohenzollern uninterested in military affairs, he had a weakness for colourful parades and could be carried away, on these or other more convivial occasions, into using violent language. His occasional lapses were soon ruthlessly exploited by the caricaturists and in this way the Germans were able to indulge vicariously in political comment in a way they would not have dared to do on their own initiative.

Contemporaries rapidly sensed a difference in the atmosphere of the forties from that of the decade which had just ended. There was a perceptible quickening of interest in national life, a sense of unlimited possibilities just around the corner. Social and political tensions were present in specific regions but there was not that sense of nationwide crisis which existed in England or France in the same period. The Chartist agitation or the industrial slump of 1842 in England had a far greater immediate effect on the mind of the English nation than any of the events of the forties on Germany. The economic factor however was crucial. Although the thirties had been a time of modest prosperity in comparison with the lean years after Napoleon's defeat, by the early 1840s the gradual expansion had begun to be checked. Harvests, which in 1834 and 1835 had been magnificent and in the other years of the decade good, now began to fail. In 1845 famine came to East Germany, a famine worse than in any other region of Europe save Ireland. There were bread riots in Posen and Berlin in the next years and near starvation in Vienna. The artisans and lower paid salaried workers were worst hit; the factory workers, a small minority still, were substantially better off. The Silesian weavers' revolt began to concern people in the highest places, among them the King of Prussia.

The middle classes in Germany did not have the financial resources at this time to alleviate distress on a large scale, but they were not insensitive to its existence. Associations for the benefit of the working classes sprang up. 1845 saw a flood of philanthropic pamphlets and reform programmes on the social question. As early as 1835 Franz von Baader, the scientist and social thinker, had written: 'the civilisation of the few can only exist through the un-civilisation of the many.'[7] Men as different as the poet Heine, Radowitz, the Catholic statesman and confidant of Frederick, and Lorenz von Stein, the political theorist of the Prussian conservatives, drew attention to the problem of the poor. From the late thirties onwards the word *proletariat* was suddenly in everyone's mouth, a term intended by contemporaries quite consciously to signify something new in social relationships. The main cause of the emergence of the proletariat has since come to be seen by social historians as the extraordinary growth in population in

Germany after the Napoleonic wars, particularly in the East. Farms could not support such an increase while industry was as yet too little developed to absorb the unemployed. What distinguished the 1840s was the extent to which public opinion in Germany became aware of the social changes created by these developments.

Yet when 1848 came it was not, despite Marx, a social revolution. 'They would have laughed at me or pitied me if I had called myself a Communist,' wrote Stephan Born, one of the radical leaders of the working class some years later.[8] Engels and Moses Hess agitated for a year among the workers in Wuppertal without success, and even in Vienna and Berlin the workers did not man the barricades in March. They were only later persuaded to take part in street demonstrations at the behest of others. The leaders of revolutionary activity were almost always middle class and usually intellectuals. The workers were not socialist or even liberal in their economic thinking. Paradoxically it was the bureaucracy and not the workers who advocated freedom for workingmen to move about and change their trades. The distressed textile workers and other craftsmen agitated in 1848 to have the guild system restored; their revolutionary aims were to secure cheaper raw materials and free education. These people did not regard themselves as members of the proletariat; despite the hardships they endured they considered themselves part of the middle class, since their social position in almost every region of the country was unchallenged. It was only when economic or political events (the slump of 1873, the defeat and distress of 1918) affected the social position of large sections of the population that revolutionary passions were aroused. In the 1840s, although of course there were considerable regional variations which make generalisation difficult, it would seem that the working men who were most affected by the 'Hungry Forties' did not share bourgeois views on the novelty or the danger of the proletarian phenomenon. They had not yet experienced the feeling which drove many of their sons to join the Socialist party, that of being by-passed by the state and society. In 1848 a well-known industrialist, Frederick Harkort, addressed a letter to working men which was read and treasured by a large number of them and copies passed down to their children. The sentiments expressed in this letter appear, from its reception, to have been more typical of the situation than those of the intellectuals or the authorities. 'People talk of the proletariat and do not know what they mean. I call someone a member of the proletariat who was neglected by his parents, unwashed, uncombed, who was never taught to behave nor sent to church or school. He never learned a trade, he married without substance, he brings into the world others like himself, who are always ready to fall on other people's property and to act as the canker of the community ... I don't call the decent working man one of the proletariat, to whom God gave capital in the strength of his hand and his own common sense, something that only sickness and old age can take from him.'[9]

The political causes of the Revolution in Prussia went back to the beginning of the new reign. The King of Prussia's initial flirtation with the liberals had led him to summon representatives from the eight provincial diets of the kingdom, but nothing concrete was achieved. In 1847 he suddenly decided to summon a United Diet of all the provincial estates to meet in Berlin, where it sat from April to June. Most members of this assembly were liberal and hoped for a constitution; the King on the other hand aimed to create a kind of patriarchal corporative state which would heal present political and social ills. The majority of the members could only see in his attitude a mockery of the expected constitutional reforms. Thus when the King agreed on the competency of the Diet to vote supplies but refused to accept the principle of regular meetings, the delegates rejected a project dear to Frederick William, although it was in the interest of many of their number: the guarantee of a loan of 25,000,000 *thaler* to build the Berlin-East Prussia railway. An important side effect of this first United Diet (it met again in the following year) was that liberal delegates from different parts of the country, notably those of East Prussia and the Rhineland, met for the first time. The debates of the proceedings were published verbatim which had an electrifying effect on political discussion both in and outside Prussia and gave substance to the feeling that great events were at hand.

The months preceding March 1848, the date of the outbreak of the Revolution in Prussia and Austria, saw an ever-increasing number of occasions for Germans from different regions to meet and discover in their common interests a novel sense of political purpose. The conference of Germanists – or 'intellectual Diets' as Treitschke called them – met in Frankfurt in 1846, in Lübeck in 1847. On these occasions Dahlmann and others of the 'Göttingen Seven' held audiences' attention. The *All-German Choral Festival* also met in Lübeck in 1847 and other activities such as shooting competitions became the opportunity for liberal agitation on a national scale. In October 1847 liberals from the west and south of Germany met at Heppenheim to discuss the project of a German parliament.

The actual outbreak of the Revolution in Germany was contingent, as had been so often the case in the last fifty years of its history, on events in France. The bourgeois monarchy of Louis Philippe was overthrown and on 26 February a republic was proclaimed. Disturbances broke out in Baden on the following day: a public meeting in Offenburg demanded a constitution for the German states, freedom of the press, trial by jury and the calling of a German parliament. These became known as 'the March demands' as they were presented to almost every German ruler in the next weeks. The first revolutionary act in the Austrian dominions had taken place in Italy: in the streets of Milan radicals snatched cigars from unsuspecting citizens and demanded that they give up smoking; the Austrian state relied on the revenue from the state-owned tobacco monopoly. For many years Metternich had feared revolution and he resigned when disturbances broke out in Vienna on 13 March and fled to England. His departure had an immediate effect on events in Germany: the Russian Tsar lost a natural ally whom he would have used to justify his intervention in Central Europe; the Federal Diet in Frankfurt, lacking the strong hand which had guided it so long, surrendered the initiative to the princes. They in their turn remembered 1789 and its consequences and showed immediate willingness to grant the 'March demands'. The main focus of interest in this first month was the calling of a national parliament.

The first practical step was taken by fifty-one liberals, the majority of whom came from South Germany, when they met at Heidelberg on 5 March. Within the next seven days the Kings of Württemberg and Bavaria had declared their willingness to call such a parliament. Thus the 'revolutionary act' of 1848 in Germany was accomplished not only with the consent but the active co-operation of the authorities. The liberals responsible for the arrangements did not feel any sense of opposition; they simply accepted the fact that their demands were reasonable and that in the light of revolutionary disturbances elsewhere in Europe, the monarchs had seen fit to accept them. The constituent assembly (*Vorparlament*) which met in Frankfurt late in March actually submitted its decisions to the old Federal Diet.* Elections took place in the next weeks, not always according to direct universal suffrage, as the liberals wished, but according to the electoral law of the different states. One member was elected for every 50,000 inhabitants, and the Assembly which met at Frankfurt on 18 May was composed of the notables of their state or locality. The authority of the academic middle class in the liberal movement before 1848 was amply confirmed by the representatives of the German people at Frankfurt. More than two thirds of the Assembly were university graduates. There was only one farmer, a few artisans, and no factory workers. We need not be surprised at this; the interests of such men were particular and local, and they would not have been regarded as fitting representatives on such a great national occasion. The 565 delegates who took their seats in St Paul's Church at Frankfurt in May to the accompaniment of the ringing of bells from the city's many churches and the firing of cannon were deeply conscious of the historic nature of the occasion. The solemnity was captured in a large number of portraits and engravings which survive. Eye-witness accounts, such as that of the distinguished noblewoman Malwida von Meysenbug, give a vivid impression of the excitement it engendered. Besides nearly 300 state officials, 100 university professors and teachers, seventy lawyers, twenty doctors and a few Catholic and Protestant clergymen who sat as delegates in the Frankfurt Assembly at some time over the next thirteen months, there were several writers who recorded their impressions. These included Arndt, now nearly eighty, and Uhland, the literary historian Gervinus, the critic and writer Vischer, as well as the writer Heinrich Laube, the political poet Anastasius Grün (Count Auersperg) and the historian Wilhelm Jordan.

The immediate task of the delegates was nothing less than the creation of a national state and the drafting of a constitution.

---

*One of the most confusing aspects of 1848 in Germany is the apparent proliferation of parliaments and assemblies: the National Assembly or Frankfurt Parliament met on 18 May, although the Federal Diet, a kind of conference of ambassadors of the rulers of the German states, had not been abolished; to add to the confusion the Prussian parliament which met in Berlin on 22 May, and the Austrian which met at Vienna on 22 July also were called 'National Assemblies'.

Germans had been so long used to regarding politics in terms of state authority that economic questions were scarcely discussed. No attempt was made to take advantage of this unique situation to unify the currency, the commercial code, or to plan a national railway network. Committees were formed but decisions were to be taken in plenary session. The prevailing theoretical approach to political questions allowed the members to devote several months to discussing the basic rights of man in the new constitution. In June the Assembly created a central authority and appointed a Regent, Archduke John of Austria. This step was approved by the German governments, an achievement which indicates the general confidence which the Frankfurt Assembly commanded at this point, for it had neither troops nor finance at its disposal.

However this represented the height of its power. The question of national minorities, which had inspired liberal sentiments among Germans in the previous decade, now began to intrude in an embarrassing manner on the awareness of the members. This was eventually to be a central factor in the failure of the Assembly and of the whole revolution. The enthusiasm of Gutzkow, Laube or Lenau for Polish freedom, which many here had once shared, disappeared overnight when the Poles in the Prussian provinces of Posen and West Prussia attempted to assert their rights. The Germans in these areas appealed immediately and successfully to the King of Prussia to intervene. In July there took place at Frankfurt a debate on the Polish question which was in fact a turning point. The debate ended with the rejection of the Polish claim by over three quarters of the Assembly. The episode pinpoints the inherent contradiction between liberalism and nationalism in Germany, which was to become even clearer in the next decades. The aspirations of the Czechs in Bohemia aroused the same passionate rejection. The Czech historian Palácky had refused an earlier invitation to send representatives from Bohemia to Frankfurt and had instead set up a Pan-Slav congress which met at Prague in June 1848. When disturbances broke out there at Whitsuntide, even the left wing members joined with the rest of the Frankfurt delegates to advocate sending in German troops to put down the Czech rebels. They fully supported General Windischgrätz whom the Austrian authorities appointed for the task. Prior to these events, the claim of Germans in the Danish ruled duchies of

Schleswig and Holstein to be incorporated into Germany had already aroused nationalist emotions in Frankfurt, particularly when the King of Prussia and federal troops entered these regions to fight against the Danes. The Germans were however defeated and in August 1848 the King of Prussia signed a treaty with the Danes at Malmö without seeking the authorisation of the Frankfurt Assembly or the Federal Diet. After initial hesitation the Assembly acquiesced in September, and both public opinion and governments alike interpreted this act as a sign of its decline.

As members of the Assembly discussed the nationalities within their borders they became increasingly aware of the implications of political and social reform. They realised their common interest with the authorities; it struck them that minority rights would be bought in each particular case at the expense of the German position which, as they were now beginning to appreciate, was a potentially powerful one. One did not have to be tempted by illusions of national grandeur to see the dangers of the minority nations for the future of Germany, let alone Austria. In the realistic appraisal of the situation contained in his *Ein Bruderzwist im Hause Habsburg,* Grillparzer rejected the principle of national rights as disruptive of the whole order of Central Europe. The motives of the German nationalists at Frankfurt were less reasoned and humane than Grillparzer's, though they shared his fear of anarchy. They acquiesced in the counter-revolutionary policies of Austria and Prussia, motivated by a new-found belief in the power of the autocrats to pursue national aggrandisement. Many of the delegates and those whom they represented were led by events to the position expressed by Wilhelm Jordan of East Prussia, who was actually a member of the radical Left. On the occasion of the suppression of the Czech riots he declared: 'My heart swells with pride ... I see at last that we mean to proceed against the attempts of puny nationalists to found their own lives in our midst, and like parasites to destroy us.'[10]

Meanwhile in Austria and in Prussia the revolution had taken a different course. After the riots in Vienna on 13 March and Metternich's flight, the revolution had spread rapidly to the other crown lands of the monarchy and naturally distracted the authorities from trying to influence events in Germany. Although in

April the first constitution in Austria was proclaimed by Metternich's successor, Prince Pittersdorf, the radicals in Vienna soon
began to dominate the revolution. The Emperor Ferdinand felt
forced to flee to Innsbruck, though he returned when the Austrian
Diet was convened in July. The delegates of this assembly met in
the building which in more peaceful days had belonged to the
Spanish riding school. The delegates' most important act was the
liberation of the Austrian peasants from feudal dues. The sessions
were interrupted by a new wave of mob violence in the autumn
instigated by a number of radical leaders who were impatient at
the slow progress of reform. Once more the Emperor left his
capital, this time for Olmütz in Moravia; the assembly transferred to the residence of the prince bishop of Olmütz at
Kremsier, and General Windischgrätz besieged Vienna. Mass
arrests and executions followed its fall. In December the agree-
able if somewhat weak-minded Emperor Ferdinand abdicated in
favour of his nephew, Francis Joseph. He lived on for thirty more
years, happily engaged in the pursuit of his hobby, heraldry.
Francis Joseph (1848–1916), who was destined to have the longest
reign of any monarch in European history except Louis xiv, was
only eighteen years of age on his accession; he immediately initiated a show of strength against the liberals; the Kremsier constitution which was the work of the assembly was rejected and his
generals in Hungary and elsewhere completed the bloody suppression of the revolution.

In Prussia meanwhile the revolution had broken out almost
by accident. The King had already conceded the regular meeting
of the Prussian Diet and other liberal demands, when on 18
March large numbers of people gathered in front of the Palace.
Some were merely excited and curious, others dissatisfied with the
royal promises. The king, however, in a moment of panic, called
in the troops and a clash occurred. Frederick William was horri-
fied and attempted conciliation. The victims of the incident
were given an impressive funeral, celebrated in a famous painting by Adolf von Menzel. When the bodies were borne in proces-
sion to the palace the King was seen to remove his headgear on
the instigation of the crowd; two days later he was seen wearing
the black, red and gold armband, colours of the constitutionalists.
Liberal ministers were appointed to the government and a constituent assembly met in Berlin. Orderliness and segregation were

the distinctive features of the German, though not of the Austrian revolution. A citizen's militia was formed in Prussia in March, and orders and military uniforms were the source of satisfaction to its members and their wives. Not being citizens the manual workers were excluded, yet there was no *bonnet rouge* to be seen. Bourgeois women continued to wear their poke bonnets, peasants their cap or hood. So orderly were the citizens that when in November the militia was commanded to return the guns issued in March, all but 150 did so.

However the Prussian assembly which met in Berlin in May was socially more representative than its counterpart in Frankfurt, though its members also spent excessive time in theoretical discussion. In August the conservative feudal landowners from the regions east of the Elbe split off to form a parliament of their own, the Junkers' Parliament, and began to put pressure on the King. They were better propagandists than their liberal rivals and a strong reactionary party grew out of their midst; a paper was founded, the *Neue Preußische Zeitung,* better known as the *Kreuz-Zeitung* from the large cross on its front page. Its brilliant editor Hermann Wagener made it one of the most successful organs of political propaganda in the century, and under the influence of the leader of the reactionary party, Leopold von Gerlach, it played a part in the political development of Otto von Bismarck, who was aged thirty-three at the time of the revolution. The natural orderliness of the Prussian people asserted itself after some disturbances during the summer; the public lost confidence in the Prussian National Assembly, which the King, after dismissing his liberal ministers, had transferred to the small provincial town of Brandenburg. It was finally dissolved in December and the King promulgated a constitution.

Up to the late summer of 1848 the events of the previous months in Germany could hardly have been said to constitute a revolution. In September and October however sporadic violence broke out in various parts of the country. It was partly the spontaneous expression of lower class unrest at the economic hardship they were still enduring, but it was also a symptom of the resentment among workers and their leaders that the revolution had excluded them from its benefits. In Frankfurt itself, in Cologne, in Saxony, Baden and Hesse-Kassel risings broke out, often the outcome of agitated discussions in the workers' clubs which had appeared in recent months in many German cities. In Baden the disturbances were protracted, for they were fed by refugees streaming southwards after the suppression of the revolution in Prussia and elsewhere, and by agitators belonging to the radical movements in Switzerland and Alsace. The Baden uprisings were finally quelled by Prussian troops in the spring of 1849. The effect of all this, an effect of such importance for the future of the liberal movement in Germany, was to rally bourgeois liberal opinion behind the state governments and to restore the self-confidence of the latter.

The decisions on which Germany's immediate future was to depend were not taken at Frankfurt, but on the periphery of German speaking territories, in Vienna and in Berlin. The Frankfurt Assembly had proposed a personal union between the German and non-German Austrian dominions, and the inclusion of the former in the new German state which was to be set up. The new prime minister of Austria, Schwarzenberg, however began to restore authoritarian rule in the winter of 1848–9 and so the Frankfurt delegates decided to turn to the so-called 'little German solution', that is, Germany without Austria. In March 1849 Frederick William of Prussia was offered the elective imperial crown of Germany. He refused 'a crown from the gutter' as he put it and his refusal split the Assembly. It had already been in session for one year. What had it achieved? A rump parliament, largely democrat in composition, withdrew from Frankfurt to Stuttgart; in September it was scattered by Prussian troops at the instigation of the King of Württemberg. From there the troops proceeded southwards to crush the risings in Baden and the Palatinate. The Prussian troops remained in occupation for several months. Back in Prussia itself order had been restored in the previous November when the army under General Wrangel had scattered the Prussian assembly. It is significant that the Revolution, tame affair that it had been in most regions, was suppressed almost everywhere by the armed forces. The politically aware drew the conclusion over the next decade that military power was a necessary agent of political change. However, the population of Prussia and of the other German states, whether liberal or democrat in sympathy, remained thoroughly hostile to the army. Their animosity was not overcome until the victories of the mid-sixties and in the rest of Germany later still.

The national character of the Germans as it appeared to contemporaries in the first half of the nineteenth century was confirmed by their conduct during the Revolution of 1848. Heine's
dire warning of the *furor teutonicus* which a German revolution
would unleash was not fulfilled, at least not at this time. Instead
German liberals impressed observers by their sincerity, orderliness
and responsibility. The only passion displayed by the majority
concerned national, not liberal goals. No prince in any of the
thirty-nine states lost his realm, and there was remarkably little
violence done to persons in all the months of the revolution. There
was a tragically ironical side to the general docility of the revolutionaries. They wanted to impress on their rulers their sense of
responsibility in crisis, to prove their political maturity. Similarly
the bands of artisans who flocked to Berlin and Frankfurt to receive the liberty they had heard about, were careful to respect
property for the same reason. The rulers of Germany however regarded such behaviour simply as a display of weakness and did
not hesitate to exploit middle class fears of the workers. The outbreak of violence in the autumn of 1848, the extremist views
provoked by the brutal repression by Austrian and Prussian
troops, had the effect desired by the authorities. The middle
classes began to doubt the practicality of the liberal reform programme or at least to look to the authorities to do what was best.
They lost confidence in their own political ability. Börne's acid
comment on the bourgeoisie after the promulgation of the
Carlsbad Decrees in 1819 could be applied to the atmosphere in
1849: 'The thinking part of the German people will shortly return to its studies – already the German is reposing on his stomach; and while he is surrounded by smoke and fire and war . . .
he remarks calmly: "that's not my business . . . my government
does all that".'[11]

An important obstacle to liberal thinking before 1848 had been
the bureaucratic tradition in all German states. Many educated
Germans believed and the less educated assumed that bureaucratic
administration was more efficient and therefore necessarily better
than responsible cabinet ministries and elective assemblies. Even
in Baden, which was celebrated as being the only German state
which had a parliament that actually met and worked, some deplored the waste of time involved in this kind of government. The
experiences of 1848 confirmed these convictions among the public

at large. After the initial disappointment at the failure of the 'revolution of the intellectuals', as 1848 in Germany is sometimes called, the German middle classes were not wholly dissatisfied with the way things had turned out. The events of the autumn and winter of 1848 had awakened fears that liberty meant licence and given substance to their belief that order and efficiency were more essential to human well-being than freedom. In Prussia the constitution of December 1848 and the three-class franchise of May 1849 contained several liberal features. The judicial powers of the landowners were abolished, the press was granted greater freedom and letters were no longer to be censured. The extent of the Prussian estates' power to vote taxes remained ambiguous, however, and the King retained his right of veto. On the other hand the new franchise was based on taxes paid, a system which remained in force until November 1918. This pleased those who had become more fearful of social upheaval in the course of the previous months and who, as the economy began to expand in the next decade, gained an increasing stake in the country's wealth.

One of the inevitable consequences of the revolution was emigration, and it was most widespread in those parts of Germany which had been more liberal before 1848. Germany had lost large numbers of her subjects, particularly agrarian workers, to the United States even before 1848. The poor German *emigrés* who had left Germany in the depressed years after 1815 or in the forties had been the victims of unscrupulous profiteers. The economist List, who spent some years in America, had tried to use his *Zollvereinsblatt* and his own major work *The National System of Political Economy* (1846) to encourage industrial projects at home in order to put a stop to the human misery and economic loss involved in mass emigration. List argued in favour of the exploitation of the German hinterland and the use of surplus population to develop *Mitteleuropa*, as he termed the Danube basin. Although his views became popular later in the optimistic climate of the German Empire, in the disillusioned years after the Revolution they were ignored. One million Germans left their homes in the years 1848–55; Baden alone lost one tenth of its population. Only a minority were political refugees. The rest doubted their ability to keep up with the rising cost of living or simply shared the prevailing sense of depression after months of expectation during 1848–9. The United States had been the only power to recognise the Frankfurt Assembly and for this reason alone many were persuaded to seek their fortune in the new world. The more affluent and talented expected and usually found sympathy and opportunities there. The actual loss of national wealth was considerable and continued to be so. It was not until the 1890s that the trend was halted and by 1900 it was estimated that seven million American citizens were either German born or had one German parent.[12]

The attitude of intellectuals to the failure of 'their' revolution reflected the response of the middle classes to which most belonged. They were disappointed that German unity had not been achieved but were relieved that things had not got out of hand. The negative response of Grillparzer, Stifter and others like them was not typical. Grillparzer's last tragedy, *Libussa* (1848), illustrates the anguish and fear of the future which characterised some of his nationality and background. Stifter, a somewhat younger man, felt an obligation to try and provide his readers with moral values in an age of disruption; he was at pains to stress the ethical content of his short stories and novels written after 1848. Gutzkow tried to do something similar in his long novel, *Die Ritter vom Geiste,* which he began just after the suppression of the revolution in 1849. He showed his awareness of the role of class differences in destroying the impact of the revolution by introducing into his novel of contemporary society a moral elite – the 'Knights of the Spirit' – which was drawn from all classes and kinds. Nietzsche later spoke of the 'fetid air of the fifties' and Schopenhauer's pessimistic philosophy became popular among a select few. These however represented the minority. Intellectuals in general found distraction like the rest, either in the greater material prosperity or in the national movement.

The consequences of 1848 made themselves apparent in political attitudes rather than in institutions. The Confederation was restored after a barely perceptible tussle between Austria and Prussia in which Schwarzenberg successfully asserted Austrian authority in Germany. Most German state governments indulged in a policy of reaction or simply stagnated. The most far-reaching consequence of the recent events was unquestionably their effect on the middle classes. The sense of elation felt during the Revolution, for all its pedantic discursiveness, had derived from the new political and national awareness. This had grown up slowly over the previous decades and was reflected in the character of contemporary writing. The protracted nature of the Revolution, the variety of events, the impassioned debates and the contacts between Germans from different regions during these months made people conscious of belonging to one nation. The disappointment of the hopes placed in the Revolution made the people of Germany lose faith in the idea of liberal reform as a prelude to national unity. They did not give up the vision they had glimpsed during the years 1848-9 of a united Germany. Thereafter however they looked increasingly not to their own efforts but to the state to bring it about.

9

The 1850s: An Age of Prose?

The immediate consequence of the suppression of the Revolution in Germany and Austria was a return to reactionary rule. In Austria the new prime minister Schwarzenberg and a number of able cabinet colleagues created the policy known as neo-absolutism in the 1850s. If the rebellious were treated with great severity, belying the legend of dear fumbling Austria, the nobility, officer corps, bureaucracy and the middle class at large were for their part satisfied with an enlightened economic policy and the impression of firmness at the top. Alexander Pope's

> For forms of government let fools contest,
> What'er is best administered is best

could be an apt summary of Austrians' feelings about their state in the fifties and early sixties.[1] In Germany itself, and particularly in Prussia, the repressive measures after 1848 tended to be disconcerting rather than harsh. While Napoleon III and Francis Joseph had the walls of their capitals dismantled and cobbled streets paved and widened to prevent future revolutionaries from raising barricades, Frederick William regarded the city as the source of modern ills. People, he felt, should try to live in the country more; certainly young minds must be protected from contamination by the metropolis by having their schools, where possible, transferred to rural areas. He pronounced excessive education to be the chief source of unrest among his subjects and advised primary schools to concentrate only on the three R's and the catechism. He even had a number of teachers' training colleges opened in remote country districts in order to ensure that future teachers were exposed only to the 'right' influences. In his novel *Der Hungerpastor* (1864) Wilhelm Raabe sketched the story of a product of the Prussian King's educational policy, and won wide acclaim among the public. His hero, the generous-hearted but naive Hans Unwirsch, is born and educated in the provinces and eventually comes as a tutor to Berlin. Here he is so upset by the materialism and corruption of life in the big city that he flees to the 'true life' in a tiny village in the Baltic, where he lives happily ever after. The enormous success of this novel in Germany for many decades suggests that Germans liked to see themselves as unspoiled by the corruption of modern society, and to imagine to themselves the joys of Hans Unwirsch's quiet country retreat, without actually following his example.

Another aspect of reaction was much more significant. The Prussian bureaucracy was weeded of 'undesirable' elements on the basis of two laws passed in 1850 and 1853, and lost the moderately liberal character which had attracted able and enlightened men to its service previously. In the years following 1848 conformist officials began to penetrate parliament in Prussia, and the other German states.

The precarious mental stability of the Prussian ruler was permanently affected by the events of 1848–9. This brought about a change in the character of government in Prussia. Frederick William felt hurt and misunderstood in his affection for his people, but much more keenly he felt a sense of having betrayed a God-given trust in permitting the Revolution to advance as far as it had. He never, even now, doubted his own capacity or aims, and in 1850 tried to rectify matters by asserting Prussian leadership and royal authority in the Confederation. Austria reacted sharply and the two states came to the brink of war in November 1850 over the question of primacy in German affairs. However Prussia capitulated before Austria's demands to desist, and Russian intimidation, at the meeting between Prussian and Austrian ministers at Olmütz in the same year. This was widely accepted as a public humiliation of Prussia. The whole affair was not much more than a diplomatic incident, but was to become significant for its effect on the middle classes. It marked the end of Frederick William IV's political ambitions and the rise to eminence of Bismarck, then thirty-five years old. German public opinion, prompted by Bismarck, came to see Olmütz as a turning point in the relationship between Austria and Prussia. Hitherto Prussians had accepted the Austrian supremacy in Germany as a matter of course. The years of the Revolution had brought a rapid growth of political consciousness among Prussians, but Austria now had chosen to humiliate Prussia as she was taking hesitant steps in self-assertion. The conclusion subsequently drawn among Prussians was that Austria must be excluded from German affairs.

The strain of these years caused the King to rely more and more on those whose background and outlook approximated to his own. In 1850 he transformed the upper house of the Prussian Diet (*Landtag*) into a hereditary House of Lords. He allowed himself to be directed by the small group of landowners who dominated this upper house and who had created that influential organ of agrarian conservatism, the newspaper, *Die Kreuzzeitung*. This group, which came to be known as the *Camarilla,* included the two Gerlach brothers and the King's favourite Radowitz, a Silesian nobleman whom Bismarck once called 'valet to the King's imagination'. Their conservatism was less forceful and less relevant to the general economic situation in Germany in the fifties than was contemporary liberal thinking, but as Prussian Junkers they shared the desire for power of their class. They advocated a return to an organic society based on Christian principles, and thus disapproved of the economic and social aspects of post-revolutionary Germany. The *Camarilla* very often bypassed the official Prussian cabinet under the Prime Minister Otto von Manteuffel. Although its influence disappeared when William became Regent in place of his brother Frederick William in 1858, the Prussian Junkers retained an influence quite out of proportion to their number and their wealth, for they continued to dominate the upper house and the army. There was much in Prussian and indeed in German society in the second half of the century in their favour, especially the strong tendency towards conservatism in society which was part of a general reaction to too rapid industrialisation. There was also the fact of their physical proximity to the ruler which stemmed from the rigidly hierarchical structure of the Prussian court, and which was retained after Germany was unified under Prussia in 1871. The Junkers acted as a kind of filter between the King, later the Emperor, and external reality of which they, by reason of their narrow background and education, knew little.

As far as the authorities were concerned, the ten years between 1849 and 1858 deserve to be called an era of reaction. The fifties have therefore been characterised as a time of repression and disillusionment. It was only, now thirty years after its publication, that Schopenhauer's pessimistic *Die Welt als Wille und Vorstellung* became popular with intellectuals. The pessimism of Grillparzer's last plays, Stifter's reaction to the Revolution, the disappearance of the radical element in German politics with the exile of its leaders, and the quiescence of the working class movement between 1849 and 1863, all give substance to this picture. And yet it would be misleading to deduce from official policy or from the prophetic vision of a number of intellectuals the prevailing mood of the German people in the years after 1848. Taking Germany as a whole the overall impression is one of cautious confidence, not passive resignation. Despite the failure of the Revolution, the German bourgeoisie felt that their methods, not their aims, had been at fault. There was also a perceptible satisfaction that things had not got out of hand, while the curtailing of certain aristocratic privileges inspired them with confidence in the future. Indeed in the course of the fifties and sixties the bourgeoisie in Germany and particularly in Prussia went over from fear of revolutionary change to enthusiastic acceptance of evolutionary change, and looked to the future to remedy the ills of society. The belief grew among them that education and increasing material affluence opened up endless possibilities of dominating their surroundings. The decisive factor in moulding this attitude was the revolution in the economy.

The Revolution had lost much of its force when it became apparent in the winter of 1848–9 that the economic crisis of the last decade was already receding. The harvest of 1848 was good, food became cheaper, mills and factories began to open up, sugar refineries and chemical plants followed. These new enterprises were generally financed by foreign capital to begin with, and later by joint stock companies, using the capital of small investors. The first of the famous banks were founded in the fifties: the Dresden Bank in 1853, the Darmstadt Bank in 1856. Unemployment receded all over the country, partly owing to the judicious encouragement of emigration by the authorities. Although a brief setback to economic advance and social complacency came with the recession in 1857, affecting in particular West Germany, this was short-lived and by 1860 a period of consoidation had begun which lasted until the more serious crisis of 1873. By this later date the material wealth of the country and its inhabitants had increased vastly by comparison with 1850. Manteuffel in Prussia had pursued a vigorous economic policy in the fifties: he had extended the Customs Union and foiled Austria's attempt to penetrate and dominate it. Thus the confidence of commercial circles in the Prussian government grew, however much individuals might criticise the authorities' illiberal measures in the political sphere.

The industrial revolution came to Germany, and particularly to Prussia, with extraordinary suddenness; and it was as much the speed of change as the phenomenon itself which was to have such far-reaching consequences. Prussian encouragement of middle class participation in the industrial revolution has sometimes been presented as a clever political manoeuvre. But it was not simply a question of a reactionary government providing a distraction from politics, a 'sop' for which the people sold their birthright of political self-determination and their chance of a parliamentary democracy. Germain history in the fifties and sixties has too often been seen in terms of a 'betrayal' of the 'other Germany', since many writers of this time, members of an earlier idealistic generation, such as Gervinus, Gutzkow or Heine did see contemporary developments in this light. But for the majority of people in this period, the conditions of life and the needs of society were indeed changing. Christianity lost much of its appeal in public life; there was a general decline in the belief in the existence of immutable laws governing the universe. Speculative philosophy no longer attracted the middle classes; the country had produced no great systematic philosopher since Hegel. People were instead drawn to history, which they felt provided useful analogies with the present, and to the natural sciences, particularly chemistry and biology, which they thought would provide the means to enable them to dominate their environment. The ideas of the French thinker, Auguste Comte, found favour in Germany at this time, if only briefly. Positivism, as his thought was called, postulated an analogy between the laws of the physical sciences and the laws of human society; its followers rejected the existence of ultimate moral principles. Positivism was an apt creed for a period in European history when men's minds were absorbed with the present age, when tremendous changes in the economy, presaging even greater changes in society, made people feel the need for a philosophy based on empirical data, which would help them to orientate themselves in this new world. A growing number of Germans found themselves in a position, whether in commerce, industry or journalism, to regulate their lives and influence their surroundings in a manner unknown to them before. For the large class of state employees in Germany, the extension of the administrative machinery appeared to offer similar possibilities. All these factors combined to encourage Germans to concentrate more than before on contemporary affairs. National issues began to take precedence over regional ones in people's minds; current affairs in Europe engaged people in all walks of life. Germans read more widely, if perhaps less deeply, than in former times. The image of the German character began to change with the much greater mobility of life. It was in the fifties that construction of railway lines and new highways went forward apace; one of the most admired achievements of the decade being the great Semmeringer railway over the lower slopes of the Alps from Vienna to Italy, completed in 1854.

The importance of the press was even greater than it had been before 1848. The family journal became a kind of institution in the national life, the most popular of all being *Die Gartenlaube* (1853); with the astonishing increase in circulation figures of the daily and weekly press, a much greater variety of readers was reached than had previously been the case. An enormous public appetite for information was both fostered and satisfied and its political significance recognised. A genial press policy on the part of the Prussian prime minister Manteuffel and his assistants, Constantin Franz and Ryno Quehl, was able to win sympathy among large sections of the press which had formerly been hostile to Prussia; Manteuffel set up press bureaux, which won confidence for their reliability and their rapid transmission of news. The leading articles of many a non-Prussian newspaper in the fifties were quite obviously inspired by the Prussian news-agency. Manteuffel thus exploited in the Prussian interest the journalists' need to satisfy their editors. As Wuttke, a Saxon professor and a sharp critic of Prussia, wrote:

Thus all opponents were silenced and certain opinions on public affairs or views of prominent personalities were disseminated through the largest possible number of pages; the confidence of the reader who did not share these views was undermined, the enthusiasm of another was dampened, while that of a third was framed : every modification and deviation of Prussian policy was praised and the atmosphere made receptive to the line the Berlin cabinet wished to follow. A uniform picture was reflected in countless newspapers and so it was easy to identify the press agency with public opinion.[2]

Manteuffel's economic and press policies persuaded the middle class German of liberal opinions in this period that Prussia was in fact changing and that he could confidently look forward to enlightened Prussian leadership. But it was not Manteuffel, but Bismarck who profited by this.

The German industrial revolution brought a change in technique, not a new way of life. The industrial revolution in England and France had produced important technical inventions. In Germany it was characterised by the application of ideas and processes to the German industrial situation. In England it stretched over three quarters of a century, in Germany little more than three decades. This was possible because here industrialisation came late; Germany learned from her western neighbours and she already possessed the basis of a modern transportation and communications system before large-scale expansion began, which it did in the fifties. From the beginning the state was much more closely associated with industry and finance than was the case in England. State intervention was necessary owing to the structure of the economy, and also for political reasons. Such integration made for a high degree of rationalisation in manufacture, distribution and pricing, and towards the end of the century, it facilitated the forming of cartels. Public opinion in favour of state intervention in this period was stimulated by the work of the economist Friedrich List, who had not been read much in his lifetime. His *National System of Political Economy,* which had appeared in the year of his death, in 1846, advocated a planned national economy. Germany was late in the industrial field; direction by the state would help her through the difficult period when the economy was being transformed from an agrarian to an industrial one; individual liberty, he suggested, would be subordinated to a powerful administration during this period, but controls would cease once the process was complete. Germans found List's arguments persuasive in the fifties and sixties, and in subsequent decades he impressed them with his idea of a great economic continental block in Central Europe.

One of the positive aspects of state investment in industry became apparent in the chemical industry, which was rightly regarded as one of the best examples of German enterprise. The state subsidised scientific research at the universities, among other things in order to discover a substitute for indigo and so break the British monopoly. Such discoveries benefitted industry; thus German agriculture was helped by the artificial fertilisers developed by the great German chemist Liebig in his laboratories at Giessen. He taught for twenty-eight years at Giessen and twenty-one at Munich, investigating and stimulating inquiry into the fundamental processes of animal life. Foreign observers began to speak of German achievements with a new respect. Thus *The Engineer* of 25 March 1870 declared the state laboratories in Berlin, Leipzig and Bonn to be 'the nearest approach that has ever been made to realising Bacon's grand imagination of the New Atlantis – a university for experimental knowledge of the cosmos.'[3] Englishmen, such as John Cobden, admired the achievements of German education in promoting the industrial revolution. Colleges of technology, *Realschulen,* and commercial and technical schools were almost always pioneered by the state in Germany, and not, as in England, by individuals. These educational institutions increased in the fifties, for there was much talk of 'educating for industry' and its benefits. The technical schools laid the foundation on which the material prosperity of the nation was to be built. An industrialist, Joseph Mayer, whou founded the Penny Library in Germany in the fifties, coined the slogan 'Knowledge is freedom; knowledge is power!' In Germany the supply of technically-trained manpower was as essential to the expansion of industry as the high educational standard of entrepreneurs. Even at this time the Germans already set great store by the trained expert; this partly explains why the increasingly prosperous middle classes from the 1860s onwards were prepared to leave politics to state officials, who were, after all, the experts in their field. The social stigma attached to trade was less pronounced in Germany than in England in the second half of the nineteenth century, and it was said that, whereas in England the younger son of a good family went into the army or the church, in Germany he was destined for industry. In the fifties too the Junker code, whereby a landowner might not work his land for profit, but only to support his family, was relaxed; however, few Junkers had the necessary capital to invest. Their lack of contact with the world about them made them cling the more determinedly to their privileged social and political position.

The pre-capitalist classes that were opposed to social change in the 1850s and 1860s – privileged landowners, artisans and peasants – survived the period of industrialisation better than in other western countries and helped to inhibit social mobility in Germany. The efforts of the liberal civil servants in Prussia and elsewhere to abolish the monopoly of the guilds in the early decades of the century had been opposed by the paternalistic policies of the Prussian Kings, Frederick William III and IV. Other German states made concessions to the guilds at the height of the industrial revolution. It was not until the late 1860s that the principle of freedom of workers to move about the country and change their trade was legally established in Germany. Influential aristocratic circles in Prussia set the artisan and peasant classes apart as morally superior and politically more reliable than the factory workers. This paternalistic attitude was incorporated in commercial and industrial legislation and, besides acting as a brake on social mobility, helped to foster resentment among the less successful members of the lower middle class towards the industrial workers. The large stake held by the state in industry and commerce encouraged a bureaucratic structure in industry. The so-called open society of western industrial countries did not emerge in Germany, for the social rigidity characteristic of Germany before 1848 was not modified in any significant way by her industrial revolution. Titles, symbols of the small man's vicarious satisfaction, remained as coveted as they had been in the days before the bourgeoisie became wealthy.

The pace of industrialisation in Germany and its effects on society varied according to region. It was most rapid in West and Central Germany, and, apart from Lower Silesia, slow in the East and South. The main industrial regions were centred around the coalfields of the Ruhr, the Saarland and Silesia, and around the lignite and mineral deposits of Saxony. Thus all the major industrial regions, with the exception of Saxony, lay within Prussian territory. It is understandable that liberal businessmen found themselves in the fifties able to forget the repressive political role played by Prussia and concentrate instead on the benefits to be derived from her enlightened economic policies. The Prussian state actually owned the coalmines in the Saar as well as some of the deposits in Silesia and she attracted foreign investors. Saxony on the other hand had the highest concentration of urban centres within a comparatively small area; in 1846 she had the highest proportion of artisans in her population, and had the oldest manu-facturing and mining industries in Germany. Her important mineral deposits, her central position in the country, enabling her businessmen to derive maximum benefit from the railway net-work, brought a rapid changeover from domestic manufacture to factory work. The social changes brought hardship to many and in Saxony, in contrast with the rest of Germany, the 1848 Revolution was caused by economic and not political unrest. It was in Saxony that modern German socialism was born, and within her borders, in Gotha in 1875, that the Social Democratic Party emerged. (In later years it was in this state that the Communist party was to have its largest membership.)

The concept of two Germanies, the one north, the other south of the river Main, which people had begun to remark upon in the early nineteenth century seemed confirmed by the course of the industrial revolution. South Germany lacked the mineral deposits of Prussia or Saxony, though she had a longer commercial tradi-tion. Bavaria and Baden had little industry, indeed Munich had few factories before the outbreak of the First World War. The ruling classes, the artisans and the small farmers who made up Bavarian society until the 1880s showed little interest in the liberal and socialist ideas which engaged their fellow countrymen in the North in the second half of the nineteenth century. The contrast between Bavaria's provincial outlook and her relative lack of influence in national affairs, which was aggravated after 1871, and the development of the rest of the country, fostered her resent-ment towards Prussia. The Protestant areas of Bavaria, that is, in Franconia and the former free cities of the Holy Roman Empire such as Nuremberg, Ulm and Augsburg, developed somewhat differently from the rest of Bavaria. They could look back on a long trading history, and in these parts liberal enterprise devel-oped industries. Neighbouring Württemberg was largely Protes-tant and here too a native tradition of individual enterprise and self-help created family firms which prospered in the years of the industrial revolution. The liberal parties found here their strongest support south of the Main, and the Swabians were also the first in South Germany to recognise the economic as well as the political advantages of Prussia in the late fifties and in the sixties. Co-operative movements were started successfully in Württemberg and benefitted Swabian agriculture. Baden, in contrast, remained relatively backward, both in agriculture and in industrial development.

The main social consequence of the industrial revolution was the movement of population from the areas mentioned above towards the big cities – Hamburg, Frankfurt, Vienna and Berlin. Domestic industries inevitably declined and the Junkers, many of whom had such on their estates, suffered a further economic setback. It was not until the 1880s that legislation was introduced to deal with the consequences of rural depopulation and overcrowding in the cities. Society did not seem particularly aware of these problems, apart from some philanthropically minded individuals; few writers mentioned them in their work. German governments, although they intervened in the financing and organisation of industry, did not feel called upon to deal with its social effects; it was widely asserted that it was wrong to disturb the 'paternal' relationship between employer and employed by restricting hours and conditions of work. Indeed most of the early factory owners were *'Fabrikherrn'* (masters), like Herr Schmidt in Spielhagen's *Sturmflut*, who treated their employees much as they had been treated while still workers on the land; they regarded the idea of self-help among the workers in terms of disloyalty to themselves.

Germany was relatively slow in adapting herself to new methods of farming in the nineteenth century, at least by comparison with the United States and England. Agricultural production lagged well behind that of England, Denmark or Holland, although it is still true to speak of a 'revolution' in agriculture arising out of the industrial revolution. Among many innovations the most significant was the application of Thaer's theories and the discoveries of Liebig, 'the father of organic chemistry', to soil cultivation. Farm machinery began to be used more widely, especially after Germans had visited the Great Exhibition of 1851, which they did in large numbers. Here they also learned new methods of stock-breeding. West German industrial regions created a growing demand for food and the farming areas nearby were rationalised to cater for the need. In the remoter parts of Germany, such as Mecklenburg in the North and Pomerania in the East, the older methods continued; here a form of three-field cultivation continued to be practised well into the twentieth century; in Mecklenburg farm labourers were treated in practice, if not in theory, as no more than serfs, for the backwardness of these regions was proverbial. In the north west and in the south of Germany conditions of life on the farms were more congenial, but peasant proprietorship and lack of ready capital stood in the way of advance. Nevertheless it is a striking fact that by the end of the century, when Germany as a whole was highly industrialised and more than half the population was living in towns and cities, she still managed to produce nearly 70 per cent of her own food. Although the revolutionary methods in stock-breeding and cultivation were of course primary factors here, the dietary habits of the vast mass of Germans were almost equally important. Germany had gone over to large-scale cultivation of sugar beet in mid century; she produced her own pork and veal; but above all there was the native devotion to the potato, which was almost as unswerving as that of Irishmen.

The political aspect of the industrial revolution did not engage people's attention as immediately as might be supposed. As things stood in mid century, Austria and Prussia obviously offered alternatives to those who looked for direction in German affairs. Most people thought that the confrontation at Olmütz had settled the matter for the time being in favour of Austria, and right up to the actual outbreak of war between the two states in 1866, observers tended to assume the superiority of Austria. But she failed to consolidate her influence after 1848 in South and Central Germany whose common bond with Austria had been their dislike of the Prussian regime and their distrust of Prussian ambitions. Few people in Germany in the fifties recognised the fortunate timing, for Prussia, of the industrial revolution. They were hardly aware that between 1856 and 1867 Prussia's dexterous economic policy was preparing the way for the relatively smooth passage to German unity under Prussia in 1871. Bismarck, who became Prussian Prime Minister in 1862, inherited a very favourable situation from Manteuffel and his successor, and by exploiting Prussia's commercial treaties with France (1862) and Belgium (1863) and by his threat to dissolve the Customs Union in 1864, he established the fact of a community of interest between Prussia and the Central and South German states. This they were not prepared to sacrifice in support of Austria. Success was the real factor in attracting the *'Realpolitiker'* among the German bourgeoisie to Prussian leadership.

Towards the end of the fifties it became clear that Germany's political backwardness was standing in the way of her economic progress. A new urgency made itself felt in discussions on German politics, and when Austria was defeated by France and Sardinia in Italy in 1859, observers in Germany, particularly in Prussia, began to draw analogies between the situation in Italy and that in Germany. If Austria's defeat in Italy had so signally advanced Italian unity, could not something similar be achieved in Germany? A year previously Prince William, Regent of Prussia since 1858, had spoken of the 'moral' duty of Prussia to intervene in German affairs. Academic commentators, such as the historians Droysen and the young Treitschke, began to advocate unification on ethical, as well as economic and geographical grounds. In the course of the sixties the debates, letters and diaries of members of the union of liberals founded in 1859 (the *Nationalverein*) give evidence of an increasing preoccupation with the issue of unity, and the gradual conversion of the majority to the view that Prussia, whatever her faults, was most likely to achieve this.

'The old local and national self-sufficiency is being replaced by communications in every direction, by an all-round interdependence of nations.' Marx declared after 1848.[4] The growing awareness of national rather than regional questions in the years after 1848 was matched by a general sense of Germany's being part of a wider whole. This openness did not outlive Bismarck's wars, and already by the beginning of William I's reign (1861–88), the liberal German historians were beginning to show a sense of national exclusiveness. The years 1849 to the early sixties are in fact the period in the nineteenth century when the attitudes and aspirations of Germans approximated most closely to those of her neighbours in the west. Commercial circles stressed the similarities rather than the idiosyncrasies of European nations. Most Germans and the large number of sympathetic English and American observers began to look on the political and economic differences between their countries as merely stages of the same process. The political problems of Germany were widely felt to be something that time would solve.[5] Sympathy with England was general in Germany in these years. After all, Albert, brother of the patron of German liberalism, Duke Ernst of Saxe-Coburg-Gotha, had married Queen Victoria of England; their daughter Victoria married the heir to the Prussian throne, Frederick, in 1858 and began to exert her influence on behalf of liberal reform. These were the halcyon days of German middle-class liberalism, and just as a generation earlier English writers like Carlyle and George Eliot had been fascinated by German thought, so now English political writers and social novelists, especially Dickens and Thackeray, enjoyed a brief vogue in Germany. In the event it was Darwin and Spencer rather than Bentham or Mill who influenced German life and institutions. That German liberalism was not in fact a way of life, but a sectional commercial interest, at best the creed of a small number of idealists, only became apparent later. In the fifties and early sixties, to be middle class was to believe oneself a liberal, and the natural gregariousness of Germans, which had acted as a stimulus to political agitation before 1848, now received constant satisfaction in the form of associations and conferences. These culminated in the founding of the first liberal body on a nationwide basis, the German *Nationalverein,* one year after the Prussian regent had inaugurated the so-called New Era of liberal government in Prussia. The president of the *Nationalverein* was Duke Ernst of Saxe-Coburg-Gotha and it included among its members the leading figures in public life of the next decades, such as Bennigsen, leader of the National Liberal party (formed in 1867), and Schulze-Delitsch, founder of the co-operative movement in Germany.

In the period of 1848–71 the academics and in particular the historians contributed significantly to the growth of national consciousness in Germany. This was the great age of German historiography. In mathematics, physics and the social sciences, Germany was conscious of her debt to England and France; in history she led the world. A new generation of historical scholars emerged, who built on the foundations of the historian of Rome, Barthold Niebuhr and his pupil Leopold von Ranke. They investigated Germany's past, in particular the policies and achievements of her great medieval Emperors (Giesebrecht and Sybel), drawing analogies between Rome and Germany, as did Mommsen in his superbly written *Römische Geschichte* (1854–6), and they helped to focus interest in and sympathy for Prussia through their accounts of her past glories (Droysen's *Geschichte de preußischen Politik* 1858ff.). In the fifth volume of his monumental *History of Germany in the Nineteenth Century* (1878ff.), Treitschke proudly quoted Ralph Emerson's words: 'Germany thinks for others; these semi-Greeks grasp the science of all other peoples.'[6] As advocates of the constitutional state, and as opponents of Austrian autocracy and of German particularism, the German historians of these years regarded themselves as liberals. Few, apart from Mommsen, were to remain so. They were realistic, they felt, in their appraisal of the current situation, and as academics with experience of 1848 they thought it was their duty to direct public opinion in favour of a particular solution to the problem of German disunity. Ranke's seminar system, which he had employed to train his many students in his exact methods of scholarship, was now adapted by Sybel and others for political purposes. They chose periods for research which reflected Germany's past glories. They founded, and wrote for, periodicals which combined scholarly and political objectives. Sybel's *Historische Zeitschrift,* which became a leading periodical for historical research up to our own century, was founded in 1859. Sybel, then a professor at Munich, refused to accept contributions from monarchists, clericalists or radicals; the journal was intended to inform liberal opinion in Germany. The literary historian Haym, author of *Hegel und seine Zeit* (1858), one of the finest studies of contemporary literary history of these decades, edited the *Preußische Jahrbücher*; he was successful in attracting the services of the most able literary stylist and political propagandist amongst German historians: Heinrich von Treitschke (1834–96). At a different level and with a more educated readership in mind, these historians, few of whom were Prussian, played an important part in directing middle class opinion in Germany towards the notion of a German state that would exclude Austria; many of the best-known ultimately became Bismarck's most vociferous supporters.

Hermann Baumgarten, a South German historian and publicist, declared in retrospect that he and his colleagues had 'wanted to influence the world as much as promote scholarship'.[7] The political development of the German historians in these years was analogous to that of Germans in general. During the course of the war with Austria (1866) Baumgarten wrote to Heinrich von

Sybel: 'liberalism, I fear, has spoiled its chances. If the good people of Berlin had heeded my warnings at the end of May' (before war broke out) 'something might have been saved. Now, I fear, my prediction will come true: the people will turn its back on liberalism. But these anxieties are now secondary. Once we have a great state everything else can wait.'[8] In the half century from 1840 to 1890 the German academic moved from a position of moderate liberalism to conservative and often chauvinistic nationalism. Their stress in 1860s, during the period of Bismarck's wars of unification, on the need for a strong central authority in the state showed that these men were heirs to the Revolution of 1848 which had failed by parliamentary methods to solve the disunity of Germany. Bismarck's 'blood and iron' speech of 1862 has received more than its share of attention as a milestone in the evolution of German political attitudes, as well as in the process of unification. Three years earlier, Julius Fröbel, nephew of the great pedagogue, and himself a former democrat, had anticipated him. Sizing up the situation with penetration and with the acidity of the returned political exile he declared: 'The German nation is weary of principles and doctrines, literary renown and theoretical existence. What it wants is power – power – power. Whoever gives it power will be rewarded with honour beyond his wildest imaginings.[9] Rudolf Haym declared in an editorial in the *Preußische Jahrbücher* in 1863, following Bismarck's repressive law against the press: 'A nation is ready to give up much of its domestic freedom if, in return, it gains more power and prestige in the foreign field.'[10] Most other returned political exiles did not share Fröbel's critical attitude though they agreed with his analysis. Thus Arnold Ruge, or the lawyer Ludwig Bamberger, a liberal member of the Reichstag, became ardent nationalists; Ruge, the former Young Hegelian radical, had defended Prussian discrimination against the Polish minority in the Frankfurt Parliament in 1848 on the grounds of 'historic necessity'. By 1870 he was a fervent admirer of Bismarck from whom he eventually accepted a pension.

Thus the period between the end of the 1848 Revolution and the unification of Germany in the Second Empire in 1871 has the interim character of what was essentially a formative period. It determined the political and economic structure of the Empire and the social attitudes which were to persist until 1918. It was a time of opportunities, and most contemporaries were aware of them.

There existed conflicting theories on the function of the state and the role of the individual in society: the conservative romantic, the secularist liberal and the biological materialist. No one body of ideas is completely characteristic of the age. Literature and the arts reflected the lack of uniformity which the foreigner regarded as typical of the German scene, and which they, like the Germans themselves, held responsible for the relative backwardness of the country.

Karl Gutzkow and the Nineteenth Century German Novel

The German Romantics, who had such a complex and lasting influence on the theory and practice of nineteenth century literature, believed that the novel was a literary genre particularly suited to the age. Writers of successive generations in Germany from Immermann to Raabe and Fontane strove to comprehend contemporary reality in great epic works which took the form of novels. And yet despite their efforts the German novel is neither well known nor highly regarded today. In the years before 1848 few German critics or the reading public looked on the novel as a genre in its own right; it was still considered modern to write one. Schiller's patronising reference to the novelist as 'half-brother of the poet'[1] was more often quoted than the Romantics' advocacy of the genre, and as if to confirm prejudice Hegel hardly mentioned the subject in his aesthetical writings. When Gervinus asserted in his influential literary history that 'that hotchpotch known as the novel'[2] was unfortunately supplanting the epic, he was referring to the specific instance of the novels of the Young Germans and their imitators, which he did not admire.

This low opinion of a great literary form was partly the result of the fact that many German writers in the first half of the century were not quite certain as to what actually constituted a novel. The boundary between the various forms of prose fiction was at that time by no means as clear as present day literary historians assume.[3] Would-be novelists had no tradition to draw upon.*

*This helps to explain the extraordinary influence of Goethe's novel, *Wilhelm Meisters Lehrjahre* (1795–6), which dominated not only the so-called *Bildungsroman* of which it was the prototype, but also the sentimental family novel which became widely popular in the second half of the century.

Their readers were not acquainted with the novel as a vehicle of social criticism. There is no equivalent in nineteenth century Germany of the long social novel which was dominant in England from about 1840 to the time of Galsworthy. Germany had no Dickens, Eliot, Thackeray or Gaskell. Nor were English novelists well known in Germany, although for a time after 1850 Dickens and Thackeray became popular. However Dickens was chiefly admired as the creator of amusing characters and ingenious plots. The English had almost no influence in the direction of social comment, while the French novelists such as Balzac and Stendhal were scarcely read and were disliked as being materialistic and cynical.

The writer of serious novels in Germany at least up to the 1880s felt constrained to invest his work with some 'higher significance', some idea which would edify his readers. This almost always precluded the portrayal of contemporary social reality. The only writer, apart from the rather special case of Gotthelf, to merit consideration as a social novelist before 1880, Karl Gutzkow, failed to write a great novel of the times because he felt it necessary to add some sort of pseudo-philosophic justification to his work. Thus in *Die Ritter vom Geiste* (1850–2), his best novel, the idea of a moral élite which will bring about the spiritual regeneration of Germany is awkwardly superimposed on his portrait of society in Prussia at the end of the 1848 Revolution.

Gutzkow's fame as a novelist belongs to the fifties, but it owed a good deal to his own efforts as a young man to draw attention to the novel as a serious literary form. As the acknowledged spokesman of the Young Germans, his own novel, *Wally die Zweiflerin,* had certainly brought him more criticism than praise. However it had won the novel many new readers. Gutzkow's publicity encouraged young writers to try their hand at a novel in defence of whatever cause lay close to their hearts, whether Polish liberty, the emancipation of the Jews, the improvement of woman's place in society or the iniquity of machines. Women writers in particular took advantage of the new interest in this literary form. The most successful in the 1840s were Countess Hahn-Hahn and Fanny Lewald, whose first novel, *Jenny,* an autobiographical account of the social and professional difficulties of a Jewish woman writer, won great acclaim on its appearance in 1842. The bulk of novels which appeared in the next two decades were tendentious. Far more care was lavished on the 'idea' of the novel than on its character or plot, and indeed many of the figures were mere mouthpieces for their authors. But to be called tendentious was not considered derogatory by German writers. Indeed the reverse was true: English novelists were often dismissed as superficial precisely because they lacked '*Tendenz*'. It scarcely needs to be said that the vast majority of German works of this type are not read today.

After about 1871 Gutzkow's reputation as a writer and critic declined rapidly. His unattractive personality made him many enemies among his fellow writers whom he liked to improve and correct. Many of these writers were also literary critics whose views were incorporated into the standard literary histories. They villified him in his lifetime and after he died in 1878, also because he was one of the few German liberals who refused to be drawn into the wave of national enthusiasm which accompanied unification. Their view of Gutzkow as a derivative writer who enjoyed a brief notoriety has persisted largely to the present time. Some modern critics have even found it necessary to restate old prejudices. Thus in the recent edition of *Deutsche Literaturgeschichte in Grundzügen*, Karl Fehr in his essay on realism suggests that Gutzkow, author of 'unintelligent and boring' works would hardly be worth mentioning but for the fact of his critical reception of 1871.[4] A student reading this would naturally deduce that Gutzkow's novels are not worth bothering about. Since he makes things difficult for potential readers by the sheer length of his works, very few find themselves in a position to challenge the accepted view of Gutzkow as a novelist. His allusions to contemporary figures are a further obstacle, since no critical edition exists of either *Die Ritter vom Geiste* or *Der Zauberer von Rom* (1858–61), and copies of the latter are hard to come by.

Yet Gutzkow merits closer examination for several reasons; in particular because he came closest of any German writer between 1830 and 1880 to making good the obvious omission of German literature in this period, namely the social novel of the times. He took for granted that society was man's natural element. He was curious about the way people behaved and what they talked about, nor did he confine his curiosity to a particular class. He was amused at the discrepancy between people as they saw themselves and as they really were. Gutzkow is not usually credited with humour, but in fact he created several humorous and witty portraits, particularly of women, in whom he felt this discrepancy was most common. Examples of these are the political hostess Pauline von Harder and the middle-aged provincial Frau von Salm, married to a man much older than herself and with a penchant for sentimental young men (*Die Ritter vom Geiste*), or Herta Wingolf in *Die Nihilisten* (1853), an emancipated young woman who smiles as she surveys the lace napkins and shining silver on the tea table set for an intimate tea with her gentleman friend, before curling up in an armchair to peruse a work by the atheist philosopher Feuerbach. (This lastnamed short novel contains one of the funniest incidents in nineteenth century German fiction, the episode of the capture of a pet goat from the local Junker, who eventually marries the ringleader of the plot.) Very few German novelists thought it of interest to the reader to include the kind of realistic details in their narratives which reflect a way of life of a society. Even a novelist like Spielhagen, who expressly wrote about middle class society, used a stereotyped setting for almost all his many novels. Thus such features of Gutzkow's art as the indirect characterisation of Pauline von Harder through a description of her town residence,[5] or the wonderfully vivid rendering of a country child's impressions of city life from the narrow quarters of her mistress's flat in the early chapters of *Der Zauberer von Rom* were rarely equalled by his contemporaries.

Die Ritter vom Geiste was written in 1849–51 and published in serial form; the action was set in the present. It is a portrait of state and society in Prussia in the uneasy years immediately following the Revolution, and it presents a story of love, intrigue and moral development of a number of characters drawn from every social class. On this, his original plan, Gutzkow superimposed the story of the 'Knights of the Spirit' which gives the book its title, a sort of new masonic order which sets itself the task of restoring idealism to society. His canvas was immense. There are some seventy characters in the story, whose destinies are linked in mysterious ways. A good deal of Dickensian contrivance is of course required to connect the lives of the main characters through illicit unions and secret documents so beloved of serial readers; for the novel is almost 2,000 pages long.

Gutzkow anticipated his critics to some extent by providing them with a new theory of the novel. As a critic himself and a

journalist of some twenty years experience he knew what the
public liked, and rightly felt they would accept his work more
readily if it were based on some aesthetic theory. The forties and
fifties were something of a heyday of aesthetic discussion. Writers
introduced their imaginative works with solemn prefaces or filled
the columns of literary journals with their deliberations, as for example Hebbel, Stifter, or the minor writers like Otto Ludwig,
Vischer and Spielhagen. And, true enough, Gutzkow's contemporaries spent much more energy and ink on the merits and demerits
of what he termed the 'novel of *Nebeneinander*' than on the book
itself. We need not bother too much about Gutzkow's theory. What
it meant in practice was that his purpose was to present the reader
with a truly representative cross-section of contemporary life within
a sharply defined period.

The principal characters in the story are the brothers Dankmar
and Siegfried Wildungen, who represent the intellectual capacity,
the willpower and the creative imagination of the middle class.
Representatives of the nobility are Prince Egon von Hohenberg,
who succeeds to his father's impoverished estate at the beginning
of the story, and the politically ambitious Pauline von Harder, once
a close friend of his mother Amalia, who is in possession of the
secret knowledge that Egon is in fact the illegitimate son of the
lawyer Heinrich Rodewald, now known as Ackermann. Egon's
old teacher Rudhard is the type of traditional Lutheran clergyman
and is contrasted with the modern cleric of social ambitions and
literary pretensions, Guido Stromer. In Louis Armand, a former
friend of Egon's in his radical youth, and Luise Eisold and their
circle we have the artisan and factory working classes, while the
young sergeant Sandrart provides a link with the peasant world.
In no. 9 Brandgasse, where Luise Eisold and her younger sisters
and brothers live with their great-grandfather, and where much
of the action takes place, we also meet criminals, prostitutes and
spies. Finally, in Ackermann Gutzkow included a topical portrait
of the returned American.

Ackermann plays an important structural role in the novel: his
return from America sets events in train, for he is not only the
possessor of several guilty secrets involving other persons, but he
has had liaisons with three principal characters and is the father
of two more. Ackermann's character is based to a large extent on
that of Henry Simon (cf. p. 25), the lawyer and revolutionary,

whose brief affair with the popular novelist Countess Hahn-Hahn in the 1840s had provided gossipmongers with such promising material. *Die Ritter vom Geiste* abounds in portraits of Gutzkow's contemporaries, not usually flattering to them; these include the new Prussian Prime Minister Manteuffel (Egon), Radowitz, the King's adviser and intimate friend (General Voland von der Hahnenfeder), Prince Pückler-Muskau (Otto von Dystra), presented here as an ugly old man who proposes marriage to almost every young girl he meets. The King of Prussia, Frederick William IV, does not actually appear, but an extremely lifelike and critical portrait of him is painted by the main protagonists. This is a feature of the novel which certainly appealed more to contemporaries than it does to modern readers.

Apart from his personal role in the novel, Ackermann is interesting in his public capacity. He uses his considerable wealth to try and remedy the wretched state of agriculture, one of the immediate causes of the Revolution, by introducing new farming methods learnt in the United States. Ackermann's technical knowledge of machinery – 1851 was the year of the Great Exhibition in London which many Germans visited – and his readiness to supervise and discuss new methods with his employees, suggest the ideal type of entrepreneur in these early days of the industrial revolution in Prussia. In the figure of Ackermann and in his sympathetic portraits of the factory and domestic workers in this novel, Gutzkow was perhaps attempting to counter the harsh polemics against industrialism of Ernst Willkomm in his novel *Die Sklaven* (1845). Ackermann's successful career reflects the current optimism in Germany engendered by the promise of material improvements and prosperity. The same optimism is not extended to the political scene. The effect of the policies of the authorities after 1848 are described, as are the fatuous attempts of the monarch and his court to restore piety as an alternative to political reform. The activities of the 'Knights' themselves are not particularly fruitful, though Gutzkow undoubtedly did not intend to give this impression. However he does succeed very well in representing the variety of political opinion in the state. Unlike his rival Freytag he is not prejudiced in favour of a specific political viewpoint, but shows how people's political opinions are formed by their personal circumstances, experience and character. The scenes where he provides a cross section of current attitudes are among the best in the book, such as the scene in the inn early on in the story, where the laywer and political intriguer Schlurck argues with the cabinetmaker Armand and Prince Egon in the disguise of an artisan, and Justus Heidekrüger, a former democrat, joins in,[6] or the political dialogue between the brothers Dankmar and Siegfried, stimulated by the avid curiosity of their barber, Herr Zipfel.[7]

The most original feature of this novel is the portrait it contains of the German working classes. Like Dickens, who influenced him, Gutzkow's working-class girls, such as Luise Eisold and her friend Fränzchen, are somewhat idealised figures, and occasionally he assumes an air of middle class satisfaction at the sight of the industrious poor. In general however his portrait of working-class life is realistic and unsentimental. He showed in precise detail how this first generation of urban workers settled and made a living in Berlin in mid century. There is a wonderfully plastic scene in which the author describes the living conditions of a poor artisan family such as that of the Eisolds: the eighteen year old Luise Eisold sets up the beds for her family of eight from drawers, chairs, straw mattresses etc. The brothers Wildungen, who are visiting the Eisolds' tenant Hackert, look on, but soon find there is no room for them as Luise, perhaps impatient at their unnecessary admiration of her, finishes her task.[8] On the bottom floor of the same house in the Brandgasse, Frau Mullrich, the first of a long line of evilly minded concierges in German fiction, watches the movements of her tenants. With her husband, a police spy, she supplements the house-keeping with a little blackmail, for both are fully aware of the dubious character and connections of most of the house's inhabitants. Gutzkow had lived as a child in surroundings such as he described, and he continually reminds his readers of the force of character needed to live a decent life in such circumstances. There is none of the 'rustic idyll' of working-class life which occurs, for example, in Fontane. Gutzkow was probably the first German novelist to show the importance of working men's associations in helping them to retain their self-respect: the appeal of such associations or clubs to the *déraciné* agricultural workers was the sense of belonging which they gave them. 'If a man is not working in the evening, he goes to the association,' Alberti, one of Karl Eisold's colleagues, tells Ackermann.[9]

Although the novel is so long, it is – apart from the solemn passages on the 'Knights of the Spirit' – very readable. The portraits of women contribute much to the reader's entertainment, and the most successful of these are undoubtedly his middle-aged and aging women, notably Pauline von Harder and her confidante Charlotte von Ludmer. Pauline is a former society beauty, whose literary reputation some years earlier was less a tribute to her talents as a novelist than to her generosity with her favours. (In this clear allusion to Countess Hahn-Hahn, Gutzkow betrayed the fact that the former Young Germans had now little time for literary or indeed emancipated women.) Now of mature years, she decides that political intrigue is likely to be of more lasting value to her than her remaining charms. She is not, however, prepared to admit this even to herself, as is clear from a conversation with Schlurck: ' "Yes, indeed, Schlurck, I'm nearly fifty. I'm heroically outspoken about the truths which one can no longer deny!" .... Schlurck ... smiled for he knew she ought to have said, "nearly sixty".'[10] The politically engaged woman was a phenomenon of mid century and soon disappeared. Gutzkow showed he was aware of the change of taste by making Pauline seem an archaic figure before the novel ends, and in bringing about a change in the character of his middle class heroine, Melaine Schlurck. Her vivacious personality and mental alertness give place to sober respectability after her marriage to Egon, who has discovered the true story of his origins; in the same way the pert Fränzchen and her friend Luise Eisold became model housewives.

Besides this and other modifications of social types in the novel, which reflect contemporary changes, Gutzkow includes allusions to almost every aspect of life which engaged his contemporaries: the advent of the railways, their impact on social as well as economic life, the growth of factories, of industrial speculation, the influence of the journals on public opinion, the efforts of the Prussian Junkers to organise a conservative league in defence of agrarian interests, and the prevalent fear of communism. However for reasons stated he could not trust his public to be satisfied with the human scene alone. This is why he felt it necessary to impart some 'message' by means of the élite, the 'Knights of the Spirit', which would make the contemporary scene meaningful; in this he was being true to the didactic tradition of German prose. It was an unfortunate decision, and the main cause of his failure to write a great novel. It seems as if he was unconsciously aware of this, for the *Ritter* episode is not properly integrated into the novel.

The association of the 'Knights' was essentially a middle-class one, though it drew members from all social classes. By showing its practical achievements to have been negligible and by allowing the documents which were to finance their philanthropic activities to be destroyed at the end of the novel, Gutzkow anticipated the failure of German middle class efforts at self-assertion in the political field in the years 1848–71.

As a work of art *Die Ritter vom Geiste* is not comparable with the works of the great English social novelists, but the difference is one of degree, not of kind, as is the case with the other German novelists of this time. Gutzkow was concerned with relationships in society and with how the physical circumstances of a person's environment influence his social character. The case of Gutzkow seems to confirm the thesis that Germany's lack of a capital city goes far to explain the weakness of the social and political dimension in her literature. A city child, he had grown up in the centre of Berlin; the squalid atmosphere of his native city had had a formative influence on his imagination.[11] Gutzkow was the first German novelist to show what it was really like to be a poor artisan or an escaped prisoner or a prostitute in metropolitan Berlin. *Die Ritter vom Geiste* has obvious aesthetic flaws. It does not perhaps deserve to be included among the great imaginative novels of nineteenth century Germany, Goethe's *Die Wahlverwandtschaften*, Keller's *Der grüne Heinrich*, Stifter's *Der Nachsommer* or Fontane's *Unwiederbringlich*. But its many merits seem the greater because they are uncommon in German writing. It is a novel of the age and in it Gutzkow wished to entertain and inform the widest possible section of society about contemporary Prussia. The most obvious defects, the idealistic fancies of the 'Knights', the tendency of leading figures, particularly Dankmar and Siegfried, to philosophise when we might reasonably expect them to act, are aesthetic ones; as the observations of a social critic they are accurate: they do reflect the propensity of the middle classes of the time and their habits in social intercourse and political life.

The novel was well received by the public. It was very expensive, costing eleven *thalers*, but it sold well and attracted the praise of such different critics as Keller and Hebbel. It was however greeted with almost frenzied condemnation by the editors of an influential literary journal, *Die Grenzboten,* namely Gustav Freytag and Julian Schmidt. It is ironic that critics have since habitually linked Gutzkow with Freytag (and Spielhagen) as the popular novelists of the time. Certainly all three wrote about society and they appealed to a growing public which was eager to be entertained and edified. But whereas Freytag and Spielhagen made ready concessions to the taste and prejudices of their readers, Gutzkow did not. Freytag presented middle-class society in the fifties and sixties as the middle class liked to see themselves. Spielhagen did much the same, and if after 1871 his novels satirised the new rich, he was always careful to provide a manly, idealistic and successful hero with whom his readers could identify themselves. The wrongness of bracketing Gutzkow with his two younger contemporaries is further demonstrated if one compares their styles. Gutzkow is admittedly an uneven writer and in his love scenes is inclined to rely too much on literary models. These apart, he writes with vigour, with an eye for detail and atmosphere and the propensity we associate with the European novel of the nineteenth century for sage and witty observation of the common run of humanity. How flat and contrived Spielhagen seems after reading Gutzkow (except in his comic scenes); while Freytag in his best known novel *Soll und Haben* is a typical example of the *Bildungsphilister*, continually using the expressions of earlier writers, especially Goethe, as if they were his own.

The reading public were able to follow the feud between Gutzkow and Freytag through the literary reviews each wrote in the periodicals with which they were associated, Gutzkow in his *Unterhaltungen am häuslichen Herd* (1854), which he had founded in imitation of Dickens' *Fireside Chats,* and Freytag in *Die Grenzboten*. The quarrels between prominent writers in the 1850s actually increased public interest in their work. But whereas Gutzkow's popularity declined in the next decade, Freytag and Spielhagen continued to be read enthusiastically for many decades, and had the highest sales amongst the nineteenth-century German novelists. Freytag and Spielhagen owed their popularity largely to their choice of subject, the milieu and aspirations of the German middle class at the time in which they wrote. It was partly in reaction to 1848 that all three novelists were able to awaken public interest in developments outside Germany: the vision of the brotherhood of nations and the progress of knowledge and human happiness, evoked by Prince Albert at the opening of the Great Exhibition in 1851, had struck a chord in German breasts.

The more lasting popularity of Freytag and Spielhagen derived from their interest in nationalism. This was particularly the case with Gustav Freytag (1816–95), who helped to create a kind of mythology of German nationalism through his writings in these years. Thus the rising of 1813, which for a novelist like Immermann had been simply a patriotic incident, in which he and others like him had taken part, appear in Freytag's novels as 'a popular rising'. His most successful novel *Soll und Haben* (1855), like his *Bilder aus deutscher Vergangenheit*, (1859–67) a kind of historical chronicle, and *Die Ahnen* (1872–80), a family chronicle stretching back far into Germany's past, presented an idealised version of German history to middle-class readers. One aspect of his interpretation found great favour and did much to boost national self-confidence among Freytag's readers: this was the notion of the 'cultural mission' of Germany in Central Europe, which had been fashionable with the Romantics. In Freytag's work this was elaborated to demonstrate Germany's ethical as well as cultural superiority over her eastern neighbours. In *Soll und Haben* the lack of a cultural tradition among the Slavs and the Jews in eastern Europe is shown to degrade them to a point where they cannot improve themselves; not only are they physically unattractive, but they lack the morality of the German. Freytag's influence was considerable in Germany. He owed his position initially to the patronage of Duke Ernst of Saxe-Coburg-Gotha, who conferred on him the title of *Hofrat* to save him from Prussian persecution for his liberal ideas in the reactionary climate of the early fifties. But Freytag is typical of many middle-class Germans, who in the fifties became ready to overlook Prussian reactionary policies for the sake of her potential ability to lead Germany. He concurred in the view expressed by German historians such as Heinrich von Sybel, that the 'true' Germany was Protestant and Prussian, and that the connection with the Holy Roman Empire and with Austria had been against her national interests. He certainly inspired others with his own enthusiasm for Prussia: on the occasion of his seventieth birthday, in 1886, many tributes were paid to him such as that of the philologist Scherer who declared that he owed his nationalist feeling to the work of two people, Jakob Grimm and Gustav Freytag. In his own person Freytag linked 1848 and 1871 and blended the abstract idealism of the liberals with practical Prussian politics.

Soll und Haben was probably the most widely read novel of the century. It is the story of the material and moral triumph of a self-made man in contemporary Germany. It describes the early years of the industrial revolution, the first fruits of which are shown in the form of greater material wealth among the enterprising bourgeoisie, pledged to uphold authority in their families and in their business. This seems to Freytag synonymous with culture: he draws a sharp contrast between the world of his hero, Anton Wohlfahrt, and the Jews and Slavs among whom he works in his native Silesia. His Jewish counterpart is shown to be not only morally inferior but physically repulsive, a significant association for future anti-semitism. Although ostensibly exalting bourgeois morality, Freytag makes no attempt to conceal his adulation of the nobility. A contemporary English commentator on the novel, three translations of which had been published in England by 1858, pointed out that an English reader might find it hard to understand how a *von* before the name of Fink, one of the characters in the commercial house where Wohlfahrt works, was sufficient to ensure his social position and authority.[12] An interesting feature of the novel is that it foreshadowed the self-imposed limitations of the German middle class. Anton does not exploit his position at the end of the novel to marry into the aristocracy and enter public life; he prefers the hand of the elderly and domesticated sister of his late employer and the life of commerce. Neither politics nor public affairs attract the successful businessman who is concerned merely with the exercise of his profession. According to Freytag he is therefore a moral example worth following. Another point of interest arising from this social compendium of the contemporary middle-class mind is the snobbery associated with education and material possessions, the one seen as the preliminary to the other. The mania for titles was growing more marked in this and the following generation: as the content of the classical humanist ideal of education diminished, outward marks received greater emphasis. The extent to which bourgeois self-respect depended on outward forms only became fully apparent when they were robbed of these by the upheavals of the post-war world in the twentieth century.

From 1860 to the beginning of naturalism in the 1880s, the serious German novel was dominated by Friedrich Spielhagen (1829–1911), whose novels run into thousands of pages. The novelist, according to Spielhagen, is at one and the same time agitator, pedagogue and poet; though his own works are contemporary novels of manners, their purpose is to acquaint men with the 'challenge of the age'. Spielhagen's attitude contrasts with the prevailing note in Stifter, Keller or Storm, his contemporaries. We are not used to optimism in German writers. The positivist Spielhagen extols the potentialities of economic and political reform and of scientific discoveries: men will be better for responding to the opportunities of the age. The doctor in *Problematische Naturen* (1861) excitedly anticipates the future benefits of medical research; others look to the day when class barriers will fall in the general search for a better world. Although the pessimism of some of his heroes shows that Spielhagen had fallen under Schopenhauer's spell, the minor characters, which are much the most convincing, present the positivist position. Like most Germans he stressed the growing importance of the state, but he also gave due importance to economic questions. He was bitterly attacked by the naturalists in the 1880s, but he remained popular: the eighty-first edition of his *Problematische Naturen* appeared in 1918. The exaggerated pathos and wishful thinking of the middle-class protagonists of Spielhagen's novels was an accurate reflection of the contemporary mood especially from the mid sixties onwards. Occasionally he satirised their pretensions, as in the character of the vicar's wife and would-be poetess Primula and her circle (see p. 29), but he generally took his solemn heroes and heroines seriously. Perhaps in his desire to write novels of lasting fame – he was a tireless theoretician of the novel and published his disquisitions, *Beiträge zur Theorie und Technik des Romans* in 1882 which were respectfully received – he neglected his real talent, which was for comedy. Almost all his novels contain robust and witty minor characters, or brief humorous scenes, as for example the exploratory conversation between the valet and the coachman of two Prussian noblemen in chapter seven of *Sturmflut* (1875) which begins: 'We are widowers' (referring to his master, von Warnow), 'What are you?'

In his later novels, most notably in *Sturmflut,* a study of the social causes and the course of the financial speculation and crash of 1873, Spielhagen showed himself to be an acute observer of contemporary society. The same type of blue-eyed and manly hero of hard working middle-class origin which we encounter in earlier works, manages again to bring events to a happy conclusion. However, whereas formerly Spielhagen had indulged in moral condemnation of the Prussian aristocracy, now he was more interested in social analysis and more penetrating in his interpretation of social change. The action of the later novels is set, not in some remote country estate, but in Berlin. This novel excels in the portrayal of social functions, in a manner which anticipates the achievements of Fontane in his novels of the 1880s. The party in von Warnow's house in *Sturmflut* deserves special mention, with the long conversation among the guests about Wagner, in which the tyrannical old gossip and society figure, Baroness von Kniebreche, tries to probe the matrimonial projects of the younger members of her 'set'.[13]

In the history of the German novel Spielhagen is an interesting if minor figure; his work and its appeal for the German reading public in the second half of the nineteenth century is relevant in this context because it reflects so accurately the self-analytical spirit of the German middle classes just before and immediately after the unification of the country.

11

The German Form of Realism
1840-80

The years between the Revolution of 1848 and the founding of
the German Empire in 1871 can be seen in retrospect as forming a
political and economic unity of a kind, but little such unity can be
discerned in the literature of the time. The year 1871 certainly
brought a change of emphasis in most writers' work, but if one
wishes to characterise German literature in general terms, it is
necessary to consider the period from about 1850 to the late 1880s.
This is the age of European realism and Germany too had her
place in it. However, although human experience was now presented in more concrete terms, German writing showed many features
not usually prominent in realist fiction or poetry. It is true that
German realist writers, among whom Stifter, Keller and Storm, and
also Fontane and Raabe (see Chapter 14) may be included,
appeared to avoid the specifically nineteenth-century scene as a
subject of literature: realism understood as the objective representation of contemporary life against a background of gradual
historical change is not characteristic of German imaginative writing between 1850 and 1885. Much of the criticism levelled at nineteenth-century German realism derives from the fact that it is not
naively mimetic.[1] Stifter, Keller and Raabe were keenly sensitive to
the changes going on around them, but their interpretation of these
in their work as problematical and contradictory is often dismissed
by critics as evidence of failure to come to grips with the times.
Unlike their European contemporaries, they tried to represent the
ethical rather than the social or political import of the revolutions
they witnessed. In doing so they were following the tendency
traditional since the eighteenth century among German writers to
stress the ethical dimensions of man's experience, and to regard
the individual's relationship with society as problematical.

Certainly the relationship of the artist to society as Stifter,

Raabe, Fontane, and to a lesser extent Keller experienced it was not a particularly happy one. It was not simply that they were unsuccessful in capturing the attention of the public for what they wrote, but that the type of work which the educated middle classes admired was so very inferior. At least it seemed so to them, and their judgement was confirmed by later generations. There was throughout the second half of the nineteenth century a marked imbalance between literary achievement and popularity. As has often been pointed out, rarely has any period experienced such a radical reversal of its literary preferences than these years in Germany. An uneasy relationship between the serious writer and society thus determined the character of German, as against European creative writing at this time. The way in which a French writer could take his position in French society for granted remained an object of wonder and envy now as it had been for Börne in the thirties. But whereas in the earlier period the writer had faced primarily political difficulties, now he experienced a loss of the sense of community of which he was part and to which he might speak. Nearly every important writer came from a relatively stable provincial background, and the process of his outgrowing this background (Stifter, Keller, Storm) coincided with his development as a mature artist. And yet the 'cultural centres' in which this experience was gained – Stifter in Vienna, Keller and Storm in Berlin – proved narrow indeed. They discovered that fashion dictated taste in art as well as in dress and décor, and that popularity and literary seriousness were apparently mutually exlusive. That a rather superficial interpretation of their work allowed them a brief vogue – such as Stifter enjoyed for his early work – can hardly have consoled them. They shared an acute sense of misrepresentation or ignorance on the part of the critics and the public. They sought understanding in each other, and their correspondence, in particular that of Keller with Storm and with their young friend Paul Heyse, affords interesting reading on the social and material aspects of a writer's life. A good deal of space in their letters is occupied with the discussion of literary genres, a preoccupation of German aesthetics since the eighteenth century. It is entertaining to contrast the sober domesticity of the three above-mentioned writers as reflected in their correspondence with the ebullience of the Romantic poets fifty years earlier. The mid century writers were not only domestic, they wished to seem so;

they wanted an integral position in the social structure of their time as artists, and this they did not feel they had achieved.

Many of course did have their work published in the literary journals with responsible editors, such as Julian Schmidt's *Grenzboten, Westermanns Monatshefte* edited by Julian Rodenberg and the *Deutsche Rundschau,* modelled on the *Revue des deux mondes.* Of these journals the *Rundschau* deserves special mention, although the period of its greatness belongs a little later: from its founding by Rodenberg in 1874 until 1888. If the novelists Gotthelf, Alexis, Auerbach and Ludwig and the dialect writers Reuter and Groth became well-known names through their association with the *Grenzboten,* Rodenberg introduced writers to the public who had less immediate popular appeal. He not only published the work of Storm, Keller, Meyer and Fontane, as well as the essayists Grimm and Hillebrand; he also coaxed and encouraged writers whom he, a novelist himself, recognised as having great talent. In fact he helped to create a market for the late works of many of the realist writers; although often recognition came too late to restore their self-confidence as artists in society.[2] Book publication usually followed serialisation, but in the face of the post-1850 phenomenon of the bestseller, where a writer like Freytag or Scheffel might see close on one hundred printings of a work in his life time, less successful writers who maintained high artistic standards did feel their failure to reach the reading public.

The characteristics of German literature in its major and minor writers distinguish the first half of the century clearly from the first. There are no more Christian writers after Gotthelf. The metaphysical dimension gave way to a brief optimistic positivism in Freytag and Spielhagen, and later, in Meyer and others, to a relativisation of values which is strikingly modern. The prose fiction of this period generated little of that moral energy in Germany which one associates with English fiction in the same era; this was in keeping with the noticeably weaker belief in the individual's ability or his right to influence his surroundings. The literary genres favoured by writers also altered after 1850. It was, as Heine had said of the pre-revolutionary years, an age of prose. The drama declined, although it remained very popular as a form of entertainment. French plays by Dumas, Sardou and Feuillet, captivated middle-class audiences. But after Hebbel's *Nibelungen* (1861), which owed its success mainly to its national theme, Germany produced no major dramatic work for over twenty years. The popular theatre declined also, and although Keller expressed hopes as to its future after seeing a Viennese company perform in Berlin in the fifties, these were not fulfilled. A native tradition of satire in the form of political cabaret did not establish itself in Berlin until the end of the century. The operettas of the German-born French composer Offenbach satisfied the taste for spectacle in Vienna and in other big cities; they played to bourgeois audiences whose new and increasing affluence gave them cosmopolitan airs.

The taste in lyric poetry also changed about mid century; the 'confessional' type of lyric associated with Goethe and his successors became less popular after the early 1850s. Most of Keller's poetry of this type had already appeared by 1851; the additions in his *Gesammelte Gedichte* (1883) tended to be patriotic poems or ballads, types of poetry which retained their popularity in Germany throughout our period. The same can be said of Storm, whose *Gedichte* (apart from the wonderfully moving poems in memory of his wife, 1825–65) were published in 1852. Fiction in the form of the novel and short story dominated the literary scene. The *novella* had a special place in the work of Stifter, Keller and Storm, and they produced a remarkable variety within the genre. It would appear that the historical situation was the common factor in accounting for its popularity among these writers. In general, character replaced incident as the motive force of the narrative, while a veritable cult of form offered a semblance of objectivity to the story told. The psychological penetration of character was one of the finest achievements of the German *novella* at this time, but among readers it was not a popular form. They preferred the long novel with 'contemporary' themes and ideal heroes with complicated relationships and destinies.

As the distance between the artist and the society in which he lived grew greater, serious prose fiction made fewer concessions to the age, preferring the private world to the historical events of the time, and depicting man in his relations with himself, his family, his daily life. The literary language of these major writers began to differ from that spoken in the street or written in the press. In the late works of Stifter, such as his novel *Witiko* (1865–7), in the novellas of Meyer, such as *Der Heilige* (1871) or *Die Versuchung des Pescara* (1887), or those of Storm and Heyse, this led to the use of archaic expressions, a mannered effect, which was also part of the general fondness for historical costumes. After 1871 German realist writers also represented the claims of the different regions against what they felt was the increasing and soulless centralisation of Germany under Prussia. Some writers were didactic in their use of regional and dialect expressions, such as Rosegger and Anzengruber, from Austria. Many writers experienced a dilemma in thus defending a provincialism which they regarded as confining, but at the same time they felt too much out of sympathy with the way Germany was developing: this was certainly true of Stifter and Keller. The language and the form of their works retained historical features, as though they were trying unconsciously to hold back the age. It is not surprising that there was little in the realist generation of the formal experimentation of a Grabbe or a Büchner.

For the German realist writer the 'modern world' signified potential chaos rather than opportunity, and his first task was to discover coherence in what he saw around him. He did not in general allow confrontation between 'permanent values' and 'modern times', but rather set his tales in the historical past, in the countryside, in specific regional areas, all of them real but peripheral. The heroes of German realist fiction and their milieu are presented in more concrete terms than in the Biedermeier period, but the most successfully drawn are still, as it were, on the periphery of life: the young and the old; sensitive youths who find refuge in a landscape or small town; eccentrics of various types. These traits are present even in the most urbane German writer of the second half of the nineteenth century in Germany – in Fontane. Unlike his fellow-writers, Fontane had travelled extensively and lived abroad for many years; he is a prime example in his time of that exceptional being: the German social novelist. Yet even Fontane's social comment is circumscribed as to milieu. His most successful works deal with a class which he knew only indirectly, the Prussian Junkers. Yet the class which obtruded most forcibly on the public consciousness at the time of his writing, the industrial proletariat, is hardly ever mentioned in his work. Where it does appear, it is in the form of a rustic idyll – in *Irrungen Wirrungen* (1888), where the wives of the factory workers in Berlin bring their husbands' lunch and spread out an enticing meal upon the grass at the factory gate. Fontane's sentimental attachment, despite growing reservations, to the Prussian aristocracy, made him a sensitive observer of their decline. However he did not convey in his work that sense of historical development and its impact on the Junker which Freytag attempted to provide in his *Soll und Haben*. Like many other great German realist writers, Fontane seemed to prefer nostalgia to confrontation.

Although Stifter, Keller and Raabe recognised their great debt to Goethe, the sense of tutelage, of being an imitator, disappeared. Instead they experienced a sense of transience, a sense of the relativity of things, which grew more acute towards the end of their lives. At its weakest this degenerated into sentimentality, as occasionally in Storm, Raabe or Fontane, or into elaborate stylisation, as in Meyer, for these writers were seldom able to create a tragic vision to give it significance. Keller and others could smile at the excesses of the materialists, but at the same time they were disturbed by the popular acclaim given to such men as Ludwig Büchner or Karl Moleschott, and by the feeling that the values they were presenting in their own work were no longer relevant to the age. The debasement of culture found active critics from the late eighties onwards; the criticism of the realists however was often little more than a passive gesture of distress or at times despair. The German realist writers shared the desire for familiar things characteristic of an earlier generation; in many of their works a fear of change is evident, a fear which is never exorcised nor even openly acknowledged, and which accounts for example for the concept of fate in writers like Stifter or Storm. One critic prescribed the remedy for such a state of things: in his *Einleitung zur Kritik der Hegelschen Rechtsphilosophie* Karl Marx wrote: The Germans mustn't be allowed a single moment of self-deception and resignation. . . . Every sphere of society must be described as the *partie honteuse* of German society; we must get these fossilised conditions moving, by singing them their own tune.'[3] But Marx had virtually no influence on German literature in the nineteenth century.

223

Masters of the Realist Novella: Stifter, Keller, Storm

I Adalbert Stifter

The Austrian Stifter seems in many histories of literature to hover uncertainly between the Biedermeier and realism. His life span covers both, for he was born in 1805 and died in 1868, one year after Zola's *Thérèse Raquin* was published. Like Gotthelf, who was eight years older, and Fontane, who was fourteen years younger, Stifter did not begin to publish until middle life, and his first works have a quality of faint middle-aged regret. His first stories were published in local Viennese journals in 1840, followed by collected editions under the modest title *Studien* (1844, 1847, 1850). Some were issued in revised form after 1848, notably the six novellas, *Bunte Steine,* which are his best known work. Stifter spent much time rewriting his works in conformity with his high ideals on art and its function in the community. He also wrote two novels, *Der Nachsommer* (1857), a *Bildungsroman,* and a long historical novel, *Witiko* (1865–7), as well as several other short tales and a chronicle in novel form, *Die Mappe meines Urgroßvaters,* of which four versions exist.

Stifter's origins were modest. The son of a linen weaver in South Bohemia, he was educated by the Benedictines at Kremsmünster and sent to study law at Vienna. Something of an eternal student, he failed to take examinations and spent much of his life as private tutor to noble families. He was accepted socially in these circles once he had become known as a writer and as a painter, for the tradition of patronage of the arts by the nobility survived longer in Austria than in Germany. In 1850 one of Stifter's ambitions was fulfilled when he was appointed inspector of schools in Upper Austria; but his enlightened policies found no favour with the authorities in these years of conservative reaction and he was relieved of his post in 1856. In the last years of his life he turned increasingly to his art as a compensation.

There is much poignancy in his work and little passion. There is evidence everywhere of reflection and the endeavour to understand men through experience of life. Everywhere, just below the surface, one is aware of tensions overcome. Stifter is master of the unspoken in narrative prose, as Grillparzer is in drama. The circumstances of Stifter's life seem at several points to provide the key to his work: his passionate nature, which he strove to subdue, his unhappy marriage, his childlessness, his need of friends and difficulty in communicating with them. Yet, as with all great writers, this interpretation is inadequate. His life and times provided the impulse to write; his work was the product of great personal solitude and is in accord with the often unconscious currents of his age. But contemporary events as such play no direct role in any of his works, to the disappointment of those who admired him, and who urged him to 'turn his attention to the history of mankind'. Sometimes an indirect reference is apparent, as the plague in *Der Pechbrenner* (later included among the *Bunte Steine* under the title of *Granit*) which recalls the horrors of 1848. Stifter was deeply and anxiously concerned about his age, but this is barely evident on first reading his work.

With rare exceptions, Stifter's stories are set in the countryside in the remote past or, as in the later works, in pre-revolutionary days. References to town life are few; the centres of human civilisation are made to seem of little consequence and are referred to as 'the world outside', somewhat in the way present day Austrians refer to Germany as '*draußen*'. But Stifter is no writer of village tales; there is nothing of the sentimentality of Riehl or Auerbach, nor of the patriarchal didacticism of his fellow countrywoman Marie von Ebner-Eschenbach. The house is one of the central symbols of his work, yet his houses are invariably solitary buildings set in a forest, valley or plain, far from human habitation. The characters in his stories are few, they are not usually psychological character studies, they live their uneventful lives in a vast landscape, which Stifter describes with great power and a wealth of concrete detail. For all the elusiveness of his art – and Stifter is in many ways a difficult writer – he never leaves the concrete world and always writes about what he knows.

There was obviously something of a *déraciné* peasant about

Stifter, as many critics have pointed out, something of the nostalgia of the first generation city dweller for the once familiar country-side.[1] In one of his early works, *Wien und die Wiener* (1844), Stifter recorded his shock on first coming to Vienna as a young man at 'this colossal wilderness of walls and roofs, countless crowds of human beings, all strangers to one another as they hurry past.'[2] It was his evocation of the countryside which first made Stifter popular in Germany as well as in his native Austria. Like Grill-parzer and many other nineteenth century writers in German, he won acclaim for his early works, and little thereafter. In England he gained an enthusiastic following of which he remained unaware; the London *Athenaeum* of 26 August 1848 drew its readers' attention to the writer of the first four volumes of the *Studien*, set in Bohemia:

It [the Bohemian Forest] is one of the few districts still remaining in the heart of Europe, where Nature may still be found . . . where a lover of her looks and voices may still for a time forget the restless work of human energies and human wants, that has nearly effaced her original features from the Europe of our day.[3]

In Germany, Stifter appealed to those who disliked the contem-porary obsession with social and political problems in art. He seemed to be tacitly attacking French and Young German ideas on literature; yet in fact he was little aware of contemporary influences which he either ignored or misunderstood. He revered Goethe and was greatly influenced by him, as also by Schiller's concept of the educative function of art, though he expressed his impatience at the adulation of Schiller at Goethe's expense which was common in his own time. 'I am no Goethe,' he wrote to his publisher Heckenast in 1854, 'but one of his family,'[4] and with a typically Austrian blend of modesty and dignity he believed he was entrusted with a mission to make men aware of permanent moral and aesthetic values in an age of change. In the same letter he implied that his own achievement measured in relative terms might in fact be greater than that of his predecessors, given the unpropitious times in which he lived. Stifter was by background and tempera-ment a moderate liberal, a product of the enlightened bureaucratic state in its pre-revolutionary form. While he made it his task to draw attention to the deeper meaning of existence as embodied in great art, in morality and religion, he also understood and accepted the scientific discoveries of his time. Nineteenth century belief in progress, in the efficacy of social and political reforms as universal panaceae, was in Stifter's view, not wrong; it simply left too much unexplained. As an Austrian civil servant for part of his life, he was often made painfully aware of the limited sphere of action open to the average individual, and while he had contact in the hospitable aristocratic homes of the Viennese nobility with the cultural, political and military leaders of his day, he never quite overcame his feeling of social inferiority. He was therefore less inclined to challenge existing practices and institutions and associated himself after 1848 with conservative tendencies in desiring 'organic' or 'natural' change. He lacked the Viennese resilience of Grillparzer who could relieve his frustrations in caustic epigrams. Stifter instead put his trust in the inner resources of man and in education.

The Revolution of 1848 administered a violent and lasting shock to Stifter: he saw in it the failure of reason and education. 'The ideal of freedom has been destroyed for many years to come,'[5] he wrote. Like the dramatists, Grillparzer, Bauernfeld, Anzengruber and many other Austrians, after a brief period of enthusiasm he soon identified the revolutionary disturbances of 1848 with mass rule and chaos. He saw a parallel with the chaotic forces in himself. 1848 was in every way a turning point in his life. With endearing pedantry and great idealism he now rewrote his earlier work in order to eliminate all subjective elements and stress its exemplary character. He felt called upon to act as a publicist, and wrote for and edited the *Constitutionelle Donau-Zeitung,* the *Wiener Bote* and the *Linzer Zeitung.* He began to plan a series of novels, as being more weighty than the short tale or novella which he had hitherto preferred. The stress he laid on order was merely a more elevated version of post-revolutionary Austrian and German parternalism. But before any of his novels appeared, he published two volumes of novellas under the title *Bunte Steine,* three of which, *Kalkstein, Granit* and *Bergkristall,* can be read as children's stories; the remaining three are arresting, sombre tales, on themes which make their appearance again and again throughout Stifter's work, solitude and tragic fate. It is impossible not to be struck by the disparity between what Stifter claimed to have demonstrated in the stories (as elaborated in the *Vorrede zu den Bunten Steinen*) and what he actually wrote. That Stifter was trying to convince himself as much as his readers that this was a good world, became apparent in *Der Nachsommer,* which he had been writing since the time of the Revolution and which appeared in 1857, the same year as *Madame Bovary* and *Les Fleurs du Mal.* The story takes place about thirty years earlier in a remote country estate. In his novel Stifter tried to demonstrate classical humanist ideals in a modern setting. The title, *Indian Summer,* refers to the late flowering of the love between von Risach, owner of the *Rosenhaus* where the action is set, and his neighbour Mathilde, to whom he was once secretly engaged. Von Risach, who has had long and bitter experiences of public life, now undertakes the education of the son of an acquaintance of his, the young Heinrich Drendorf. Through contact with mature minds, with nature and the beautiful objects assembled in the *Rosenhaus* which give the latter the atmosphere of a museum, the slow process of Heinrich's education is achieved. All the characters in the novel, like those of *Die Mappe meines Urgroßvaters* and of the poignant story, *Der Waldgänger* and many more, collect, catalogue and arrange various objects such as plants, shells and precious stones in the process of self-education. Through study, self-discipline and contemplation, men discover, so Stifter would persuade us, the unity of art and nature which he believed was based on universal laws. Stifter differed from his contemporaries in his assertion of the existence of an underlying harmony in the world, but it was a belief he had to struggle to uphold. For him education and nature were complementary; education is the process of becoming aware of nature. Again and again in his works, the reader is struck by the sensation that his nostalgia for such harmony was stronger than his belief in its existence: the atmosphere of *Der Nachsommer* as of *Die Mappe,* the nobility of the characters, the ritual of daily life are too remote, for all the concrete language he uses to describe them, to be completely convincing.

Stifter's prose does not lack immediacy of feeling, but this is presented indirectly. The theme of guilt and expiation which appeared early in his work is presented after 1848 in more general terms, and is more clearly symbolical of the forces in human history. Human passions, the chaos of war and revolution, are seen in perspective, as a stage in the development of human beings or communities. Time and education are seen to subdue passion and to channel energy to creative tasks. There is no dramatic confrontation, only a slow imperceptible growth expressed in the leisurely flow of Stifter's wonderful prose style. The period covered by a single short tale often spans an entire adolescence, the years of early manhood, and even a whole life. Stifter made one or two attempts to explain his theoretical position, as in the opening passages of *Abidas* (1843) and the well-known preface to the *Buntie Steine*. The latter, though more persuasive than the first, may seem an inadequate appraisal of his ideals, and, as so often happens with the pronouncements of artists on their work, the *Vorrede* tends to be interpreted as a measure of Stifter's whole achievement. Whereas in his early work – notably in *Abdias* and in the bitterly autobiographical *Der Waldgänger* (1846) – the expiation demanded of a human being seemed out of all proportion to the guilt he had incurred, in the *Bunte Steine* and subsequent works, another person takes the task of expiation unwittingly on himself and brings about a harmonious conclusion (*Bergkristall, Kalkstein, Granit*). Stifter's views on tragic guilt are directly related to the sense of guilt he felt towards his wife and to his effort to project a meaningful relationship into his marriage. Late in life he wrote passionate love letters to his cold and ignorant wife; his intention was not least to leave an impression of a harmonious life to posterity, which would, in the contemporary manner, verify the truth of his poetic creation by relating it to his biography. In most of the works he wrote after 1848 he tried to stress the positive aspects of suffering. Thus the unhappy experiences of Freiherr von Risach (*Der Nachsommer*) and of Brigitta in the eponymous novella mature and refine them through suffering. Their experiences equip them emotionally and mentally for their task of educating the young. Education, Stifter said, is contact, with people and things. Drendorf is prepared for an unspecified life of usefulness, Brigitta and Stefan's son will carry on their work of cultivating the barren steppe and ruling their people, Augustinus in the *Mappe* and the young Witiko are made ready for service to the community, whose work will perpetuate their name.

Despite the references to a Christian pattern of living, Stifter did not interpret the world in Christian terms, except in *Kalkstein* and *Bergkristall*. The nineteenth-century Austrian's attitude to his inherited religion was a complex one. Stifter showed nostalgia for the Christian world, but was not part of it; yet unlike Storm he did not draw explicit conclusions from his inability to be convinced by the Christian faith. He found no solution to the problem which haunted him and which found expression in almost all his works: why must men suffer and what do they leave after them? In *Brigitta, Der Waldgänger, Turmalin* and other works he described intense suffering and the ennobling effect it may have on a man or woman of exceptional character; but the problem remained. For Stifter, the figure of the child is a symbolic link between the present and the future (as is the family house in Storm's work); a child is the pledge that a man has left his enduring mark on the world, no matter how slight the memory of him. In the *Mappe* Stifter showed how the life of a descendant, many years later, may be ennobled through the memory of his ancestor's virtuous life. Stifter's acute sense of man's vulnerability was given poignancy by his own childlessness. Again and again in his novellas happiness is depicted as the association, often ephemeral, between an elderly man and a young child. In the ancient symbol of the withered tree in *Der Waldgänger* he evoked the tragedy of childlessness; on another occasion he likened it to being shut out of the human community: 'for his existence left no image and his traces are not borne down by the river of time.'[6]

The human beings in Stifter's prose fiction often seem dwarfed by the landscapes which dominate it. His exact observation and description of landscape and the changes wrought in it tend to make readers forget that he sees it symbolically. Stifter's landscape is a symbol of humanity, and the passing of the seasons, as in ancient times, recalls the cycle of human life. It is natural that the individual should seem diminished in stature against a background of centuries, just as the cycle of a single year seems to leave little permanent record of its passing on the countryside. Yet the cumulative efforts of men do indeed leave their effect behind them: the simple priest in *Kalkstein* is an instance of the power of an insignificant life. It is not for nothing that men have lived. In his late work Stifter was fond of the *topos,* the great river of life, as in *Witiko*: 'In the historical novel history is the main consideration, the human beings of secondary importance, they are borne by the great river of time and help to form it.'[7] He devoted much space in his work to the task of building a house, cultivating land, planting a garden. His characters show an almost pedantic love of arranging objects in a room. Only slow patient labour gives results, never, in the cultivation of nature or of the mind, the sudden spurt. Brigitta makes even the barren steppe bear fruit, the surveyor in *Kalkstein* discovers the beauty and colour of the *Kar,* the stony landscape around him, the symbol in each case of their growth to maturity.

Stifter's fascination derives from the fact that he can be read on many levels. He has elements of the pastoral writer, something of the Biedermeier eccentric, but his major works are examples of symbolic art unequalled in his age. Contemporary illustrations of himself, as for example the cheerful chubby-faced man who peers from Daffinger's portrait, prefacing an edition of the *Studien,* perpetuated the first image of Stifter, while the illustrations provided by Ludwig Richter for the *Bunte Steine* showing angelic looking children and benign old men, provoked the author to a rare outburst of anger, as being wholly foreign to the idea of the tales. It is significant that it was two of Germany's greatest writers in subsequent generations who acknowledged his genius by reading him on a symbolic level: Nietzsche and Rilke. In more recent times Thomas Mann challenged the then prevalent sentimentalist view of Stifter: in *Die Entstehung des Doktor Faustus* (1949) he called him rather 'one of the most elusive and significant . . . writers of world literature.'[8]

The private tragedy of childlessness, the disappointment of 1848 and its consequences heightened Stifter's awareness of his art. He hoped his work would give permanence to his life, although he might not be understood while he was still alive. People would only understand what he was aiming at in *Witiko* in a hundred years, he wrote – we are reminded of Annette von Droste-Hülshoff's wish to be read a century hence. To achieve what he hoped, his work must make the deeper springs of humanity apparent to his readers; in the frequent images of nature growing over the ruins of man's habitation (*Die Narrenburg,* 1843, *Zwei Schwestern,* 1846) we are made to witness the nullity of man's achievement unless the moral law be realised in his life and in the education of the next generation. When he planned the novel *Witiko* in 1847 he intended to illustrate the relationship of the state to morality and culture. In the actual course of writing it, Stifter became more concerned with what he regarded as the insignificance of his own age against the background of centuries. Although he was certainly influenced by the current vogue for

Tradition and Revolution

recreating great ages of the past in this work, he was quite without
the nationalist prejudice which marred the historical novels of his
lesser contemporaries.

In his last stories he turned once more to the education of
children and adolescents. Stifter's view of the child was wholly
unsentimental. His pioneering work on primary school education
had developed out of his recognition of the distinctive personality of each individual child, its intellectual and emotional needs
at the different stages of its development. One of his last stories,
Der Kuß von Sentze (1886) illustrates his pedagogic ideas in
practice. Stephan, who is living in the countryside with his two
children, befriends a wild gypsy girl and adapts his educational
methods to her particular and difficult circumstances with notable
success. Stifter designed an educational reader which has since
won the approval of educationalists, but it was rejected by the
ministry in his lifetime.

In his increasing concentration on the private sphere of the
family which he regarded as representative of the good society,
Stifter was influenced by the Biedermeier and by the political
events of his middle years. Von Risach declares in *Der Nachsommer:* 'it is the family that is needed by our times; more than
art, science, more than trade and commerce, prosperity, progress
or whatever may be called desirable, we need the family. Art,
science, human progress, the state, all rest on the family.'[9] In late
Stifter, as in the late works of Keller, Storm and Raabe, the private
sphere became a refuge from an unsympathetic world. If Stifter's
younger contemporaries concentrated on psychological realism in
their character studies, he was concerned to present exemplary
types. He was more troubled than they were by the decline of
spiritual forces in the community; they made less absolute claims
than he for their art. Indeed few of his contemporaries, whether his
friends or his critics, could appreciate his exalted view of the ideal
poet: 'Teacher, guide, friend of his fellow men ... interpreter,
priest of the All Highest.'[10] Stifter stands at the end of a tradition
of idealism in art. His awareness of his position created tensions
not wholly resolved in the harmonious endings of his later tales
and in the pregnant silences in his characters' dialogue. 'Our time
demands greatness, a national effort, something relevant to our
world, but it is these things which show the poverty of our age,'
Stifter remarked in 1857.[11] Concerned as he was with the inner

world of human beings, his concentration on 'inner action' and the power and simplicity of his nature descriptions made him a master of the novella form, although his novels also command admiration. And yet at the end of his life and for many decades after his suicide he was little read except as an Austrian regional writer.

II Gottfried Keller

The first works of Stifter's younger contemporary, Keller, began to appear only a few years after his own. Keller was born in Switzerland in 1819 and lived in Zurich for most of his life. He seemed at first to wish to identify himself with the political trends of the 1840s. 'The poet,' he wrote in 1843 at the age of twenty-four, 'must raise his voice in the service of the suffering and the needy; having done this his art should then provide the flower garden and recreation ground of life.'[12] This sententious pronouncement was part of a 'poetic plan' of his own devising and echoes the blend of the didactic and sentimental in poets like Freiligrath and Herwegh, who were popular in Keller's youth. The 'vital call of the age' gave him his first stimulus to write, and as a defender of the liberal cause against the Jesuits in his native country he produced some stirring verses. These were the days when Switzerland was regarded as the hotbed of dangerous radical movements: the word *Putsch,* of Swiss dialect origin, was incorporated into standard German in these years. Keller frequented émigré circles in Zurich in the forties; he met Arnold Ruge as well as Freiligrath and Herwegh, and his first poems, *Lieder eines Autodidakten,* were published by a German bookseller, August Follen in 1845. Appreciative notices prompted the city fathers of Zurich to award Keller a two year travelling scholarship in Germany. In this and in their later patronage they showed unusual foresight and an admirable degree of consistency, for Keller developed slowly and did not show immediate signs of providing a return on the capital investment of his thrifty fellow citizens. He had already spent two years in the pursuit of an artistic career in Munich (1840–2) and had returned with nothing to show for it. It was at the age of twenty-nine and still a student that Keller set out for Heidelberg on his scholarship in 1848. He did not return to settle in Zurich for seven years.

If Keller's beginnings were not propitious, the next years did not seem more so. Plagued by debts and determined to prove himself before his return, he was only able to do so through the generosity of his mother in 1855. He had only just finished his first novel, *Der grüne Heinrich* (1854–5), which was conceived before his departure to Germany, and he had published another collection of poems, *Neuere Gedichte* (1851). In 1856 the first volume of his immortal *Die Leute von Seldwyla* appeared, a cycle of novellas. He was relieved of financial stress by being appointed town clerk of Zurich in 1861 and he held this post until his retirement in 1876. These years produced only a few works, *Sieben Legenden* (1872) and the second volume of *Seldwyla* (1874) many of which had been written earlier. The years following his retirement saw a rich harvest: the *Züricher Novellen* (1877–8), the revised version of *Der grüne Heinrich* (1879–80), *Das Sinngedicht* (1881), his most perfect work, and *Die gesammelten Gedichte* (1883), which included a number of patriotic poems and ballads written under the influence of the ballads of C. F. Meyer. A second novel, *Martin Salander*, was published in 1886, but it showed evidence of the diminishing powers of the aging Keller.

Keller had a quality which the Austrian novelist Robert Musil also shared: the ability to make his friends concern themselves about his own artistic and physical well-being. These friends included many great names of the day, for although he was not in the strict sense of the word popular in his day, he did gain recognition from leading critics. F. Th. Vischer and Hermann Hettner remained close to him throughout his adult life; he corresponded with Storm for years, although they never actually met; while a mutual friend, Paul Heyse (1830–1914), was instrumental in drawing public attention to the works of both Keller and Storm while they were still little known. Berthold Auerbach, who enjoyed considerable fame in the fifties and sixties as the author of the *Schwarzwälder Dorfgeschichten* (and also as a notorious wife-beater), praised Keller's work. Although such acknowledgement encouraged him, Keller's *Seldwyla* tales were thereby stamped as sentimental village tales of the type written by Auerbach himself. Keller vigorously refuted Auerbach's criticism of his *Romeo und Julia auf dem Dorfe* (1855) and made pungent comments on contemporary notables and on current literary taste in his letters to Hettner. Vischer prophesied that Keller would never be popular because he was too much of a poet; but in his last years he did gain sufficient recognition to support himself by his writing. The turning point in his fortunes came when he was taken up by the influential literary publishers Goeschen and by the journal *Deutsche Rundschau,* which also published Storm, Fontane and Raabe. Keller's academic reputation in the nineteenth century, in contrast to that of Mörike or Stifter, was gradually established because his friends Vischer and Hettner, who were university professors, praised him to their students. Keller's blend of ethics and patriotism corresponded to the mood of the seventies, and if his serious intention was often overlooked by the public at large, his humorous portrait of contemporary reality found favour. In 1890 Otto Brahm, the naturalist critic and dramatist, could write that 'Keller came nearest of all the older writers to contemporary taste.'[13]

Keller's friends encouraged him, lent him money and tried to speed up the painfully slow progress of his creative work. They confirmed his belief in himself, but at bottom he did not need them. The years of self-imposed exile in Berlin, his 'penitentiary' as he called it, had been a protracted apprenticeship: in the process of writing *Der grüne Heinrich* and in his abortive attempts to become a dramatist, Keller had found himself as an artist. Nearly all his later works were planned or partly written in the Berlin years: the *Galatea* novellas, to be published as *Das Sinngedicht,* and most of the *Seldwyla* tales, the *Sieben Legenden* and the projected revision of his novel. The slow maturing of his artistic vision, the constant revising of his work before the final version was produced, made Keller one of the great masters of form in the nineteenth century, particularly in that exacting prose narrative form, the cyclical novella. In all his narrative prose he retained his position as the omniscient, at times quite paternal narrator and form never threatened to become a fetish with him as occasionally with Heyse, who also wrote a very great number of novellas, or Keller's fellow countryman Meyer. From his Berlin period onwards, though frequently hard pressed for money, he consistently refused to commercialise his talents in the service of popular taste, as Auerbach, Freytag, and Lewald were doing. He was a stern critic of the contemporary phenomenon of the *Literat* and in his novella *Die mißbrauchten Liebesbriefe* (1873) he paid off old scores against the pretensions of the Berlin literary cliques.

He shared with Stifter and Meyer a high regard for the calling and integrity of the artist, though he did not put it in so many words, and in his later years he too became distressed by what he regarded as the ambiguous position of the artist in modern society.

Keller's whole work however is a comment on contemporary social reality and in this he is closer to his contemporaries in England, France and Russia than to German writers of the time. This was due chiefly to his national origin, to his contact with the philosopher Ludwig Feuerbach at a crucial stage in his literary development, and, not least, to his own personality and temperament. Keller and Gotthelf might at first seem to have little in common, yet both were formed by the same local tradition and particularly by eighteenth-century Swiss rationalism with its belief in the value of educating the citizen; this was to have a profound influence on their view of literature and on the forms they adopted. All Keller's stories have a pedagogic intention, both his novels are *Bildungsromane* of a sort, and while fervent preaching was foreign to him, he shared Gotthelf's belief in the important role played by popular literature. Keller was acutely concerned at the contemporary distinction between 'literature' and 'what the people read'; he believed this was a trend which could only be harmful to literature by creating artificial barriers between the writer and his public. For this, amongst other reasons, Keller chose the cyclical novella form, which establishes a relation between narrator and reader. In *Das Sinngedicht* he restored the earlier conception of the cycle as an oral tradition.

The sense of community which Keller owed to his Swiss origins was brought home to him through his meeting with Feuerbach in Heidelberg in 1848. He had gone there to study history as a preparation for a dramatic career. The structure of Europe in this 'year of fate' was in Keller's mind particularly suited to dramatic treatment; like many others at the time he felt that the drama could command a more serious and also wider public, as the most social art form; he illustrated this in his treatment of the performance of Wilhelm Tell in *Der grüne Heinrich*.[14] Keller's evolutionary view of history was not in fact suited to drama, but it was nearly ten years before he gave finally up his plans. The historians who lectured him at Heidelberg, Gervinus and Häusser, seemed to him excessively theoretical; Feuerbach offered a far more stimulating experience, and when the authorities refused to confirm

Feuerbach's university appointment because of his atheistic views, the students persuaded him to lecture in the town hall. For Keller this meeting gave him a new sense of liberation and of artistic purpose which never afterwards left him, even in the difficult years which followed. He learned to see how his background, his age and his own particular situation could provide the subject material of his creative writing. Feuerbach taught him to focus his attention firmly on the world about him, he stimulated him to produce that wonderful blend of observation of humanity and eccentric fantasy which is so distinctive and so original.

Keller's great merit as a writer is his ability to illuminate aspects of human behaviour in all their complexity within a narrow local world. As a narrator he remained within the world he wrote about; and in contrast with his countryman Meyer in his prose work the framework of Keller's novellas conveys a sense of the social bond linking the role of the listener and narrator with that evoked in the tale; or shows how they both share in the same Swiss historical tradition, as in the story of the governor of Greiffensee and his five former sweethearts (*Züricher Novellen*). In the latter cycle and in *Das Sinngedicht* the framework has a clear didactic function: to cure folly by demonstrating its foolishness. Keller's admirers never tire of his portrayal of the Swiss milieu in his works, of the interaction between environment and character. The private world and the public world are rarely far apart in Keller, quite in contrast with his fellow German writers. The unity between the two worlds is shown in his popular festivals, which so often provide a turning point in the history of hero or heroine or in their development. Examples of this abound in his work, in *Das Fähnlein der Sieben Aufrechten* written in 1860 or, *Frau Amrain und ihr Jüngster, Dietegen* or *Das verlorene Lachen (Leute von Seldwyla* II). *In Der grüne Heinrich* the popular festival is clearly an integral part of the social life of the community, whereas the artists' carnival, which Heinrich attends in Munich, is shown to be artificial and meaningless. On occasion, too, the small world which Keller evokes so beautifully is shown capable of tragedy, and in the case of *Romeo und Julia auf dem Dorfe,* tragedy of classical proportions: a stark tale of love and self-destruction of two young lovers with its wonderful social, psychological and moral motivation. The story has rightly attracted a great deal of critical appreciation, but its tragic outcome is not typical of Keller's work.

Keller's slow growth to maturity allowed him to digest the social implications of Feuerbach's thought without indulging in the somewhat ludicrous fantasies of other enthusiasts, such as Ludwig Büchner, author of the phrase *Der Mensch ist, was er ißt* (man is what he eats). Feuerbach's optimistic view of man's nature and Keller's own warm friendliness encouraged him to believe in the existence of perennial forces in the world which contain man's folly: youth, love and good sense. For all the singularity of his appearance and way of life, Keller had in abundance that quality which Hebbel, Stifter and Meyer, his contemporaries, lacked: humour. Keller's humour is social, it draws people to his works and allows them to share in his tolerant delight in humanity. One can argue as to the origins of Keller's balanced view of man and society; his humour is uniquely his own, its quizzical tone a sign of maturity. It was not evident in his early correspondence and only made its appearance in the more successful parts of *Der grüne Heinrich*. If folly, meanness and some more extreme forms of eccentricity are symbolic in Keller's work of the destructive passions of the world, his humour has the function of reducing these to manageable proportions and underlies his basic optimism. Humorous exaggeration serves to diminish the stature, though not the impact on the reader, of the grotesque figure of the gossip in *Das verlorene Lachen,* of the uncannily virtuous combmakers in *Die drei gerechten Kammacher* (*Die Leute von Seldwyla* I), or of the citizens of Ruechenstein in *Dietegen*. The robustness of Keller's heroes, their equanimity and trust in a reasonable and even benevolent fate, derive from his own position as an artist. His view of the artist, at least up to his late middle age, as a member of the community (at times an uncomfortable one!), his belief in the social function of art, and his own tried and buoyant personality, gave him an assurance which his fellow writers in Germany did not share.

For all the differences between them, Keller shared Stifter's view of life as a process of education, largely self-administered. His novel, *Der grüne Heinrich,* traces the story of the childhood, youth and early manhood of an aspiring artist. It has distinct autobiographical undertones. The early version (1854–5) is told from the viewpoint of the subjective individual; in the revised version Heinrich takes his place after many vicissitudes as a responsible member of the community. This ending pleased contemporary opinion, both in Germany and Switzerland, but today we see the achievement of the novel as lying rather in the fine delineation of childhood, which is represented as an adult might recall it in later years, in a series of phases, not in continuous progressive development. Keller's rejection of the supernatural after his meeting with Feuerbach made him more acutely aware of the material and accidental factors of environment and circumstance in forming a child's character. He showed the inborn sense of right and wrong with great insight: the effect on a child of sensitive character of the early loss of its father; the subtle moral contamination at school and play is presented most convincingly. Keller demonstrated how complex is the influence of the world about him on a growing child: history and nature, education and religion, the nation and the family are shown as influences in a series of specific incidents, as for example Heinrich's visit to his cousins or the performance of *Wilhelm Tell.*

If one compares the first version of the novel with Keller's original plan to write a *Künstlerroman* on the lines of Mörike's early work, *Maler Nolten,* one can see how far he progressed as an artist in the course of writing. In the section on Heinrich's life in the artists' world he clearly relied on literary prototypes: these German artists are stereotype figures and their surroundings lack the visual reality and humour of the Swiss milieu. *Der grüne Heinrich* has been called Keller's workshop; it is easier to point out individual merits and shortcomings than to appraise it as a whole. It was not very successful; twenty years after publication over one hundred copies of the original 1,000 remained unsold. Those who believed in his talents seemed disappointed and argued heatedly about the ending. Their criticisms influenced him and he almost immediately planned a revision. After giving it serious thought over many years he eventually rewrote it in the winter of 1879–80.

The integration of the artist into the community is shown in the second version as being the goal of his progress to maturity. Keller often ended his stories in this way – *Pankraz, Frau Amrain, Das Fähnlein* and many more. Put that way it sounds a little dull, and when, as in *Frau Amrain* or in his last novel, *Martin Salander,* the didactic intention is too overt, the result is laudable rather than satisfying. When Keller presents the community itself, as he did in his novellas, he is irresistible. The prejudices and preoccupations of the people of Seldwyla, his fictitious community, are characteristically smalltown, but they are also universal aspects of men's relationships with one another. Keller is a supreme storyteller with an engaging gift for exaggeration. The form of his five collections of novellas suggest a return to the earlier moral or exemplary tale of the late eighteenth century and this is confirmed by the unusual events and persons of the tales. The humorous undertone in almost all of them shows them to be variations on the theme of folly, usually in the form of pursuit of an ideal which turns out to be the reverse. On the basis of Keller's belief in the good sense of man and his world, his characters learn to distinguish reality from appearance, an educative process which redounds to their benefit as well as that of the community. An example of this is *Die Sieben Legenden* (1872) ostensibly seven legends about the intervention of the Virgin in the lives of those under her protection, with the humorous twist that in each instance young people are cured of misplaced asceticism and directed to a normal life of wedded bliss. In Keller the women usually teach the men, and they certainly emerge as the most engaging and persuasive in most of his works. Though Germany had few feminists in the nineteenth century and few women novelists of quality, the portrait of woman in literature evolved impressively in the second half of the century, particularly with regard to women's personal freedom in marriage. Keller's women do not inspire their menfolk to great deeds, but cure them of eccentricities, usually marrying them and awakening in them a sense of purpose in the process.

His tales have a special quality of timelessness in form and theme and yet almost all rest on contemporary preoccupations or topical events. *Romeo und Julia auf dem Dorfe* was inspired by a notice in a newspaper in 1847; Spiegel, in *Spiegel das Kätzchen,* (*Seldwyla* I) mocks at the excesses of contemporary materialist thought; Spiegel's moral sense fluctuates in direct relationship with his diet. The combmakers' eccentricities in *Die drei gerechien Kammacher* and their passion for security at any price recall the contemporary crisis of the artisans in Central Europe. The *Züricher Novellen* and one or two of the second volume of the *Seldwyla* tales breathe an atmosphere of transience which is part of a general reaction of serious writers in Germany to the climate the seventies. Death is made to seem almost homely in *Der Land-*

vogt von Greiffensee, being referred to as *Skelettchen* or *Tödlein,* but the main characters stand under its shadow.

Keller's work progresses from Romantic subjectivism in his early work to belief in the liberal bourgeois community in his mature writings. Like Raabe, he liked to satirise the bourgeoisie; both distinguished between the responsible citizen and the philistine, the latter being a butt of nineteenth-century criticism from the Romantics to Ibsen. In the late works of Keller and of Raabe, the ideal bourgeois is the exception; in common with the general trend of German realist writing under the impact of the industrial revolution and post-1871 nationalism, the bond between the thinking citizen and the community becomes tenuous. Only a special kind of person can overcome the pressures of society. The attractive Lucie in *Das Sinngedicht* (1881) is such a person. *Das Sinngedicht* is the story of a young scientist Reinhard in search of a wife, who chances on the home of Lucie and her uncle and who discovers with the aid of stories told by all three the sort of qualities which the partners of a happy marriage should have. The tales are set in different ages and different regions; the protagonists entertain and instruct in a happy Kellerian manner. It can hardly be claimed that Lucie – or the marriage of Lucie and Reinhard – are representative of the average citizen in 1881 in the same way as the hero and heroine of *Das Fähnlein* might be said to have been in 1860. Lucie's educated mind and forthright character are not the products of an orthodox education; she is the exception, not the rule. Their home stands aside from the road as does Stopfkuchen's 'castle' in Raabe's eponymous novel. Their way of life is different in almost every respect from the 'normal'. Like Raabe or Fontane, Keller seems to say that the individual must needs cultivate true *Bildung* – and acquire a thick skin of humour – to preserve his sense of proportion. Love and laughter are preserved intact in Keller, but in his later works only in the private sphere.

Keller's artistic maturity is everywhere evident in *Das Sinngedicht,* his finest work; his tolerant irony and delightful humour, as he depicted the ideal relationship between man and woman in marriage, was matched by profound symbolism and a fascinating use of traditional literary motifs. By contrast, his late novel *Martin Salander* (1886) seems the product of an ageing man. Like Goethe in his old age, in later life Keller became preoccupied by the extent to which utilitarian concepts governed men's lives. In *Das ver-*

lorene Lachen (Seldwyla II) the 1,000 year old oak is felled for what it can command in the money market. If material success and possessions are the only touchstones of a man's values, human relationships are threatened. Moral and ethical problems absorbed Keller's attention in *Martin Salander* to the exclusion of social and political ones. The novel reflected his unease when he observed the changing world beyond the horizons of his Swiss home; it is set in Germany, once his spiritual home, which had now become strange to him as it had to his fellow countrymen Burckhardt and Meyer, in the years after 1871. What J. M. Ritchie calls Keller's 'choir of active onlookers',[15] who provide so much of the substance of his other work, is absent here, and the reader misses the sense of joy and wonder at creation, which is so attractive in his novellas. *Martin Salander* was an attempt on Keller's part to write a novel of the times, influenced by his reading of Flaubert and Zola and of Spielhagen's theories on the modern novel. It is of interest in that it showed how even an optimistic writer like Keller was affected by the materialist climate of his time, but the misanthropy evident in his interpretation of the characters of the story is a-typical, the product, in part, of his increasing infirmity.

Keller's fantasy and his highly individual turn of phrase delights the reader; his gallery of eccentrics has surely few rivals in German literature, and yet his characters are but extensions of traits we know in others and ourselves; Keller's humour makes them credible. For all his appreciation of the earnestness of life and his times, for all his didactic intention, Keller obviously delighted in humanity. His humour derived from the constant discovery of oddity in himself and others. What is so attractive about him is the presence of this personal characteristic in his every work. While commentators have naturally stressed the importance of his Swiss background for his generally positive attitude to man in an age where most major German writers were pessimistic, in the last analysis it is largely a question of temperament and natural gifts: 'my style is part of my personality.'[16]

Keller deserves also to be remembered for his letters. His eye for humorous detail and his warm humanity made him a delightful correspondent. One of the most interesting collections of his letters is the one of those he wrote to Theodor Storm (1817–88) who like him was a gifted writer of novellas and a lyric poet of great distinction. They were introduced to each other by a mutual friend when both were in their late fifties but they never actually met. For a decade they conducted a wide-ranging correspondence, including careful and often inspired analyses of each other's works, and critical and humorous comments on their contemporaries. Thus Keller dismissed the nationalistic dramatist Wilhelm Jordan, who in the seventies was exploiting the current vogue for successful authors' lecture tours by referring to 'that coquettish rhapsodist, Jordan'.[17] The letters also contain an illuminating discussion of literary genres, interesting details about artists' emoluments, and occasionally the domestic preoccupations of both writers: on one occasion Keller tactfully reminded Storm that Switzerland was abroad and would he remember to put the equivalent stamp; he didn't of course mind about such things, but his thrifty spinter-ish sister disturbed the peace of their somewhat eccentric house-hold each time the postman demanded double payment.[18]

III   Theodor Storm

In a felicitous phrase Keller once spoke of Storm as one of 'those quiet goldsmiths, filigree workers in silver'.[19] Storm was a master of complex narrative forms, who identified himself closely in his work with a particular region, his native Holstein, and represented the changing moods of the local landscape in his work. He com-bined a reverence for the poet's vision with a critical awareness of the limitations imposed on him by his talents and his times. Thus he never attempted either the novel or the drama; his work com-prises some fifty novellas and short stories and a few collections of short lyrics. He was not a professional writer, although he started to write early in life; he chose a legal career and wrote many of his works at night in the company of some or most of his eight child-ren. His early stories, from *Immensee* (1850) onwards, have the form and structure of lyric poems, rich in atmosphere and with little action. (Paul Heyse, a close friend of both Storm and Keller, coined the phrase 'lyrical novella' to describe Storm's early work.) Like other major writers of his age, Storm wrote his greatest prose works at the end of his life, particularly in the eight years before he died, after he had retired as a judge.

Perhaps in no other writer of the time does one get a greater sense of the contrast between the German novella, the most dis-tinguished achievement of her literature in this period, and the

European novel. Virtually every one of Storm's prose works is centred on the intimate family circle and the setting is invariably the small seaport town of Husum in which his mother's family had lived for many generations, or the countryside nearby. Even his historical novellas, the product of his later years, seem to be extensions into the past of the life of this small world; its seafaring inhabitants, who might have seen China on their voyages, are in all other ways quite remote from the revolutionary developments of the Germany and Europe in which they now live. There is no perception in Storm of the social changes characteristic of his age, no sense of history in the making. The past strengthens the sense of unbroken tradition of which the citizens of Husum feel proud. Often in his novellas Storm depicted the slow passage of time, sons following in their fathers' footsteps, improving their financial and thus their social position, or, as in *Hans und Heinz Kirch* (1881–2) or *John Riew* (1884), failing with tragic consequences through some personal fault or blow of fate to take their rightful place in this stable and sober world. The appeal of Storm to his contemporaries was that his isolated world so vividly evoked seemed out of reach of change; his characters, drawn from life, solid citizens, covetous of recognition by their peers, retired sea captains, sailors with their English phrases and Spanish curses, the busy *Hausfrauen* and their blonde, well-brought up daughters seemed in a sense outside time. The political and technical upheavals of the century, even the state itself, barely obtruded. Even if new houses were built, telegraph wires erected, the old customs remained unchanged, 'the end of the railway line lay many a mile inland on the other side of the hills.'[20] Towards the end of his life and in later years Storm's work won admirers – among them Thomas Mann – for the way he managed to imply, beneath all this appearance of stability, the fragile nature of his 'safe' bourgeois civilisation.

For Storm, openly hostile to churches and religions, was obsessed with a sense of the mutability of things, which haunts both his poetry and his prose. In his early works, most notably in *Immensee,* this appears as a sustained mood of resignation, when an old man, Reinhard, relives in his imagination his past life and his failure to win happiness. This short tale is, perhaps surprisingly, probably the most widely read German story; in the nineteenth century it was already well known outside Germany and frequently translated; its simplicity of language is something rarely found in a work of comparable poetic achievement. Modern readers often find it hard to make the imaginative effort necessary to understand the passivity of the young lovers, Reinhard and Elizabeth, and are surprised to learn from Thomas Mann that his *Tonio Kröger* was but a modern version of the story. Few however can fail to admire the perfect stylistic harmony of technique and content in *Immensee,* the manner in which action and passion are revealed symbolically, despite the remote quality they take on in Reinhard's distant memory.

In Storm's novellas written in the seventies and eighties, this sense of transience shows itself as the efforts of individuals – the anonymous painter in *Aquis Submersus* (1875–6), the ambitious father in *Hans und Heinz Kirch,* the *Deichgraf* Hauke Haien in *Der Schimmelreiter* (1888) – to defy time by making an enduring mark on the world. Storm's basic concern remained unchanged throughout forty years of creative life: how does a man come to terms with existence, knowing as he does that there is no life beyond the grave? Though the historical and social circumstances are ostensibly the cause of individual tragedy, as for instance the failure of the painter Johann to marry the noblewoman Katherine because of the difference in their social status (*Aquis Submersus*), or the way in which John Glückstadt is driven to despair and death because of the inability as an ex-convict to get work (*Ein Doppelgänger,* 1886), in fact the story of human failure merely serves to illustrate the irrationality of human life. His later novellas are far removed from the elegaic mood of his early stories: *John Riew* is about hereditary alcoholism; in *Ein Bekenntnis* (1887) a doctor adminsters poison to his much loved wife on her own request to relieve her from the agony of a fatal disease. And yet Storm seemed often to draw back from the tragic implications of these tales of human inadequacy and inexorable fate which provide the substance of the novellas of his maturity; he frequently exploited his narrative mastery to soften the harsh impact of events. The use of more than one narrator in his novellas, of indirect or 'broken' narrative and framework tales, of chronicles and manuscripts, served to remove the figures of these stories from the familiar world of the listener. In many instances the sufferings of an individual are made meaningful in the lives of the next or later generations. Thus the wretchedness of Wieb's life, once Heinz

Kirch's sweetheart, is alleviated as she tends his ageing father, while the character of Christine, John Glückstadt's daughter (*Ein Doppelgänger*) is strengthened by the memory of her convict father's noble efforts in spite of society to bring her up decently.

If the modern reader often reacts unfavourably to the muted or even idyllic endings of Storm's novellas, these were very much to the taste of his contemporaries. Storm was perhaps the only major writer of fiction in the second half of the century who could be called popular. Discriminating colleagues admired him, he was the correspondent and friend of Turgenev, and the general reading public thought highly of him. This is not surprising. The domestic setting of most of his stories, the psychological realism of his portrait of family life, of love and happiness, tensions and conflict, appealed to them, while his narrative brilliance set him apart from the many other writers who chose similar themes. Two examples may serve to illustrate different aspects of Storm's achievement here, *Viola tricolor* (1874) and *Hans und Heinz Kirch*. If the themes of these novellas are commonplace, the treatment is not. *Viola tricolor* is the story of a second marriage, of the efforts of a young wife married to a man many years her senior to win the love of her ten year old stepdaughter. The story opens with the child Agnes (Nesi) waiting at the top of the stairs to greet her new step-mother Ines. Everyone in the household including her father, has been especially, perhaps excessively tactful in preparing her for the ordeal; Nesi is prepared to love Ines for herself and as her father's wife, but refuses to accept the idea that she should now become her mother; she had promised her own mother on her deathbed, that she would never forget her. Storm's portrayal of the conflict and deep unhappiness of stepmother and child, of the incomprehension and impatience of Rudolf, the husband, during the first months of their life together is very moving: so much is implied and so little actually said of their real feelings. Ines becomes pregnant and the situation becomes more tense; Rudolf's very effort at forebearance towards his young wife makes him seem old to her and lacking in feeling. The child begins to feel unloved and shut out, Ines to regret her marriage. Tragedy seems imminent, but is averted by the intuitive discovery by Ines and her step-daughter of their true feelings for each other through the overgrown garden at the side of the house. This garden had been at first a symbol of past happiness for Rudolf and Nesi, for Ines a reminder of an oppressive past and of her own failure, but together they explore it and understand one another. Particularly memorable in this story is the insight and delicacy with which Storm uncovers the feelings and relationships of the three protagonists without recourse to emotional effects in what was a potentially lachrymose subject.

By contrast the story of the father and son in *Hans und Heinz Kirch* is starkly tragic. Hans Kirch had risen through his own efforts to be a man of wealth in his native town and destines his only son to take his place among the leading families, a place he, because of his lack of education, could not aspire to. Heinz becomes the symbol for him of his own achievement; he loves him possessively, and when, in his early childhood the boy is in danger of losing his life through some foolhardy exploit, Hans gives vent to his terror by beating an older boy mercilessly. This episode makes a lasting impression on Heinz. Many years later a quarrel breaks out between the hot-tempered father and son prior to Heinz' departure on his first long voyage as a sailor; Hans sends a violent letter after his son which leads to an estrangement. For two years no more is heard of the boy and then he sends a letter begging for help. He is penniless and the letter is unstamped: such a blatant disregard of bourgeois convention by one who in his father's eyes is a pledge of his own future name is too much for Hans. To the horror of the postman and without the knowledge of his family, he refuses to accept the letter; it is returned unopened to Heinz. As in *Viola tricolor* and in Storm's major stories of this period the psychological realism of *Hans und Heinz Kirch* is of a high order, especially his depiction of the psychological barriers between father and son and the ineffectual attempts of Hans' wife and daughter to influence a man obsessed by a single idea. Fifteen years later, after his mother's death and the marriage of his sister, Heinz comes back to his father's house. But is it he? The doubt in the minds of the father and his son-in-law that this prematurely aged and scarred sailor could be their close relation grows as the days pass. They persuade themselves that he is an impostor and Hans' relieved (thank God) he is a stranger, expresses the feelings of them all: Heinz, if it is he, has so obviously excluded himself from the bourgeois order that the rest of them recognize. When Heinz discovers that his only refuge, Wieb, who does not belong to 'respectable' society, is also lost to him through her marriage, he becomes a symbol of the homeless one, a kind of drop-out in an exigent and conformist society. There is no place for Heinz and he disappears, this time for ever. The bitter father, whose ambitions have been at least outwardly realised by his daughter's advantageous marriage, comes to understand that Heinz is still an extension of his own self. He ages prematurely and in an uncanny vision sees his drowned son before him and he knows that he is dead. The old man seen looking out to sea at the end of the novella is only a shadow of the real Hans.

In his last novella, *Der Schimmelreiter*, Storm brought together the familiar themes of his prose and poetry: his experience of love, the family, landscape and history, in one of the most compellingly told stories of German realist fiction. Suffering from stomach cancer and knowing himself close to death, he created the almost mythical figure of Hauke Haien, the poor boy who rises to become *Deichgraf* in his village. Hauke tries to overcome the hostility of the villagers, to challenge time's inevitable obliteration of human endeavour by building a great dyke; he is swept with his wife and child to his death in the course of its erection. The powerful imagery of this novella draws together the different strands of its author's lifework: symbols of nature in her more tranquil moods go back to the earliest stories; the predatory birds and animals, common in the stories of his middle years, stand for the irrational impulses in human beings and in nature. Above all, the sea and the sky, the most striking components of the landscape of his native Holstein, evoke the wonder and the incommensurability of life but also of fate, Hauke's fate. So many of Storm's figures lose their lives by drowning and Hauke is almost a mythical figure to the villagers before he too meets his end in the waves. The sea is without contour, it buries without trace, an apt image to set against man's unavailing yet inspired efforts to overcome his destiny.

Stifter, Keller and Storm have an abiding place in German literature as writers of fiction. There are many minor figures, whom their contemporaries rated higher and who are still remembered for one or two fine works. Otto Ludwig (1813–65), author of the short novel *Zwischen Himmel und Erde*, wrote about small town life with a graphic visual sense; Paul Heyse (1830–1914), something of a prodigy in his early manhood for his success as a writer and author of formally exquisite novellas, is through some quirk of fate remembered today chiefly as the protagonist of a particular theory of the novella, and as the first German to receive the Nobel Prize (1910). Born in the same year as Heyse, the Austrian noblewoman Marie von Ebner-Eschenbach (1830–1916) is still deservedly read today for her portrait of rural life in the Austrian monarchy. She spent most of her life in Vienna or on her country estates in Bohemia, and her warm and humane personality informs her work. Like many Austrian writers her approach was didactic; she attacked the neglect by the aristocracy of their social obligations to the poor and their deliberate brutality toward dependents. Perhaps her formally most distinguished story is also that in which she appealed most strongly to the social conscience of her kind, *Er laßt die Hand küssen*. Here the narrator tells of his aristocratic grandmother, a woman of cultivated tastes and author of a pastoral romance, *Lex adieux de Chloë*. It flatters her vanity to undertake the moral reform of her less fortunate dependents, and when Mischka, a labourer on her estates, fails to respond to her efforts, she has him flogged for a slight transgression. The action and characterisation are almost entirely achieved through scraps of conversation in the countess's mansion, as she and her circle are performing *Les adieux de Chloë*. The cries of the tortured creature barely penetrate to the drawing room, when she decides to show clemency and stops Mischka's punishment. She calls the butler, but he anticipates her and announces in the conventional phrase with which all servants in Imperial Austria prefaced their remarks to a superior : *Er laßt die Hand küssen, er ist schon tot* (He kisses your hand, he is already dead). Marie von Ebner-Eschenbach's *Dorf- und Schloßgeschichten* contain vivid portraits of character and life in rural communities – reactionary landowners, idealistic doctors, gamekeepers, ambitious Jewish traders and beggars. Her novel, *Das Gemeindekind* (1887), is a more deeply felt work, an indictment of the village community's failure to care for its less fortunate members. In the story of Pavel Holub, the child of a murderer and therefore a kind of social outcast with no family, its author described the degradation of the rural proletariat in grim detail. Like her fellow countryman Anzengruber, the Austrian novelist sought to counter the sentimental concept of life in the country current in family journals and popular novels with the real thing.

Marie von Ebner-Eschenbach's social position and literary connections, her Austrian nationality and the fact that she wrote most of her work in the last decades of the century places her apart from the other realist writers treated here. At the same time her straightforward didactic approach made her a less penetrating observer of the ethical implications of change than Stifter, Keller or Raabe, who was born one year after her, in 1831. None of these writers were able to identify themselves with the Germany they experienced in the decades after 1848.

13

Imperial Germany:
Doubts and Fears 1871-90

The Empire, in which the realist writers were to feel increasingly estranged, was proclaimed on 18 January 1871. Victory was celebrated, victory over France and also victory over past disunity. No representative of the middle or lower classes was present at the ceremonial coronation of William I as Emperor of Germany in the Hall of Mirrors at Versailles. And yet there was little doubt that the nation as a whole identified itself with the sense of achievement. So much had changed so quickly in the last seven years and so much excitement had been engendered by events and by the reports of the local and national press that the public had had little time to see it all in perspective. The man in the street became suddenly converted to the view of the *Kleindeutsch* intellectual of eight or ten years earlier. Victory was now made to look like the outcome of wise foresight rather than the result of a mixture of able political and military leadership and fortuitous circumstance. It was attributed to the spirit of self-sacrifice of the Prussian-German rulers and people. Prussia was seen as the embodiment of the German nation because she had made herself heir to the traditional national spirit, exemplified both by Frederick II's war against the Austrians in 1740 and the so-called Wars of Liberation from the French in 1813. Thus even in this most revolutionary event in the history of nineteenth century Germany, the unification under Prussia, German fear of change expressed itself in the fiction of the historical legitimacy of the new state. In the years to come a great deal of effort was to be lavished on the 'image' of the Empire by all those concerned with the directing of public opinion: the authorities and their bureaucratic representatives, as well as the teachers in schools and universities, the writers, sculptors, scholars and journalists. The very name *Second* Empire sought to demonstrate legitimate descent from the Holy Roman Empire to which it bore no resemblance. In fact it ran counter to the federalist tradition of German history which had existed since the late middle ages.

Success is a great persuader and because history is written by the victors the official version established itself and remained largely undisputed (except in Austria) for the next seventy-five years. People accepted the new form of state, as they accepted the military élite in society, the military discipline in life and work, because it gave them a vicarious share in the great events of their time. Pressure was brought to bear on dissident opinion. The conformity to social convention which had characterised German life before 1871 became even more marked afterwards, and was characteristic also of political opinions and attitudes to the state. Uniformity was achieved in all sorts of ways, most effectively through education. *Großdeutsch* sympathisers, that is, those who regretted the exclusion of Austria from Germany, as well as Catholics and Socialists, found it difficult to get appointments to university chairs and senior school teaching posts from the 1870s onwards. Given the authoritarian character of German education, the appointment of men with the 'right' political views ensured the correctness of opinions and loyalties in the next generation. Even before 1871 the nomination of pro-Prussian university teachers in Württemberg, Baden and Central Germany – such as Treitschke to Heidelberg in 1867 – had done much to influence the intellectuals in favour of unification under Prussia. Loyalty to the state as an ethical duty had acquired greater appeal with the decline of classical humanist ideals and in consequence of the powerful influence of Hegel in German political education. The German state in 1871 did not represent in the eyes of her citizens a universal idea such as freedom, democracy or international solidarity; it was rather a symbol of security, of economic progress and of unity in its military and bureaucratic aspect.[1] Germans however felt the need for some kind of ideology and this was satisfied by resurgent German nationalism in the form of loyalty to the state. The state had been successful in war, in fostering commerce, industry and science; it was now represented with increasing frequency by publicists as the fountainhead of law, culture and ethical conduct. Since confessional and regional differences continued to create tensions within the Empire, the authorities and the people themselves made an effort to overcome them by stressing their common national character and ethos. It is a striking fact that all the basic ingredients of German nationalism, as the twentieth century was to experience it, emerged in Germany in the first decade or so of the new Empire. (In Austria they were also present in a more extreme form, but for different reasons.) Even the German cultural heritage was submitted to a 'nationalising' process: in 1885, on the occasion of the founding of the Goethe society, an appeal was launched 'to all admirers of Goethe'. The admirers learned that 'with the new Reich the time has arrived ... for a national and political way of thinking; those limitations which in past decades have kept many from due knowledge and appreciation of Goethe have now been removed.'[2] After about 1880 the moral and the aesthetic value of a work of art in popular estimation was judged according to its national sentiment.

In an effort to reassure people, Germany was now represented as a bulwark in an age of change, and the national myth of Germany's cultural superiority and mission, favoured by the Romantics, and more recently, by the liberal nationalists such as Freytag, was resurrected. It was not long before Germany's superior morality was being contrasted with the materialism or decadence of western European nations. Though the monarchy and the army had their critics, public comment in the seventies and eighties was much more inclined to stress the 'moral strength' of these institutions, compared with the institutions of other nations. One consequence of this attitude was the endemic dislike of England, which became widespread towards the end of the century. Much play was made of the materialism of the English – a charge which had often been levelled by Germans in earlier decades of the century; this accusation was not without irony when one considers the worship of the golden calf in German plutocratic circles after 1871. Towards the end of the eighties Germans expressed their envy of Britain's power and irritation at British condescension by drawing analogies for her future: all empires decline and soon it would be England's turn. Of the many critics of England, Treitschke was the most vocal, and in his years as professor of history at the University of Berlin (1874–96), he exercised considerable influence. The characteristics of modern nationalism – the suspension of logic, the crusading tone – were apparent in his lectures and his writings: the fortress of Metz in German hands means peace, he declared in the seventies, in French hands it will precipitate war. All the opponents of Germany were wicked as well as wrong. Chauvinism of course was not exclusive to Germany, it would not be difficult to find parallels in France and England even to Treitschke's nationalist posturings. The essential difference was that in other countries such utterances were not representative of official and popular attitudes as became the case in Germany. Moreover the growing tensions within German society and the German state made the isolation from contemporary Europe, which these attitudes brought with them, potentially more destructive than in other western nations.

It was not only the nationalist hotheads but Bismarck himself who began to use dislike and fears of neighbouring states to distract the German people from internal dissensions. Politicians and journalists encouraged the population to regard the recent victories as having been gained at the expense of other nations and warned of the constant danger that these nations might challenge the status quo. Some indication of the strength of these attitudes may be gained when we find them expressed in the diary of a sophisticated and cosmopolitan noblewoman, the Baroness von Spitzemberg. The daughter of a former Württemberg minister and now the wife of a diplomat living in Berlin in the last three decades of the nineteenth century, Baroness Spitzemberg made constant references in her diary to the 'hatred and envy' of Germany's neighbours at her recent success.[3] The kind of Darwinist thinking – the idea of the survival of the fittest – which was applied to aggressive business ethics in the United States,[4] was used in Germany as a guide to international relations, although Bismarck personally disavowed it. In the United States and England Darwinism was a working hypothesis; in Germany, in the interpretation of Ernst Haeckel (1834–1919), it became a philosophy of life. German success, in business as in war, was represented in terms of peculiarly German loyalty, endurance and strength. Darwin's famous 'tree of life', showing the young buds and branches replacing weak and dying ones at every stage of evolution, made an immediate impact on a new generation of Germans schooled into thinking of success as something that had to be won at the expense of others, as survival in a hostile world. As the period of recession from 1873 to the end of the eighties drew to a close, Germans became obsessed with the idea of competing with the other powers for the supposedly limited markets and raw materials available. This attitude accounts for the rapid growth of the pan-German and other nationalist associations in the 1890s and the enthusiasm engendered by the Fleet programme.

Nationalist propaganda, to use a modern term, had its most lasting effects in the field of education. It is here that the full force of the contrast between Germany at the beginning and the end of our period is most strikingly apparent. In his illuminating article on the German school reader, Walter Killy names the years immediately after 1871 as the time when classical humanist principles, on which German secondary education had been based, were abandoned.[5] Echtermayer's *Auswahl deutscher Gedichte für höhere Schulen* first appeared in 1836 and was re-issued in new editions over the following decades. In 1874 the twentieth edition appeared, edited by Herman Masius, who introduced it in the following words: 'This collection aims at bringing young people to a knowledge of the ideal world of our nation ... only what is truly exemplary and national is included.'[6] The thirty-second edition some two decades later omitted many excerpts from the German classical writers in order to remedy the need felt for more patriotic material:

> thus we make the minds and hearts of young people receptive to patriotic greatness and national honour by including ... more works of E. M. Arndt, tribune of the Germans against Gallic treachery, of Körner, the heroic bard, and of Emanuel Geibel, herald of the new Reich; than previously, while with the same intention in mind we introduce Ernst von Wildenbruch.[7]

Many liberally minded Germans, as for example the later President of the Federal Republic of Germany, Theodor Heuss, recalled in after years, how their teachers in the eighties and nineties imposed conformism to the national spirit upon them, even to the point of discriminating against Jewish children or those whose parents had socialist sympathies.[8]

The external appearance of German towns and cities helped to promote a new degree of uniformity throughout the Empire. It is true that in the architecture of her civic buildings, Germany had retained her regional diversity much longer than France – one has only to recall the uniformity of the neoclassical *hôtel de ville* from Montpellier to Lille; now however this was changed:

in the mania for erecting monuments to national figures and in the naming of streets after recent victories, North and South Germany came closer together. The late nineteenth century was an age of monuments throughout Europe; German monuments were conspicuous in their preference for 'architects of the Fatherland', kings and soldiers in preference to artists or philanthropists. Schiller and Goethe owed their inclusion to what was referred to as their 'national moral stature', and not to their art. The unveiling of statues had something pseudo-religious about it, as indeed had so much of contemporary German nationalist doctrines and their external symbols.[9] The spate of public and private building which followed the founding of the Empire was of course partly the result of the very great increase in public wealth and the desire to display it.

German capitalism began to dominate public life in these years and to penetrate the public mind at all levels. During the course of the period covered in chapter eight Germany had acquired the technical equipment as well as the organised institutions generally associated with a capitalist society. Transport, inventions and research, methods of production, the financing of industry through the joint stock companies and the state, all these had developed with great rapidity during those years: now expansion became prodigious. Between 1870 and 1874 more engineering firms and more iron foundries opened in Germany than in the preceding seventy years. After her defeat of France in the Franco-Prussian war, Germany acquired the Lorraine iron ore and potash deposits which furthered the growth of the Ruhr complex. Vast firms emerged: Krupp, who had made a fortune out of the Crimean war and was to do so again by financing both sides in the Russo-Turkish war of 1877–8, Borsig, the manufacturer of rolling stock, and new names in industry like Thyssen, Stumm-Halberg or Prince von Donnersmarck. The shipping lines, German Lloyd and *Hamburg-Amerika-Linie*, expanded all over the world; Germany exported rolling stock and armaments to a world market. The first period of industrialisation had been dominated by the steam engine, leading to large industrial units because of the capital requirements; the second phase was initiated by Siemens' discovery of the dynamo and the electric motor, which was sufficiently cheap to be available to small firms. Modern technology appealed to the popular mind partly because of its contribution to recent victories. Prussia had exploited her technical advance in the wars against Austria and France, with the use of the fast-loading needle gun and efficient transport of troops on the railways. Apart from the military and political aspect, modern technology brought benefits to society at all levels. Transport facilities enabled food to be brought from distant countries such as the United States and Russia, while at any rate until the crises of 1873 and 1879 high employment ensured a degree of social stability.

The frontiers of knowledge seemed to expand almost daily, and Germans showed themselves brilliantly adept at applying new discoveries to everyday life. German interest in optics led to the development of research based on the use of the microscope: the surgeon and liberal politician, Virchow, the discoverer of cellular pathology, is one of the leading names in this field. A country doctor, Robert Koch, isolated the cholera and tuberculosis bacilli, and as a persistent advocate of fresh air in home and classroom, aroused great hostility in his time. Medical hygiene brought striking benefits : epidemics were eradicated, while Dr Semmelweiss' researches into puerperal fever, which became generally known about this time, greatly reduced the number of deaths of women in childbirth. Anaesthetics were introduced into Germany in the early sixties. Many changes took place in daily life in consequence of technological and commercial innovation: oil lamps were used in the home, coal began to be used for domestic as well as industrial consumption. Better drainage and sewage disposal made life healthier for everyone. Walking in the clean, well-paved and well-lit streets and in the public amusement parks of Berlin and other German cities in the seventies and eighties, citizens of the Second Empire felt rightly proud of their country's achievements.

Some tensions in German society made themselves felt soon after the financial crash of 1873 which had been provoked by foolhardy speculation and the unexpectedly rapid payment of the French war indemnity. However, the overall picture of Germany in the first years after unification is one of self-confidence and growing ostentation. The economic boom had created a new plutocracy within a few years and when recession followed the 1873 financial crisis, it was the small investors and not the directors of industrial enterprises who were its chief victims. It was the latter who gave this era its name, the *Gründerzeit* or era of the Promoters, and many novelists of the time, notably Fontane, have left us portraits of these men – the *Kommerzienräte* van Straaten (*L'Adultera*) and Treibel (*Frau Jenny Treibel*), or the recently ennobled von Gundermanns (*Der Stechlin*). The epoch had its own characteristic style, a style favoured by men who wished to display their wealth and improve their social position. The style in architecture resembled that of late Victorian England; it was pseudohistorical, a not always happy combination of architectural elements copied from earlier European models. The representational buildings, the villas of the wealthy and even their factories bore Renaissance or Gothic façades: the tastes of Prussian industrialists were not so very different from those of the Lancashire or Yorkshire millowners. The interiors of town halls, libraries and museums were adorned with murals and paintings representing Germany's glorious past, while the furnishings of houses showed a preference for luxurious materials and fabrics. The word 'culture' was much in evidence in conversation.

In these years successful painters were not only the social equals of those who employed their services as portrait painters, they also made fortunes never dreamed of before: the fashionable society portrait painter Lenbach, who painted among others Bismarck and Moltke, owned a number of city mansions; Hans von Makart, famous for his imposing paintings of historical events, used to charge admission to admirers visiting his studio. It was common practice for a wellknown artist to receive generous payment for gracing a banquet or other social occasion with his presence. These painters and others besides painted successful industrialists as well as princes and statesmen. For the aristocracy, though it retained its position as an élite, was forced to accept the presence at court and at official functions of those whose loyalty to the conservative Empire had been rewarded with patents of nobility and titles. The less well-to-do aristocrats, higher civil servants and army officers could not absent themselves from the continual round of social occasions if they wished to continue to be 'in' society. There was much irritation felt among the nobility in these years at having to associate with 'recently ennobled civil servants, rich men with or without a patent of nobility, baptised or unbaptised Jews from the rag-trade, indeed on occasions even with intellectuals, long-haired and shorn alike.'[10] Yet, as was also the case in England, the nobility in Germany found it necessary to intermarry into the new plutocracy in order to maintain its social position.

The German middle classes believed that they possessed a monopoly of culture, as evidenced by their collections of paintings and
patronage of the arts. It was important to the self-esteem of its
members to appear well-read; it was at this period that the title
of *Herr Doktor* became an accepted social asset. Conversation was
sprinkled with quotations and allusions, although the poet Geibel
was now more popular than Goethe. Perhaps Fontane's most
delightful satire in his novels of Berlin life in the 1870s and 1880s
is contained in his use of G. Büchmann's *Geflügelte Worte* for the
conversations of the middle classes which constitute such a large
part of his novels; from Büchmann's collection of 'suitable' quotations from the classics and popular works of the time enjoyed
enormous success among well-to-do Germans from its first appearance in 1864. The pretensions of the epoch represented the debasement of the traditional culture of the German middle classes, and
they help to account for the growing separation between the artist
and the general public in the last decades of the century.

In all this ostentation there was a deadening conformity of
taste and conversation; or so it seemed to critics. The celebrated
actress, Helene von Racowitza, a Prussian Junker's daughter,
contrasted German life in the eighties with that of Munich and
Berlin two decades earlier: 'in those days one knew no better; it
seemed to them of greater importance that the occupant of a chair
should be clever and amusing than that the chair itself should be
of a certain design.'[11] With greater humour Fontane criticised the
pretentiousness of contemporary society, the blend of ruthlessness
and sentiment which he found characteristic of it. He also depicted
the way in which the bourgeoisie emulated the aristocracy and
showed themselves in agreement with the well-ordered authoritarian principles according to which life was conducted. They were
in favour of military service and compulsory education which
'knocked sense' into radical elements. They admired Bismarck and
rejected criticism of his domestic policy; they were proud of his
diplomatic success and basked in the reflected glory of Germany's
greatness. If they had voted liberal in the sixties, they were in
general supporting one of the conservative parties in the eighties.
Many prosperous businessmen stood as conservative candidates
for the Reichstag or the Prussian Diet at the end of our period,
more perhaps for the contacts and social status involved than for
hopes of political influence. Indeed the Reichstag counted for

relatively little as an influence on government policy. The Prussian Diet, on the other hand, offered valuable contacts with official circles and became the spearhead of reaction in the Empire, after its brief liberal period in the 1860s. Since it had control of senior administrative appointments and since such matters as education and religion in the state of Prussia came under its provenance, the Prussian Diet was very influential in shaping both official and social attitudes from 1871–1918.

For all property-owning classes, but also for salaried officials lower down the social scale, the question of 'the masses' took on a new urgency in the last decades of the century. Before 1871 'the people' were generally regarded by the authorities and the middle classes as loyal and well-disposed towards their superiors. Thus Bismarck could write to his wife after visiting the Prussian troops after the victorious battle of Königgrätz (Sadowa) over the Austrians:

> Every one of them so brave, so composed, so polite, despite empty stomachs, wet clothes, wet quarters, little sleep, the soles falling off their boots; friendly to everybody, paying what they can and content to eat mouldly bread. Fear of God must be deeply engrained in our common people or this could not be![12]

Although Bismarck was reluctant to acknowledge the existence of an industrial revolution, he was perfectly willing to use the bogy of the proletariat as a kind of political red herring, and spoke in the Reichstag of dangerous radical tendencies among the masses and of irresponsible leaders. He even accused these leaders – on negligible evidence – of complicity in two attempts on the Emperor's life in the late seventies. The German public was very ready to accept Bismarck's version. The later Emperor, William II's (for once) laconic comment on the leaders of the socialist movement: 'they should all be shot!' was not un-typical of public opinion on the subject of the organisation of the working classes in Germany.

The founder of the first German workers party was Ferdinand Lassalle (1825–64). Lassalle, though not really an original thinker, was a man of strong personality and powerful intellect. He founded the *Allgemeiner Deutscher Arbeiterverein* in 1863 with a programme that was both social and democratic: he planned the improvement of the working man's lot through self-help and an enlightened state welfare policy. Bismarck took him seriously and had several meetings with him in 1863-4; it is possible that he even contemplated some sort of alliance with his movement in order to put pressure on the liberal opposition of the time. Lassalle was a notorious figure in Berlin in the 1860s. He was the son of prosperous Jewish parents, who lived in Breslau, the Silesian capital, and as a young lawyer he had defended Countess Hatzfeldt, a red-wigged and cigar-smoking noblewoman, in a divorce suit. After winning the case he had lived openly with the Countess who was several years his senior; later, in 1864, he was killed in a duel fought over Helene von Racowitza. He did not seem a likely person to lead a working man's party, but in fact several thousand joined his movement in 1863-4. The membership consisted of journeymen, rather than factory workers, and after Lassalle's death, his movement was absorbed either by the co-operative association founded by a philanthropic businessman, Schulze-Delitsch, or by the Social Democrats under Bebel and Liebknecht. The *Allgemeiner Deutscher Arbeiterverein* was not Marxist in origin; it had its roots in the democratic radical movements which had emerged in 1848. Unlike the Marxists Lassalle favoured co-operation with the state, for Germany had a strong tradition of social activity on the part of the state.

In the same year as Lassalle's movement, the *Verband Deutscher Arbeitervereine* was founded by August Bebel (1840–1913), one of the most colourful figures in Imperial Germany, and Wilhelm Liebknecht (1826–1900). The *Verband* was anti-Prussian and had an immediate appeal in Saxony, which was now highly industrialised, and also in South Germany. Both Bebel, who was the son of a master turner and non-commissioned officer from Saxony, and Liebknecht, who came from an academic family which counted Luther among its ancestors, had fought as democrats in 1848. Both won fame when they were imprisoned in a Prussian fortress in 1870 for opposing the Franco-Prussian war; they led all the socialist groups in Germany at the time in opposing the annexation of Alsace-Lorraine after Prussia's defeat of France. In 1869 the *Verband* was reorganised on a Marxist basis at Eisenach, being re-named the *Sozialdemokratische Arbeiterpartei*; in 1875 it formed a union with the Lassallean movement under the able leadership of Bebel. By 1890 with its massive organisation from local clubs to state associations it was the leading Socialist party in Europe.

Socialism emerged in Germany after the financial crash of 1873 and the subsequent recession. The Marxist elements in its doctrine, particularly those relating to monarchy and state, were anathema to all but the working classes and a relatively small number of intellectuals of strong personality and convictions. Critics of the movement chose to ignore the fact that the theory of socialism was much more revolutionary than its practice: no revolution took place nor any act that could be termed revolutionary. And yet when Bismarck exploited the attempts to assassinate the Emperor in 1878 to legislate against the socialists, there were very few in or out of parliament who criticised his policy. It is difficult to understand the degree of hysteria with which socialism was regarded in this new and successful Germany after 1871. In England and Belgium, two highly industrialised countries, the resentment of poor workers against the rich was just as real and apparent, yet even in the Hungry Forties public opinion in these countries did not become unduly alarmed. The endemic fear of revolution and its consequences among Germans has something to do with this hysteria in the last decades of the century: it was fed by the fear of losing what had been so recently achieved in the political and economic sphere, and by the readiness of the German public to believe in the jealousy other powers were said to feel of the new Empire. The international character of socialism made its German opponents see the masses as the instruments of hostile foreign powers, a view which prevailed up to the time of Hitler and even of Adenauer. In this fear there were elements too of the Social Darwinism which seemed such a persuasive philosophy to a materialistic age. Critics of socialism were often heard to say that the movement should be crushed before it was too late: a verse in Viktor von Scheffel's epic poem, *Der Trompeter von Säckingen* (1854) which went into one hundred and sixty-eight editions in the nineteenth century, was frequently quoted in support of aggressive action against the socialists : 'For the big eat the little, and the biggest eat them all; and so the social question is in Nature easily solved.'[13]

The German Socialist party was more preoccupied with theory than any other socialist movement in Europe. However the behaviour of its growing band of followers gave a lie to the apprehension of the propertied classes. The workers in general showed themselves more concerned with standards of living than with revolution or the classless state. As a new period of prosperity succeeded the recession in the last years of the century, the German working classes began to accept the nationalist ideals of the rest of society, although they still gave their allegiance to the Socialist party. In his inaugural address in Freiburg in 1895 the young sociologist Max Weber could say with some justification: 'The workers belong to the petty bourgeoisie. Economically they are far more mature than the egoistic property-owning classes wish to believe ...; politically they are far less mature than leftwing journalists would make them believe they are.'[14]

Social democracy as a way of life answered a real need among the industrial working classes which had so recently left the farms and villages. Moreover the proverbially pious lower orders in Germany lost their religious belief with unexpected suddenness in the course of the nineteenth century. Germany had no tradition of Nonconformism as a substitute for the state church, which meant little to the working man in the Protestant regions. The messianic element in Marxist thought had a wide appeal, and in addition the social aspect of the new creed was all important. Lily Braun, an aristocratic supporter of the movement, married to an intellectual socialist (*Kathedersozialist*) at Berlin university, George von Glyzcinski, recorded a vivid illustration of this in her memoirs. On a visit to a poor shoemaker, whose daughter, Marta Bartels, had joined the party, she learned their story. The father had lost his livelihood, Martha could not get work to support them; then she met the socialists: 'The old man stroked his daughter's cheek with his wrinkled hand. "And so she saved my life! Suddenly we weren't alone in the world any more: we had something to live for".'[15] Socialism helped people to overcome the loneliness that threatened the uprooted and small craftsmen after their migration to the big cities. In addition, apart from the more obvious achievement of the movement as a protector of workers' rights, socialism appealed to high-minded people desirous of helping their fellows and gave many a new sense of belonging, of security in a world without God and without a feudal overlord.

If the political rulers and the socially secure were hypersensitive to the 'socialist menace', the less well-off in society were becoming preoccupied with a 'threat' from a different quarter: from the

Jews. The lower middle classes in the last decades of the century were a large but heterogeneous group, comprising the numerous small businessmen and shopkeepers and minor officials on a low salary, a class which had always been numerous in a bureaucratic state like Germany; after 1871 a new element appeared: the office workers. These last-named regarded themselves as middle class, feeling neither solidarity nor sympathy for the factory workers, who might be financially better off than themselves; they were perhaps the most conservative group in Germany at the time. Most of these, or their families, had been radical in their political allegiance at the time of the 1848 Revolution; they had become disillusioned in their political loyalties afterwards without finding a substitute. In Germany in the second half of the nineteenth century, political parties tended to become identified with economic interest groups. The lower middle class had no particular party to represent them, since the two liberal parties in the Reichstag, the National Liberals and the Progressives, were the parties of industry and commerce the one, of the professional classes the other. In the fever of speculation which gripped Germany in the sixties and early seventies, the lower middle classes set aside their traditional sobriety and thrift and began investing their savings in joint stock companies. In 1873 the Vienna and Berlin stock markets collapsed and the small investors lost heavily. The conservative Prussian *Kreuzzeitung* reported an alleged bankers' conspiracy: the national and local press carried daily reports and photographs of those who had absconded with their company's funds. Novels of the time – such as Spielhagen's *Sturmflut* – contained portraits of such villains who prospered at the expense of the poor. As a result of the crash many small businessmen and officials lost their life savings; some were reduced to penury. They looked in vain to the established parties to do something for them, and when rumour had it that 'the Jews' were responsible for their ruin, many showed themselves ready to believe this. It was from such classes that support for the radical nationalist antisemitic parties or extra-parliamentary associations was won in the following twenty years. The Jew was an obvious scapegoat: he had 'come up in the world'; the Jews were rootless, it was said, but their international connections gave them the wherewithal to speculate at other people's expense without loss to themselves. Almost all the familiar arsenal of Nazi antisemitism was already present in this situation; it is significant that political antisemitism made its first appearance on a wide scale in Germany during a period when wealth was amassed by those who were already well-to-do, while a large section of those living on a fixed salary or savings suffered a significant reduction in their standard of living.

The Jews had won emancipation only recently. Their legal and social position varied from state to state, being better in the Protestant North than the Catholic South. The largest Jewish communities were in Prussia and in Bavaria. Under Napoleon Jews in the western parts of Germany had won emancipation, but in 1815 the old disabilities were re-imposed, despite energetic protests from the Jewish communities of the three Hanseatic towns and Frankfurt. In subsequent years sporadic attacks of violence took place throughout Germany, more particularly in the South, until the Federal Diet took steps to restore order. The rise of liberalism naturally favoured Jewish aspirations; the Prussian United Diet lifted several religious disablities, but in most states the Jews suffered political and civil disadvantages. From the first, Jews took an active part in the 1848 revolution, above all in Austria; they were prominent in the street fighting and in the assemblies. Reißner from Hamburg, Viet from Berlin, Kuranda and Hartmann from Vienna took an active part in the work of the Frankfurt parliament. In the spring of 1849 the parliament promulgated the *Basic Rights of the German People,* granting equality to all religious creeds, and although some states retained aspects of these in their constitutions, they never became law. Formal equality of Jews with Christians before the law existed in almost all the states after 1848, even in the reactionary states of Saxony and Mecklenburg; in practice the Jews might exercise their right to vote but were impotent against discrimination. Bavaria managed to resist pressure to moderate its policy towards the Jews by simply refusing to discuss the matter.

The fifties saw a worsening of their position: for the Jews were associated in the minds of the authorities with the recent revolutions. Jews were discriminated against in appointments to public offices and local assemblies in the provinces. Particularly obnoxious were the police regulations governing the right of domicile, movement from place to place and the right to prosecute a trade. After 1858, when a liberal ministery came to power in Prussia, piecemeal granting of rights gave place to comprehensive legislation. Full legal emancipation was finally obtained in Germany in 1871 (in Austria in 1866, in Switzerland in 1874). The Jews who benefited most from emancipation were the old-established who were socially assimilated. Antisemitism was directed in general against the prosperous 'liberal' Jews who dominated certain professions, such as law, medicine and journalism, and was continually stimulated by the great influx of Eastern Jews who were only gradually assimilated or not at all. Antisemitism became common among intellectuals in the 1880s. It was symptomatic of the widespread disregard for liberal beliefs in Germany at the time, and at a deeper level of the cultural pessimism which characterised many leading thinkers. One of the most influential of these was Paul de Lagarde (1827–91), an original scholar and author of the *Deutsche Schriften*. Lagarde championed a new aggressive nationalism and was one of the first to advocate a form of pan-Germanism for Central Europe. He condemned Bismarck's moderate policy and proposed the extension of Germany's frontiers 500 miles eastwards. This drive would be led by a small élite chosen for their ethical character and intellectual endowments: Jews were to be automatically excluded from such a society. These ideas were contained in Lagarde's collection of philosophical and political observations, the *Deutsche Schriften* (1886), which had wide and diverse influence on young intellectuals and on such dissimilar figures as Nietzsche, the historian Treitschke, the popular antisemitic preacher Adolf Stöcker and Langbehn, author of the racist interpretation of society contained in *Rembrandt als Erzieher* (1891). It seems strange that a man like Lagarde, a recluse who spent most of his life in his study amassing prodigious knowledge of the Orient, including some dozen languages, should have had such an impact. His writings provided a vague national mysticism which was to the taste of those who resented the shallowness of their prosperous society.

Dislike of the Jews was exploited by people for their own particular interests. The conservatives appealed to such prejudice to alienate sympathy from clever critics of the authoritarian system, such as the Progressive politicians Lasker and Bamberger, both Jewish lawyers. Bismarck defended the Jews in finance, because they performed a useful function, but he was prepared to see as a danger the presence of Jews in parliament and the press. The large Jewish interest in the press and entertainment made them an easy target for those convinced of the decline of public and private morality in the last years of the century. Atavistic prejudices against the Jews were rationalised by influential figures like Treitschke who attributed to them all current social evils; his views gained support because emancipation was so recent, and because the physical appearance of the eastern Jews was not calculated to lessen prejudice. Wilhelm Busch, one of Germany's greatest graphic artists, contributed his part to prejudice: the last letter of his pictorial alphabet for children (1874) showed a long nosed and sinister figure in a dirty kaftan chewing an onion. It carried the caption: *Die Zwiebel ist der Juden Speis'* (The onion is the Jews' food) and referred to the habit of eastern Jews of chewing onions or garlic in public.[16] In contemporary literature it is more usually the assimilated Jew who is the object of dislike. Undoubtedly such popular novels as Freytag's *Soll und Haben* and Raabe's *Der Hungerpastor* helped to encourage these feelings, and indeed Raabe's book became a school textbook in 1880. In both novels there is a strong emotional pressure for the reader to identify himself with the hero, who is made to suffer or is betrayed by a Jew.

The essential difference between prejudice against Jewish citizens of Germany before and after about 1871 is that, whereas formerly it had been largely religious, now it was based on racial differences. The French writer Gobineau's assertion of the moral superiority of certain races over others in his *Essai sur l'inégalité des races lumaines* (1853-5) became widely discussed in the latter period. But German racialists could refer to far more widely known authorities than Gobineau: namely to Fichte and Wolfgang Menzel. As long ago as 1797 Fichte had warned: 'a mighty and hostile state is spreading through Europe, which is at war with every other state; in some cases it imposes a dreadful burden on the citizens – it is the Jews.'[17] Menzel in his *Geschichte der letzen vierzig Jahre* (1857) spoke of 'the deep hatred of the Christian religion and the German nations' which allegedly was characteristic of the Jews.[18] In 1880 considerable impact on public opinion was made by the Antisemitic Petition organised by students and others at Berlin, demanding discrimination against the Jews. Very few public figures chose to disassociate themselves. The future Frederick III of Prussia (1888) was heard to say that antisemitism was 'the disgrace of the century'; the historian Theodor Mommsen was almost unique in the vigour of his protest in *Auch ein Wort über unser Judentum* (1880). He castigated Treitschke for his irresponsibility as a university teacher in not publicly denouncing the use of his name in connection with the petition and for encouraging chauvinism in his lectures. As a liberal Mommsen was just as keen as Treitschke to eradicate social, regional and religious problems in the new Germany, but he was one of the few to recognise the truth of Moltke's dictum: the victorious general of Prussia's wars (1864–71) had once said that what had been won on the battlefield needed thirty years to be assimilated. It was Treitschke, not Mommsen, who won the attention of the younger generation, who became progressively more extreme in their views on German superiority and racial purity. Student associations, especially athletic clubs, showed a marked tendency to exclude Jews, or even to threaten fellow students, who happened to be Jews, with violence. In 1903 the Minister of Education in Prussia considered the situation serious enough to warn teachers about it in a circular. Meanwhile the so-called Berlin Movement under Adolf Stöcker, the court preacher, tried to win people back to church by alleging a Jewish conspiracy against Christian workers in the late 1880s. He was successful in fomenting ill-feeling among the lower middle classes, though less so in increasing worship, and in conjunction with the lunatic fringe of German politics, the Dührings, Försters and Sonnenbergs, the Berlin Movement helped to win seventeen Reichstag seats for the Anti-semitic Party in 1896.

The verbal violence of antisocialites and antisemites alienated some sections of German society in the last years of the century. The position of another minority in the new Reich, the Catholics, had apparent similarities but even more significant differences. Bismarck's *Kulturkampf* (see p. 41) and the support it gained despite its illiberal character was part of the effort lavished by official and popular agencies on the image of a united and powerful Germany. From 1873 onwards he helped sponsor a series of bills designed to break the Catholic Church's monopoly in education for its members and to override its ruling that the children of mixed marriages must be Catholic; its legislation was also designed to weaken the Catholic Centre Party. As a political effort the *Kulturkampf* was one of Bismarck's most notable failures, and it had a serious effect on its liberal supporters: an anomalous situation arose when the allegedly less educated deputies of the Centre

Party quoted Goethe and Humboldt to the liberals in the Reichstag in defence of tolerance and freedom. Although the Centre Party emerged greatly strengthened from the affair, it could be said that it suffered politically in the long run: instead of becoming the moderate bourgeois party its founders in 1848 had envisaged, it became strictly Catholic. When Bismarck made his peace with the Catholics he found himself able to rely on their support. The conservative sympathies of the German state, the piety of her rulers and the economic prosperity of the 1890s almost completed the integration of the Catholics into the Reich. After this time opposition to the Empire from the Catholic territories, such as Bavaria, was based on regional loyalties rather than religion.

14

Two Novelists of the Empire: Fontane and Raabe

It was against this background that Germany's first genuine social novelist emerged in the late seventies. Theodor Fontane was born in Neu-Ruppin in 1819, the son of a pharmacist of French extraction. In *Meine Kinderjahre* (1894) he left a portrait of his father and of his childhood, a most entertaining and informative social document. He took up his father's profession, but soon changed to journalism; he became known as a writer of ballads, and produced some 3,500 pages on the history of the three Prussian wars, as well as a new type of local history, the *Wanderungen in der Mark Brandenburg*. Had Fontane died (as Hebbel did) at the age of sixty, he would have been a peripheral figure in German literature; commentators might have reiterated the words he wrote to his English friend James Morris in the year of his death: 'the little I had to give came out despite all; I have no complaints to make about my fate.'[1] In 1878, at the age of fifty-nine, Fontane published his first novel and followed this with fifteen more over the next twenty years. He made a point of ironic self-disparagement, but there was exceptional dedication in the way he set aside the last years of his life for creative writing, having worked hard all his life to make a modest living; despite only moderate success, he resolutely refused attractive financial offers for alternative work. Fontane and Keller were born in the same year. When Keller, published his mature work, *Das Sinngedicht,* Fontane had not yet published his first 'Berlin' novel, *L'Adultera* (1882). In the subject matter of his novels, in his openness as a critic to contemporary life and art, his appreciation of Zola, Ibsen and others, and also in his recognition and encouragement of such German naturalist writers as Hauptmann, Holz and Schlaf, Fontane seems to belong to a later generation than that to which he belonged by the date of his birth. But in his literary conventions, in his moral and social attitudes, he looks back to the German realist writers such as Keller.

It was fashionable among German scholars some decades back to look upon Fontane as a 'lightweight' and to attribute his urbanity to his French ancestry: there is no-one quite like him in nineteenth-century German narrative writing. He belongs more to European realism than to the literary tradition of his native country; his work was influenced by Jane Austen, George Eliot, Thackeray and the Russian realist writers. Like Switzerland in Keller's novellas, Prussia in Fontane's novels is a natural part of the European world. However he quite obviously preferred to portray a specific social class, despite his claim to be depicting 'the whole of life in its abundance, the great and small alike.'[2] Almost all his novels are set in aristocratic circles, with some bourgeois characters and a variety of old retainers; although he personally was in sympathy with social democracy, he tended to ignore or to prettify the working class of the Berlin of his time.[3] These self-imposed restrictions set boundaries to his social comment, but he owed his success to his basic assumption, uncommon among his predecessors and contemporaries in Germany, that novels are in the first place about people.

Fontane's intellectual personality was the product of a rather haphazard education supervised by his father. He worked as a dispenser in various pharmacies from 1839–49; in 1844 he joined the Berlin *Tunnel,* a literary club of a type common enough in those days, which met at regular intervals and brought him into contact with Prussian officers, officials and professional men who served him as models for his characters. Like Lewin, the hero of his first novel, *Vor dem Sturm,* Fontane read his ballads on patriotic subjects to his fellow members. Although a moderate liberal by conviction, his feelings about the 1848 Revolution were ambiguous, and from 1850 onwards he moved mainly in conservative circles. He became a journalist in 1849 and for many years struggled to support his wife and family by his writings alone. He gave private lessons, and spent three years in England as a press correspondent, having got a post in Manteuffel's press bureau (see p. 192) through a *Tunnel* friend. From 1860–70 he was employed by the reactionary *Kreuzzeitung.* He now had time to write what he enjoyed, and in company with a friend, W. Hertz, he began to explore the countryside of Brandenburg. Hertz published the *Wanderungen* in five instalments 1862-84. It was at this time that Fontane also wrote his history of the Prussian wars. He spent some time in France as a prisoner of war in 1870 and on his return found a congenial post as theatre critic from 1870-89 with the *Vossiche Zeitung*. To his wife's dismay he resigned a well-paid sinecure as secretary to the Royal Academy of Arts in Berlin in 1876 after only a few months, because they treated him not as an artist but as 'some poor pilgrim who should consider himself lucky to find a refuge'.[4]

At the end of his life Fontane asserted that the year 1870 had made him into a writer. He did not share the almost ritual feelings towards their art which animated his contemporaries Storm and Heyse. His impatient reference to Storm's 'eternal *Husumerei*' was prompted by what he wrongly regarded as Storm's artistic posturing; he did not understand the concern felt for German literary tradition by Stifter, Keller or Storm. He would prefer, he once said, to write leading articles than prize-winning tragedies.[5] Journalistic expressions and colloquialisms are said to mar his narrative prose in some novels, as for example *Die Poggenpuhls,* but this is not true of his major works. He won recognition from his younger colleagues, the naturalist writers; his obvious interest in social environment appealed to them. He encouraged Hauptman telling him 'to go on as he was doing',[6] and he explained his own position to Otto Brahm:

it would cost me nothing to transfer my allegiance to the side of the 'moderns' with all due solemnity. The moral aspect of the thing would n't worry me. The only thing I lack is a couple of hundred weight of conviction. I see the positive and the negative side and then I simply settle back into my armchair. You can afford to do that at the age of seventy-one.[7]

Thus, although he was influenced by many writers, Fontane's work belongs to no specific literary movement. His conciliatory if sceptical portrait of human nature is characteristic of a man grown old in the world without losing his curiosity.

Fontane's novels are generally of two kinds: the historical and the social or 'Berlin' novels. He also wrote two novels, *Ellernklipp* (1881) and *Unterm Birnbaum* (1885), which anticipate the modern detective story. His first fictional work was *Vor dem*

Sturm, which was set in Brandenburg in the months between Napoleon's defeat in Russia and the Prussian rising against the French. 'History', says Professor Schmidt in *Frau Jenny Treibel,* 'nearly always passes by what it should record'.[8] One of Fontane's central concerns in his novels is the reaction of great events in history on ordinary people's lives: *Vor dem Sturm* is full of interesting information about how people lived in those days, 1812–3, and has a broad social canvas. The action takes place mainly on the estates of the Prussian Junker von Vitzewitz and his relatives, and in the Berlin of the professional classes and the respectable poor. It is in the portraits of Berlin and of local life that he anticipates his characteristic art: the Vitzewitz family servants, the war veterans at the inn and the impressively grotesque evening entertainment given by Frau Hulen, Lewin von Vitzewitz's landlady.

The patriotic impulse analysed in the novel and the choice of the year 1812–13 were on the face of it highly suited to the temper of German readers after 1871; Fontane too was quite capable of intense patriotism as is shown by his war histories or his poem to 'Bismarck-Siegfried' of 1885. But he surprised and disappointed his readers by his lack of bias against the French and the Poles, by his lack of the chauvinism to be found in those contemporary historical novels which commanded a wide public, such as Dahn's *Kampf um Rom* (1876). Only 510 copies of his novel were sold. Patriotism was by this time almost synonymous with virtue and readers were displeased to note that the French officers in the novel were invariably chivalrous, that the Pole made a penetrating criticism of the Prussian mentality, and that Bernd von Vitzewitz's chauvinism was gradually revealed as a grotesque fantasy. Fontane's portrayal of the national question links him with his own generation which had experienced the 1848 Revolution as young men; it also shows him to be possessed with a levelheadedness uncommon among Germans when discussing such matters. The central events of this novel are the development of Bernd von Vitzewitz from extreme to moderate nationalism, his son Lewin's story, and the heroic death of two minor figures, the middle class historian, Hansen-Grell and the lawyer Othegraven. Fontane was here concerned with the nature of genuine patriotism, which can countenance apparent disloyalty to one's class or country of origin. Thus the inspiration of Othegraven's heroism is not Prussian chauvinism but the ideas of the French Revolution, which has helped men to realise that noble action in defence of freedom is open to all. Fontane tried to show that patriotism was not, as many liked to think, the prerogative of the nobility or the establishment. It is made clear that he was arguing here in favour of individual initiative and his – in a German context – most original acceptance of the French Revolution is based on his appreciation of the opportunities and energies which it liberated.

Fontane conceived this novel during his time on the *Kreuzeitung*. The Prussian nobility provided him with his most rewarding theme, but his attitude to this class underwent a significant change: this was already apparent in his next novel, *Schach von Wuthenow*, written between 1878 and 1883. This is the story of a Prussian officer in the years before the battle of Jena (1806), who lacked the moral courage to face mockery from his companions by marrying the pocked-marked but intelligent Victoire, whom he has seduced, or to flout social convention and impugn his 'soldier's honour' by refusing. In the end Schach satisfies convention but shoots himself immediately after the wedding ceremony. Here Fontane first achieves that economy of narrative and that indirect characterization which are the outstanding qualities of his best works. As in his previous novel, he depicts the dichotomy in social, military and national life in Prussia by means of the interplay of related characters. Schach's refinement and honesty side by side with his lack of moral fibre is paralleled by the weakness of the state on the eve of Prussia's greatest military defeat. The distinction between authentic and conventional patriotism and honour in both novels was certainly prompted by Fontane's impatience at contemporary preference for the extravagant gesture over true feeling.

In the novels written in the eighties Fontane chose unconventional themes: in *L'Adultera* (1882) he depicted adultery in a respectable bourgeois setting, in *Cécile* (1887) he told the story of the former mistress of a prince who kills herself after her present husband has killed her new admirer in a duel. *Irrungen Wirrungen* (1888) and *Stine* (1890) are finely drawn portraits of milieux and social types, the theme in each one being a love affair between an aristocrat and a 'girl from the people'. The title of his first Berlin novel, *L'Adultera*, recalls the vogue for 'shocking' titles, such as *Fräulein Mutter* and the like, which became common in the 1880s, but though numerous suicides and violent deaths occur in his novels, their presentation is entirely undramatic.[9] In *L'Adultera* Melanie, married to an affectionate parvenu husband, deserts him for the bohemian Rubehn. The world of the nouveaux riches, which he was to portray so pungently in *Frau Jenny Treibel* a decade later, was drawn with great sophistication here. By far the greater part of this novel (as also of the other three Berlin novels mentioned above) is taken up with Fontane's description of his milieu, which is conveyed through his splendid dialogue, especially around the breakfast or dinner table. He himself was a renowned conversationalist – *causeur* is the word most often used by his critics – and the conversations occurring in his novels, during the typical dinner parties and excursions, were unequalled in German literature. Frequently, as here, in *Irrungen Wirrungen,* and in a later novel, *Effi Briest,* these social occasions provide a turning point in the action or serve to crystalise a relationship. Such is the author's delight in talk that he seems on occasion to leave the plot aside for a while and continue and elaborate the dinner table conversation as the guests return home in their carriages. Human relationships fascinated him; he did not bother with the meticulous description of the scene of action, which his naturalist contemporaries favoured. In these short novels of the eighties his historical and journalistic interests were still much in evidence. Numerous aspects of the time are gently ridiculed: the contemporary, arrogant belief of the middle classes that they have the prerogative of education; the vogue for Wagner; the military quality of life in the Empire, and the *Kulturkampf,* which had only just drawn to a close, as in *L'Adultera, Cécile, Frau Jenny Treibel* (1892) and many others. Fontane takes a subtle revenge on hidebound attitudes by making their representatives into bores: as for instance the ultraconservatives Rossow (*Cécile*) and Lieutenant Vogelsang in *Frau Jenny.* The conversation about Bismarck on the eve of Melanie's departure (in *L'Adultera*) reflects the complexity of Fontane's own feelings about Bismarck, and it also contains some ironic criticism of the contemporary adulation of success. It is a fine example of Fontane's narrative art, for it further serves to show how irrevocably Melanie is separated from her husband and how little he has understood her.

In his last years Fontane achieved mastery. *Unwiederbringlich,* published in 1891, is a psychological study of married life in early middle age and of the incompatibility of temperaments. It was written just after Fontane suffered the loss of his own son, George, and is the most deeply felt of all his novels. As it was based (like *L'Adultera*) on a contemporary incident, he set it in a world that was unfamiliar to most of his readers, namely in Schleswig-Holstein and Copenhagen. Whether because of this or because of its wholly unsentimental portrayal of suffering and disillusionment, the novel was not popular. C. F. Meyer, as always, perceptive and original in his literary judgement, called it 'the finest thing . . . which the *(Deutsche) Rundschau* has ever published in the pure novel form.' Countess Christine von Holk alienates her husband by her rigid piety at a time of incipient crisis in their relationship. Her emotionalism in matters of worship is an outlet for her frigid nature, which is one of the principal factors in the estrangement between husband and wife. Christine insists on sending their two teenage children to pietist boarding schools, and Helmut, her husband, who is easy-going and kindly, and essentially more interested in the planning of new cow sheds for his shorthorns than in the education of his children, allows himself to be irritated by her dominance and her sentimentality. At this point in the story, he is called to attend the Danish court; his wife, on the plea of attending to the children's schools, does not accompany him, and in the subsequent months in Copenhagen he gradually becomes estranged from her. The novel is told from both points of view, and the formal balance of the four parts, the first and last set on the Holks' estate, the second and third in Copenhagen, was something Fontane had not yet previously achieved. The relationships of the principal characters are explored and the inner tensions revealed in the many social occasions that occur in the course of the novel. The report of Christine's suicide in the sea just in front of the house is very moving; suddenly we realise the complete necessity of her fate from the moment the book opens.

The public responded much more positively to Fontane's second great novel, *Effi Briest* (1895), than to the stark unspoken tragedy of *Unwiederbringlich*. *Effi Briest* was his first novel to win popular acclaim and in the first year it went into five editions. It is the story of the only daughter of a noble country family, who marries a former suitor of her mother's, Baron von Innstetten, when she is only seventeen years of age. Many years later Innstetten discovers evidence of a brief and frivolous affair between Effi and a Major Crampas, which had taken place while the couple were living in a lonely Baltic spa. Innstetten feels obliged to avenge himself. He fights Crampas in a duel and kills him; Effi he condemns to the solitary life of a divorcée in contemporary Berlin, not to avenge himself on her, but because he believes it to be his duty to separate their only child from a mother who could behave so irresponsibly. In his portrayal of Innstetten, Fontane touches once more on the concept of Prussian honour, which he had treated in *Vor dem Sturm* and *Schach von Wutenow,* and implies the fundamental wrongheadedness which could make a man feel obliged to inflict such suffering on himself and on Effi, and affect their child so adversely. One of the finest scenes which Fontane ever wrote is to be found in this novel, when her ten year old daughter is allowed to visit Effi a couple of years after the divorce. The child's emotions have become confused by the picture she has been given of her mother, and she answers each of Effi's agonised efforts to elicit a gesture of affection by an almost mechanical phrase: 'if I'm allowed.'[10] The achievement of *Unwiederbringlich* and *Effi Briest,* the sustained evocation of an entire social world, is even more impressive when one considers the rarity of this type of novel in Germany. The ambivalence of social convention is made wonderfully apparent in the conversations Innstetten has with his friend Wüllersdorf before deciding to divorce Effi, and between the servants, the Protestant Johanna and the Catholic Roswitha, who eventually leaves the household to join her mistress. Mercifully, Fontane had no message to preach, he had nothing of the social reformer in him.

Frau Jenny Treibel, which appeared in 1892, is Fontane's one overtly satirical novel. Frau Jenny personifies that type of middle class lady about whom in his diaries and letters he makes his most bitter observations – if it is correct to speak about bitterness in one so tolerant and sceptical as Fontane.[11] She is hardheaded, ruthless and nauseatingly sentimental, but neither she nor her rivals and associates ever learn their lesson. After inevitable marital complications, the two worlds depicted here, the commercial and intellectual bourgeoisie, remain tidily separate, and ironic humour replaces the original satirical intention. Fontane's observation of the German scene since 1848 had made him sceptical of the middle classes as a social and political entity. His attitude towards the liberals both before and after unification (1871) was tinged with irony; towards the end of his life, when this novel was written, his strictures had become almost harsh. When one reviews the body of his work, his portrait of the middle class is indeed an unfavourable one: egocentric to the point of being social boors – Eginhard von dem Grund in *Cécile* – ignorant and intolerant as the Gundermanns in *Der Stechlin* etc. The only exceptions are the eccentrics, whose humanity reflects Fontane's own personality, such as the chemist Gieshübler, who proves such a friend to Effi Briest, or Professor Schmidt, the verbose and affectionate father of Corinna in *Frau Jenny,* and at one time favoured by Frau Jenny's regard. As a study of eccentricity on the one hand, and egocentricity on the other hand, *Frau Jenny Treibel* is marvellously varied. The professor, his colleagues and his housekeeper, a policeman's widow, are all of them eccentric, while Jenny herself, Corinna and the reactionary Lieutenant Vogelsang are egocentrics of one kind and another. The conversation is superb and all but replaces action, conjuring up a precise and at all times entertaining picture of Berlin of the newly rich commercial counsellors and their 'courts' and the pedantic but rewarding life of grammar school teachers.

Splendid conversation and much inner action are characteristic of Fontane's last novel, *Der Stechlin,* published in 1898 in the year of his death. *Der Stechlin* had not the development of his two finest novels, but just as *Ein Bruderzwist im Hause Habsburg* will always have a particular appeal to a lover of Grillparzer, this novel must always be a favourite with any admirer of Fontane, since it contains so much of the personality and the creative world of its author. Fontane's conciliatory scepticism with regard to humanity and human aspirations permeates the novel, which has for its theme the situation of the Prussian country nobility in the contemporary world. In the aphoristic style of this late work Fontane gives free play once more to his tolerance and his dislike of intellectual and moral dogmatism: 'There are no such things as absolute truths and if there are they're tedious,' Stechlin observes in the opening chapter.[12] The character of this old Prussian nobleman, Dubslav Stechlin, reflects Fontane's delight in the variety and the contradiction in human life, often present in one and the same character. He often used linguistically antithetical names to express these contradictions – as the compound of Slav and German here or in the composer Niels Wroschowitz in the same novel, or puns, like Frau Dörr of a fat woman, Fräulein Honig of a soured spinster (in *Irrungen Wirrungen* and *Frau Jenny Treibel*) and antithetical pairs of characters like Dubslav and his sister Domina Adelheid Stechlin. In a sense Dubslav was Fontane's self-portrait in the setting of the Germany of his old age: like the author the hero is aware of the fact of change, of the disappearance of the society and the nation which he had known in his prime, and sceptical of the ability of the individual to avert social and political change, however he might regret it. Fontane like his chief characters lacked passion but had conviction and moral earnestness; he also shared another quality with them, uncommon in the prosperous Second Empire, namely humour.

As a writer and commentator of his time both in his novels and his historical and journalistic work, Fontane is an example of the intelligent and moderate critic so uncommon in Germany and Austria.[13] He reminds his readers that most of us have preconceived notions and that we are inclined to attribute base motives to the actions and attitudes of people in society, which rather have their origin in the narrow confines of the world in which they live. Perhaps no German writer before Thomas Mann conveyed social reality with such richness and such subtlety as he did. His biography as well as his work are most illuminating for what they tell us about the development of social attitudes in Germany during the second half of the nineteenth century, in particular the failure of liberalism. Thus at the end of his life he wrote to his son on the occasion of the 1898 election:

> this whole election business cannot possibly be wisdom's final and most splendid stage. In England or America perhaps, or even certainly – but in Germany, where first a policeman, and then a battalion and then a battery stand behind each voter, it all seems like a waste of time to me. What must stand behind a popular election is popular sovereignty and if that is missing, none of the rest matters.[14]

Fontane was a critic in the nineteenth-century tradition, but less rigorous, and indeed less far-seeing than Kierkegaard, Marx or Nietzsche. He however did not believe in the necessity for absolute choice. He was more of a child of his time than these critics were, possessed of more commonsense than vision, and despite his criti-

cism: 'so long as one takes all things around one for granted, everything is fine; but the moment one begins to criticise, it all collapses.
Society is a horror,'[15] he identified himself by and large with the
world in which he lived. He had no regard for moral and social
utopianism; ethical problems were treated as relative, not absolute
in his work; he drew no prophetic conclusions. His modesty, his
humanity and his humour made him a perceptive critic of his
countrymen in a specific historical situation. Perhaps his most telling comment on that situation and one that was to remain valid
for many years was made to his son in 1890: 'We somehow can't
manage to be sure of ourselves.'[16]

Wilhelm Raabe

Unlike Fontane, the novelist Wilhelm Raabe enjoyed considerable popularity in his lifetime and even received some official
recognition. In our own time he has become highly regarded in
serious literary circles, though not for those works which made
him known in the nineteenth century. He has often been described
as the German novelist *par excellence*: nationalists in his own time
and since have praised his portrayal of 'German' virtues. It was
Raabe who said: 'the French conscience is in Paris, the English in
London, but do not let us fool ourselves, the German is by no
means in Berlin.'[17] A keen observer of his own times, and a far
more complex and sophisticated writer than readers of his early
and popular works might have foreseen, the basic theme of
Raabe's work is man in an age of social change. His intuitive perception of the specific local and temporal situation is apparent in
all his major works. He combined a grasp of the anomalous
position of the German writer and man of letters in the society of
his time, with his own generation's political passivity. The particular interest of his work is that he wrote in the context of the everyday world of the German middle class: Raabe was clearly identified with a particular section of society; this had never been the
case with Stifter or Keller. In the works of his maturity and old
age, he developed a personal ironic style which was most perceptive in its evaluation of that section of society at a particular and
significant stage in its history.

Raabe was born in 1831, one of the few major figures to be born
in Germany in that decade, and he produced his first novel, *Die*

Chronik der Sperlingsgasse in 1857, some twenty years before Fontane published his. His birthplace was Echtershausen in Brunswick, and he spent almost his whole life in small towns. He never knew the formative influence of life in a city and he had no contact with his fellow writers. He did not exercise a bourgeois profession as they did: after a brief period at university he relied wholly on his writing for a living, something which often entailed personal sacrifice and hardship. His first novel was his most popular and drew warm praise, among other critics, from the historical novelist Alexis. Raabe employed the reminiscence technique used by Storm and others: the story probably earned its popularity from its portrayal of ordinary German folk as they liked to see see themselves then, affectionate, impractical and patient in times of trial. There are many contemporary allusions in the book: while in the 1830s these tended to be literary, now such references were consciously political and social.

The success of his first novel helped him to find a publisher for his next works, which he wrote in fairly rapid succession on contemporary or historical themes. His publisher followed the common practice of the time, in that the novels were serialised and then, if successful, were published in book form. Raabe's novels usually appeared in *Westermanns Monatshefte,* which had been founded in 1856 as an organ of the mildly liberal middle classes. In 1862 he moved to the South, for eight years, to Stuttgart, which was then a town of some 62,000 inhabitants. The experience was crucial to his work. His next novels, even where unsuccessful in execution, showed a new awareness of the moral problems of contemporary life. Raabe followed events in Prussia closely and rightly regarded these years as the turning point of the century for Germany. Württemberg was of all southern states the most receptive to Prussia's point of view, as Treitschke noted with satisfaction. (This did not prevent great bitterness against Prussia among Raabe's circle of friends, for not all Swabians were in agreement on the subject.) He wrote three of his best known novels while in Stuttgart: *Der Hungerpastor* (1864), *Abu Telfan* (1867) and *Der Schüdderump* (1870). He refered to them, without much justification, as a trilogy. They represent stages in the development of his art and his social attitudes.

Artistically *Der Hungerpastor* is one of Raabe's weaker novels, but since all the evidence over the next decades suggests that the

Tradition and Revolution

attitudes it expressed were to become widely representative of the
German public, it is worth examining it more closely. The 'Hungerpastor' of the title is Hans Unwirrsch, the orphaned son of a poor
tailor, who follows the familiar path of the impoverished but noble-
minded German novel hero: diligent schoolboy and idealistic
student, he later becomes tutor in a commercial family and finally
a parson in an obscure East Prussian village. The period as tutor
gives the author an opportunity to digress on the spiritual and
social horrors of the modern city, as Berlin seemed to many
provincials in the 1860's – 'a fearful lurking monster'.[18] The title
of the book refers less to Hans' poverty than to his hunger for truth
and goodness; to make his point Raabe associates his hero with a
Jew, Moses, somewhat in the way Freytag had done in *Soll und
Haben*. Moses is in every respect Hans' opposite; early in the story
Hans saves the little Jewish boy from the cruelty of the other
children who are taunting him with cries of 'Hep! Hep!'[19] In the
scenes which follow in the home of the boy's father, the pawn-
broker Samuel, Raabe includes interesting social material to show
the historical reasons for the peculiar character of the Jew in
German society. The product of this environment, Moses, is
thoroughly unpleasant but extremely talented. Hans' hunger for
spiritual goods contrasts with Moses' hunger for success and riches.
Both achieve what they desire, but whereas Hans remains innocent,
Moses becomes morally and intellectually corrupt. It is probably
true that Moses stands, not for the Jew as such, but for the renegade,[20] but the portrait of his character and the continual references to the contrasting 'German' virtues in Hans certainly appealed
to contemporary prejudices against the Jews. Whereas Freytag's
Veit Itzel was a superficial caricature, Raabe's portrayal of Moses
was much more subtle. It is astonishing how Raabe foreshadows
the prejudices of anti-Jewish feeling, directed principally at the
intellectual or emancipated Jew: the Germans love animals while
the Jews are cruel or at best indifferent to them; the Jew is a cold
rationalist, using knowledge as a means to an end; he is incapable
of the love of learning for its own sake, or indeed of the emotional
depth of the German; he will succeed at the expense of the
German. The impression left on the reader was of the deep alienation of the Jew from that humanity which is the most prominent
feature of the German character. *Der Hungerpastor* was immedi-

ately popular and became a best seller toward the end of Raabe's life.

Raabe shared the fate of many great writers when he outgrew the views expressed in his early work to which his readers still clung. His impatient comment in 1902 was still valid some forty years later : 'people are quite happy with the stale fare of my youth, with the *Chronik* and the *Hungerpastor,* they don't bother with the rest.'[21] Towards the end of the latter novel, he introduced an ironic note, questioning the excessively black and white picture he has drawn, though without properly integrating this. Ironic questioning lends a note of appeal to *Abu Telfan,* which is concerned with one of Raabe's most fruitful themes: the antithesis between freedom and conformity. Leonhard Hagebucher returns to his provincial home in Germany after ten years of slavery in Africa. With his new understanding of human nature which he has learned in captivity he tries to put life into the archaic self-satisfied community of his home, and to come to terms with everyday life himself. This novel contains Raabe's celebrated statement that the German genius draws a great part of its strength from German philistinism, a theme many of his later novels also dwell upon.[22] Here he depicted the narrow world of most Germans on the eve of unification – it was finished at the moment when the North German Confederation was formed by Bismarck in 1867. He included some bitter satire on court life in the small state where Leonhard had his home, but the main interest was focussed on the provincial bourgeoisie, whose virtues Hagebucher eventually acknowledges. The minor figures are the most memorable, as in his previous novel; they serve to encourage the hero and to mediate between him and the world. One such figure is cousin Wassertreter, the ex-revolutionary and near-alcoholic. Like Stifter, Keller, and to a lesser degree Fontane, Raabe expressed his feelings about society by investing the many eccentrics of the novels with greater vision than their fellows, and like these writers he often invested these eccentrics with many of his own traits of character. Certainly odd and even freakish characters abound in Raabe's work. In *Abu Telfan* as elsewhere the eccentrics help to bring about the process of disillusionment to which the chief figures are subjected. These learn to differentiate between ideals in theory and in practice, a reference no doubt to the facile optimism of intellectual and political liberals at the time of writing. The social setting of this novel is full of interest; essentially it tries to show the clash of two worlds as in *Der Hungerpastor,* but in the later novel Raabe showed a far greater awareness of the complexity in their relationship than had the naive antithesis of the earlier.

Raabe was forty years old when the Empire was declared. As with most of his generation, the following years wrought changes in him. His political views were fairly typical of his class: he had undergone the conversion of most moderate North German liberals to Bismarck's national policy, and he shared in the initial sense of exaltation in 1870–1. But almost immediately he became disillusioned. However, instead of drawing into a fictional world of his own making, as some Germans did in these years, he depicted the contemporary scene in a series of fine novels in the 1870s and 1880s. *Christian Pechlin* (1872) described the rapid transformation from patriotism to the 'moneybag mentality' (Fontane's phrase). Raabe accepted the fact of change; he accepted, as perhaps Stifter and Storm did not, that time cannot be held back and that change is irreversible. In *Horacker* (1876), *Alte Nester* (1880) and *Unruhige Gäste* (1886) he showed the disadvantages of provincial life whose passing was making people idealise it. For him, change in the physical appearance and social patterns of life were governed by the same inevitability and irrevocability as the passage from childhood to adult life. *Villa Schönow* (1883) and *Pfisters Mühle* (1884) discuss the process of transforming the rural landscape into an industrial one. This last is a remarkable work, something between a long short story and a short novel. Its realism was rejected by the first publisher to whom Raabe offered it on account of 'its bad odours'. The action of *Pfisters Mühle* takes place within the space of a short holiday; Raabe often compressed the external action of his novels into a single day. He extended this day backwards in time as the plot unfolded and thus anticipated, as modern critics have noticed, the spatial form of twentieth-century novels. The brief period in which change is accomplished at Pfister's mill reminds the reader of the extraordinary rapidness of the industrial revolution in Germany. The story ends on an optimistic note, suggesting that it is possible to marry the new world with the old. However the opposite is the case with Raabe's subsequent novels on the same subject, *Im alten Eisen* (1887) and his late work *Die Akten des Vogelsangs* (1896). The too rapid transformation of Germany from a rural community with its traditions stretching far back into the past to an industrial, a – historical world is seen to destroy the human community without finding an adequate substitute.

In his sixtieth year Raabe published his masterpiece, *Stopf-kuchen* (1891). It was the summary of his achievement, though not his last novel. The story and its hero are made up of a series of paradoxes and double meanings, which represent the author, his work and his philosophy of life. It shows Raabe's unswerving concern with the lower middle class world from which he came and in which he lived most of his life, his strictures on it and his need for it. The language in which the story is told is a parody of the style of the contemporary semi-educated man, or *Bildungsphilister*, who is often the butt of Raabe's sarcasm as for example the splendid character study of Dr Brokenkorb in *Im alten Eisen*. At the same time his narrative method pokes fun at its author's own narrative habits in all his works, in particular his use of literary allusions and quotations. Even the book's sub-title teases the reader and mocks gently at the public demand for sensation. He called *Stopf-kuchen* 'a murder and sea story', which in one sense it is, but he arouses expectations which are not fulfilled. Stopfkuchen, the hero, so named for his greediness as a boy, is like Raabe in making a virtue of his defects and at the same time mocking himself. Familiarity with this great novel makes one ever more aware of its artistry, which is most notable in the treatment of time and in the astonishing diversity of narrative perspectives. The novel offers a unique picture of the world of Raabe's generation and a subtle commentary on the last quarter of a century which had wrought such changes in Germany. Perhaps such ironic detachment as he achieved here was only possible in an older man, but the fact remains that his novel is remote from the world of other realist writers in Germany in these decades, apart from Fontane's later novels, which were being written at this time. Both writers provide a wry commentary on their age, and both have in common the fact that they utter far harsher criticism in their letters than in their novels. Raabe here gradually deflated the contemporary cult of personality, the admiration afforded to 'the man of action', prompting a critic to call *Stopfkuchen* an 'anti-Faust'.

The narrative is shared between two former school-mates, Stopf-kuchen and Eduard. Eduard is a successful merchant living overseas, who has returned home for a holiday (aboard a ship called *Leonhard Hagebucher* – a nice touch of self-irony on Raabe's part!). Stopfkuchen, or Heinrich Schumann, to give him his real name, has never left home, having made it his life's aim to clear the name of a man accused of murder and win the hand of his daughter. At the opening of the novel he appears as a comfortable bourgeois, with every appearance of the philistine, with his sententious conversation and his idiosyncratic museum of antediluvian remains (Dubslav Stechlin also had a museum full of the most extraordinary objects, dear only to himself). Raabe employs a very complex reminiscence technique and the effect of the story is derived from the gradual process of revelation through narrative and monologue. The merchant adventurer Eduard is seen to be a very ordinary hero while Stopfkuchen's intellectual and human stature and his moral superiority over his former companion became apparent. Slowly Eduard is stripped of his illusions, of his sentimental picture of an idyllic childhood and of nature, while his heroism and his nostalgia appear as conventional and even contemptible instincts. Stopfkuchen by comparison is not clever, but wise and humane. The warmth and human concern embodied in the hero of *Stopfkuchen* is again and again offered by Raabe as the only worthwhile thing to offset the materialism of the time: see the historical novels *Das Odfeld* (1887) and *Hastenbeck* (1898), or *Horacker* and *Im alten Eisen*. With the characteristic artistry of this astonishing novel Raabe poked fun also at his own earlier taste for the sentimental and idyllic and at the public's continued preference for his youthful works. But there is a certain earnestness behind it all. 'I got them there right enough, the human *canaille*,' Raabe commented to Max Adler with a Stopfkuchen-like satisfaction after finishing the book.[23] While he clearly accepted the fact that values no longer exist which can have an absolute claim on man, he unmasked the vested interests which pose as substitutes. Injustice, persecution of the innocent and wanton destruction of the historical landscape are shown to be the pattern of the modern world, under the guise of 'progress' and 'development'. Raabe's *Stopfkuchen* is not meant as a 'solution' to the problem of the individual and society at such a time; the language of the book stresses its essentially private character. Perhaps the only message it offers is the belief in the power of humanity to come to terms with life in any situation.

Despite the relevance of his themes to the German society of his time, Raabe cannot be called a social novelist in the accepted sense. Rather he presents metaphysical problems in a precisely described social and historical milieu. At the same time he is surprisingly ready – for a German writer – to accept the fact of social change and to concentrate on trying to ensure the individual's ability to lead a worthwhile existence. The individual is thrown on his own resources: the images of refuge abound in his later work, like the Red Redoubt in *Stopfkuchen,* the cave in *Das Odfeld* and the tower in *Hastenbeck*. Raabe elaborates the idea of literature as an 'ark' preserving the intrinsic values of an existence in which he wished to believe. There are few more revealing allusions to the position of the artist in German society at the time. His late work shows how well he understood the combination of culture, sentimentality and self-irony, which he, and others since, have regarded as peculiarly German. He lacked like Fontane the passion of the truly involved writer and disappoints his readers occasionally by avoiding confrontations. He would not be without order in the world. The bitterness evoked by his sense of exclusion from life in his earlier novels gives way to a philosophic and humorous detachment. The questions he asked in his last novels are penetrating ones. Should life be lived in conformity with changing patterns of society at the cost of spiritual and intellectual values, or in self-imposed seclusion? Are these in fact mutually exclusive? Can one be involved in the process of historical change without sacrificing one's humanity?[24] Raabe presents honestly, and in his late works with very great subtlety, the ambivalence of this moral problem as he and his generation experienced it.

The Cultural Split
in Imperial Germany

The humour of Fontane or Raabe seems curiously remote from the spirit of the *Gründerzeit,* the first decades of the Second Empire. Although some of Germany's most gifted artists – Nietzsche, Wagner, Brahms, the historian Jakob Burckhardt, the painter von Marées – were living and working at the time, the arts in general declined. It was in these years that there emerged in Germany a sense of dichotomy between serious art and that favoured by official and popular taste: this development was later given the name of Germany's two cultures. It had been foreshadowed in the lack of popularity accorded to her major writers in the previous decades and was to become much more pronounced in the reign of Kaiser William II (1888–1918). Serious writers wrote for a diminishing public and felt cut off from society. On the other hand a large number of artists devoted their talents to supplying popular demand, with considerable profit.

Such artists, painters, writers and musicians earned acclaim for two main reasons. Firstly in their subject matter they contributed to the myth of national vigour and greatness which the new Reich sought to embody: the historical paintings of the Austrian Makart and of Lenbach, the historical novels of Felix Dahn, the dramas of Ernst von Wildenburch, who became a kind of 'house dramatist' of the Hohenzollerns, are cases in point. Secondly they favoured in their work the heroic and monumental, a deliberate stylisation which satisfied a current need. Official policy and popular taste were in general agreement: the new monuments, such as the massive *Germania* near Rüdesheim on the Rhine, showed the partnership at work. The authorities chose the subject and approved the style of execution; the public contributed handsomely. The cult of personality in art during this period was an

aspect of the widely felt desire for symbols of Germany's new position in the world and her recently acquired wealth. Writers who
had already made a name for themselves, such as the lyric poet
Geibel, responded to the situation in the works they produced after
1871, as for example Geibel's *Heroldsrufe* (1871), with the line,
a subsequent pan-German slogan: '*Am deutschen Wesen soll die
Welt genesen!*' (The German spirit shall cure the world!). The
historians, biographers and essayists of the time stressed the importance of the great man in history, the monumental figure who stands
above his age. They largely ignored the effects of environment on
character and attributed a mythical stature to those of whom they
wrote: thus Hermann Grimm in his essays on great men in the
recent past, Treitschke in his stylistically compelling and highly
partial *History of Germany in the Nineteenth Century* (1878-94),
Wilhelm Jordan, who liked to call himself the 'Homer of the North',
in his *Nibelungen* (1868–74). Intellectuals, artists and politicians
attributed to themselves and their work a similar exalted character.
They wrote their memoirs as they executed their work 'for posterity'. Anselm Feuerbach the painter called his memoirs:
Vermächtnis (Legacy), stating openly : 'I am indeed aware that I
have been called to great things.'[1] The language of literature and
criticism, of public speeches and the press favoured highflown
pathos in keeping with the pretensions of life.

In these years Richard Wagner (1813–83) was raised by popular
esteem to being the most celebrated artist in Germany, although he
was still a controversial figure for many. He had left Germany after
the collapse of the 1848 Revolution in which he had taken an active
part, and only returned in 1861. His *Ring of the Nibelungen* had
been composed in exile and during his wanderings in Europe he
had elaborated his ideas on the national regeneration of his own
country. Patronised by Ludwig II of Bavaria, who succeeded to
the throne in 1864, he followed a similar pattern to that of many
other ex-revolutionary Germans in his acceptance of Bismarck's
Germany. Wagner's interest lay in the 'national community', not
the German state, but, as on subsequent occasions in Germany's
history, the representational character of his music and his musical
festivals was very acceptable to the authorities in the 1870s and
1880s. In the forties he had written on revolution, two decades
later he was writing on the Germans, and in 1871 he composed a
triumphal march in honour of the German troops' entry into

Paris. In the following year, through the money made available by Ludwig II, the building of the festival opera house at Bayreuth began. In this context the reception of Wagner's music and the Bayreuth festivals are of particular interest as the implementation of his ideas on the national community. Wagner saw himself doing for Germany what Sophocles had done for Athens, creating the sense of a nation or 'folk' community through the active participation of the audience in the stage performance of his work.

The ritual aspect of Bayreuth struck all its visitors. It was in fact an extension, with a new stress on its specifically German character, of the traditional attitude towards theatre-going. German demeanour in the theatre had for many decades resembled that thought proper in a church. The sense of a whole people enacting a solemn ritual in celebration of their nationhood did attract many people, quite apart from the sheer enjoyment of Wagner's music and his magnificent staging. There were plenty of critics too, indeed the controversial nature of Wagnerian performances was an additional attraction: it was an unending source of dinner table conversation.[2] The staging of his music dramas, the idea of the *Gesamtkunstwerk* embracing music, literature, philosophy, metaphysics and mythology, gave substance to the exalted national idea of the time. Wagner did much to make the new sense of nationhood articulate among Germans. The myths he incorporated into his work, Germanic and Celtic in origin, came alive to audiences in combination with his modern psychology. His romantic vision of a specifically German culture which would bring about a rebirth of the German race was persuasive, since it rested on ideas familiar to many. Above all, he appealed to the German bourgeoisie's new taste for pomp and magnificence. The theatre of Bayreuth was intended to be like the amphitheatre of ancient Greece in having none of the distinctions of rank and wealth of the European theatre, but in the event the 'national community' was not present there during the enactment of Wagner's works, primarily for financial reasons. Bayreuth became instead the centre for the wealthy of Europe and Germany and even attracted potentates from distant countries. Cosima, Wagner's second wife and the daughter of Franz Liszt, entertained the guests in famous open air parties. Although on a more lavish scale, these entertainments were on a par with the receptions the painter Makart gave in his home, an aspect of the association between the successful artist and the plutocracy in Imperial Germany.

Some other artists of the older generation began to respond to the public demand for patriotic and representational art. One of these was Adolf Menzel (1815–1905). After Menzel's death it was said disparagingly of him that he was 'a realist and lacked knowledge of the realm of higher ideals and thought'. Menzel was one of the few naturalists in nineteenth-century painting and certainly one of her greatest graphic artists of all time. In an age which was very conscious of history and of historical models in art, he was distinguished by the individuality of his work. He made several thousand sketches of contemporary uniforms and costumes before he executed his famous woodcuts to illustrate Franz Kugler's *Le Friedrichs des Großen* (1840–42). His historical work was close in conception to Ranke's 'history as it really was', by contrast with the stage representations of the past favoured by the much more popular painters Makart and Piloty. The same natural quality which appeared in this, his first major work, marks his impressionist paintings of 1845–50, which many consider his finest work – *Room with a balcony, The Berlin-Potsdam railway, The artist's sister with a candle* etc. After the period flavour of his paintings of Frederick II and his court executed in the fifties, Menzel turned his attention to contemporary subjects which suited his naturalist style: the 1866 war with all its 'horror, misery and stench' (Menzel's phrase), and industrial Germany, a theme very few of his fellow artists even attempted: *The rolling mill* (1875) is his most famous work in this field. Under the Second Empire he painted subjects in more popular taste, *William I leaving for the war* (1871) and scenes from contemporary society life: *Ballsouper* (1878) and showed on occasion a sardonic humour, absent from the work of his younger contemporaries in this period, with the exception of the illustrator Wilhelm Busch. Perhaps Menzel's greatest achievement lay not in his paintings but in his graphic art. His sketches of social types are a wonderfully comprehensive record of his age; his drawings are of real people, not, as for example in the work of the popular portrait and landscape artist Anselm Feuerbach, abstractions of some idea.

Successful painters during the Empire would have rejected Menzel's advice to a young artist who complained of having to earn his living in commercial art: 'accept everything as a genuine artistic problem.' Where Menzel, like the German realist writers, found subject matter even among insignificant people, most artists at this time were concerned with the idealised figure, the great personality. The inspiration of painting was for the majority primarily literary; it has been well said of Böcklin (1827–1910), whose paintings hung in most bourgeois homes, that his work was 'thought', not seen. Figural paintings predominated, and the draping of the figures received special attention (as in Feuerbach's *Iphigenie* or *Medea with a dagger,* both 1871 with their voluminous flowing garments). The flesh of the nude figures in paintings of the time had a curiously unreal quality, like that of marble angels on gravestones or the sculptured figures adorning public buildings. We can see a parallel here with the very popular novellas of Paul Heyse (1830–1914) written in the 1870s and 1880s, where the characters are always ideal figures, the women invariably beautiful and passionate, the men noble, intelligent and virile.[3] The painters Feuerbach, Makart, Lenbach and Böcklin personified ideas rather than painted human beings. The stylisation of painting and prose of the time gives their work a lifeless quality, or at least so it seems today: in their own time they emanated a sacred aura, in keeping with contemporary views on the function of art. It was the prevailing need for a sense of lofty purpose which thus encouraged the cult of the heroic in art. Undoubtedly this reflects in some degree the disappointment of the post-war years after the excitement of the founding of the Empire, and artists and public alike sought in this idealised monumental art an illusion or a mystery. Böcklin's most popular paintings – *Island of the dead* (five different versions exist, the first dated 1880), *Ruins by the sea* (three different versions 1880 ff.), *Vita somnium breve* (1888) – seemed impressive and meaningful to the thousands who hung copies of them in their drawing-rooms.

Perhaps Germany's finest painter in these years was the colorist Hans von Marées (1837–87). He showed the dedication of solitary and unrecognised artists and might have starved had not Franz Lenbach, the painter of Bismarck, Moltke and other notables of the Empire, supported him. His work was limited to a few canvases in which he made use of symbolic colour, anticipating the work of twentieth century expressionist painters. Like Feuerbach and Böcklin, von Marées spent most of his creative life in Rome. This was in the tradition of the nineteenth century German painter from the time of the Romantics onwards; it suggests that, for all the 'cash payments to culture', in Nietzsche's phrase, Germany of the *Gründerzeit* did not provide a climate favourable to artistic work. Another fine painter, Wilhelm Leibl (1844–1900), whom Courbet had acclaimed as Germany's leading painter when he was only twenty-five, exhibited in Paris but not in his own country. Apart from the Bavarian villagers whom he painted, Leibl won little recognition in Germany; his most distinguished work includes the character paintings, *Village politicians* (1876) and the enthralling study of village women listening to a sermon *Three women in a church* (1878–81).

Germany of the Second Empire found its chronicler in one of the most brilliant caricaturists of nineteenth century Europe and a great graphic artist, Wilhelm Busch (1832–1908). In several series of illustrated verse tales Busch presented a whole galaxy of German middle-class types in the years of the industrial revolution. He was the artist of solid domestic comforts, of the joys and irritations of family life, with children and pets figuring largely in the last category. He was not a political caricaturist, unlike those whom his penmanship inspired in the last years of the century, Th. Th. Heine or Olaf Gulbransson of *Simplicissimus*. His satire was social, and he invented and perfected the cartoon story, writing the verses himself, many of which have long since become household words in German. He poked fun at all the traditional foibles of the German bourgeoisie, their love of food and drink, of feather beds and nightcaps, their capacious waists in middle life, their womenfolk's passion for cleaning and the men's for smoky pipes. In *Tobias Knopp* (1876) he presented the life cycle of the average burgher, his abortive attempts at courtship, his eventual practical choice of Dorothea, his housekeeper, as his bride; his delight in the pleasures of the table increases still further after marriage and Busch depicts him with his serviette tucked round his chin, its corners sticking up like ears, making him look like a friendly pig; the final part deals with the birth and education of his daughter Julchen, introduced by the now famous lines: *Vater werden ist nicht schwer, Vater sein dagegen sehr.* (It's not hard to become a father, being one is very different.) Everybody finds happiness in cosy domesticity. The poet Balduin Bählamm (*Balduin Bählamm, der verhinderte Dichter*, 1883) yearns for liberty and leaves his dear ones to seek inspiration in the countryside. Here however he is subjected to all sorts of torments, from milkmaids and mosquitoes to jealous farmhands, earwigs and goats. Finally a terrible toothache sends him hastening home to the bosom of his family.

Busch, who originally wanted to be a painter, accepted a position on the staff of the satiric journal *Fliegende Blätter* in 1858. He made his reputation with *Max und Moritz* (1865), the tale in pictures and rhyme of two wicked schoolboys who play infamous pranks on the neighbours but are eventually brought to justice by a sly farmer. Like Nestroy, Busch was most popular among those whom he satirised. His wit was crude but of a kind that has entertained men for centuries. The villains fall headlong into thorny hedges; the scheming Jesuit Filucius and his associates in *Pater Filucius* (1872), which was written in the anticlerical spirit of the *Kulturkampf*, are kicked into a muddy duckpond. Virtue in general triumphs, but the punishment allotted to the wicked is usually far in excess of their villainy. Thus Max and Moritz are ground by the local miller and the bits are gobbled up by some ducks who happen to be passing; the tiresomely pious Helena (*Die fromme Helene*, 1872) indulges in so much liqueur to assist her devotions that she sets herself on fire from a nearby lamp and is burnt to death. Everyone is encouraged in Busch's drawings to see his neighbour in the satirical portrait, not himself, and the characteristic response of the Busch burgher to the fate of another: 'What's that to me?' was often the characteristic response to the artist's own message. Essentially however Busch was popular in his own day as he still is in our time for the brilliant penmanship and the superb economy of his line.

Critics of the Empire

Literature, thought and philosophy in the twentieth century owe an immense debt to Friedrich Nietzsche (1844–1900). In his own time he was truly a prophet without honour. His family background and youth – he was the son of a Lutheran parson in Saxony – was not untypical of many gifted Germans; in the insularity of the Second Empire his thought and its implications have no place. His countrymen were hardly aware of Nietzsche's existence until after his lapse into insanity in 1889. Nietzsche is that passionately committed critic so rare in nineteenth-century Germany, a moral reformer and a prophet. In his comments on the post-1871 period, he reminds one at times of Heine, whom he admired and whose wonderful command of language he shared. He lacked Heine's urbanity, and also his frivolity, but he was just as open to the ideas and achievements of other nations, a quality uncommon in his time. It is possible to relate many stylistic features in Nietzsche's work to the age in which he wrote, but it could dwarf his statutre and distort his thought to present him as a product of the *Gründerzeit*. The cultural criticism of a few of his contemporaries stimulated him, while the state of nineteenth-century Europe gave him the starting point from which he re-examined Western civilisation. Nietzsche accepted that he had failed to win recognition in his own country, but he showed pleasure when the Norwegian literary historian Brandes, Strindberg and the French philosopher and critic Taine paid tribute to him at the end of his active life. His strictures on the German mind suggested that he did not believe his contemporaries capable of grasping what he was trying to say; he was witty but malicious in his commentaries on German nationalism: 'The cost of power is a heavy one; power makes one asinine.' Or ' "*Deutschland, Deutschland über alles*", I fear that was the end of German philosophy.'[4]

The isolated figure of Nietzsche is a reminder of the fact that hardly any subject of the Second Empire submitted the new system to a searching criticism. The many who felt disappointed or disillusioned kept their comments to themselves or to a small circle, or they concentrated as artists on formal problems. Wilhelm Busch, Fontane and the older realist writers did not dissociate themselves from the age, despite their many anxious fears for the future of Germany. Even the liberal historian Mommsen, whose *Testament* (Will) carried such a harsh indictment of his fellow countrymen and the times, was criticising what its author had praised before 1871.[5] Moreover the *Testament* was suppressed after his death by his own wish and was not published until 1948. The orientalist Paul de Lagarde also provided criticism of the establishment in his *Über die gegenwärtige Lage des deutschen Reiches* (1875), but it is symptomatic of contemporary German attitudes that his strictures were almost entirely overshadowed in the public mind by his antisemitic views.

The last decades of the nineteenth century were probably the most self-conscious in Germany's history up to that time. People's obsessive concentration on the nature of Germany and the Germans

had its roots in the unsolved problem of her national identity. This
was a problem which went back to the origins of German nationalism in the late eighteenth century, and which has continued to
complicate her development ever since. The deliberate grafting
of the new Reich on to fictitious traditions made people attribute
a special significance to the role of German culture. For the
Romantics the idea of German culture offered a substitute for her
lack of political unity. Later in the nineteenth century Wilhelm
Riehl (1823–97) had introduced cultural history as a distinct
discipline; Riehl and Gustav Freytag had written popular novels
and stories on aspects of German cultural history. In his seminal
work, *Die Kultur der Renaissance in Italien* (1860), Jakob
Burckhardt explored the relationship between culture, religion
and the state. He however knew nothing of the notion of a German
culture morally superior to that of other nations, which historians
and journalists of the Empire proclaimed.

Jakob Burckhardt (1818–97), citizen of Basle and professor of
history and art, was a profound and farseeing critic who has
attracted greater attention in our own time than he received when
he was alive for his cultural criticism of Germany in the last decades
of the century. Burckhardt had turned down the chair of history
at Berlin after Ranke's death, before it was offered to Treitschke.
He was one of the first people to appreciate the nature of the
changes taking place in Germany in the years 1866–71 and to
record simply and dispassionately what was being lost. Unlike
liberal politician or academics of these years he was not emotional
in his disappointment; his criticism was that of a man with an
acute political sense. His cultural pessimism is recorded in his posthumously published *Weltgeschichtliche Betrachtungen,* a series
of lectures given to his students in Basle. In these and in some letters
he wrote at the end of his life, as for example the one written to
the ecclesiastical historian Ludwig von Pastor in 1896,[6] he made
a striking analysis of developments in Germany, and incidentally
revealed his unfashionable dislike of the heroic pose.[7] At the time
of the Franco-Prussian war and the founding of the Empire some
twenty-five years earlier, his comments centred on the break with
tradition which he rightfully regarded as the most serious result
of recent German history. His letters make most interesting and
entertaining reading, and are full of wise and astute comments

on his time. He made frequent sardonic references to the part played by academics, particularly the university professors – *viri eruditissimi* in his ironic phrase – in the betrayal of German cultural traditions in favour of a new glorification of power. He shows a certain affinity with Raabe on occasions, as in the letter to his Prussian friend, von Preen in 1870 : 'I really no longer know what can be the value of German culture in making the individual inwardly happy; all those small centres of culture, where the German spirit was sitting pretty *next door* to German philistinism, are being blown skyhigh with *éclat,* and after all, the chief consequence of centralisation is spiritual mediocrity.'[8]

Such criticism is particularly understandable coming from a citizen of Switzerland, with its traditions of democracy and decentralisation, but Burckhardt, like his countrymen, felt part of the wider German cultural tradition and thus experienced developments in the Empire after 1871 particularly keenly. He himself spent nearly all his life in Basle, where he met Nietzsche. The younger man was impressed by Burckhardt's rejection of the contemporary European belief in progress and his dislike of the nationalist myth. Burckhardt feared for Germany's future also, since he was convinced that the recent events in her history were creating a situation favourable to eventual domination by the masses. This, in his view must, necessarily end in despotism. 'People no longer believe in principles,' he once alleged, 'but they do believe in saviours.' Ideological tyrannies come in the wake of modern warfare such as Germany had just experienced, and in this country such a tyranny might come. Burckhardt was detached and solitary in his private life. His pessimism contrasts with the gracious, educated and stable world from which he came, a world which recognised a scale of values very different from that of the Second Empire.

Burckhardt was never affected by the conflicting claims of Switzerland's two dominant cultures, the German and the French, as was the Zurich-born poet and writer of *novellas,* Conrad Ferdinand Meyer (1825–98). He wrote on the occasion of the Franco-Prussian war in his diary : 'In this historic moment I was overwhelmed by an awareness of newfound maturity: I cast off my French being, and obeying an inner dictate, wrote *Huttens letzte Tage.*'[9] This was a verse cycle on Ulrich Hutten, a South German knight prominent during the Reformation in Germany for his challenge to papal authority, and regarded in the nineteenth century as one of the first German nationalists. *Hutten* (1871) was not Meyer's first work; a few years earlier he had had *Zwanzig Balladen von einem Schweitzer* published in Germany, but their reception was not auspicious. Prior to this he had written poetry in French, but from 1871 he wrote all his creative work in German, several lyric poems and some fourteen novellas of great artistry. Although he came from a wealthy patrician family and his comfortable circumstances aroused a certain envy in his compatriot Keller, Meyer seems a stranger to the secure world which Keller inhabits. His family background was most unstable; he inherited his mother's nervous instability and suffered deeply when she committed suicide by drowning: he too felt a strange fascination for water, which is a central symbol in his poetry. The effect of his nervous temperament on his work appeared in his reluctance to reveal his inner world, his preference for indirect narrative technique in his prose and for symbolist language in his poetry.

Meyer's art was his life. The energy that many other German writers had to use in earning their living was spent by Meyer in pursuit of ideal form. 'He was a *poeta,* a craftsman, whose poems have the quality of something handmade, like the products of a carpetweaver or a potter.'[10] He determinedly destroyed the manuscripts which did not satisfy him and he wrote and re-wrote his poems. There exist as many as fourteen different versions of a single poem and nearly all of his finest poems have at least four or five versions, usually composed over a period of several years. Meyer was influenced by the German Romantics, by that great master of form, August von Platen, and by contemporary French poets and prose writers. His work has many of the stylistic marks of the *Gründerzeit*: the preference for great historical personages as heroes of his stories, the quest for formal beauty, the stylisation of his landscape and costume. However, in his interpretation of historical figures and in the symbolic patterns of his poetry and narrative prose, he seems rather to belong to the European *fin de siècle*. The themes and images of his poetry are few. The matter of the poem is of secondary importance. Thus for example a lighthearted love poem such as *Die Ampel* and a serious religious poem such as *In einer Sturmesnacht* share the same central symbol of light. Often, in the course of rewriting a poem, he took an image, a phrase, even a line from one poem and used it in another quite dissimilar context. The effect of the final version is static and remote, but in his finest lyric poems it seems as if feeling has become pure form. In 1882 Meyer published a collection of his poetry. He wrote to Luise von François, a well-known historical novelist, who showed a kindly interest in the artist and his work: 'In *Jenatsch* and the *Heilige*' (two prose works) 'there is far more of myself, under various disguises, of *my real sufferings and passion*, than in these lyrics; they are little more than trifles or at most the expression of a subordinate aspect of my being.'[11] Even to a close friend with whom he liked to discuss artistic problems, Meyer feared to reveal himself. The lack of self-assurance expressed itself in the relentless pursuit of his art, in his effort to exclude subjective elements from his work, to translate atmosphere into symbol. Critics are in general agreement on the uneven quality of his work. Some of his poems and some of the figures in his stories recall Hofmannsthal's judgement: 'anecdotes from the chronicles made into pictures, doublets and armour, out of which voices speak . . . we feel the breath of a moribund century.'[12] Other works, his poems *Spätboot, Firnelicht, Der römische Brunnen, Die tote Liebe* etc, rank among the finest examples of German symbolist poetry. Meyer recognised that his uneasy relationship with the physical world was a source of his art, but he was also aware of the danger of empty stylisation: see his poem *Möwenflug* (final version 1882).[13]

Meyer's experience of life and art as an antithesis is perhaps more readily apparent in his stories. He is rightly regarded as one of the masters of the novella technique, particularly of the frame-work tale. No-one ever wrote novellas of greater artistry; sometimes, as in *Die Hochzeit des Mönchs* (1884), the intricate form is more arresting than the content of the tale. The figures of his stories are invariably persons of consequence at key points in history. Although his choice of characters and period reflected contemporary interest in the High Middle Ages, the Renaissance and the Counter-Reformation, Meyer's interpretation is ironic and his ambiguity modern. His figures tell us more of the unfathomable nature of man than of his vital and aggressive character. The contradictory quality of life is reflected in the different forces motivating one and the same individual. Stimulated by his travels in Italy in the late 1850s and by his reading of Burckhardt's *Die Kultur der Renaissance in Italien,* Meyer became fascinated by the a-moral character of Renaissance man and the aesthetic way of life; yet his own essentially religious nature is constantly evident. Meyer was influenced by his Reformed Protestant upbringing and the rather morbid religious views of his mother, which influenced his concept of fate in the stories. He found one of his most fruitful themes in the confrontation of the ethical and aesthetic, often in the same person. These opposing impulses motivating human action show the equivocal character of man at odds with his age, and make man unfathomable even to himself. The age in which Meyer lived encouraged scepticism, and like Keller, he soon became disillusioned with the new German Empire. The ambiguity of Meyer's 'heroic' characters show that fallacy of attributing his choice of the warrior, statesman, saint or reformer simply to a desire to compensate for his own weakness and instability, as some critics have alleged.

From his earliest prose tale *Das Amulet* (1873) to his last work *Angela Borgia* (1891), Meyer was concerned with illusion and reality, and he used this motif consistently to show the relativity of ideals and values in the modern world. Thomas à Becket, chancellor of Henry II and central figure of the elusive and compelling novella *Der Heilige* (1879), undergoes a change of personality when the King appoints him archbishop of Canterbury. From being a calculating statesman he becomes ascetic to the point of fanaticism. And yet even this central event of the story is made to seem ambiguous. There are contradictory explanations for every act and every speech of Thomas. Thus when he has been murdered at Henry's instigation, a relic is taken from the body of the man whom many now believe to have been a saint, and is brought to a sick girl. But she dies. Perhaps Thomas was never a saint; perhaps his whole career as archbishop was a magnificent deception to revenge himself on the King for having brought about the death of his, Thomas's, daughter, Grace. How can we know that truth and holiness and greatness exist? How can we recognise their existence, since the evil prosper and the mighty perish? *Der Heilige, Plautus im Nonnenkloster* (1882) and *Die Hochzeit des Mönchs,* showed deceit and brutality in alliance with religion. Later Meyer expressed his own his satisfaction with *Der Heilige*. He had set out, he said, to present the mind and life of a saint, and this equivocal portrait had emerged.

Seven years before the appearance of his finest novella, *Die Versuchung des Pescara* (1887), he declared it his intention: 'to proclaim with bugles and trumpets the might of the ethical.'[14] This intention was not realised. The problem of ethical choice is never relevant to Pescara himself, who is dying of a fatal wound received in his victorious battle of Pavia (1526) before the story opens. The 'temptation' only exists for Pescara's entourage and his contemporaries. The world of the Renaissance, the vital, a-moral men and women of the Italian courts, of the Spanish and French monarchies, reveal themselves in their reactions to the central character, a static and enigmatic figure, who becomes stylised into a sort of Christ. All the characters have something of the actual and potential Pescara in them, and all impute to him their own self-interest. The story portrays the world of politics as a world of wholly cynical intrigue yet one not lacking the aesthetic quality of a game. Religion, humanity, loyalty, justice are shown to be things to which men cling for self-preservation or cite in self-defence; Meyer failed signally to establish 'the might of the ethical'. In *Pescara* the conflict of the ethical and the aesthetic is unresolved at the end. Like Jürg Jenatsch in the story of the same name (1874), like Thomas, Pescara is released from his equivocal position by death. Death in Meyer's prose and poetry is represented as a supreme moment beyond good and evil, not the antithesis of life, but its fulfilment. The individual shows a heightened perception of beauty – as Pescara contemplating his wife Vittoria – a tranquil acceptance of fate at the moment of his dissolution.

In all the stories he wrote up to *Die Hochzeit des Mönchs* (1884), Meyer employed the fiction of a framework tale to exclude the omniscient narrator. The teller of the story is often used to draw attention to the essential ambiguity of the tale. Thus Poggio in *Plautus im Nonnenkloster* remarks: 'there is no such thing as a conscience common to all men: even among those of us who have a conscience it appears in different forms and guises.'[15] Or Hans, the narrator in *Der Heilige:* 'in passing judgement on anything, as in shooting, it is all a question of one's own point of view.'[16] Although Meyer retains in some stories the traditional framework tale set in an aristocratic society, as Boccaccio had used it, the didactic purpose as well as the desire to entertain are no longer present; the relationship between the framework tale and the story itself are explored by Meyer to create an ambivalent effect. Such characteristics of his narrative art separate Meyer clearly from writers like Keller, Storm or Raabe, with whom, solely because he was born in 1825, he has been long associated. After 1884 Meyer abandoned the framework technique and used instead a more refined version of indirect narrative and characterisation, making use of allegorical pictures, statues and tableaux; significant gestures and facial expressions, contrasting or parallel sub-plots are common in his last works.

Meyer's relationship with the past as represented in his work illustrates his ambivalent position at the end of one period of Germany's cultural history and on the threshold of another. He shared a common tendency of the *Gründerzeit* to stress the theatrical quality of history; he was fond of using archaic phraseology and even spelling, and of historic costume. He went to great pains to produce authentic historical colour and incidental detail. He seemed to feel he owed this to the genre, for unlike Fontane, he was not interested in the past for its own sake. The historical setting of his stories recall the stylised and lifeless historical paintings of Kaulbach, Piloty or Makart. Recourse to historical costume as a means of lending significance to art was too widely accepted in the 1870s and 1880s for a writer like Meyer to ignore it. He was far removed from the realists' awareness of tradition manifested in a way of life, which provides a link between the past and the present of an individual or a nation. Despite the patriotic impulse which prompted him to write his ballads and *Huttens letzte Tage*, Meyer had no interest in the origin and historical development of the nation. What interested him was the mystery of the individual: the epoch in which he places his characters is largely incidental except in so far as it can be understood as analogous to Meyer's own time. The historical setting of his novellas lent distance and, therefore, a semblance of objectivity, which he strove to achieve in the lyric poetry and prose of his maturity. Meyer was original in his disregard for the evolutionary process of history which informed the vision of most of his contemporaries. He anticipates the twentieth century in his concentration on the subjective individual, without particular regard for his environment. Finally the ambiguity of human motivation, the unfathomable nature of man, the blurring of the distinction between reality and illusion, which emerge from Meyer's narrative work, show that he is concerned with a crisis of moral values, for which no solution is offered. In the history of German literature in the nineteenth-century Meyer, once regarded as a decadent aesthete, seems in fact closer to our own time than any other writer, apart from Nietzsche.

Conclusion

The comprehensive character of change in the period 1830–90 affected virtually every German and elicited some kind of response in him. Political awareness had come to the nation as a whole in this period, but compared with Western nations such as England, France or the Netherlands, it had come relatively late; this, and the Germans' lack of experience in the process of government, encouraged the development of extreme political views. Towards the end of Bismarck's administration, which also coincides with the end of our period, the interaction of foreign affairs, domestic problems and the expansion of industrial markets beyond Europe made Germans and their rulers attribute too much importance to national militancy and a homogeneous national outlook. The Second Reich implicitly ignored Germany's historical character, which had been heterogeneous and regional. The constant effort to give substance to the desired ideal of national unity heightened the excessive self-consciousness of its subjects. The German scale of values changed; amiability and contentment gave place to aggressive and rather humourless efficiency as the national ideal. Great significance was attributed to appearances and material possessions. The typical Germans, Michel and Gretchen, who so aptly represesented their countrymen in 1830, were no longer acceptable; their place had been taken by the lieutenant of the Reserve or the uniformed *corps* student, who brought colour and dash – *Schneid* – to German streets and German drawingrooms.[1]

The tone of foreigners towards Germany became noticeably less patronising, but also less affectionate. If progress in transport and technology had brought the nations closer together physically, it had not brought friendship with it; in the case of Germany's relations with England, a surprising change is apparent. In the last years of the century the misgivings of the authorities and certain circles in England towards Germany received disturbing confirmation in the hostility expressed towards the English in the German press.[2] Many British newspapers responded with equal animosity, particularly when Germany's colonial and naval ambitions became evident. Some lovers of Germany, such as Viscount Haldane, a member of Asquith's government who visited Germany in 1912 in a last effort to salvage relations between the two countries, clung to the idea of the 'two Germanies', the 'true' Germany of Goethe, Schiller and Humboldt, and the modern militaristic state which had temporarily overshadowed it. Germans were of course by no means the only people to cultivate national exclusiveness in the last years of the nineteenth century, but the basic social instability of Germany, the tensions within the Reich, and Germany's geographical position made such attitudes potentially more inflammatory there than in other European countries of the same standing. As early as the 1890s intelligent foreign observers were talking of the 'German problem'.

Perhaps in no other country were there so many pious patriotic speeches and festivities commemorative of the past and so much earnest talk of tradition. And yet the main source of the nation's excessive self-consciousness lay precisely in its own uneasy relationship to its own past. There was some truth in Marx's observation that Bismarck's Reich was a 'military despotism with parliamentary trimmings and an admixture of feudalism, influenced by the bourgeoisie, put together by the bureaucrats and under the care of the police.'[3] In 1871 most Germans accepted and identified themselves with the triumph of the German national state. They saw their country as the embodiment of culture in an age of decline, dominating Central Europe and based on growing industrial and commercial wealth in which the majority could hope to share. By 1890 the ideal had become more elusive. The leading German writers of the previous decades had anticipated in their work the growing disillusionment of the nation. They had stressed the moral consequences of change for the national character and they had found no reassurance in the political and social developments they witnessed. Now, in the disciplined and dedicated, but spiritually and intellectually arid world of the Reich in 1890, two years after the accession of the new Emperor and in the year of Bismarck's fall, they could only confirm that the tradition of German culture, as they knew it, had been lost.

Notes and References

Part I THE SOCIAL BACKGROUND 1830–90

1 Carl Gustav Carus, *The King of Saxony's Journey to England in 1844*, translated by S. C. Davison (London 1846), p. 355.
2 Bisset Hawkins, *Germany: the Spirit of her History, Literature, Social Conditions and National Economy; illustrated by Reference to her Physical, Moral and Political Statistics, and by comparison with other Countries,* (London 1838), p. 39.
3 Baumgarten in the *Preußische Jahrbücher* (1866), quoted in Hans Kohn, *The Mind of Germany,* (London 1965), p. 158.
4 Hawkins, *Germany: the Spirit of her History,* p. 55.
5 Ignaz Castelli, *Memoiren meines Lebens (Denkwürdigkeiten aus Alt-Österreich* 10) (Munich 1914), vol. 2, p. 128.
6 'Ist überhaupt in einer Fabrik, (wie der hiesigen) anders als in einem meisterlichen Haus und kein Zusammenhalt nit unter den Gesellen. Läuft jeder seinen Weg und dreht sich nit viel nach dem anderen.' Johann Eberhard Dewald, 'Biedermeier auf Walze, Briefe und Aufzeichnungen des Handwerksburschen Johann Eberhard Dewald' in: *Deutsche Selbstbiographien,* ed. Gisela Moeller, (Munich 1966), p. 476.
7 'Dies alles aber, weil wir mit den Studenten ein Lied auf das ganze Deutschland gesungen hatten! Machen es einem wahrlich nit leicht auf sein Vaterland stolz zu sein.' Dewald, 'Biedermeier auf Walze', p. 453.
8 *Our Summer in the Harz by a Scotch Family,* (Edinburgh 1865), p. 96.
9 Fontane, *Meine Kinderjahre,* (Munich 1963), p. 30.
10 'Gar oft schon fühlt' ich tief/Des Mädchens Seele wird nicht sich selbst/ Dem Liebsten nur Geboren,' Eichendorff, *Werke,* (Leipzig 1931), vol. 1, p. 1129.
11 'Bettinens Liebe, Charlottens Tod und Rahels dunkle Weissagungen sind durch unsere Brust gefahren,' Quoted in E. M. Butler, *The Saint-Simonian Religion in Germany,* (Cambridge 1926), p. 374.
12 William Howitt, *The Rural and Domestic Life of Germany, with Characteristic Sketches of its Cities and Scenery,* London 1842, p. 235.
13 Immermann, *Münchhausen,* in *Werke* (Meyers Klassiker, Leipzig and Vienna), vol. 1, chapter 13, pp. 28–37.
14 *Our Summer in the Harz by a Scotch Family.*
15 In mid century a *Reichsthaler* or *thaler* was worth slightly more than 3s; a *groschen* (30 gr. = 1 *thaler*) about one penny; a *florin* was approximately 1s. 6d, a silver *ducat* about 3s, and a *louis d'or* about £1 or 6 *thalers*. In 1837 some South German and Central German states adopted the Rhenish florin to counteract the profusion of currencies, while in 1838 Prussia made a convention with some of her neighbours in the North to

adopt the *thaler*. When in 1857 a monetary convention was negotiated in the German Confederation, the *thaler* became in effect the German currency. Cf. Agatha Ramm, *Germany 1789–1919, A Political History*, (London 1967), p. 228.

16 Ilse Barea, *Vienna*, (London 1966), p. 131.

17 Henry Simon, Unpublished Diaries in the possession of the University Library of Manchester. (Quoted with permission of the Librarian.)

18 Spielhagen, *Problematische Naturen*, (Berlin 1918), book II, chapters 14 and 15.

19 E. Kohn-Bramstedt, *Aristocracy and the Middle Classes in Germany. Social Types in German Literature 1830–90*, (London 1937), p. 200 ff.

20 'Mir ist nicht bange, daß Deutschland nicht eins werde. Unsere guten Chausseen und künftigen Eisenbahnen werden das ihrige tun.' Quoted in A. Sarter, *Die deutschen Eisenbahnen in Kriege*, (Stuttgart, Berlin, Leipzig and Yale), 1930, p. 21.

21 Franz Gall, *Kleiner Fuhrer durch die Universität Wien*, (*im Auftrag des Akademischen Senats der Universität*), (Vienna 1965), p. 88.

22 Hawkins, *Germany: the Spirit of her History*, pp. 329–31.

23 'Wahrlich mit diesen göttlichen Bengels wollt ich die ganze Welt erobern.' Quoted in E. W. Dobert, *Karl Gutzkow und seine Zeit*, Bern and Munich 1968, p. 50.

24 Hawkins, *Germany: the Spirit of her History*, p. 311.

25 Howitt, *Rural and Domestic Life of Germany*, p. 429.

26 Carus, *The King of Saxony's Journey etc.*, pp. 359–60.

Part II LITERATURE AND SOCIETY 1830–90

Chapter 1 THE LITERARY SCENE 1830–90

1 For this chapter and also chapter 4 see George Eliot's most illuminating comments in her review of W. H. Riehl's *Die bürgerliche Gesellschaft* and *Land und Leute* which appeared in the *Westminster Review*, July 1856, pp. 51–79.

Chapter 2 WHAT WAS BIEDERMEIER?

1 'Der Fleiß ist unser Apollo und die Mühe unsere Muse,' 24 February 1824. Quoted in Martin Greiner, *Zwischen Biedermeier und Bourgeoisie*, (Göttingen 1953), p. 82.

2 See Rudolf Stadelmann, 'Soziale Ursachen der Revolution von 1848', pp. 145–6, in Hans-Ulrich Wehler, *Moderne Sozialgeschichte*, (Berlin, 1966).

3 See Walter Höllerer, *Zwischen Klassik und Moderne*, (Stuttgart 1958).

Chapter 3 THE BIEDERMEIER WRITERS 1820–50

1 '(Aber wie immer man es wendet, Vergangenheit ist der Schlüssel zur Zeit.) Und gerade das macht Tiecks Menschen zu unermüdlichen

Erzählern.' Marianne Thalmann, *Ludwig Tieck, Der Heilige von Dresden,* (Berlin 1960), p. 145.

2 'Schon früh dachte ich darüber nach, wie edel im Menschen der Trieb sei, alles, was sein Bedürfnis erfordert, neben dem Notwendigen noch mit einer gewissen Zugabe von Schönheit zu umhängen, so daß der Reichere und Gebildetere keinen Hausrat haben möchte, der nicht durch hinzugefügten Zierat in etwas Höheres verwandelt war.' Ludwig Tieck, *Romane,* ed. Marianne Thalmann, (Munich 1964), p. 244.

3 Dewald, *Biedermeier auf Walze, Briefe* . . .

4 'Alles muß der Dichter verantworten, nur nicht Influenzen; die sind die reine Last des Schicksals.' *Die Papierfenster* (1822), quoted in Greiner *Zwischen Biedermeier und Bourgeoisie,* p. 92.

5 'Wir müssen durch das Romantische . . . hindurch in das realistisch-pragmatische Element. Immermann, *Memorabilien,* (Munich 1966), p. 149–50.

6 'Mein Sinn stand darauf, eine Geschichte der Liebe nachzuerzählen, der Liebe folgend bis zu dem Punkte, wo sie die Menschen für Haus und Land, für Zeit und Mitwelt reif, mündig, wirksam zu machen beginnt. Immermann, *Werke,* vol. 2, p. 415.

7 Th.Fontane, *Schriften und Glossen zur Europäischen Literatur,* (Zürich1965), vol. 1, p. 124.

8 *Liechtenstein-Einleitung* in Wilhelm Hauff, *Werke,* (Munich 1966), vol. 2, pp. 564–9.

9 'Seit man nicht mehr in die Kirche geht, ist das Theater das einzige öffentliche Gottesdienst, sowie die Literatur die Privatandacht.' (Tgb. 3505, 1839–40), Grillparzer, *Sämtliche Werke,* (Darmstadt 1964), vol. 3, p. 860.

10 'Gerade jenes Mittelding zwischen Goethe und Kotzebue, wie ihn das Drama braucht.' (Tgb. 1626, 1828), Grillparzer, *Sämtliche Werke,* vol. 4, p. 442.

11 'Der wahre dramatische Dichter *sieht* sein Werk darstellen, indem er es schreibt.' Grillparzer, *Werke,* vol. 3, p. 830.

12 Grillparzer, *Selbstbiographie,* in *Sämtliche Werke,* vol. 4, p. 26.

13 'Ein Trauerspiel, so traurig es sein mag, doch immer auch ein Spiel bleibt.' Grillparzer, *Selbstbiographie,* p. 80.

14 'O, prüfe nicht die Stützen, beßre nicht,' Act III, line 1, 1640, Grillparzer, *Werke,* vol. 2, p. 405.

15 Raimund, *Sämtliche Werke,* ed. Fr. Brukner and Ed. Castle, (Vienna 1934), vol. 2, pp. 434–6.

16 S. S. Prawer, *Mörike und seine Leser,* (Stuttgart 1960).

17 'Sohn des Horaz und einer feinen Schwäbin.' Quoted in Benno von Wiese, *Eduard Mörike* (Tübingen 1950), p. 217.

18 'Uhland, ohne Zweifel der erste Repräsentant der Lyrik'. Friedrich Hebbel, *Sämtliche Werke,* (Berlin 1903), vol. 12, p. 343.

19 'Die Poesie immer mehr ins Sinken gerät und immer mehr ein Gegenstand des Luxus, anstatt eine Sache des Volkes wird.' Quoted in W. D. Williams, 'August von Platen' (*German Men of Letters,* vol. 5), (London 1969), p. 140.

Chapter 4 PEASANT LITERATURE IN NINETEENTH CENTURY GERMANY

1 Karl Fehr in his *Gotthelf*, (Stuttgart 1966), p. 40, justifiably compares this work for originality of thought on the social question with the *Communist Manifesto*.

2 H. Waidson, *Jeremias Gotthelf, An Introduction to the Swiss Novelist*, (Oxford 1953), p. 211.

3 'Dieses Leben mußte sich entweder aufzehren oder losbrechen auf irgendweine Weise . . . Hätte ich alle zwei Tage einen Ritt tun können, ich hätte nie geschrieben.' Gotthelf, *Sämtliche Werke, Briefe*, (Zurich 1948), vol. 4, p. 280.

4 'Es haben gar unendlich viele Kinder ihrer Großmutter viel mehr zu verdanken als den gelehrtesten Herrn Professoren, welche oft nicht viel anders sind als vertrocknete Haarseckel.' Gotthelf, *Werke*, 1921 ff., vol. 2, p. 261.

5 'Kapitale, die man zinsbar zu machen habe, nämlich Kräfte und Zeit,' and 'Ein gutes Auskommen in der Welt . . . (und) den Himmel und seine Schätze.' Gotthelf, *Werke*, vol. 4, p. 30 and p. 32.

6 Hermann Boeschenstein, *German Literature of the Nineteenth Century*, (London 1969), p. 83.

7 In: *Dorf- und Schloßgeschichten*, (1883 and 1886).

Chapter 5 THE GERMAN WRITER BETWEEN REVOLUTIONS, 1830–48

1 'Die Dichter und aesthetischen Prosaisten stehen nicht mehr wie vormals allein im Dienst der Musen sondern auch im Dienst des Vaterlands und allen mächtigen Zeitbestrebungen sind sie Verbündete.' L. Wienbarg, *Aesthetische Feldzüge*, ed. Jürgen Jahn, (Berlin 1964), p. 188.

2 'recht war, indem sie dem Tage gedieh,' quoted in Franz Schnabel, *Deutsche Geschichte im neunzehnten Jahrhundert*, (Freiburg 1934), vol. 3, p. 132.

3 *Preußische Jahrbücher* 32 (1889), pp. 379 ff.

4 'Wir wollen nicht glauben, daß diese Nation in Kunst, Religion und Wissenschaft das Größte vermocht habe und im Staate gar nichts vermöge.' Quoted in Peter Demetz, *Marx, Engels und die Dichter*. (Stuttgart 1959), p. 22.

5 'Allerdings war die Literatur, die Kunst der Dichtung und der Prosa, nicht auszuschließen, aber, was das Object der Darstellung betrifft, forderten die Religion, die Wissenschaft, die bildende und zeichnende Kunst, die Natur, das öffentliche und bürgerliche, das häusliche und gesellige Leben, die Geschichte, Vaterlands- und Völkerkunde vollkommen gleiche Rechte.' Gustav Schwab, *Die deutsche Prosa von Mosheim bis auf unsere Tage*, (Stuttgart 1843), p. 11.

6 'Sie wird tanzen. . . die Mimik der Grazien der Taglioni haben die drohenden Zeichen der Zeit verdrängt.' Quoted in Georg Brandes, *Main Currents in Nineteenth Century Literature*, (London 1905), vol. 6, p. 11.

7 Gutzkow habe gewagt, 'die französische Affenschande, die in Armen von Metzen Gott lästert, aufs neue nach Deutschland zu überpflanzen.' Karl Gutzkow, *Wally, die Zweiflerin*, ed. Jost Schillemeit (Göttingen 1965), p. 79*.

8 'Das deutsche Volk hat noch zu wenig politische Aufklärung.' Ludwig Börne, *Kritische Schriften*, ed. E. Schumacher, (Zurich 1964), p. 326.

9 'Thiers ... wird Unterstaatssekretär für Finanzen, ohngefähr so viel wie Minister ... Wie man hier sein Glück macht! Möchte man nicht vor Ärger ein geheimer Hofrat werden! Es ist geradeso, als wäre der Heine Minister geworden oder der Menzel oder ich! Und was sind wir?' L. Börne, *Sämtliche Schriften*, (Düsseldorf 1964), pp. 56–7.

10 Hawkins, *Germany, the Spirit of her History*, p. 87.

11 P. Demetz, op. cit., p. 37.

12 'Laßt nur den Zufall an den Tag bringen, daß sich unter den spanischen Jakobinern ein Mathematiker befinde und sogleich wird euch der Bundestag die Logarithmen untersagen.' Quoted in Demetz, *Marx, Engels und die Dichter*, p. 39.

13 'Hinter, oder vielmehr mit Hoffmann von Fallersleben hat die Poesie ein Ende.' Heinrich Heines *Sämtliche Werke*, (Leipzig 1915), vol. 10, p. 256.

14 *Zeitgedichte (Nachlese)*, Heinrich Heine, *Werke*, (Frankfurt 1968), p. 278.

15 Text and genesis in S. S. Prawer, *Heine, the Tragic Satirist*, (Cambridge 1961), pp. 288–301.

Chapter 6 YOUNG GERMANY 1830–48

1 'Dir, junges Deutschland (widme ich diese Reden), nicht dem alten.' Wienbarg, *Aesthetische Feldzüge*, p. 256.

2 'Ich gehe morgen nach Warschau, um für das heilige Recht eines Volkes gegen die Tyrannen zu fechten. Ich liebe das polnische Volk eben nicht sehr, aber für seine Sache will ich bluten und sterben.' Heinrich Laube, *Gesammelte Werke*, vol. 1, *Das junge Europa*, (Leipzig 1908), p. 178.

3 'Seit dieser zu singen begonnen hat, sind wir Spatzen.' Quoted in Ferd. Freiligrath, *Werke*, ed. W. Ilberg, (Berlin 1967,) p. 7.

4 Freiligrath, *Werke*, p. 89.

5 'Wir sind Freiligrath in einer Weise verpflichtet wie vielleicht seit dem Tode Schillers keinem zweiten und erweisen ihn kaum Ehre genug, wenn wir ihn den "Bürger" unserer Epoche nennen.' Quoted in Freiligrath, *Werke*, p. 40.

6 'Obwohl unsere Dichter auch schon anfangen, die Leier anstatt sie zu spielen, dem Gegner an den Kopf zu werfen.' Philip Glander, *The Letters of Varnhagen von Ense to R. Monckton Milnes* (Heidelberg 1965,) p. 22.

7 Fanny Lewald, *Meine Lebensgeschichte*, (Berlin 1862), vol. 2, p. 111.

8 'Nur Operntex te zu schreiben oder ... eine Geschichte der Deutschen herauszugeben, in der alle anderen Nationen erbärmlich, die Söhne Thiuskons aber einzig und erhaben dastehen.' Karl Gutzkow, *Wally, die Zweiflerin*, p. 20*.

9 'Wie damals der Mönch, so ist es jetzt der Philosoph, in dessen Hirn die Revolution beginnt.' Quoted in Karl Buchheim, *Handbuch der deutschen Kulturgeschichte*, vol. 1, (Frankfurt 1966), p. 150.

10 'So sind die Neulinge fast alle. Uns verdanken sie, daß sie lesen und schreiben können, und ihre erste Tat ist geistiger Vatermord.' Quoted in Demetz, *Marx, Engels und die Dichter*, p. 54.
11 Norbert Fürst, *The Victorian Age of German Literature*, (London 1966), p. 188.

Chapter 7 REVOLUTION IN DRAMA: GRABBE, BÜCHNER, HEBBEL

1 'Ich möchte Sie dann warnen, diesem Zerstörungsprozesse des Lebens nachzugeben, der sich in der Maske seiner geborenen Feindin, der Poesie, aufdrängen will.' Chr. Dietrich Grabbe, *Werke* (Detmold 1960), vol. 1, p. 5.
2 'Krieg und Frieden, Lieb und Glück, und Gott/Und Glauben, nur die Worte sind, von dem /Was sie gewesen.' Grabbe, *Werke*, p. 420.
3 'Deutschland ... Europas Herz- - ja ja, zerrissen.' Grabbe, *Werke*, p. 433.
4 'In Grabbe wird zum ersten Male die Geschichte selbst lebendig.' Quoted in Benno von Wiese, *Von Lessing bis Grabbe* (Düsseldorf 1968), p. 309.
5 'den gräßlichen Fatalismus der Geschichte.' Georg Büchner, *Sämtliche Werke*, (Berlin 1966), p. 401.
6 J. P. Stern, *Reinterpretations* (London 1964), p. 89.
7 'Die höchste Stufe der Poesie und der Kunst überhaupt.' Quoted in Fritz Martini, *Deutsche Literatur im bürgerlichen Realismus 1848-98* (Stuttgart 1962), p. 116.
8 'Nie verwinde ich das wieder, nie, darum habe ich nicht das Recht, es zu verzeihen.' Quoted in Fritz Martini, *Deutsche Literaturgeschichte*, 4th edition, (Stuttgart 1952), p. 368.
9 (daß) 'Herodes das Christentum als erhabenstes Kulturinstrument feiert, daß Michelangelo die tiefste Demut predigt, daß Agnes Bernauer den Staat als die Grundbedingung alles menschlichen Gedeihens hinstellt, der jedes Opfer fordert, und daß Gyges an die ewigen Rechte des Herkommens und der Sitte mahnt.' Quoted in Helmut Kreuzer, *Hebbel in neuer Sicht*, (Stuttgart 1963), p. 320.
10 'Das Individuum, wie herrlich und groß, wie edel und schön es immer sei, sich der Gesellschaft unter allen Umständen beugen muß, weil in dieser und in ihrem notwendig formalen Ausdruck, dem Staat, die ganze Menschheit lebt, in jenem nur eine einzelne Seite zur Entfaltung gelangt.' Hebbel, *Sämtliche Werke*, vol. 4, pp. 258-9.
11 'Du bist nichte wie ein anderer, der die Gerechtigkeit dadurch versöhnen kann' etc., *Agnes Bernauer*, act V, scene x, in Hebbel, *Werke* (Meyers Klassiker), vol. 3 (Leipzig and Vienna), p. 427.
12 'Das moderne Theater ... war von jeher Unterhaltungsmittel, Zeitvertreib.' Hebbel, *Sämtliche Werke* op. cit., vol. 11, p. 15.
13 Kreuzer, *Hebbel in neuer Sicht*, p. 324.
14 'Das nationale Motiv, die Unterwerfung des Einzelnen unter das Überpersönliche, die Staatsidee, die steigende Monumentalisierung, alles Züge, in denen eine Mittelstellung zwischen der Verwerfung der

Achtundvierziger Revolution und dem Geist der Gründerzeit verrät.'
Kreuzer, *Hebbel, etc.*, p. 331.

Chapter 8 THE 1848 REVOLUTION

1 Agatha Ramm, *Germany 1789–1919*, p. 172.
2 Th. Fontane, *Sämtliche Werke*, (Munich 1966), vol. 5, p. 353.
3 'Die Justiz ist in Deutschland die Hure der Fürsten.' Georg Büchner,
Ludwig Weidig, *Der Hessische Landbote*, (Frankfurt 1965), p. 22.
4 'Glauben Sie, meine Herren, es wird kein Haupt über Deutschland
leuchten, das nicht mit einem vollen Tropfen demokratischen Öls gesalbt
ist.' *Über die Wahl des Reichsoberhaupts*, 1849, quoted in Walter Killy,
Die deutsche Literatur VI: Neunzehntes Jahrhundert, (Munich 1965), p. 168.
5 Karl Gutzkow, *Die Ritter vom Geiste* (Hempels Klassiker), (Berlin), book 2,
chapter 13, p. 372.
6 Quoted in Heinrich von Treitschke, *History of Germany in the Nineteenth
Century*, (London 1919), vol. 6, p. 361.
7 'Die Zivilisation der wenigen (besteht) nur durch die Unzivilisation der
vielen.' Quoted in Werner Conze, 'Vom "Pöbel" zum "Proletariat"',
in *Sozialgeschichte*, p. 118.
8 'Man hätte mich ausgelacht oder bemitleidet, hätte ich mich als
Kommunist gegeben.' Quoted in Golo Mann, *Deutsche Geschichte des 19.
und 20. Jahrhunderts*, (Frankfurt 1958), p. 238.
9 'Da spricht man viel von Proletariern, ohne das Wort zu deuten. Einen
Proletarier nenne ich den, welchen seine Eltern in der Jugend
verwahrlost, nicht gewaschen, nicht gestriegelt, weder zum Guten
erzogen noch zur Kirche und Schule angehalten haben. Er hat sein
Handwerk nicht gelernt, heiratet ohne Brot und setzt seinesgleichen in
die Welt, welche stets bereit sind, über anderer Leute Gut herzufallen
und den Krebsschaden der Kommune bilden ... Nicht aber rechne ich
zu den Proletariern den braven Arbeiter, dem Gott durch die Kraft
seiner Hände und den gesunden Menschenverstand ein Kapital verlieh,*
welches ihm niemand rauben kann, es sei denn durch Krankheit und
Alter.' Quoted in Conze, *Sozialgeschichte*, p. 120.*
10 Roy Pascal, see 'The Frankfort Parliament, 1848 and the Drang nach
Osten', in *Journal of Modern History* 18, (1946), p. 112.
11 'Der denkende Teil des deutschen Volkes wird sich bald wieder dem
Studium ergeben – auf dem Bauch liegt er schon; und wenn ihn Rauch
und Flamme und Krieg umgeben ... sagt er ganz gelassen: "Was geht's
mich an? ... das ist die Sache meiner Regierung".' Ludwig Börne,
Kritische Schriften, pp. 324–5.
12 Joachim Remak, 'Friends of the New Germany: The Bund and German-
American Relations' in *Journal of Modern History* 29 (1957), pp. 38–41.

Chapter 9 THE 1850S: AN AGE OF PROSE?

1 Heinrich Benedikt, *Die Monarchie des Hauses Oesterreich*, (Munich 1968),
p. 124.

Notes and References

2 'Also wurden die Gegner übertäubt, wurden bestimmte Ansichten über die öffentlichen Verhältnisse, bestimmte Urteile über die hervortretenden Persönlichkeiten durch möglichst viele Blätter in Umlauf gesetzt, hier der anders denkende Leser in seiner Überzeugung verwirrt, dort der Begeisterung ein Dämpfer aufgesetzt, an einer anderen Stelle geschürt, jede Wandlung und Windung der preußischen Politik belobigt und die Stimmung vorbereitet auf das, was den Ansichten des Berliner Kabinetts entsprach. Ein und dasselbe Bild spiegelte sich in einem Heer von Zeitungen wieder: da konnte man getrost die Ansicht der Preßstelle als die Volksmeinung austragen.' Heinrich Wuttke, *Die deutschen Zeitschriften und die Entstehung der öffentlichen Meinung*, (1866), in Buchheim, *Handbuch der deutschen Kulturgeschichte*, p. 207.

3 Quoted in W. H. Armytage, *A Social History of Engineering*, (London 1961), p. 185.

4 Quoted in Ernst Nolte, *Three Faces of Fascism*, (London 1965), p. 435.

5 See for example T. Theodores, *On the Study of the German Language* in *Introductory Lectures on the Opening of Owens College* (later the University of Manchester) (London 1852), pp. 134–53.

6 Treitschke, *History of Germany in the Nineteenth Century*, vol. 5, p. 570.

7 Baumgarten, quoted in A. Dorpalen, *Heinrich von Treitschke*, (Yale 1957), p. 40.

8 W. H. Simon, *Germany in the Age of Bismarck* (London 1968), p. 115.

9 'Die deutsche Nation ist der Prinzipien und Doktrinen, der literarischen Größe und der theoretischen Existenz satt. Was sie verlangt ist Macht – Macht – Macht. Und wer ihr Macht gibt, dem wird sie Ehre geben, mehr Ehre, als er sich aus denken kann.' Quoted in Heinrich, Ritter von Srbik, *Deutsche Einheit*, (Munich 1935), vol. 3, p. 5.

10 Haym, quoted in Dorpalen, *von Treitschke*, p. 77.

Chapter 10 KARL GUTZKOW AND THE NINETEENTH CENTURY GERMAN NOVEL

1 'Halbruder des Dichters,' quoted in Friedrich Sengle's essay, 'Der Romanbegriff in der ersten Hälfte des neunzehnten Jahrhunderts' in his *Arbeiten zur deutschen Literatur 1750–1850*, (Stuttgart 1965), p. 178.

2 'Jene große Zwittergattung des Romans', also quoted in Sengle, 'Der Romanbegriff', p. 179.

3 Sengle, 'Der Romanbegriff', pp. 175–96.

4 'Langweilig und geistlos', *Deutsche Literaturgeschichte in Grundzügen*, ed. B. Boesch, 3rd edition, (Bern 1967), p. 362.

5 *Die Ritter vom Geiste*, book 4, chapter 1.

6 Book 1, chapter 6.

7 Book 3, chapter 9.

8 Book 4, chapter 6, pp. 70–2.

9 'Wer Zeit hat des Abends, der geht in den Verein.' Book 4, chapter 11, p. 113.

10 ' "Ja Schlurck, fast fünfzig Jahre.' Ich besitze den Heroismus der Wahrheiten, die unleugbar sind"'. . . Schlurck . . . lächelte, da er wußte,

Tradition and Revolution

daß Frau von Harder hätte sagen müssen, fast sechzig Jahre.' Book 3, chapter 5, p. 421.

11 See Gutzkow's arresting account of his childhood in *Aus der Knabenzeit* (1852).

12 J. S. Andrews, 'The Impact on Nineteenth Century Britain of Freytag's "Soll und Haben" ' in *Proceedings of the Leeds Philosophic and Literary Society, Lit. and Hist.* Section 8, iv, (1959), pp. 315–331.

13 *Sturmflut* in Spielhagen, *Werke*, book 3, chapter 8, pp. 312–26.

Chapter 11 THE GERMAN FORM OF REALISM 1840–80

1 J. S. Ritchie, 'Realism' in *Periods of German Literature*, (London 1966), p. 176.

2 Martini, *Bürgerlicher Realismus*, pp. 93–4.

3 'Es handelt sich darum, den Deutschen keinen Augenblick der Selbsttäuschung und Resignation zu gönnen . . . Man muß jede Sphäre der Gesellschaft als die partie honteuse der deutschen Gesellschaft schildern, man muß diese versteinerten Verhältniße dadurch zum Tanzen zwingen, daß man ihre eigene Melodie vorsingt.' Quoted in H. A. Glaser, *Die Restauration des Schönen*, (Stuttgart 1965), p. 77.

Chapter 12 MASTERS OF THE REALIST NOVELLA: STIFLER, KELLER, STORM

1 Stern, *Reinterpretations*, p. 247.

2 'In dieser ungeheuren Wildnis von Mauern und Dächern, diesem unermeßlichen Gewimmel von Menschen, die sich alle fremd sind und aneinander vorübereilen.' Quoted in Urban Roedl, *Stifter (Rowohlts Monographien)*, (Hamburg 1965), p. 25.

3 Quoted in Fürst, *The Victorian Age, etc*, p. 64.

4 'Ich bin zwar kein Goethe, aber einer aus seiner Verwandtschaft.' Stifter, *Sämtliche Werke*, (Prague 1918), vol. 18, p. 205.

5 'Das Ideal der Freiheit ist auf lange Zeit vernichtet.' Quoted in Urban Roedl, *Stifter (Rowohlts Monographien)*, Hamburg 1965, p. 98.

6 'Denn sein Dasein hat kein Bild geprägt, und seine Spuren gehen nicht mit hinunter in dem Strom der Zeit.' Quoted in Roedl, p. 79.

7 'Es erscheint mir daher in historischen Romanen die Geschichte die Hauptsache und die Menschen die Nebensache, sie werden von dem großen Strome der Zeit getragen und helfen den Strom bilden.' Stifter, *Sämtliche Werke*, vol. 19, p. 282.

8 'Stifter ist einer der merkwürdigsten, hintergründigsten . . . Erzählern der Weltliteratur.' Thomas Mann, *Die Entstehung des Doktor Faustus* in *Werke*, (Frankfurt 1960), vol. 11, p. 238.

9 'Die Familie ist es, die in unseren Zeiten Noth thut, sie thut mehr Noth als Kunst und Wissenschaft, als Verkehr, Handel, Aufschwung, Fortschritt, oder wie alles heißt, was begehrenswerth erscheint. Auf der Familie ruht die Kunst, die Wissenschaft, der menschliche Fortschritt, der Staat.' Stifter, *Sämtliche Werke*, vol. 18, p. 217.

314

10 'Er ist der Lehrer, Führer, Freund seiner Mitbürger . . . Dolmetscher und Priester des Höchsten.' Stifter, *Sämtliche Werke*, vol. 18, p. 209.

11 'Unsere Zeit verlangt Großes Nationales Zeitgemäßes . . . und gerade diese Dinge sind das Armuthszeugnisz der Zeit.' Stifter, *Sämtliche Werke*, vol. 18, p. 209.

12 'Der Dichter soll seine Stimme erheben für das Volk in Bedrängnis und Not, aber nachher soll seine Kunst wieder der Blumengarten und Erholungsplatz des Lebens sein.' Quoted in *Der Briefwechsel zwischen Keller und Hettner*, ed. Jürgen Jahn, (Berlin 1964), p. 9.

13 'Unter den deutschen Poeten der älteren Generation steht uns Keller am nächsten; denn keiner rückt näher als er an den gegenwärtigen Geschmack heran.' Otto Brahm, *Kritiken und Essays*, ed. F. Martini, (Stuttgart 1964), p. 343.

14 Book 2, chapter 14.

15 J. M. Ritchie, 'The Place of Martin Salander in Gottfried Keller's Evolution as a Prose Writer', *Modern Language Review* 52 (1957), p. 216.

16 'Es liegt mein Stil in meinem persönlichen Wesen.' Keller, *Gesammelte Briefe*, vol. 3 (1), (Bern 1952), p. 197.

17 'Den kokotten Rhapsoden Jordan'. Keller, *Briefe* 3 (1), p. 435.

18 *Briefe* 3 (1), p. 437.

19 'Solche stille Goldschmiede und silberne Filigranarbeiter'. Keller, *Briefe* 3 (1) op. cit., p. 190.

20 'Das Ende der Eisenbahn lag noch manche meilt landeinwärts hinter dem Hügelzuge.' Theodor Storm, *Sämtliche Werke*, (Munich 1969), vol. 2, p. 185.

Chapter 13 IMPERIAL GERMANY: DOUBTS AND FEARS 1871–90

1 See H. Plessner, *Die verspätete Nation*, 4th edition (Stuttgart 1966), p. 72.

2 W. Leppmann, *The German Image of Goethe* (Oxford 1961), p. 122.

3 *Aus dem Tagebuch der Baronin Spitzemberg*, ed. Rudolf Vierhaus, (Munich 1965), p. 146.

4 See V. C. Hopkins, 'Darwinism and America', in *Darwin's Vision and Christian Ethics*, ed. Walter Ogg S. J. (London 1960).

5 Walter Killy, 'Zur Geschichte des deutschen Lesebuchs', pp. 61–78, in *Nationalismus in Germanistik und Dichtung*, ed. B. von Wiese and R. Henß (Berlin 1967.)

See also here Helmut Hartwig, *Ältere Erläuterungen zu Heines Gedicht 'Deutschland'* and Winfried Pielow, *Nationalistische Muster im Lesebuch*, pp. 229–60.

6 'Es ist daher der Zweck dieser Sammlung, die Jugend einzuführen in die ideale Welt unseres Volkes . . . (Es darf) daher nur das wirklich Mustergültige und Nationale hier zugelassen werden.' Killy, 'Zur Geschischte des deutschen Lesebuchs . . .', p. 71.

7 'Kommen wir diesem Verlangen entgegen, machen wir ihr (der Jugend) das Auge groß und die Brust weit für das, was vaterländische Größe und

nationale Ehre ist . . . Darum erheben Männer wie Ernst Moritz Arndt, der Tribun der Deutschen gegen welsche Tücke, Theodor Körner, der Sänger und Held, Emanuel Geibel, der Herold des neuen Reiches, häufiger als bisher ihre Stimme, und neu erscheint auf dem Plane Ernst von Wildenbruch.' Killy, *Zur Geschichte des deutschen Lesebuchs*, p. 71.

8 Theodor Heuß, *Vorspiele des Lebens, Jugenderinnerungen*, (Tübingen 1952).

9 Lukács aptly refers to 'das denkmalsüchtige Deutschland' in *Deutsche Realisten des neunzehnten Jahrhunderts* (Berlin, 1952), p. 146.

10 'Frischem Beamtenadel, geadelten oder nicht geadelten Plutokraten, getauften oder ungetauften Kleiderjuden, ja, bisweilen selbst... gekämmten oder ungekämmten Gelehrten.' Robert Michels, *Probleme der Sozialphilosophie*, quoted in Hans Rosenberg, 'Die Pseudodemokratisierung der Rittergutsbesitzerklasse', *Sozialgeschichte*, p. 288.

11 Princess Helene von Racowitza, *An Autobiography*, (London 1910), p. 2.

12 Quoted in Gordon A. Craig, *The Battle of Königgrätz*, (London 1965), p. 178.

13 'Denn der Große frißt den Kleinen/und der Größte frißt den Großen,/ also löst in der Natur sich /einfach die soziale Frage.' Quoted in H. A. Glaser, *Spießer-Ideologie*, (Freiburg 1964), p. 107.

14 'Ökonomisch weit reifer, als der Egoismus der besitzenden Klasse zugeben möchte... Politisch (ist) sie unendlich unreifer, als eine Journalistenclique... sie glauben machen will.' Quoted in Golo Mann, *Deutsche Geschichte*, p. 408.

15 'Der Alte streichelte mit der runzligen Hand die Wange der Tochter. "Sehen Sie, und damit hat mir die Kleine das Leben gerettet. Auf einmal waren wir nicht mehr allein und der Mühe wert war es auch für uns arme Leute zu leben".' Lily Braun, *Memoiren einer Sozialistin*, (Munich 1910), p. 601.

16 Wilhelm Busch, 'Naturgeschichtliches Alphabet für grö ere Kinder und solche, die es werden wollen' in *Das Gesamtwerk*, (Olten 1959), vol. 2, p. 32.

17 'Fast durch alle Länder von Europa verbreitet sich ein mächtiger, feindselig gesinnter Staat, der mit allen übrigen im beständigen Kriege steht, und der in manchem fürchterlich auf die Bürger drückt: Es ist das Judentum, ein... Staat im Staate.' Quoted in Ludwig, Graf Westphalen, *Quellenhefte zur Geschichte und Gemeinschaftskunde*, (Stuttgart 1965), p. 7.

18 'Tiefer Haß gegen die christliche Religion und die deutsche Nationalität.' Westphalen, *Quellenhefte zur Geschichte ...*, p. 7.

Chapter 14 TWO NOVELISTS OF THE EMPIRE:
FONTANE AND RAABE

1 'Das bißchen, was in mir war, ist auch so rausgekommen. Ich habe mein Schicksal nicht anzuklagen.' 14 March 1898, quoted in Jost Schillemeit, *Theodor Fontane*, (Zurich 1961), p. 7.

2 'Der Realismus umfasst das ganze reiche Leben, das Größte wie das Kleinste.' Quoted in Peter Demetz, *Formen des Realismus*, (Munich 1964), p. 218.

3 As for example in *Die Poggenpuhls*, where the factory at night seems like an enchanted castle to Sophie, in Fontane, *Sämtliche Werke*, (Munich 1963), vol. 4, p. 539, or in *Irrungen Wirrungen* (see p. 222.)

4 'Wie einen "matten Pilger", der froh sein könne, schließlich untergekrochen zu sein.' 1 July 1876, quoted in Schillemeit, *Theodor Fontane*, p. 10.

5 Theodor Fontane, *Gesammelte Werke*, (Berlin 1905–10), 2nd series, vol. 10, p. 198.

6 'Gerhart Hauptmann aber darf aushalten auf dem Felde, das er gewählt. *Causerien über Theater*. (Munich 1964), vol. 2, p. 713.

7 'Mit klingendem Spiel in das Lager der "Neuen" überzugehen, wäre eine Kleinigkeit und mir moralisch ganz unbedenklich. Aber dazu fehlen mir einige Zentner Überzeugung. Ich sehe das Gute aber auch das Nichtgute und drücke mich in die Sofaecke. Mit 71 darf man das.' Quoted in Schillemeit, *Fontane*, pp. 23–4.

8 'Die Geschichte geht fast immer an dem vorbei, was sie vor allem festhalten sollte.' Fontane, *Sämtliche Werke*, vol. 4, p. 459.

9 'Das Vorzüglichste, . . . das die Rundschau in der reinen Kunstform des Romans je gebracht hat.' Quoted in Schillemeit, *Fontane*, p. 7.

10 'Wenn ich darf'. Th. Fontane, *Effi Briest*, (Munich 1969), ch. 33, p. 279.

11 See letters to his wife (21 July 1883) and his daughter Mete (18 April 1884) in Fontane, *Briefe*, (Berlin 1968), vol. 1, pp. 221–4, and vol. 2 (1969), pp. 62–5.

12 'Unanfechtbare Wahrheiten gibt es überhaupt nicht, und wenn es welche gibt, so sind sie langweilig.' Fontane, *Sämtliche Werke*, vol. 5, p. 10.

13 Joachim Remak, *The Gentle Critic, Theodor Fontane and German Politics 1848–98*. (Syracuse 1964).

14 Quoted in Remak, *The Gentle Critic*, p. 12.

15 Quoted in Stern, *Re-interpretations*, p. 343.

16 Remak, *The Gentle Critic*, p. 77.

17 'Das französische Gewissen sitzt in Paris, das englische Gewissen sitzt in London, aber das deutsche sitzt schon lange nicht in Paris', Lukács, *Deutsche Realisten . . .*, p. 149.

18 'Drohendes Untier.' Wilhelm Raabe, *Werke*, (Munich 1966), vol. 1, p. 680.

19 'Hierusalem est perdita', see p. 60.

20 Hermann Pongs, *Wilhelm Raabe Leben und Werk*, (Heidelberg 1958), p. 224.

21 'Das Volk ist ja völlig befriedigt mit dem mir abgestandenen Jugendquark: Chronik und Hungerpastor und läßt mich mit allem übrigen sitzen.' Quoted in *Der deutsche Roman*, ed. B. von Wiese, (Dusseldorf 1963), vol. 2, p. 142.

22 'Wohin wir blicken, zieht stets und überall der germanische Genius ein Drittel seiner Kraft aus dem Philistertum.' Quoted in Martini, *Bürgerlicher Realismus*, p. 700.

23 'Da habe ich die menschliche Canaille am festesten gepackt.' Quoted in Pongs, *Wilhelm Raabe*, p. 552.

24 See Marketa Goetz, 'The Short Stories: A possible clue to Wilhelm Raabe', *Germanic Review* 37 (1962), pp. 55–67.

Chapter 15 THE CULTURAL SPLIT IN
IMPERIAL GERMANY

1 'Ich bin zu Großem berufen, das weiß ich wohl.' Quoted in Richard
Hamann/Jost Hermand, *Gründerzeit*, (Berlin 1965), p. 45.

2 See for example *L'Adultera*.

3 Hamann/Hermand, *Gründerzeit*, p. 118.

4 'Es zahlt sich teuer zur Macht zu kommen: die Macht verdummt,' and
'"Deutschland, Deutschland über alles", ich fürchte, das war das Ende
der deutschen Philosophie'. *Götzendämmerung: Was den Deutschen abgeht* in
Friedrich Nietzsche, *Werke*, (Munich 1966), p. 983.

5 'Politische Stellung und politischen Einfluß habe ich nie gehabt und nie
erstrebt; aber in meinem inneren Wesen, und ich meine, mit dem besten,
was in mir ist, bin ich stets ein animal politicum gewesen und Wünschte ein
Bürger zu sein. Das ist nicht möglich in unserer Nation, bei der der
Einzelne, auch der Beste, über den Dienst im Gliede und politischen
Fetischismus nicht hinauskommt. Diese innere Entzweiung mit meinem
Volke, dem ich angehöre, hat mich durchaus bestimmt, mit meiner
Persönlichkeit, soweit mir dies möglich war, nicht vor das deutsche
Publikum zu treten, vor dem mir die Achtung fehlt.'
Quoted in Alfred Heuß, *Theodor Mommsen und das neunzehnte Jahrhundert*,
(Kiel 1952), p. 282.

6 *The letters of Jakob Burckhardt*, ed. Alexander Dru, (London 1955), pp.
234–5.

7 See Jakob Burckhardt, *Weltgeschichtliche Betrachtungen*, especially Chapter
V: 'Das Individuum und das Allgemeine (Die historische Größe)', ed.
Rudolf Stadelmann, (Pfullingen 1949), pp. 253–99.

8 *Letters of Jacob Burckhardt*, ed. Dru, p. 140.

9 'Von einem unmerklich gereiften Mannesgefühl jetzt mächtig ergriffen,
tat ich bei diesem weltgeschichtlichen Anlaß das französische Wesen ab
und, innerlich genötigt, dichtete ich Huttens letzte Tage.' C. F. Meyer,
Werke, (Stuttgart 1960), vol. 2, p. 582.

10 'Er war ein Poeta, ein Macher oder Verfertiger, dessen Gedichte den
Charakter von Produkten haben, ähnlich den Werken eines Teppich-
webers oder Töpfers.' H. Henel, *Gedichte Conrad Ferdinand Meyers*,
(Tubingen 1962), p. 158.

11 'Im Jenatsch und im Heiligen ist in den verschiedensten Verkleidungen
weit mehr von mir, meinen *wahren Leiden und Leidenschaften*, als in dieser
Lyrik, die kaum mehr als Spiel oder höchstens die Äußerung einer
untergeordneten Seite meines Wesens ist.' Quoted in Emil Staiger,
Die Kunst der Interpretation, (Zurich 1955), p. 239.

12 'Anekdoten aus der Chronik zum lebenden Bilde gestellt-Wämser und
Harnische aus denen Stimen reden-... das halbgestorbene Jahrhundert
haucht uns an.' Hofmannsthal, *Prosa IV*, (Frankfurt 1955), p. 279.

13 'Und du selber? Bist du echt beflügelt?/Oder nur gemalt und abge-
spiegelt?/Gaukelst du im Kreis mit Fabeldingen?/Oder hast du Blut in
deinen Schwingen?' *Gedichte* op. cit., p. 79.

14 'Ich fühle immer, was für eine ungeheure Macht das Ethische ist; es

soll in meinem neuen Buche mit Posaunen- und Trompetenstößen verkündet werden.' Quoted in Martini, *Bürgerlicher Realismus*, p. 839.

15 'Das Gewissen ist kein allgemeines und auch unter uns, die wir ein solches besitzen, tritt es, ein Proteus, in wechselnden Formen auf.' Meyer, *Sämtliche Werke*, (Bern 1959) vol. 11, p. 155.

16 'Es kommt. . . beim Urteilen, wie beim Schiessen lediglich auf den Standpunkt an.' Meyer, *Werke*, vol. 13, p. 24.

CONCLUSION

1 See Werner Ross, 'Die Stellung der deutschen Sprache in der Welt', *Nationalismus*, ed. von Wiese and Henß, p. 220.

2 See Oron Hale, *Germany and the Diplomatic Revolution*, (Philadelphia 1931), especially the opening chapters.

3 'Ein mit parlamentarischen Formen verbrämter, mit feudalem Besitz vermischter, schon von der Bourgeoisie beeinflußter, bürokratisch gezimmerter, polizeilich gehüteter Militärdespotismus.' Quoted in Golo Mann, *Deutsche Geschichte*, p. 404.

Bibliography

The following is a guide to further reading. The reader who requires full bibliographies should consult *The Year's Work in Modern Language Studies*, which is published annually by the Modern Humanities Research Association, and *A Guide to Historical Literature*, published and periodically revised by the American Historical Association.

General works

Karl Buchheim: *Deutsche Kultur zwischen 1830 und 1870*, Frankfurt, 1966, is a very fine introductory work on the subject and has a short but useful bibliography of primary sources, especially of contemporary newspapers and journals.

William Carr: *A History of Germany*, London, 1969.

Arnold Hauser: *Sozialgeschichte der Kunst und Literatur*, Munich, 1953, is the only full length work of its kind on the subject but it is disappointing for nineteenth-century Germany.

Ernst Heilborn: *Zwischen Zwei Revolutionen* (2 volumes), Berlin, 1927–9: *I Der Geist der Schinkelzeit 1789–1848; II Der Geist Bismarckzeit 1848–1918*, is written in a rather journalistic manner but contains a great deal of information on daily life which is difficult to come by.

E. J. Hobsbawm: *The Age of Revolution 1789-1848*, London, 1962, is a mine of information on all aspects of life in this period. The small amount of space devoted to events and developments in Germany is an accurate reflection of her relative unimportance in contemporary early nineteenth-century estimation.

Golo Mann: *Deutsche Geschichte des 19. und 20. Jahrhunderts*, Frankfurt, 1958: Journalistic and occasionally irritating in its presentation of factual information but often very successful in conveying the 'feel' of the age.

Bibliography

Otto Pflanze: *Bismarck and the Development of Germany, The Period of Unification: 1815-71,* Princeton, 1963. A clear and useful account.

Otto Pflanze: *Bismarck and the Development of Germany, The Period of Unification: 1815-71,* Princeton, 1963. A clear and useful account.

Ed. Werner Pöls: *Historisches Lesebuch I, 1815-1871,* Frankfurt, 1966. Documents drawn from a wide range of sources on political and social life in Germany.

Agatha Ramm: *Germany 1789-1919. A Political History,* London, 1967. A most useful reference book.

Gerhard Ritter: *Staatskunst und Kriegshandwerk,* volume 1, Munich, 1954.

Franz Schnabel: *Deutsche Geschichte im neunzehnten Jahrhundert,* 4 volumes, Freiburg, 1948–51, is still the most comprehensive account of the life and times but only goes as far as 1848. It gives very full treatment to the churches.

W. J. Simon: *Germany in the Age of Bismarck,* London, 1968 (Historical Problems: Studies and Documents). Mainly political, but with a section on social life.

Heinrich, Ritter von Srbik: *Deutsche Einheit,* Munich 1935-42. Also his great biography: *Metternich, der Staatsmann und der Mensch,* Munich, 1925-54.

Heinrich von Treitschke: *Deutsche Geschichte im 19. Jahrhundert,* Berlin, 1879-94, 5 volumes. Still fascinating reading although his pro-Prussian bias is everywhere apparent.

Hermann Kinder and Werner Hilgemann: *Atlas zur Weltgeschichte,* vol. 2: *Von der Französischen Revolution bis zur Gegenwart,* Munich, 1967.

R. Streit-Scherz and H. Klüter (editors): *Facsimile Querschnitte durch alte Zeitungen und Zeitschriften,* Bern, Stuttgart and Vienna, 1963. Most informative on social and political life are these facsimile selections from nineteenth century German newspapers and journals, among them *Die Gartenlaube, Kladderadatsch, Simplicissimus* etc.

Contemporary accounts

G. Carus: *The King of Saxony's journey to England in 1844,* English translation, London, 1846.

George Downes: *Letters from continental countries,* volume II, Dublin, 1832.

De Forest: *European Acquaintance. Sketches of people in Europe,* New York, 1858. An American traveller's account of the German spas and their society which is informative and entertaining.

Bisset Hawkins: *Germany: the spirit of her History, Literature, Social Condition and National Economy, illustrated by reference to her physical, moral and political statistics and by comparison with other countries,* London, 1838. A very full account.

William Howitt: *Rural and Domestic Life of Germany with Characteristic Sketches of its Cities and Scenery.* London, 1842. A very detailed treatment, strong on the different regions and social classes.

J. Russell: *A Tour in Germany, and some of the southern provinces of the Austrian Empire in the Years 1820, 1821, 1822,* Edinburgh, 1824. Very well-informed.

Anon.: *Our Summer in the Harz by a Scottish family,* Edinburgh, 1865, gives an impression of the provincial character of life in the German countryside and makes a meticulous comparison of the cost of living for Scottish and German professional families.

Anon.: *German Home Life* (Reprinted from *Fraser's Magazine*), London 1877, (3rd edition).

Edward Vehse: *Memories of the Court of Prussia,* English translation, London, 1854.

Carl Julius Weber: *Deutschland oder Briefe eines in Deutschland reisenden Deutschen,* 6 volumes, 3rd edition, Stuttgart, 1855.

Memoirs and letters

(i) *Men in Public Life*

August Bebel: *Aus meinem Leben,* 3 volumes, East Berlin, 1964.

Otto von Bismarck: *Gesammelte Werke,* Berlin, 1924-35. Vol. 14: I/II *Briefe,* ed. W. Windelband and Frauendienst. Vol. 15: *Gedanken und Erinnerungen,* ed. G. Ritter and R. Stadelmann.

Ernst II, Duke of Saxe-Coburg-Gotha: *Aus meinem Leben und aus meiner Zeit,* Berlin, 1887-9.

Großherzog Friedrich I von Baden: *Großherzog Friedrich I von Baden und die deutsche Politik von 1854-71, Briefwechsel, Denkschriften, Tagebücher,* 2 volumes, ed. Hermann Oncken, Stuttgart, 1927.

Julius Fröbel: *Ein Lebenslauf. Aufzeichnungen, Erinnerungen und Bekenntnisse*, 2 volumes, Stuttgart, 1890-1.

Julius von Hartmann: *Lebenserinnerungen, Briefe und Aufsätze*, 2 parts, Berlin, 1882.

Karl Mathy: *Aus dem Nachlaß von Karl Mathy. Briefe aus den Jahren 1846-8*, Leipzig, 1898.

Helmuth von Moltke: *Briefe des General-Feldmarschalls Grafen Helmuth von Moltke*, volumes IV and V of the *Gesammelte Schriften und Denkwürdigkeiten*, Berlin, 1891.

J. M. von Radowitz: *Aufzeichnungen und Erinnerungen aus dem Leben des Botschafters J. M. von Radowitz 1839-90*, 2 volumes, ed. H. Holborn, Stuttgart, 1925.

Carl Schurz: *Lebenserinnerungen*, 3 volumes, Berlin, 1906-7.

Friedrich August Stägemann: *Briefe und Aktenstücke zur Geschichte Preußens unter Friedrich Wilhelm III. vorzugsweise aus dem Nachlaß von F. A. Stägemann*, 3 volumes, Leipzig, 1899-1902.

Freiherr du Thil: *Denkwürdigkeiten aus dem Dienstleben des Hessen-Darmstädtischen Staatsministers Freiherrn du Thil 1803-48*. ed. Heinrich Ulmann, Stuttgart and Berlin, 1921. Of particular interest as representing the 'middle states' of Germany as for example in his account of the formation of the Customs Union (*Zollverein*).

Karl August Varnhagen von Ense: *Denkwürdigkeiten des eigen Lebens*, 6 volumes, 3rd edition, Leipzig, 1871.

(ii) *Men and Women of Letters*

Lily Braun: *Memoiren einer Sozialistin*, volume 1, Munich, 1910. An account of the early days of Socialism and the ostracism by society of the few intellectuals who sympathised with the movement. Lily Braun was a noblewoman, whose first husband was George Glyczinski, one of the *Katheder* or academic socialists.

Jakob Burckhardt: *Letters*, edited by Alexander Dru, London, 1955.

Ignaz Castelli: *Memoiren meines Lebens (Denkwürdigkeiten aus Alt-Oesterreich 10)*, 2 volumes, Munich, 1914. His insufferable vanity does not, however, prevent this dialect poet and well-connected man of affairs from being a most informative commentator on his times.

Maria von Ebner-Eschenbach: *Meine Kinderjahre*, Vienna,

323

1906. The social life and education of a young Bohemian aristocrat in mid-century.

Theodor Fontane: *Briefe,* 3 volumes, ed. Kurt Schreinert and Charlotte Jolles, Berlin, 1968 ff.

Theodor Fontane: *Meine Kinderjahre,* Berlin 1894. A colourful account of Fontane's childhood in the 1820s and 1830s in the Baltic sea ports of Swinemünde and Küstrin.

Karl Gutzkow: *Aus der Knabenzeit,* volume 1 1852, volume 2 1872, in *Werke* 7ter Teil. A graphic and at times harrowing account of poverty and the struggle for respectability of Gutzkow's family in Berlin in the years after the Napoleonic wars, written by one of the most astute observers of social life in nineteenth century Germany.

Karl Immermann: *Memorabilien,* Munich, 1966.

Gottfried Keller: *Gesammelte Briefe,* 4 volumes, ed. C. Helbing, Bern, 1950-4, especially those to Theodor Storm, Hermann Hettner, Paul Heyse, Emil Kuh, C. F. Meyer.

Fanny Lewald: *Meine Lebensgeschichte,* 3 volumes, Berlin, 1861-2. Probably the most informative of nineteenth century memoirs for social customs and topical matters by this deservedly popular woman novelist. The first volume *Im Vaterhause* (1861) contains a vivid account of the day-to-day life of a Jewish family and the difficulties they contended with in the provincial town of Königsberg in East Prussia.

Graf Prokesch von Osten: *Aus den Briefen des Grafen Prokesch von Osten (1849-55),* Vienna 1896.

Alexander von Uugeru-Sternberg: *Erinnerungsblätter aus der Biedermeierzeit,* ed. Joachim Kühn, Potsdam and Berlin, 1919.

David Friedrich Strauß: *Ausgewählte Briefe von D. F. Strauß,* ed. Eduard Zeller, Bonn, 1895.

(iii) *Some representatives of the different social classes*

Ed. Gisela Moëller: *Deutsche Selbstbiographien,* Munich, 1966. Contains among other interesting items the splendid account of an artisan's life in the 1830s by J. E. Dewald.

Wilhelm von Kügelgen: *Jugenderinnerungen eines alten Mannes,* Leipzig, 1911. Perhaps the most justly famous of memoirs for its comprehensive and witty picture of German provincial life in the professional classes.

Malwida von Meysenbug: *Memoiren einer Idealistin,* 3 volumes,

Berlin 1876 (published anon.) includes an eye witness account of Frankfurt in 1848 by this highly intelligent friend of Alexander Herzen, Mazzini and (later) Nietzsche.

Princess Helene von Racowitza: *Autobiography,* English translation, London, 1910. Is interesting for the actress's account of intellectual life in Munich and Berlin in mid-century.

Baronin Spitzemberg: *Das Tagebuch der Baronin Spitzemberg (1865-1914),* ed. Rudolph Vierhaus, 3rd edition, Göttingen, 1963. As daughter of the Prime Minister of Württemberg and wife of the Württemberg minister at the Prussian court, the baroness belonged to court society and gave an informative and critical account of events and personalities over half a century.

Rahel von Varnhagen: *Ein Frauenleben in Briefen,* Weimar, 1912.

Biography

The Germans do not perhaps excel in the art of biography to the same degree as the English, but the student should consult Srbik, already mentioned, and also Hermann Oncken's distinguished studies:

Hermann Oncken: *Rudolph von Bennigsen: ein deutscher liberaler Politiker,* Stuttgart, 1910, and his *Friedrich Lassalle, eine politische Biographie,* Stuttgart 1923.

Among more recent works the following contain a great deal of information on nineteenth century life and thought:

Andreas Dorpalen: *Heinrich von Treitschke,* New Haven, 1957, and

P. W. Lougee: *Paul de Lagarde 1827-91. A study of radical conservatism in Germany,* Cambridge, Mass., 1962.

Rowohlts Monographien (Hamburg), general editor Kurt Kusenberg, currently being published, contain a number of studies devoted to nineteenth century figures; these provide an excellent guide to the way of life of artists and men of letters in Germany and Austria. They also include full and up-to-date bibliographies. Among many fine studies, the following deserve special mention:

Bernd Breitenbuch: *Gottfried Keller.*

Johannes Hemleben: *Ernst Haeckel.*

Ludwig Marcuse: *Heinrich Heine.*

Hans Meyer: *Richard Wagner.*

Helmuth Nürnberger: *Theodor Fontane* (includes an absorbing account of F's impression of London as a foreign correspondent in the 1850s).

Urban Roedl: *Adalbert Stifter.*

Marcel Schneider: *Franz Schubert.*

Hans Wollschläger: *Kurt May* (includes much interesting material on the depressed artisan class from which May came and is also very enlightening on the reasons for this best-selling author's popularity).

Economic and social history

W. H. Armytage: *A Social History of Engineering,* London, 1961.

Ilse Barea: *Vienna,* London, 1966. An exemplary and beautifully written account of daily life, society and culture in the capital of the Austrian Empire.

K. E. Born: 'Sozialpolitische Probleme und Bestrebungen in Deutschland von 1848 bis zur Bismark'schen Sozialgesetzgebung, (*Vierteljahresschrift für Sozial-und Wirtschaftsgeschichte:* VSWG, 46) 1959.

O. Brunner: *Neue Wege der Sozialgeschichte, Vorträge und Aufsätze,* Göttingen, 1956.

Gerhard Bry: *Wages in Germany 1871-1945,* Princeton, 1960.

E. Cohn-Bramsted: *Aristocracy and the Middle Classes,* 2nd edition, London, 1964. A pioneering work on the sociology of literature.

Ingeborg Drewitz: *Berliner Salons: Gesellschaft und Literatur zwischen Aufklärung und Industriezeitalter,* Berlin, 1965. Volume VII in the *Berlinische Reminiszenzen* series.

H. W. Graf von Finckenstein: *Die Entwicklung der Landwirtschaft in Preußen und Deutschland 1800-1930,* Würzburg, 1900.

Ed. Walter Först: *Das Rheinland in preussischer Zeit,* Köln and Berlin, 1965. Ten essays on social and economic life.

Ed. Ruth Glatz: *Berliner Leben 1870-1900. Documents of social life,* Berlin, 1963. An interesting and unusual selection, though with the expected bias of a work published in East Germany.

Heinz Gollwitzer: *Die Standesherren. Die politische und*

gesellschaftliche Stellung der Mediatisierten, 2nd edition, Göttingen, 1964.

T. S. Hamerow: *Restoration, Revolution, Reaction. Economics and Politics in Germany 1815-71,* Princeton, 1958.

T. S. Hamerow: *Social Foundations of German Unification 1858-1871* : *Ideas and Institutions,* Princeton, 1969.

W. O. Henderson: *The Industrial Revolution on the Continent* : *Germany, France and Russia 1800-1914,* London, 1961.

W. O. Henderson: *The Zollverein,* 2nd edition, London, 1959.

W. Köllmann: *Politische und soziale Entwicklung der deutschen Arbeiterschaft 1850-1914* (VSWG, 51), 1964.

J. Kulischer: *Allgemeine Wirtschaftgeschichte,* volume II: *Neuzeit,* reprinted 1954.

Norman Longmate: *King Cholera* : *the biography of a disease,* London, 1966. Contains several references to Prussia and Austria, and to the work of German research scientists such as Koch.

M. Weber: *Wirtschaft und Gesellschaft,* 4th edition, Tübingen, 1956.

M. Weber: *Kleinbürgerliche Demokraten in der deutschen Einheitsbewegung 1863-6,* Berlin, 1963.

Ed. Hans-Ulrich Wehler: *Moderne deutsche Sozialgeschichte,* Cologne-Berlin, 1966. Contains an important collection of essays on social and economic history 1815-1918.

Specific topics

1848

Jacques Droz: *Les révolutions allemandes de 1848,* Paris, 1957. An invaluable work.

P. H. Noyes: *Organization and Revolution: Working-class Associations in the German Revolutions of 1848-9,* Princeton, 1966.

R. J. Rath: *The Viennese Revolution of 1848,* Austin, Texas (U.S.A.), 1957.

P. Robertson: *The Revolutions of 1848. A social history,* Princeton, 1952.

Veit Valentin: *Geschichte der deutschen Revolution von 1848-9,* Berlin, 1930-1. (Abridged English version: *Chapters of German History,* London, 1940.) Contains material on the regions and vivid portraits of some of the participants not found in most general accounts.

1871 and the Second Empire

Ed. Helmut Böhme : *Die Reichsgründung*, Munich, 1967.

Egmont Zechlin : *Die Reichsgründung*, Frankfurt, 1967. (Deutsche Geschichte : Ereignisse und Probleme, General Editor : Walter Hubatsch.)

Richard Hamann/Jost Hermand : *Die Gründerzeit*, Berlin, 1965. Mainly concerned with cultural history; it is very informative on painting and architecture, as well as literature and music.

H. Plessner : *Die verspätete Nation,* 4th edition, Stuttgart, 1967. A thoughtful collection of essays on the Second Reich and its consequences.

H. J. Schoeps : *Zeitgeist im Wandel,* volume 1 : *Das Wilhelminische Zeitalter,* Stuttgart, 1968.

Art

German art is usually neglected in general histories in English but

F. Novotny : *Painting and sculpture in Europe 1780-1870,* London, 1960, contains a good deal of information.

Austria

Heinrich Benedikt : *Die Monarchie des Hauses Oesterreich,* Munich, 1968. A brief but very informative study of Austrian politics, culture and society by one of Austria's most distinguished living historians.

Education

Richard Samuel and R. Hinton Thomas : *Education and Society in Modern Germany,* London, 1949.

History and historiography

G. P. Gooch : *History and Historians in the Nineteenth Century,* London, 1952, is a useful introduction to the subject for the student.

Hans Rothfels : 'Ungeschichtliches und geschichtliches Jahrhundert' in *Festschrift für Klaus Ziegler,* Tübingen, 1968.

Bibliography

Nationalism

Hans Kohn: *The Mind of Germany*, London, 1961. A most perceptive, if in some ways one-sided, account of the failure of liberalism in nineteenth century Germany.

Fr. Meinecke: *Weltbürgertum und Nationalstaat, Studien zur Genesis des deutschen Nationalstaats*, Munich/Berlin 1908.

Benno von Weise and Rudolph Henß (editors): *Nationalismus in Germanistik und Dichtung*. Dokumentation des Germanistentages in München von 17. bis 22. Oktober 1966, Berlin, 1967. Contains several illuminating studies on specific aspects of nationalist attitudes. Among many excellent papers Walter Killy's on the German school textbook in the nineteenth century deserves special mention.

Egmont Zechlin: *Die Einheitsbewegung*, Frankfurt 1967. (Deutsche Geschichte: Ereignisse und Probleme, General Editor, Walter Hubatsch.)

Political Ideologies and the Parties

L. Bergstraesser: *Geschichte der politischen Parteien in Deutschland*, 9th edition, Munich 1955.

K. W. Epstein: *The Genesis of German Conservatism*, Princeton, 1966.

F. C. Sell: *Die Tragödie des deutschen Liberalismus*, Stuttgart, 1953.

Gunther Roth: *The Social Democrats in Imperial Germany. A Study in Working-Class Isolation and National Integration*, New Jersey, 1963.

H-U. Wehler: *Sozialdemokratie und Nationalstaat. Die deutsche Sozialdmokratie und die Nationalitätenfrage von Karl Marx bis zum Ausbruch des 1. Weltkrieges*, Cologne, 1962.

Political Thought

S. Hook: *From Hegel to Marx*, Ann Arbor, 1962.

H. Marcuse: *Reason and Revolution. Hegel and the rise of social theory*, Oxford, 1941.

Religion

G. Kruger (editor): *Handbuch der Kirchengeschichte:* Part 4: *Die Neuzeit*, Tübingen, 1931.

329

Karl Buchheim: *Ultramontanismus und Demokratie,* Munich 1963. A study of the Catholic Church in nineteenth century Germany.

S. Dubnow: *Weltgeschichte des jüdischen Volkes,* volumes VIII and IX, contain a good deal of material on the Jews in Germany which is not easily available.

Peter G. J. Pulzer: *The Rise of Political Anti-Semitism in Germany and Austria,* New York/London, 1964. An excellent short account.

Walter Boehlich: *Der Berliner Antisemitismusstreit,* Frankfurt, 1965.

Literature

(i) *General*

Erich Auerbach: *Mimesis,* Bern, 1946. The chapters on the eighteenth and nineteenth century are of interest for the way they indicate the separate development of realist literature in Germany from the rest of western Europe.

E. M. Butler: *The Saint-Simonian Religion in Germany: a study of the Young German Movement,* Cambridge, 1926. Still very readable and informative on the Young Germans.

Ed. B. Boesch: *Deutsche Literaturgeschichte in Grundzügen,* 3rd edition, Bern, 1967.

Hermann Boeschenstein: *German Literature of the Nineteenth Century,* London, 1969. A most succinct and well-written account.

G. Brandes: *Main Currents in Nineteenth-Century Literature,* 6 volumes, London, 1901-5.

Anni Carlsson: *Die deutsche Buchkritik von der Reformation bis zur Gegenwart,* Bert and Munich, 1969.

Claude David: *Geschichte der deutschen Literatur: Zwischen Romantik und Symbolismus 1820-85,* Gütersloh, 1966.

Peter Demetz: *Marx, Engels und die Dichter,* Stuttgart, 1959.

Norbert Fürst: *The Victorian Age of German Literature,* London, 1966. Capricious but full of odd and illuminating bits of information.

Martin Greiner: *Zwischen Biedermeier und Bourgeoisie,* Göttingen, 1953.

Jost Hermand (editor): *Das junge Deutschland, Texte und*

Dokumente, Stuttgart, 1966. Of particular interest for evidence of the social criticism of the Young Germans.

Walter Höllerer: *Zwischen Klassik und Moderne,* Stuttgart, 1958.

Walter Killy (general editor): *Die deutsche Literatur,* Volume VI: *Das 19. Jahrhundert,* ed. B.v. Wiese. Munich, 1965. Has very wide terms of reference and under the heading *Literature* includes documents drawn from history, philosophy, and what the Germans call 'trivial' or popular literature of the penny magazine type.

Under the title *Klassiker der Kritik,* Artemis Verlag (Zurich) publish an excellent series of selections from the work of leading German critics, with introduction and notes. Already published are: *Ludwig Börne* (1964), *Theodor Fontane* (1965), *Ludwig Speidel* (1963), *Carl Spitteler* (1965).

Georg Lukács: *Deutsche Realisten im 19ten Jahrhundert,* Berlin, 1952. Probably the best known work of the distinguished Marxist critic. Although many of its views are now challenged it has had an important influence on more recent books on the subject.

Fritz Martini: *Deutsche Literatur im bürgerlichen Realismus 1848-98,* Stuttgart, 1962. Stylistically wearisome but immensely informative.

The *Metzler Sammlung* of literary criticism (Stuttgart) contains several useful monographs on nineteenth century writers with valuable bibliographical information, e.g.

E. Galley: *Heinrich Heine* (1963).

W. Hecht: *Fritz Reuter* (1966).

K. Fehr: *Jeremias Gotthelf* (1967).

R. M. Kully: *Johann Peter Hebel* (1969)

Anni Meetz: *Friedrich Hebbel* (1962).

E. Meyer: *Eduard Mörike* (1961).

J. Mueller: *Franz Grillparzer* (1963).

F. Mossé *et al.*: *Littérature allemande,* Paris, 1959.

Roy Pascal: *The German Novel,* Manchester, 1956.

Ed. S. S. Prawer *et al.*: *Essays in German Language, Culture and Society,* London, 1969.

James Ritchie (editor): *Periods in German Literature,* London, 1966. Contains useful essays on the Biedermeier and realism.

H. J. Schrimpf (editor): *Literatur und Gesellschaft vom neunzehnten ins zwanzigste Jahrhundert* (Festgabe für Benno von Wiese zu seinem 60. Geburtstag), Bonn, 1963.

Friedrich Sengle: *Arbeiten zur deutschen Literatur 1750-1850,* Stuttgart, 1965. A most penetrating study. His essays on the Biedermeier show the close connection between popular writings and literature in this period.

J. P. Stern: *Reinterpretations,* London, 1964. One of the most stimulating books on nineteenth century German literature.

Rene Wellek: *Concepts of Criticism,* Yale, 1963.

Benno von Wiese: *Zwischen Utopie und Wirklichkeit,* Düsseldorf, 1963 and *Von Lessing bis Grabbe,* Düsseldorf, 1968, contain useful essays on Immermann and Grabbe.

(ii) *Individual authors*

Peter Demetz: *Theodor Fontane: Formen des Realismus,* Munich, 1964.

Joachim Remak: *The Gentle Critic, Theodor Fontane and German Politics 1848-98,* Syracuse, 1964.

Hans-Heinrich Reuter: *Fontane,* 2nd edition, Munich, 1969. A most impressive biography of some 1,000 pages by the East German scholar.

H. Waidson: *Jeremias Gotthelf. An Introduction to the Swiss Novelist,* Oxford, 1953.

Walter Naumann: *Franz Grillparzer: das dichtesrische Werk,* Stuttgart, 1956.

E. W. Dobert: *Karl Gutzkow und seine Zeit,* Bern and Munich, 1968.

Ed. H. Kreuzer: *Hebbel in neuer Sicht,* Stuttgart, 1963.

W. D. Williams: *The Stories of C. F. Meyer,* Oxford, 1962.

S. S. Prawer: *Heine: The Tragic Satirist,* Cambridge, 1961.

H. Henel: *Gedichte Conrad Ferdinand Meyers,* Tübingen, 1962.

S. S. Prawer: *Mörike und seine Leser,* Stuttgart, 1960. Particularly interesting for what it has to say about literary tastes in Germany.

Hermann Pongs: *Wilhelm Raabe: Leben und Werk,* Heidelberg, 1958.

Ed. Lothar Stiehm: *Adalbert Stifter: Studien und Interpretationen. Gedenkschrift zum 100. Todestage.* Heidelberg, 1968.

Marianne Thalmann: *Ludwig Tieck, Der Heilige von Dresden,* Berlin, 1960.

Index

Figures in bold type indicate pages where a subject is treated at length.

Index

Index

Index

Index

In 1830, most Germans willingly accepted the rest of Europe's image of them as a complacent, amiable, and provincial people, the dutiful subjects of innumerable minor rulers, as heterogeneous and unambitious culturally as they were politically. Only sixty years later, citizens of an imperial state, they exhibited an aggressive national pride and insisted on the unquestionable superiority of German culture.

In *Tradition and Revolution*, Eda Sagarra traces, with admirable economy and an unfailing eye for significant detail, this transformation of Germany in relation to the literature of the period. The result is a uniquely deft and yet suggestive portrait of an age torn between tradition and the challenges of a dual revolution — political and industrial.

Beginning with an assessment of the Biedermeier period, Professor Sagarra outlines and evaluates all the major developments of the age: the status and preoccupations of the German writers between the revolutions of